Brief Contents

About the Authors

Donald Kagan is Hillhouse Professor of History and Classics at Yale University, where he has taught since 1969. He received the A.B. degree in history from Brooklyn College, the M.A. in classics from Brown University, and the Ph.D. in history from Ohio State University. During 1958–1959 he studied at the American School of Classical Studies as a Fulbright Scholar. He has received three awards for undergraduate teaching at Cornell and Yale. He is the author of a history of Greek political thought, *The Great Dialogue* (1965); a four-volume history of the Peloponnesian war, *The Origins of the Peloponnesian War* (1969); *The Archidamian War* (1974); *The Peace of Nicias and the Sicilian Expedition* (1981); *The Fall of the Athenian Empire* (1987); a biography of Pericles, *Pericles of Athens and the Birth of Democracy* (1991) and *On the Origins of War* (1995). With Brian Tierney and L. Pearce Williams, he is the editor of *Great issues in Western Civilization,* a collection of readings.

Steven Ozment is McLean Professor of Ancient and Modern History at Harvard University. He has taught courses in Western Civilization at Yale, Stanford, and Harvard. He is the author of eight books. *The Age of Reform, 1250–1550* (1980) won the Schaff Prize and was nominated for the 1981 American Book Award. *Magdalena and Balthasar: An Intimate Portrait of Life in Sixteenth Century Europe* (1986), *Three Behaim Boys: Growing Up in Early Modern Germany* (1990), and *Protestants: The Birth of a Revolution* (1992) were selections of the History Book club.

Frank M. Turner is John Hay Whitney Professor of History at Yale University, where he served as University Provost from 1988 to 1992. He received his B.A degree at the College of William and Mary and his Ph.D. from Yale. He has received the Yale College Award for Distinguished Undergraduate Teaching. He has directed a National Endowment for the Humanities Summer Institute. His scholarly research has received the support of fellowships from the National Endowment for the Humanities and the Guggenheim Foundation. He is the author of *Between Science and Religion: The Reaction to Scientific Naturalism in Late Victorian England* (1974), *The Greek Heritage in Victorian Britain* (1981), which received the British Council Prize of the Conference on British Studies and the Yale Press Governors Award, and *Contesting Cultural Authority: Essays in Victorian Intellectual Life* (1993). He has also contributed numerous articles to journals and has served on the editorial advisory boards of *The Journal of Modern History, Isis,* and *Victorian Studies.*

A. Daniel Frankforter is Professor of Medieval History at the Pennsylvania State University. He holds degrees from Franklin and Marshall College, Drew University, and the Pennsylvania State University, where he has taught since 1970. His books include *The Medieval Millennium, An Introduction; A History of the Christian Movement; Civilization and Survival; The Shakespeare Name Dictionary;* and a translation and edition of François Poullain de la Barre's *De l'Égalité des Deux Sexes.* He has received four awards for excellence in teaching and research from the Pennsylvania State University.

Contents

4 Rome: From Republic to Empire 75

5 The Roman Empire 101

SECOND EDITION

The Western Heritage

Brief Edition

Volume I: To 1715

DONALD KAGAN
Yale University

STEVEN OZMENT
Harvard University

FRANK M. TURNER
Yale University

with the assistance of

A. DANIEL FRANKFORTER
Pennsylvania State University, Behrend College

Prentice Hall, Upper Saddle River, New Jersey 07458

Library of Congress Cataloging-in-Publication Data

The Library of Congress has catalogued the one volume edition as follows:

Kagan, Donald.
    The Western heritage / Donald Kagan, Steven Ozment, Frank M.
Turner : with the assistance of A. Daniel Frankforter. — Brief ed.,
2nd ed.
      p. cm.
    Includes bibliographical references and index.
    ISBN 0-13-081400-8
    1. Civilization, Western. I. Ozment, Steven E. II. Turner,
Frank M. (Frank Miller), (date). III. Frankforter, A. Daniel.
IV. Title.
    [CB245.K28 1999]
    909'.09821—dc21   98-34067
                                             CIP

Acquisitions Editor: *Todd Armstrong*
Editorial Director: *Charlyce Jones Owen*
Development Editor: *Susan Alkana*
Production Editor: *Barbara DeVries*
Marketing Manager: *Sheryl Adams*
Copy Editor: *Cheryl Smith*

Editorial Assistant: *Holly Jo Brown*
Buyer: *Lynn Pearlman*
Line Art Coordinator: *Guy Ruggiero*
Artist: *Maria Piper*
Cover Design Director: *Jayne Conte*

Cover Art: Market scene. Late fifteenth-century fresco. Castello d'Issogne, Italy. Fifteenth-century
rendering of an eleventh- or twelfth-century marketplace. (Scala/Art Resource, N.Y.)

This book was set 10/12 Trump Mediaeval by The Composing Room of Michigan, Inc., and was
printed by RR Donnelley and Sons. The cover was printed by Phoenix Color Corp.

10 9 8 7 6 5 4 3 2 1

ISBN 0-13-081412-1

Prentice-Hall International (UK) Limited, *London*
Prentice-Hall of Australia Pty. Limited, *Sydney*
Prentice-Hall Canada Inc., *Toronto*
Prentice-Hall Hispanoamericana, S.A., *Mexico*
Prentice-Hall of India Private Limited, *New Delhi*
Prentice-Hall of Japan, Inc., *Tokyo*
Simon & Schuster Asia Pte. Ltd., *Singapore*
Editora Prentice-Hall do Brasil, Ltda., *Rio de Janeiro*

The Middle Ages, 476–1300

Europe in Transition, 1300–1750

Maps

Political Transformations

Preface

The heritage of Western civilization has perhaps never been the focus of so much interest and controversy as it is today. Many commentators criticize it, many praise it, but for all it is a subject of intense discussion. *The Western Heritage, Second Edition,* helps teachers introduce students to the subject of that discussion. It presents an overview of Western civilization, including its strengths, its weaknesses, and the controversies surrounding it.

On campus after campus, every aspect of Western civilization has become an object of scrutiny and debate. Many participants in this debate fail to recognize that such self-criticism is characteristic of Western civilization and an important part of its heritage. We welcome the debate and hope that this book can help raise its quality.

The collapse of communism has left the people of half of Europe struggling to reorganize their political institutions and their social and economic lives. The choices they are making and the future they are forging will reflect in large measure their understanding of their heritage. To follow and participate in that process we too need to understand that heritage.

This brief second edition of *The Western Heritage* is designed to meet the needs of those who want a succinct overview of Western civilization for quarter and semester courses and those who plan to supplement their courses with extensive outside readings. Although this version of *The Western Heritage* is indeed shorter than the full version, it covers all the same topics with the same overall or-ganization. Our colleague Dan Frankforter has skillfully reworked and revised the entire text for brevity, ensuring that it retains a consistent voice and a coherent narrative.

Goals of the Text

Since *The Western Heritage* first appeared, we have sought to provide our readers with a work that does justice to the richness and variety of Western civilization. Our primary goal has been to present a strong, clear, narrative account of the key developments in Western history. We have also chosen to call attention to certain critical themes:

The development of political freedom, constitutional government, and concern for the rule of law and individual rights;

The shifting relations among religion, society, and the state;

The development of science and technology and their expanding impact on thought, social institutions, and everyday life;

The major religious and intellectual currents that have shaped Western culture.

We believe that these themes have been fundamental in Western civilization, shaping the past and exerting a continuing influence on the present.

Balanced and Flexible Presentation. History has many facets, no one of which alone can account for its development. Any attempt to tell the story of the West from a single overarching perspective, no matter how timely, is bound to neglect or suppress some important part of that story. Our goal in this text has been to present Western civilization fairly, accurately, and in a way that does justice to its great variety. We have designed the text to accommodate many approaches to a course in Western civilization, allowing teachers to stress what is most important to them.

We do not believe that a history of the West should be limited to politics and international relations, but we share the conviction that political events have shaped the Western experience in fundamental and powerful ways. Recent events in central and eastern Europe and the former Soviet Union have strengthened that belief. We have also been told repeatedly by teachers that no matter what their own specialties, they believe that a political narrative best equips students to begin building an understanding of the past.

The Western Heritage, brief second edition, also provides a rich account of the social history of the West, with strong coverage of family life, the roles of women, and the place of the family in relation to broader economic, political, and social developments. This coverage reflects the explosive growth in social historical research in the last quarter century.

Finally, no other brief survey text presents so full an account of the religious and intellectual development of the West. People may be political and social beings, but they are also reasoning and spiritual beings. What they think and believe are among the most important things we can know about them. Their ideas about God, society, law, gender, human nature, and the physical world have changed over the centuries and continue to change. We cannot fully grasp our own approach to the world without understanding the intellectual currents of the past and their influence on our thoughts and conceptual categories.

Clarity and Accessibility. Good narrative history requires clear, vigorous prose. A survey text especially must engage students if it hopes to keep them reading. Throughout this brief second edition of *The Western Heritage,* we have sought to make our presentation fully accessible to students without compromising on vocabulary or conceptual level.

Recent Scholarship. This edition of *The Western Heritage,* like all others, reflects our determination to incorporate the most recent developments in historical scholarship and the expanding concerns of professional historians.

Features of the Brief Second Edition

The Western Heritage, brief edition, has several distinctive features designed to make it accessible to students and reinforce key concepts. Each chapter includes:

An opening *outline;*

A *key topics* list that gives a succinct overview of the chapter;

Introductory and *concluding sections;*

One or more *timelines* that help students build a chronological framework;

Chapter review questions that help students review the material in the chapter and relate it to broader themes. These too can be used for class discussion and essay topics;

A *suggested readings* list that directs students to more detailed sources on particular topics.

Maps and Illustrations. The abundant *maps* throughout the text are carefully cued to the narrative. *Photographs* and other illustrations enrich the text and help draw students in to it. *Color inserts* provide examples of fine art from the paleolithic age to the twentieth century.

Political Transformations. This new map feature concentrates on six highly significant moments of political transformation in the history of the West. These features provide a brief overview of the transformation illustrated by a map and illustrations. The features will provide opportunities for study not only by individual students, but also for class discussion. The topics for this feature are:

- Greek Colonization from Spain to the Black Sea
- Muslim Conquests and Domination of the Mediterranean to about 750
- Voyages of Discovery and the Colonial Claims of Spain and Portugal
- The Congress of Vienna Redraws the Map of Europe
- The Mandate System: 1919 to World War II
- Decolonization in Asia and Africa

Ancillary Instructional Materials

The Western Heritage, brief second edition, comes with an extensive package of ancillary materials.

An **Instructor's Manual** with Test Items prepared by Perry M. Rogers. This includes chapter summaries, key points and vital concepts, identification questions, multiple-choice questions, essay questions, and suggested films.

Map Transparencies in full color.

These include all the maps in the brief edition as well as many others.

A **Study Guide** prepared by Anthony M. Brescia and updated by James Barbieri that includes commentary, identifications, map exercises, short-answer exercises, and essay questions.

A **Computerized Study Guide** consisting of 15 multiple-choice questions from each chapter with reinforcing feedback on correct answers and clarifying feedback on wrong answers. All answers are cross-referenced to the text.

A **Computerized Test Bank** consisting of more than 1500 multiple-choice and essay questions from the Instructor's Manual for IBM compatible and Macintosh systems.

The Hammond **Historical Atlas of the World,** available with the text at a special discounted price. Please contact your local Prentice Hall sales representative for details.

Acknowledgments

We are grateful to the scholars and teachers whose thoughtful and often detailed comments have helped shape *The Western Heritage.* Our special thanks to the professors who reviewed the second brief edition: Paul DeVendittis, Nassau Community College; Eugene Larson, Pierce College; Dalton McMann, Mayville State University; Terry Reynolds, Michigan Tech University; Robin Sturgis, York Technical College; and David Valone, Quinnipiac College.

We would also like to thank the many dedicated people at Prentice Hall who helped produce the second brief edition. Our acquisitions editor, Todd Armstrong, and our development editor, Susan Alkana, deftly shepherded us through the preparation of the second edition. Sheryl Adams, marketing manager, demonstrated an appreciation for historical scholarship as well as the history textbook market in her creative and informed marketing strategies. Holly Jo Brown, editorial assistant, took care of a myriad of details. Finally, Barbara DeVries, our production editor, managed the many aspects of guiding the project from manuscript to bound book and lent good-humored advice.

D.K.
S.O.
F.M.T.

1

The Birth of Civilization

KEY TOPICS

- ∾ The earliest history of humanity, the origins of human culture in the Paleolithic Age, the shift from food gathering to food production, and the emergence of civilizations
- ∾ The ancient civilizations of Mesopotamia and Egypt
- ∾ The Assyrians and the first great Middle Eastern empires
- ∾ The ancient Middle Eastern civilization compared with that of the ancient Greeks

For hundreds of thousands of years, human beings lived by hunting and gathering what nature provided. Only about 10,000 years ago did they begin to cultivate plants and domesticate animals. As they turned from harvesting food to producing it, settled life became possible. About 5,000 years ago the Sumerians, who lived near the confluence of the Tigris and Euphrates rivers (a region the Greeks named "Mesopotamia" or "between rivers"), and the Egyptians, who dwelt in the Nile Valley, pioneered civilization. By the fourteenth century B.C.E. powerful empires had arisen and were struggling for dominance of the civilized world. But one of the region's smaller states, Israel, made the ancient Middle East's greatest contribution to civilization, beginning the evolution of the modern West's major religions: Judaism, Christianity, and Islam.

1

⌐ Early Human Beings and Their Culture

Scientists estimate that the earth may be 6 billion years old and that its human inhabitants have been developing for 3 to 5 million years. Some 1 to 2 million years ago, erect, tool-using beings spread from their probable place of origin in Africa to Europe and Asia. Our own species, *Homo sapiens,* is about 200,000 years old, and fully modern humans have existed for about 90,000 years.

Humans are distinguished by a unique capacity to construct cultures. A *culture* may be defined as a way of life invented by a group and passed on by teaching. It includes both material things (tools, clothing, and shelter) and ideas, institutions, and beliefs. Because cultural behaviors are guided by learning rather than instinct, they can be altered at will to enable human beings to adapt rapidly to different environments and changing conditions.

The Paleolithic Age

Anthropologists identify pre-historic human cultures by the styles of their most durable and plentiful artifacts—stone tools. The earliest period in cultural development—the Paleolithic (Greek for "old stone")—began with the first use of stone tools some 1 million years ago. It continued until about 10,000 B.C.E. Throughout this immensely long era, people were nomadic hunters and gatherers who were totally dependent for their food on what nature spontaneously offered. An uncertain food supply and vulnerability to wild beasts, accidents, and environmental disasters persuaded early humans that they occupied a world governed by superhuman powers. The cave art, ritual burial practices, and other evidences of religious or magical beliefs that appeared around the globe during the Paleolithic era bear witness to a suspicion as old as humanity itself that there is more to the world than meets the eye.

Human society in the Paleolithic Age was probably based on a division of labor by sex. Males ranged far afield on the hunt. Females, who were less mobile because of the burdens of childbearing and nursing, gathered edibles of various kinds in the vicinity of a base camp. Only small groups could be supported in this way, and the human population was subject to the same ecological constraints as all other species.

The Neolithic Age

About 10,000 years ago people living in some parts of what we now call the Middle (or Near) East began to shift from hunting and gathering to agriculture. Because this change coincided with the appearance of new techniques that used carving and grinding rather than chipping to produce stone tools, this period is called the Neolithic ("new stone") Age. Hunters and gatherers are nomads, but farmers have to stay with the fields they cultivate. Agriculture produced village life, and settlement made possible the invention of materials such as pottery and of building techniques.

The Neolithic revolution paved the way for the emergence of civilization.

The earliest Neolithic communities appeared in the Middle East about 8000 B.C.E., in China about 4000 B.C.E., and in India about 3600 B.C.E. The Neolithic economy of China was based on rice and millet. The Middle East and India depended on species of wheat—the wild forebears of which were native to the foothills of the mountains north and east of Mesopotamia.

✧ Early Civilizations to About 1000 B.C.E.

The Bronze Age and the Birth of Civilization

About 4000 B.C.E., first in Mesopotamia and then in Egypt, advanced cultures began to evolve. They developed urban institutions and techniques for writing and for smelting metals—the characteristics of civilized societies. By 3000 B.C.E., when the invention of writing gave birth to recorded history, centralized states had already been established along the Tigris and Euphrates rivers and in the valley of the Nile (see Map 1-1).

Many of the people who live in cities do not grow their own food, so urban life is possible only where farmers can produce more than they need to support themselves. Urban populations appeared first in Mesopotamia and Egypt because their rivers flooded annually and deposited a new layer of silt that kept their fields permanently fertile. But since both regions receive very little rain, their rich soils could be exploited only after farmers learned techniques of irrigation. It has been suggested that urban life, literacy, and centralized states were responses to a need for a strong authority capable of constructing and managing irrigation systems. But this may be overly simplistic. Water management was probably the responsibility of local officials, not central governments, and the earliest written records do not deal with irrigation. They record transactions involving land, animals, and trade.

City life was much more complex and stimulating than life in farming villages, for people with different interests and educations congregated in cities. The great temple complexes that were central to Mesopotamian cities produced many kinds of texts that reveal the complexity of urban society. Temples employed large staffs of people who had all kinds of specialized duties. There was also enough commerce to support an urban merchant class. And since systems of writing were very complicated and took years to learn, each city also had a small group of professional scribes.

Cities that irrigated their fields from the same river were forced to associate closely. The need to avoid destructive competition while maintaining an equitable distribution of water encouraged the towns that depended on a common water source to consolidate and become centrally managed kingdoms.

A king in a typical river-oriented civilization was regarded either as a god or as a god's representative. He occupied the pinnacle of a hierarchy of rigidly defined social classes: soldier-aristocrats, priests, merchants, professionals, free peasants, and slaves. Cities were centers of administrative, commercial, religious, and military activity. Most of the farmers who supported urban com-

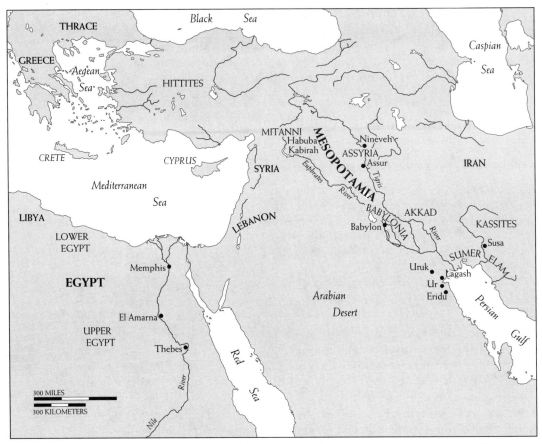

MAP 1-1 The Ancient Middle East *There were two ancient river valley civilizations. While Egypt early was united into a single state, Mesopotamia was long divided into a number of city-states.*

munities lived in outlying villages, and much of the land they worked was owned by the upper classes. These cultural patterns formed so early that they were assumed to be part of the natural order. They, therefore, changed only slowly and grudgingly.

Mesopotamian Civilization

Civilization probably made its first appearance in Mesopotamia. A people called the Sumerians founded cities close to the head of the Persian Gulf about 3000 B.C.E. For a long time the earliest known Sumerian site was at Uruk, but recent discoveries at Habuba Kabirah in northern Syria have brought to light other settlements from the same era.

Between 2800 B.C.E. and 2370 B.C.E., Sumer's Early Dynastic Period, city-

ca. 3500 B.C.E.	*Earliest Sumerian settlements*
ca. 2800–2370 B.C.E.	*Sumerian city-states, Early Dynastic Period*
ca. 2370 B.C.E.	*Sargon establishes Semitic dynasty at Akkad*
ca. 2125–2027 B.C.E.	*Third Dynasty of Ur*
ca. 1900 B.C.E.	*Old Babylonian Dynasty of the Amorites*
1792–1750 B.C.E.	*Reign of Hammurabi*
ca. 1600 B.C.E.	*Hittite and Kassite invasions of Babylon*

states such as Ur, Uruk, Lagash, and Eridu dotted the landscape of southern Mesopotamia. Each controlled about 100 square miles of territory, and they quarreled incessantly with each other over water rights and frontiers. In time the stronger towns assimilated the weaker ones and formed kingdoms.

The land upstream from the principal Sumerian city-states was inhabited by people who probably came from northern Syria. They absorbed Sumerian culture, but they did not speak Sumerian. Their language belonged to the Semitic family (that is, the same group as modern Arabic and Hebrew). These people established a kingdom with a capital at Akkad, near the site of the later city of Babylon. About 2370 B.C.E. one of Akkad's kings, Sargon, conquered the Sumerian cities and built an empire that may have reached to Lebanon and the Mediterranean coast. His dynasty endured for two centuries.

About 2125 B.C.E. the Akkadian state collapsed, and the city of Ur restored Sumerian dominance. The kings of the Third Dynasty of Ur presided over a renaissance of Sumerian culture that lasted until invaders overwhelmed Ur in 2000 B.C.E. Sumer never recovered from Ur's defeat. Sumerian ceased to be a living language, but scholarly priests and scribes preserved it and Sumer's literary legacy.

After the fall of Ur, leadership passed (ca. 1900 B.C.E.) to the Amorites, founders of the city of Babylon. The Amorite, or Old Babylonian, dynasty ruled Mesopotamia for about 300 years. It reached its peak during the reign of Hammurabi (ca. 1792–1750 B.C.E.), a king who is best known for a code of laws. Earlier collections of laws had been made by the Sumerians, but Hammurabi's code was the most extensive.

About 1600 B.C.E. invasions from the north (by the Hittites) and the east (by the Kassites) caused Amoritic Babylon to decline. The Hittites plundered and then withdrew to their homebase in Asia Minor, but the Kassites took possession of Babylon and ruled Mesopotamia for five centuries.

Government. Although some scholars claim that the Sumerian cities were originally governed as "primitive democracies," evidence for this is scant and controversial. The earliest historical records mention kings whose authority may have been little checked by their subjects. Kings led armies, administered economies, sat as judges, and served as intermediaries between the people and their gods.

The control kings had over both religious and secular institutions reflects a tendency toward centralization of power typical of Mesopotamian societies. Royal governments carefully managed each state's economy. Land was surveyed annually, fields were assigned to specific farmers, and a decision was made about how much seed would be sown. The government estimated the size of the crop and planned the distribution of the harvest before planting began.

The administration of a Sumerian city required a large staff of literate persons with specialized educations. The Sumerians invented a script that historians call *cuneiform* (from *cuneus,* Latin for "wedge"). A scribe wrote on a clay tablet by making wedge-shaped impressions with a reed or stylus. In addition to writing, Sumerians also pioneered a system of mathematics and were able to compute calendars that reconciled the lunar and solar years.

Religion. The people of Mesopotamia expected life to be difficult and anticipated no reward beyond the grave. Their religion dealt with problems of this world, which they tried to solve by resorting to prayer, sacrifice, and magic. A large priesthood existed to provide expert advice on ways to influence the gods, and many of the cuneiform tablets that have survived record prayers, incantations, curses, and omens. Sumer's gods were equated with the forces of nature, but conceived in human form. They were not very appealing, for legends often represent them as frivolous, quarrelsome, selfish, and childish. They differed from their human worshipers only in possessing greater power and immortality.

The Babylonians developed many methods for divining the will of the gods. Their conviction that the movements of heavenly bodies provided clues to the gods' intentions gave birth to astrology. They believed that abnormalities found in the entrails of sacrificial animals were significant, and they regarded all kinds of events as omens. Scribes kept extensive records of these and compiled libraries that were studied by learned priests.

Religious myth loomed large in ancient Mesopotamian literature and art, and its themes and images are still familiar. The Babylonians composed tales of the creation of the world, of a great flood that almost destroyed humanity, of an island paradise from which a god was expelled for eating forbidden plants, and of a hero named Gilgamesh who comes to terms with his mortality after a snake robs him of eternal life.

Religion also inspired the greatest achievement of the Mesopotamian architect and engineer, a building called a *ziggurat*. It was a huge stepped mound of mud-bricks surmounted by a temple. The eroded remains of these monumental structures still dot the Iraqi landscape.

Society. Tens of thousands of cuneiform texts give us a detailed picture of life in ancient Mesopotamia, and the evidence from the reign of Hammurabi is particularly good. It reveals a society legally divided into three classes: nobles, commoners, and slaves. Social status was very important, for the harshness of a punishment for a crime varied according to the class or classes to which the criminal and the victim belonged.

The space devoted to various issues in Hammurabi's code reveals his people's chief concerns. The code's third largest category of laws deals with com-

This neo-Hittite relief carving dates to the ninth century B.C.E. It comes from the citadel at Binjirli in modern Turkey and shows two banqueters. [Erich Lessing/Art Resources, N.Y.]

merce. Regulations governing debts, rates of interest, security, default, and the conduct of professionals (contractors, surgeons, etc.) testify to the complexity of Babylonian commercial life. The second largest group of laws consists of those governing land tenure. The largest deals with the maintenance and protection of families.

Parents arranged the marriages of their children. The groom made a bridal payment, and the father of the bride provided a dowry for his daughter. A marriage started out monogamous, but a husband whose wife was barren or ill for a long time could take a second wife. Men were also permitted extramarital relations with concubines, slaves, and prostitutes.

Women did not have equal sexual privileges, but a wife had some rights under the law. Divorce was relatively easy, but not entirely equitable. Women divorced by their husbands without good cause could recover their dowries. A woman could also initiate a divorce and reclaim her dowry so long as her husband could not convict her of wrongdoing. If, however, she had neglected a woman's primary duty (i.e., her home), she could be prosecuted. The law stated that if a wife "has made up her mind to leave in order to engage in business, thus neglecting her house and humiliating her husband, he may divorce her without compensation."

Although true chattel slavery did not become common until late in

Mesopotamian history (in the Neo-Babylonian period, 612–539 B.C.E.), the practice of enslaving foreigners captured in wars began very early. Babylonians also enslaved other Babylonians. Parents could sell their children into slavery or pledge themselves and their families as surety for loans. Slavery was also a punishment for certain crimes—such as kicking one's mother or striking an elder brother.

Laws against fugitive slaves or slaves who defied their masters were harsh, but Mesopotamian slaves had some legal protection. Slaves could engage in business and, with certain restrictions, hold property, and earn means to buy their freedom. They could marry free people, and the children of these unions were considered freeborn. Children of a slave by her master might also claim shares in his estate after his death.

Egyptian Civilization

As Mesopotamian civilization evolved along the banks of the Tigris and Euphrates rivers, another great civilization emerged in Egypt. Its focus was the Nile, a river that stretches from a source in central Africa some 4,000 miles north to the Mediterranean.

Ancient Egypt was shaped like a funnel with two distinct parts. Lower (downstream or northern) Egypt was the 150-mile-wide by 100-mile-deep triangular delta at the mouth of the Nile. Upper (upstream or southern) Egypt occupied a narrow valley stretching 650 miles from the delta to the First Cataract, a set of rapids that were a barrier to navigation.

The Nile alone made life possible in the almost rainless deserts of Egypt. Annually the river's floods covered the land and deposited fertile mud that enabled farmers to bring in two crops a year. Egypt's agricultural prosperity was unmatched in the ancient world.

Although Egypt was a long, narrow country, the Nile provided a kind of highway that encouraged unification. As early as 3100 B.C.E., while the cities of Mesopotamia were still competing among themselves for dominance, Upper and Lower Egypt had become a single state. The people on the open plains of the Tigris-Euphrates lived in constant fear of storm, flood, earthquake, and invasion, but nature protected the Egyptians. The Nile's unnavigable cataracts, the sea, and the desert made it difficult for foreigners to enter Egypt, and Egypt's weather tended to be stable and predictable. Consequently, Egypt was far more peaceful and secure than Mesopotamia, and Egyptian culture reflected an optimistic outlook that contrasted vividly with the pessimism expressed in Mesopotamian literature.

Events in the more than 3,000-year span of ancient Egyptian history are traditionally dated by reference to the reigns of thirty-one royal dynasties. Modern historians have clustered these into eight periods (see chronology chart). The first dynasty was founded by Menes, the unifier of Upper and Lower Egypt, and the last, by a Greek conqueror, Alexander the Great (332 B.C.E.). For most of its long history Egypt maintained its unity, for central management was vital to the success of its irrigation-based agriculture.

ca. 3100–2700 B.C.E.	*Early Dynastic Period (I–II)*
2700–2200 B.C.E.	*Old Kingdom (III–IV)*
2200–2052 B.C.E.	*I Intermediate Period (VII–X)*
2052–1786 B.C.E.	*Middle Kingdom (XI–XII)*
1786–1575 B.C.E.	*II Intermediate Period (XIII–XVII)*
ca. 1700 B.C.E.	*Hyksos invasion*
1575–1087 B.C.E.	*New Kingdom (Empire) (XVIII–XX)*
1087–30 B.C.E.	*Post-Empire (XXI–XXXI)*

The Old Kingdom (2700–2200 b.c.e.). By the time the Third Dynasty appeared, royal authority in Egypt was absolute. Ruling from their capital at Memphis on the border between Upper and Lower Egypt, Egypt's kings had the resources of a huge, prosperous nation at their disposal. The *pharaoh* (a royal title that evolved later from a term meaning "great house" or "palace") staffed his government with members of his family, appointing and dismissing them at his pleasure. Peasants were carefully controlled, and they were taxed heavily (perhaps as much as one-fifth of what they produced).

Egyptians believed their king to be a living god on whom their lives, safety, and prosperity depended. Because the law was whatever he said it was, Egypt evolved no law codes to guide its rulers. Government was part of a great religious cult that influenced all aspects of Egyptian life. Gods were conceived in many forms, both animal and human. Re, the sun god, eventually assumed a dominant role, but for centuries there was little order to the Egyptian pantheon.

Unlike the Mesopotamians, the Egyptians had high expectations for the afterlife. They had elaborate conventions for embalming and burying their dead, and they supplied graves with all kinds of things they thought the departed would need in the next world. At first, only kings were thought to merit eternal life. Then nobles were included, and finally all Egyptians—if properly buried with the requisite spells—laid claim to immortality. Tombs were beautifully decorated, and offerings of food were made to the deceased on a regular basis. Some royal tombs were provided with full-sized ships to convey the soul across the heavens.

Egypt's land belonged to its ruler, and all of its people were his servants. The extent of his power is most graphically demonstrated by the Old Kingdom's most famous monuments, the pyramids built by the kings of the Fourth Dynasty. Although many pyramids were constructed, the great pyramid of the pharaoh Khufu has cast all others in its shade. It contains 2,300,000 blocks of stone averaging 2.5 tons each. It originally rose to a height of 481 feet from a base whose sides were 756 feet long. The Greek historian Herodotus claimed that it was erected in twenty years by a work force of 100,000 men. The pyramids witness to the great technical skill of Egyptian engineers and to the power and administrative capacity of pharaonic government.

The Egyptians developed a system of writing not much later than the Sumerians. The idea of writing may actually have come to Egypt from Mesopotamia, but Egyptian script was unique. It began as picture writing and later added phonetic symbols to its pictographs. The result was a difficult and complicated script that the Greeks called *hieroglyph* ("sacred carvings"). Although Egyptian writing could be engraved on stone, it evolved from pen and ink drawings on a paper made from the papyrus reeds that grew in the delta. It bore no resemblance to the cuneiform the Sumerians developed for inscribing mud tablets.

Egyptian authors produced hymns, myths, magical formulas, tales of travel, and "wisdom literature" (bits of advice to help one succeed in the world). But Egyptian society, happier and simpler than that of Mesopotamia, produced nothing as serious and probing as Mesopotamia's heroic epic of Gilgamesh.

The Middle Kingdom (2052–1786 B.C.E.). As the government of the Old Kingdom became increasingly elaborate, power shifted from pharaohs to priests and nobles. Gradually the heads of *nomes* (Egypt's administrative districts) won hereditary rights to their offices. They slipped from the control of the central government, and about 2200 B.C.E. the Old Kingdom collapsed. An era of confusion ensued. During this First Intermediate Period (ca. 2200–2052 B.C.E.) wars raged among the nobles until the nomarchs (governors) of Thebes in Upper Egypt gained the upper hand, reunited the country, and launched the Middle Kingdom (2052 B.C.E.).

The Egyptians believed in the possibility of life after death through the god Osiris. The character of each person's life had to be tested by forty-two assessor-gods before the person could be presented to Osiris. In this scene from an illustration of the Book of the Dead, *the deceased and his wife (on the left) watch the scales of justice weighing his heart (on the left side of the scales) against the feather of truth. The jackal-faced god Anubis also watches the scales, while the ibis-headed god Thoth keeps the records. [Courtesy of the Trustees of the British Museum.]*

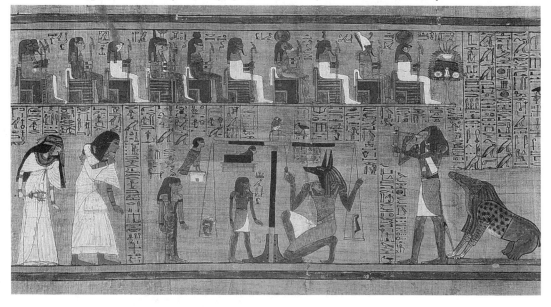

The pharaohs of the Twelfth Dynasty moved Egypt's capital to Thebes. Although they restored centralized government, their power was more limited than that of the rulers of the Old Kingdom. In tales from the period, their function is to prevent the nobility from exploiting the poor and to provide justice for all. Their statues depict them as compassionate figures burdened with care for all their people.

Order, peace, and prosperity characterized the Middle Kingdom. Trade expanded, and Egypt's influence extended north to Palestine and south to Ethiopia. The seat of government eventually shifted from Thebes back to Memphis on the border between the delta and the valley, but this did not diminish the importance of Amon, the patron god of Thebes. He was identified with Re, the sun god, and became Amon-Re, Egypt's chief deity.

The New Kingdom (Empire) (1575–1087 B.C.E.) and After. The nobles gradually eroded the authority of the pharaohs of the Thirteenth Dynasty and inaugurated the II Intermediate Period (1786–1575 B.C.E.). About 1700 B.C.E., a foreign invasion added to Egypt's confusion. A horde of Semitic peoples (probably from Palestine and Syria) crossed the Sinai and occupied the delta. The Egyptians called them the Hyksos, and they dominated Egypt until 1575 B.C.E. The nomarchs of Thebes then rallied their countrymen, drove out the Hyksos, and founded the New Kingdom or Empire.

The knowledge of new military techniques and weapons that the Egyptians had acquired from the Hyksos enabled the rulers of the New Kingdom to build a powerful army. They used it to defend Egypt and extend its territory to the south and the east. The Eighteenth Dynasty, whose most prominent pharaoh was Thutmose III (r. 1490–1436 B.C.E.), brought Palestine and Syria (as far as the upper Euphrates) under Egyptian control (see Map 1-2). Egypt's expansion was finally checked when it made contact with the powerful Hittite empire based in Asia Minor. The struggle that ensued weakened both nations, and the glory of ancient Egypt faded with the New Kingdom. During the Post-Empire period (1087–30 B.C.E.) Egypt repeatedly suffered invasion and submitted to foreign dominance.

Near the end of the Eighteenth Dynasty, when the empire was at its peak, there was a unique episode in Egypt's history. The power of the priests of Amon had increased to the point where the young pharaoh, Amenhotep IV (r. 1367–1350 B.C.E.), felt threatened. Supported by his family and advisers, he made a clean break with the worship of Amon-Re and devoted himself to the service of a new god called Aton. The pharaoh changed his name to Akhnaton ("it pleases Aton") and moved his capital from Thebes, the center of Amon worship, to an entirely new city which he called Akhtaton (modern El Amarna).

The new god was different from any that had come before him, for he was believed to be not merely an Egyptian god, but a universal deity. However, only the pharaoh and his family worshiped Aton directly. The people honored him by venerating their pharaoh. Unlike other gods, Aton had no cult statue but was represented in painting and relief sculpture as the disk of the sun. Because Aton was universal, all other gods were redundant. Their temples were shut down,

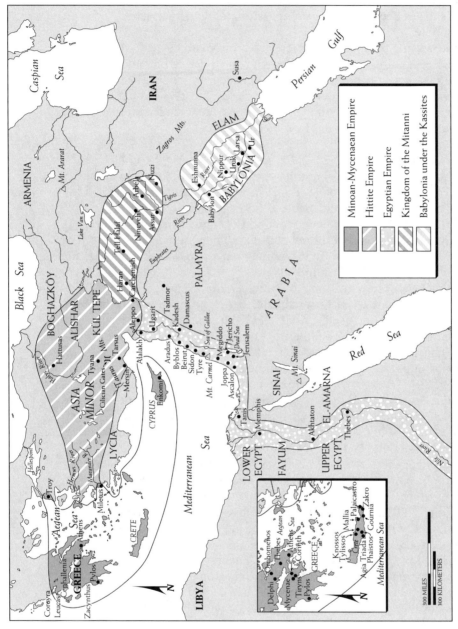

MAP 1-2 The Middle East and Greece About 1400 B.C.E. *About 1400 B.C.E. the Middle East was divided among four empires. Egypt went south to Nubia and north through Palestine and Phoenicia. Kassites ruled in Mesopotamia, Hittites in Asia Minor, and the Mitannians in Assyrian lands. In the Aegean the Mycenaean kingdoms were at their heights.*

and the name of Amon-Re, Egypt's former high god, was chiseled from monuments. The priests of the old cults were deprived of their posts, and the pharaoh appointed new people—even some foreigners—to serve him.

Akhnaton's preoccupation with religion distracted him from foreign affairs, and he allowed Egypt's Asian possessions to slip away. The military and economic consequences of their loss undercut support for the new religion, and after the king's death a counterrevolution swept away his life's work. His chosen successor was replaced by Tutankhamon (r. 1347–1339 B.C.E.), the young husband of a daughter of Akhnaton and his beautiful wife, Nefertiti. The new pharaoh restored the old religion and tried to wipe out all evidence of the Aton cult. Amon returned to the pinnacle of the Egyptian pantheon. El Amarna was abandoned, and the court sent back to Thebes. Although Tutankhamon died young and was a minor king, he is very well known today. His is the only pharaonic tomb to have survived intact from the ancient world. Its magnificent treasures were discovered in 1922.

The fall of Akhnaton restored power to the priests of Amon and to Egypt's military. A general named Horemhab became king (r. 1335–1308? B.C.E.) and recovered much of the lost empire. He branded his predecessor "the criminal of Akhtaton" and erased his name from the records. Akhnaton's city was torn down, and its memory disappeared for over 3,000 years. It was rediscovered by chance about a century ago.

Although Egypt returned to its traditional gods and culture, its confidence was shaken. At this time *The Book of the Dead* was compiled. It was a collection of spells to help the dead reach the next world safely, avoiding destruction by hideous monsters. The text was a metaphor for the fears of the nation—its awareness of powerful, menacing enemies.

✌ Ancient Middle Eastern Empires

While the Eighteenth Dynasty was ruling Egypt, new peoples who spoke Indo-European languages were moving into the Middle East: the Kassites in Babylonia, the Hittites in Asia Minor, and the Mitannians in northern Mesopotamia. The Kassites and Mitannians were small warrior castes. They dominated more civilized folk whose cultures they adopted. The Hittites founded a new kingdom and built an empire that lasted 200 years.

The Hittites

The Hittites arrived in Asia Minor about 2000 B.C.E. By about 1500 B.C.E. they had established a strong, centralized government with a seat at Hattusas (near Ankara, the capital of modern Turkey). Between 1400 and 1200 B.C.E. they contested Egypt's control of Palestine and Syria, and by 1265 B.C.E. they were important enough to merit an alliance with Egypt. Although the Hittite kingdom fell about 1200 B.C.E. (swept away by a later migration of Indo-Europeans), neo-Hittite centers survived in Asia Minor and Mesopotamia for centuries.

The Hittites adopted Mesopotamian culture, but their society had unique aspects. Hittite kings did not claim to be divine or even to be the chosen representatives of gods. In the early period a Hittite king's power was checked by a council of nobles, and the army had to ratify his succession to the throne. The Hittites were also responsible for introducing the Middle East to an important technology, iron smelting. They also helped shape history by transmitting aspects of Mesopotamian and Egyptian culture to the Greeks who lived on their frontiers.

The Assyrians

The Assyrians, who succeeded the Hittites and the Egyptians as the dominant power in the Middle East, were not invaders. They spoke a Semitic language and had ancient cultural roots in Mesopotamia. They established the first in a series of great empires that united the peoples of the Middle East and spread their ancient civilizations to new areas. The Assyrian homeland was the hill country of northern Mesopotamia and the area east of the Tigris River. Of the capitals of the Assyrian Empire, the best known was Nineveh (modern Mosul).

Before Assyria built its empire, it was ruled by Akkadians, Sumerians, Amorites, and Mitannians. The Assyrians were effectively liberated in the fourteenth century B.C.E. when their Mitannian masters were defeated by the Hittites. About 1000 B.C.E. the Assyrians entered an era of steady expansion, which by 665 B.C.E. brought them control of Mesopotamia, much of Asia Minor, Syria, Palestine, and Egypt. They owed their success to a large, well-disciplined army and a society organized to support the military. Fierce and cruel, they boasted of their brutality—a strategy designed to terrorize their enemies, control their subjects, and ease their conquests.

The Assyrian Empire was unique in its ability to exploit the people it conquered. Some simply paid tribute. Others had sustained garrisons stationed on their territory. A few were driven from their homelands and scattered about the empire (a fate that befell the people of the kingdom of Israel). The administration of something as vast and diverse as the Assyrian Empire required great skill. The state had to be policed internally and simultaneously defended from barbarians attacking its frontiers. By the seventh century B.C.E. these tasks had overextended the Assyrian government and made it vulnerable to internal upheaval. When the Chaldeans of Babylon formed an alliance with the kingdom of Media (modern Iran) and attacked the Assyrians, the empire fell very quickly. Nineveh was destroyed in 612 B.C.E., but the victorious Chaldean (or neo-Babylonian) and Median kingdoms that took its place did not last long. By 539 B.C.E., they had been gathered into a new eastern empire headed by Persia.

☞ Palestine

None of the empires of the ancient Middle East had a greater influence on the course of Western civilization than the state of Israel. This little nation evolved in Palestine, a small country between Syria and Egypt. Events here created the modern West's major religions: Judaism, Christianity, and Islam.

Canaanites and Phoenicians

Before the Israelites arrived in the land they believed their God had promised them, it was occupied by another Semitic people, the Canaanites. Canaanite culture was typically Mesopotamian in that Canaanites lived in fortified cities and practiced polytheistic religions. Pressure from the Israelites drove some of the Canaanites north to join other Semites living in a coastal district called Phoenicia.

The Phoenicians, who distinguished themselves as traders at a very early period, scattered colonies along the African coast of the Mediterranean as far west as Spain. They helped spread civilization and, in particular, literacy. The Phoenicians were among the pioneers of alphabetic scripts. An alphabet simplifies writing, for its symbols stand for the limited repertoire of sounds of speech rather than for ideas or words. It required only a small number of symbols to record everything that can be spoken.

The Israelites

Since there are few references to the Israelites in records compiled by their neighbors, most of what is known about them has to be inferred from the chief piece of literature they left behind: the Bible. It is a collection of historical narratives, ritual instructions, collections of wisdom literature, poetry, law, prophecy, and other types of documents. Although it was not designed to be read as objective history, scholarly analysis has extracted much important information from it.

According to tradition, the patriarch Abraham and his family left Ur about 1900 B.C.E. and wandered west to tend flocks in the land of the Canaanites. Some of his descendants drifted into Egypt, perhaps with the Hyksos. By the thirteenth century B.C.E., they had left Egypt (led by a man named Moses), spent some time wandering in the desert, and finally returned to Canaan. They settled down, conquered their neighbors, and established a monarchy that reached its peak in the tenth century B.C.E. under King David and his son Solomon The kingdom then split into two parts: Israel in the north and Judah in the south. Israel was larger and more advanced, but the old capital and its temple at Jerusalem were located in Judah (see Map 1-3). Assyria conquered Israel in 722 B.C.E., and dispersed its people—the "ten lost tribes of Israel." Only the residents of Judah (the Jews) survived to preserve their country's literature and culture.

In 586 B.C.E. Judah was invaded by the neo-Babylonian king Nebuchadnezzar II. He destroyed the temple that Solomon had built in Jerusalem and forced the Jews into exile. The Exile (or "Babylonian Captivity") was not permanent, for Persia soon conquered Babylon and allowed some Jews to go back to Jerusalem. The Jewish homeland continued, however, to be dominated by foreign powers for some 2,500 years. Independence returned in 1948 C.E. with the establishment of the modern State of Israel.

Significant Dates from the Early History of the Hebrew Nation

ca. 1000–961 B.C.E.	*Reign of King David*
ca. 961–922 B.C.E.	*Reign of King Solomon*
722 B.C.E.	*Assyrian conquest of Israel, the northern kingdom*
586 B.C.E.	*Chaldean conquest of Judah, the southern kingdom*
586–539 B.C.E.	*The Exile (the "Babylonian Captivity")*
539 B.C.E.	*Restoration of Jerusalem*

The Jewish Religion

The fate of the tiny nation of Israel would be of little interest were it not for its unique religious achievement. The Jews' belief in a single universal God—in an all-powerful creator who loved humankind, but who demanded righteousness

MAP 1-3   Ancient Palestine
The Hebrews established a unified kingdom in Palestine under kings David and Solomon in the tenth century B.C.E. After the death of Solomon, however, the kingdom was divided into two parts—Israel in the north and Judah, with its capital Jerusalem, in the south. North of Israel were the great commercial cities of Phoenicia.

and obedience—has become a fundamental part of the Western heritage. The Jewish concept of God is so elevated that the divine is not conceived as a force of nature, as a human being, a creature, or, indeed, pictured in any way.

Unlike other ancient peoples, the Jews intuited a link between ethics and religion. The covenant that God made with their ancestor Abraham turned them into a people who accepted the burden of revealing God in history by living according to His will. The Jewish prophets described God as a severe but just judge who was not content with mere ritual and sacrifice. God binds Himself to act righteously and expects His people to do the same. The Jewish prophets blamed the misfortunes of their nation on a just God's necessary interventions in history to punish the sins of His people. The prophets also assured the Jews that God dealt mercifully with those who repented. Gradually, the Jews came to believe that God would send them a special leader, a Messiah, to help them fulfill their mission in history. Christians maintain that Jesus of Nazareth was that Messiah.

❧ General Outlook of Middle Eastern Cultures

There were differences among the various cultures of the Middle East, but they all contrasted significantly with the way of life pioneered by the ancient people who had the greatest influence on the formation of the Western tradition: the Greeks. This becomes clear when we compare the assumptions ancient people made about how human beings were related to nature, to the divine, and to one another.

Humans and Nature

The peoples of the Middle East did not assume that there was an absolute gulf between animate creatures and inanimate objects. They believed that all things partook of life and spirit, and that the universe was an arena for a chaotic war of wills. They concluded that because the natural world seemed to have so little order, the gods who governed it must be capricious.

An Egyptian text dismissed human beings as "the cattle of god," and the Babylonian story of creation said that humanity's purpose was merely to serve the whims of the gods. In a world that powerful deities ran for their own benefit, human existence was precarious. Even disasters such as war, which we think of as human in origin, the Mesopotamians saw as products of divine wills.

The helplessness of humankind in the face of irrational divine powers is the point of the story of a great primeval flood that exists in Egyptian and Babylonian versions as well as the Hebrew Bible. In the Egyptian tale, some unspecified grievance causes Re, the god who made humanity, to loose the vicious goddess Sekhmet on his hapless creatures. He then changes his mind, and humankind is saved when Re pours 7,000 barrels of blood-colored beer in Sekhmet's path to intoxicate her. In the Babylonian story, the noise made by increasing hordes of human beings annoys the gods so much that they decide to wipe out humanity. The species is spared only because Enki, the god of wisdom, decides to rescue the family of a friend named Utnapishtim. In a world governed by such quixotic principles, humans could not hope to understand or control events. At best, they might try to pit one mysterious force against another by means of magical spells.

Humans and the Gods, Law, and Justice

Since the gods could destroy humankind—and might do so at any time for no apparent reason—people tried to win the gods over by offering prayer and sacrifice. There was, however, no guarantee of success, for gods were not bound by reason or conscience.

Human beings were different. In the earliest civilized societies rulers decreed laws to govern human relations. The challenge was to justify the authority of the law: Why, apart from a lawgiver's power to coerce obedience, should anyone obey the law? The Egyptians simply assumed that since the king was a god, he had the right to establish whatever rules seemed best to him. Mesopotamians also believed that kings were delegated divine authority over their subjects.

The Hebrews had a more subtle understanding of law. Their God was capable of destructive rages, but He was open to rational discourse and He imposed moral standards on Himself. In the biblical version of the flood story the Hebrew God is wrathful, but not arbitrary. His creatures deserve destruction as punishment for their sin. When He repents and saves Noah, He does so because Noah is a good man. The Hebrews believed that God willed human beings to live in just relationships with each other and that He was Himself an advocate for human justice.

✧ Toward the Greeks and Western Thought

Many, if not most, Greeks in the ancient world must have thought about life in much the same way as their neighbors to the east. Their gods were assumed to behave much like Mesopotamian deities; they trusted in magic and incantations to manage life's uncertainties; and they believed that laws were to be obeyed simply because the gods decreed them. The surprising thing is that some Greeks were exceptions. They conceived strikingly original ideas that charted a different path for the West.

As early as the sixth century B.C.E., Greek thinkers living along the coast of Asia Minor began an intellectual revolution. Thales, the first Greek philosopher, taught his followers to explain natural events by referring them to other natural events, not to unknowable supernatural causes. His search for naturalistic explanations for phenomena launched Western science.

Rationalism of this kind characterized the approach major Greek thinkers took to exploring all kinds of issues. Xenophanes of Colophon, Thales' contemporary, pointed out that people had no grounds for imagining gods in human form. He argued that if oxen could draw, they would sketch gods who looked like oxen. Comments like this could promote skepticism, but they could also produce valuable insights. In the fifth century B.C.E., Thucydides of Athens wrote a history that made no reference to the gods, but traced the causes of events to interactions between human efforts and chance. Similarly, Hippocrates of Cos founded a school of medicine that diagnosed and treated disease without invoking the supernatural. The same absence of interest in divine causality characterized Greek views of law and justice.

Although the Greeks' original insights account for much of the uniqueness of Western civilization, we should not forget that they built on a foundation of lore that people in the Middle East had accumulated over millennia. Phoenicia gave the Greeks a writing system, and from ancient Mesopotamia and Egypt the Greeks acquired vital technical information and models that stimulated the development of mathematics, astronomy, art, and literature. The discontinuities between the culture of the Greeks and those of their eastern neighbors are, however, more striking than the continuities.

A secular, reasoned quest for an understanding of the world that sought explanations for events in the natures of things rather than in the supernatures of gods was not characteristic of pre-Greek cultures. Nor would it appear in similar societies at other times in other parts of the world. This raises the issue of whether there was something special in the Greek experience that caused fundamental questions to be pondered in strikingly original ways.

✒ Review Questions

1. How was life during the Paleolithic Age different from that in the Neolithic Age? What advances in agriculture and human development had taken place by the end of the Neolithic era? Do they warrant referring to the period as the "Neolithic Revolution"?

2. What differences do you see in the political and intellectual outlooks of the Egyptian and Mesopotamian civilizations? How do their religious views compare? How did the geography of each region influence its religious outlook?

3. How did religious faith help bind the Hebrews together politically? Why did Middle Eastern civilizations regard the concept of monotheism as a radical idea?

4. Why were the Assyrians so successful in building an empire? How did their empire differ from that of the Hittites or Egyptians? How did their empire benefit the civilized Middle East? What caused its failure?

5. How did Greek thinkers depart from the assumptions that guided intellectuals schooled in the Middle Eastern civilizations?

✎ Suggested Readings

V. G. Childe, *What Happened in History* (1946). A pioneering study of human prehistory before the Greeks, from an anthropological point of view.

M. Ehrenberg, *Women in Prehistory* (1989). An account of the role of women in early times.

H. Frankfort et al., *Before Philosophy* (1949). A brilliant examination of the mind of the ancients, from the Stone Age to the Greeks.

A. Gardiner, *Egypt of the Pharaohs* (1961). A sound narrative history.

O. R. Gurney, *The Hittites* (1954). A good general survey.

D. C. Johnson and M. R. Edey, *Lucy: The Beginnings of Mankind* (1981). A study of the first human creatures, based on remains found in Africa.

S. N. Kramer, *The Sumerians: Their History, Culture and Character* (1963). A readable general account of Sumerian history.

J. Oates, *Babylon*, rev. ed. (1986). An introduction to the history and archaeology of Babylonia, revised to make use of newly discovered evidence.

H. M. Orlinsky, *Ancient Israel* (1960). Chiefly a political survey.

J. N. Postgate, *Early Mesopotamia* (1992). An excellent study of Mesopotamian economy and society, from the earliest times to about 1500 b.c.e., helpfully illustrated with drawings, pictures, and translated documents.

J. B. Pritchard (ed.), *Ancient Near Eastern Texts Relating to the Old Testament* (1969). A good collection of documents in translation, with useful introductory material.

C. L. Redman, *The Rise of Civilization* (1978). An attempt to use the evidence provided by anthropology, archaeology, and the physical sciences to illuminate the development of early urban society.

W. F. Saggs, *The Might That Was Assyria* (1984). A history of the northern Mesopotamian empire and a worthy companion to the author's account of the Babylonian empire in the south.

S. Sandmel, *The Hebrew Scriptures* (1963). An examination of the Bible's value as history and literature.

B. G. Trigger et al., *Ancient Egypt: A Social History* (1982).

2

The Rise of Greek Civilization

KEY TOPICS

- The Bronze Age civilizations that ruled the Aegean area before the development of Hellenic civilization
- The rise, development, and expansion of the *polis,* the characteristic political unit of Hellenic Greece
- The early history of Sparta and Athens
- The wars between the Greeks and the Persians

About 2000 B.C.E., Greek-speaking peoples settled the lands surrounding the Aegean Sea and established a culture that became one of the most powerful forces shaping the Western heritage. The Greeks' location at the eastern end of the Mediterranean put them in touch, early in their history, with Mesopotamia, Egypt, Asia Minor, and Syria-Palestine. The Greeks acknowledged their debt to these peoples, but were well aware of the importance of their own contributions to civilization.

✎ The Bronze Age on Crete and on the Mainland to About 1150 B.C.E.

During the Bronze Age, civilizations developed in three parts of the Aegean world: on the island of Crete, on the smaller islands of the Aegean Sea, and on the mainland of Greece. Crete provided a cultural bridge between the older civilizations of the East and the lands settled by the Greeks. Crete's Minoan civilization (which modern historians have named for Minos, a legendary king of the island) was the Aegean's first civilization.

The Minoans

During the periods in Crete's history known as Middle and Late Minoan (2100–1150 B.C.E.), the island evolved a unique civilization. The palace sites that modern archaeologists have excavated at Phaestus, Haghia Triada, and Cnossus are its most striking remains. Parts of the palace at Cnossus, the most important of the Minoan monuments, were four stories high. The building was a labyrinth of rooms organized around great courtyards. The main and upper floors contained living quarters as well as workshops for making pottery and

(a)

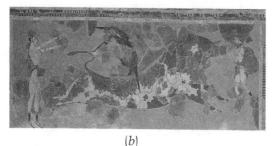

(b)

(a) The Minoan-period Palace at Cnossus on the island of Crete. (b) A fresco painting from the east wing of the palace. The fresco shows acrobats leaping over a charging bull. It is not known whether such acrobatic displays were only for entertainment or part of some religious ritual. [(a) D. A. Harissiadis, Athens; (b) Scala/Art Resource, N.Y.]

Significant Dates from the Era of the Rise of Greece

ca. 2900–1150 B.C.E.	*Minoan period*
ca. 1900 B.C.E.	*Migration of the Greeks to the mainland*
ca. 1600–1150 B.C.E.	*Mycenaean period*
ca. 1250 B.C.E.	*Sack of Troy (?)*
ca. 1200–750 B.C.E.	*Dark Ages*
ca. 725–700 B.C.E.	*Homer and Hesiod*
ca. 700–500 B.C.E.	*Major period of Greek tyranny*
ca. 650–625 B.C.E.	*Spartan constitution*
594 B.C.E.	*Solon's reforms at Athens*
546–527 B.C.E.	*Pisistratus' tyranny at Athens*
ca. 508–501 B.C.E.	*Clisthenes' democratic reforms at Athens*
490 B.C.E.	*Battle of Marathon*
480–479 B.C.E.	*Xerxes' invasion of Greece*
480 B.C.E.	*Battles of Thermopylae and Salamis*
479 B.C.E.	*Battles of Plataea and Mycale*

jewelry. The cellars had elaborate storage facilities for oil and grain. There were sitting rooms and even bathrooms to which water was piped. Ceilings were supported by columns of a unique design—tapering gracefully downward. Many walls carried murals showing landscapes, seascapes, festivals, and sports. Minoan art reflects eastern influences, but it has a style and quality all its own.

Since Minoan palaces and settlements were wealthy, they would have been attractive targets for raiders. But, surprisingly, the great Minoan structures lacked defensive walls. It may be that the protection provided by the sea made the fortification of buildings on Crete unnecessary.

The Minoans wrote on clay tablets like those found in Mesopotamia. Many of the extant specimens were preserved accidentally when they were baked into tiles by a great fire that destroyed the palace at Cnossus. The Cnossus tablets are inscribed with three distinct kinds of writing: hieroglyphic (picture writing) and two different linear scripts (A and B). Only Linear B, which records an early form of Greek, has been deciphered.

The Linear B tablets found at Cnossus are pedestrian documents. Most are inventories, the working papers of the kind of elaborate bureaucracy that was characteristic of an ancient eastern monarchy. They, however, raise an intriguing question: The Minoans were not Greeks, so why were records at Cnossus being written in Greek? What can be inferred from this about the relationship between the Minoans and the Bronze Age ("Helladic") cultures of the Greek mainland?

The Mycenaeans

During the Early Helladic Period (the third millennium B.C.E.) most of the Greek mainland was occupied by peoples who knew how to smelt metals and construct impressive buildings and who had trade contacts with Crete and the islands of the Aegean. Some of the names they gave to places have survived. These names prove that these people were not Greeks, for they do not fit the phonetic pattern of the Indo-European family of languages to which Greek belongs.

Sometime after 2000 B.C.E., many of the Early Helladic sites were destroyed, abandoned, or occupied by a new people. These are signs of invasion that probably signal the arrival of the Greeks. The newcomers took control of the entire mainland and, during the Late Helladic era (1580–1150 B.C.E.), developed a civilization that modern historians have named for Mycenae, one of its cities. The explanation for the Linear B tablets found at Cnossus is probably that at the height of Mycenaean power (1400–1200 B.C.E.), Greeks conquered Crete.

Mycenaean Culture. The Mycenaean world contained a number of independent, powerful, and well-organized kingdoms. Excavations at Mycenaean sites suggest that the culture of the Mycenaeans was influenced by, but very different from, that of the Minoans. Unlike the Minoans, the Mycenaeans were preoccupied with war. The walls of their palaces were decorated with paintings depicting scenes of battle and hunting, and defensible sites were chosen for their cities. The need for defense probably promoted the development of strong, centralized monarchies.

By 1500 B.C.E. Mycenaean kings were constructing monumental tombs that testify to their wealth and to their power to command. The *tholos* tombs of the Mycenaeans were of a unique design—beehive-like domed chambers, built of enormous cut and fitted stones buried beneath an artificial mound. The wealth that financed the construction of these monuments probably came from raids and trade. Mycenaean ships ventured west to Italy and Sicily, but most Greek commerce was with the islands of the Aegean, the coast of Asia Minor, and the cities of Syria, Egypt, and Crete.

The Rise and Fall of Mycenaean Power. At the height of their power (1400–1200 B.C.E.), the Mycenaeans enlarged their cities, expanded their trade, and established commercial colonies in the East. Mycenaeans are mentioned in the archives of the Hittite kings of Asia Minor and in Egyptian records. About 1250 B.C.E., the Mycenaeans probably sacked a city called Troy on the coast of northwestern Asia Minor (see Map 2-1). This campaign may have been the Mycenaeans' last great adventure, for by 1200 B.C.E. their world was in trouble and by 1100 B.C.E. it was gone. Memories survived, however, and gave rise to the earliest monuments of Greek literature: Homer's epics, the *Iliad* and the *Odyssey.*

The Dorian Invasion. Many Mycenaean towns fell about 1200 B.C.E., but some flourished for another century and some were never destroyed or abandoned. Ancient Greek legends imply that there may have been an attack on the Peloponnesus (the southern Greek peninsula) by Dorians, a rude people from the north whose Greek dialect was different from that of the Mycenaeans. Perhaps

MAP 2-1   The Aegean Area in the Bronze Age *The Bronze Age in the Aegean area lasted from about 1900 to about 1100 B.C.E. Its culture on Crete is called Minoan and was at its height from about 1900 to about 1400 B.C.E. Bronze Age Helladic culture on the mainland flourished from about 1600 to about 1200 B.C.E.*

this set in motion a chain of events that undermined Mycenaean civilization. The development of rigid bureaucracies may have limited the flexibility of the Mycenaean kingdoms and thus increased their vulnerability to invasion. It is impossible, however, to say with any certainty what happened at the end of the Aegean Bronze Age.

⌁ The Greek "Middle Ages" to About 750 B.C.E.

The collapse of the Mycenaean world inaugurated a long period of depopulation, impoverishment, and cultural decline in the Aegean. The palaces and the kings and bureaucrats who managed them were destroyed. The wealth and social order that made it possible for artists and merchants to thrive were swept away. Many villages were abandoned and never resettled.

Greek Migrations

The confusion that attended the Mycenaean decline caused many Greeks (including the Dorians who invaded the Peloponnesus) to migrate from the mainland to the Aegean islands and the coast of Asia Minor. These migrations turned the Aegean into a Greek lake, but trade in the region diminished with the fading of civilization. Each community was left largely to its own devices, and people turned inward. At this time the Middle East was also in disarray, so no great power was poised to take advantage of the Aegean's situation. The Greeks, therefore, had time to recover and the freedom to evolve a unique way of life. Little is known about this crucial era, for writing disappeared with the Mycenaeans and was not reinvented until after 750 B.C.E. No contemporary authors shed light on the Greek "dark age," and archaeological excavation discovers no architecture, sculpture, or painting until after 750 B.C.E.

The Age of Homer

The *Iliad* and the *Odyssey* are our best sources of information about the Greek dark ages. They are the end products of a long tradition of oral poetry with roots in the Mycenaean era. For generations bards sang tales of the heroes who fought at Troy. Since they used rhythmic formulas to aid the accurate memorization of their verses, some very old material was preserved. The poems, as they were finally written down, date from the eighth century B.C.E. and are attributed to a mysterious individual named Homer.

Although the poems narrate the adventures of Mycenaean heroes, the society they describe is not purely Mycenaean. Homer's warriors are not buried in *tholos* tombs but are cremated; they worship gods in temples, whereas no Mycenaean temples have been found; they have chariots but do not know their proper use in warfare. These inconsistencies arise because Homer's epics combine memories of the ancient Mycenaeans and material drawn from the very different world that was familiar to the poets of the tenth and ninth centuries B.C.E.

Government. The kings Homer describes had much less power than real Mycenaean monarchs. Homeric kings had to arrive at decisions by consulting with their nobles, and their nobles felt free to debate vigorously and to oppose a king's wishes. In the *Iliad*, Achilles does not hesitate to accuse Agamemnon, the "most kingly" commander of the Trojan expedition, of having "a dog's face and a deer's heart." This was impolite, but apparently not treasonous.

The right to speak before a royal council was limited to noblemen, but the common people could not be ignored. If a king planned a war or a major change of policy, he would call all his soldiers together to explain his intentions. They could express their feelings by acclamation even though they could not amend his suggestions by debating them. At a very early date, the Greeks seemed to have been accustomed to limited forms of popular government.

Society. Homeric society was sharply divided into classes. The dominant group was a hereditary aristocracy, and there were three kinds of commoners: *thetes,* landless laborers, and slaves. The *thetes* may have owned the land they worked privately, or they may have farmed hereditary plots belonging to their clans, property that could not be sold. The landless agricultural laborer had the worst lot in life. Attachment to a household guaranteed a slave protection and food, but free workers were desperately vulnerable. They were loners in communities where the only safety lay in belonging to groups that looked out for their members. There were few slaves. Most were women who served as maids and concubines. Some male slaves worked as shepherds, but most farm labor was done by free men throughout Greek history.

Homeric Values. The Homeric poems taught an aristocratic code of values that influenced all later Greek thinkers, for they became the major schoolbooks of the Greeks. The Greeks memorized Homer's texts and cherished his values: physical prowess; courage; fierce protection of family, friends, and property; and, above all, defense of honor. The *Iliad* is the story of a fight over honor. When Agamemnon, the king who presided over the Greek army besieging Troy, wounds the honor of Achilles, his most important warrior, Achilles refuses to fight and persuades the gods to heap defeat on the Greeks. Achilles finally returns to the battlefield, but he is brought back by a personal obligation to avenge the death of a friend, not by a sense of duty to his country.

The highest virtue in Homeric society was *arete*—the manliness, courage, and excellence that enabled a hero to acquire and defend honor. Men demonstrated this quality by engaging in contests with worthy opponents. Homeric battles are usually described as separate matches between great champions, not group combats. Homeric festivals usually centered on athletic competitions. Even the funeral of Achilles' friend, Patroclus, which ends the *Iliad*, is described as a series of contests for prizes.

Homer's view of life is encapsulated in the advice Achilles' father gives him as he departs for Troy: "Always be the best and distinguished above others." The father of another Homeric hero adds a codicil to this prescription: "Do not bring shame on the family of your fathers." Here in a nutshell are the values of Homer's aristocratic world: to vie for individual supremacy in *arete* and to enhance the honor of the family.

Women in Homeric Society. The male-oriented warrior society that Homer describes relegated women to domestic roles. Their chief function was to bear and raise children. The wife of a soldier was also expected to oversee his home in his absence, manage its servants, and preserve its wealth. A husband might have sexual adventures, but a wife was expected to be unswervingly faithful. Homer's ideal woman was Penelope, Odysseus' wife. Although her husband is gone for twenty years, she does not give him up for dead. She refuses the many suitors who seek her hand (and his estate) and lives in chaste seclusion with her maids. She fills her days with the labor the Greek world associated with women of all classes: weaving. Penelope's opposite, the epitome of female evil, was Agamemnon's wife, Clytemnestra. While this king is at Troy, she takes a lover. When Agamemnon returns, she and her lover assassinate him and seize his crown.

✧ The *Polis*

Classical Greek civilization emerged from an institution called the *polis* (plural, *poleis*) that evolved during the dark ages. *Polis* is usually translated as "city-state," but that implies too much and too little. All Greek *poleis* began as agricultural villages and many never grew large enough to be true cities. All of them were states in the sense that they were self-governing, but a *polis* was more than a political institution. Its citizens considered themselves a kind of extended family held together by descent from a common legendary ancestor, participation in the same religious cults, and membership in a variety of hereditary subgroups—such as *phratries* (fighting brotherhoods), clans, and tribes.

In the fourth century B.C.E., hundreds of years after the *polis* came into existence, the philosopher Aristotle outlined the assumptions that had guided its development. He argued that the human being was by nature "an animal who lives in a *polis*," for the attributes that define humanity—the power of speech and the ability to distinguish good from bad and right from wrong—require people to live together. He said that "the sharing of these things is what makes a household and a *polis*," and that people who are incapable of such sharing are not truly human.

Development of the *Polis*

Originally the word *polis* referred to a citadel, an elevated, defensible rock to which the farmers of an area retreated when attacked. (The best known example is the Acropolis at the center of the city of Athens.) Unplanned, unfortified towns tended to evolve spontaneously at such sites. Unlike Middle East city-states, locations along rivers or trade routes were not favored. Instead, the proximity of farmland to a natural fortress determined their location. Spots well back from the coast were popular, for they minimized the danger of pirate raids. Eventually an *agora*—a place for markets and political assemblies—would evolve to provide a cohesive center for the community life of a *polis*.

Poleis probably appeared early in the eighth century B.C.E. and spread widely and quickly. All the colonies that the Greeks established in the years after 750 B.C.E. were *poleis*. Monarchy declined as *polis* organizations evolved.

Vestigial kings survived in some places, but they were usually powerless ceremonial figures. A *polis* was often founded as a republic dominated by an aristocratic class, but various developments tended to broaden political participation. About 750 B.C.E., coincident with the development of the *polis*, the Greeks borrowed a script from one of the Semitic peoples of the Middle East. By adding vowels to it, they created the first true alphabet and invented a method of writing that was easy for the common person to learn. This empowered the ordinary man at a time when changes in military technology were also enhancing his importance.

The Hoplite Phalanx

Early Greek warfare was a disorganized free-for-all. Small troops of cavalry led by aristocratic "champions" cast spears at their enemies and then engaged individual opponents with swords at close quarters. Late in the eighth century B.C.E., a true infantry soldier called a *hoplite* began to dominate the battlefield. He was a heavily armed footsoldier, equipped with a spear and large round shield, who fought in a tight formation called a *phalanx*—a block of men at least eight ranks deep. The success of a phalanx depended on the discipline, strength, and courage of its members. A phalanx could withstand cavalry charges and rout much larger armies consisting of less disciplined men. The phalanx reigned supreme in the ancient Mediterranean world until the more flexible Roman legion appeared.

A phalanx was effective only when all its members worked together as a team and learned to rely on one another in the field. Hoplite tactics produced brief, violent battles that resolved disputes quickly with minimal risk to the property on which citizen families depended for their survival. It was warfare intended to kill or drive off an enemy, not enslave him or hold him for ransom.

Greeks had traditionally thought of war as an aristocratic profession, but in the era of the hoplite no *polis* could afford to limit recruitment to a small group of nobles. The strength of an infantry depended on numbers. Farmers working relatively small holdings had to join aristocrats in defending their cities. When they did, shared military responsibilities led inevitably to demands for shared political privileges.

✦ Expansion of the Greek World

About the middle of the eighth century B.C.E., the Greeks launched a colonization movement that planted *poleis* from Spain to the Black Sea. They avoided the eastern end of the Mediterranean, which was well populated and defended, and searched for western sites that were sparsely settled or whose natives were not well organized to resist. So many Greek colonies were established in southern Italy and Sicily that the Romans named the region *Magna Graecia*, "Great Greece."

POLITICAL TRANSFORMATIONS

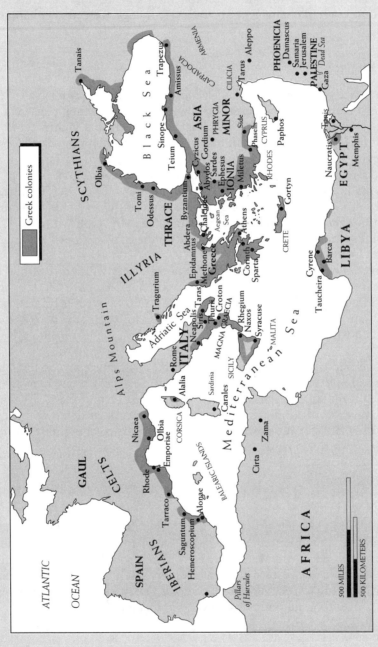

Greek colonies

ATLANTIC OCEAN

GAUL

CELTS

SPAIN

IBERIANS

Tarraco
Rhode
Emporiae
Alonge
Saguntum
Hemeroscopium
BALERIC ISLANDS
Nicaea
Olbia
CORSICA
Alalia
Sardinia
Carales
Cirta
Zama
Pillars of Hurcules

AFRICA

Alps Mountain

ILLYRIA

Tragurium
Adriatic Sea
Rome
Neapolis
ITALY
Siris
Taras
MAGNA GRAECIA
SICILY
MALTA
Thurii
Croton
Rhegium
Naxos
Syracuse

Mediterranean Sea

SCYTHIANS

Tanais

Black Sea

Olbia
Odessus
Tomi
THRACE
Byzantium
Abdera
Epidamnus
Methone
Chalcidce
Aegean Sea
Greece
Athens
Corinth
Sparta
CRETE
Gortyn
Taucheira
Barca
Cyrene
LIBYA

Sinope
Teium
Cyzicus
Gordium
ASIA
PHRYGIA
MINOR
Abydos
Sardes
IONIA
Ephesus
Miletus
KHODES
CYPRUS
Paphos
Side
Phaselis

Trapezus
Amissus
CAPPADOCIA
ARMENIA
CILICIA
Tarus
Aleppo
PHOENICIA
Damascus
Samaria
Jerusalem
PALESTINE
Gaza
Dead Sea

Naucratis
Tanis
EGYPT
Memphis

AFRICA

500 MILES
500 KILOMETERS

MAP 2-2

Greek Colonization from Spain to the Black Sea

Between the mid-eighth and mid-sixth centuries B.C.E. the Greeks scattered colonies from Spain to the Black Sea coast of Asia Minor. A colony was established for the good of the colonists, not the mother city that founded it. Colonists tended to divide the land they settled into equal shares, to copy their home constitution and its egalitarian values, to worship their former city's gods at the same festivals in the same way, and to trade with the mother city. Although a city and its colonies were supposed to maintain friendly relations and possibly help one another in time of trouble, each was politically independent.

The Athenians had colonies of this kind, but during their imperial period (478–404 B.C.E.) they began to treat *all* the members of their empire as if they were Athenian colonies—requiring them to bring offerings of cows and suits of armor to the Great Panathenaic festival, just like the colonies that Athens had actually founded. This cloaked imperial dominance in the friendlier garb of a colonial family attachment.

The best known exception to the general rule of friendly relations between colony and mother-city is the case of Corinth and its colony Corcyra. They quarreled and fought for more than two centuries. Thucydides tells of a fateful conflict between them that played a major role in causing the Peloponnesian War.

Corcyra: An Exceptional Colony

In 435 B.C.E., the people of Epidamnus, a colony of Corcyra torn by civil war, asked the Corinthians to accept them as their own colony. In the excerpt below, Thucydides explains why the Corinthians agreed.

The Corinthians undertook the task ... through hatred of the Corcyraeans, because they, although colonists of Corinth, neglected their mother-city. They would not grant the customary privileges to Corinthians at their common festivals nor allow a Corinthian representative precedence in beginning the ritual at sacrifices, as the other colonies did, but treated them with contempt.

(Thucydides, *History of the Peloponnesian War, 1.23*)

The ruins of the Temple of Apollo at Corinth. The colony of Corcyra failed to show customary respect to its mother-city of Corinth. [Anne van der Vaeren/The Image Bank]

The Greek Colony

The pressures of overpopulation probably explain why thousands of Greeks left the cities of their birth to found new *poleis*. Emigration was difficult, but potentially rewarding. Colonies were carefully planned, and most had excellent prospects as centers of trade. Many copied the constitutions and the religious rites of the cities that founded them, but they were not controlled or exploited by those cities. Each colony governed itself, and its wealth was not siphoned off for the homeland.

Colonization strengthened the Greek civilization as it spread across the Mediterranean. Over 1,000 *poleis* were established, and these helped the Greeks maintain peace among themselves by providing outlets for excess population. Colonization also heightened the Greeks' sense of their uniqueness by bringing them into contact with other cultures. *Poleis* across the Mediterranean established celebrations (the Olympic Games among them) to promote their common heritage.

The colonies also transformed the Greek homeland. The market they created for certain products had both economic and socio-political impacts. Farmers concentrated less on local consumption and more on producing specialized crops (e.g., olives and wine) for export. Demand also increased for manufactured goods such as pottery, tools, weapons, and fine artistic metalwork. Expanding commercial opportunities enlarged the class of independent commoners, and their increasing prosperity led them to resent the aristocrats' traditional monopoly of governmental authority. The political turmoil this generated brought tyrants to power in some *poleis*.

The Tyrants (About 700–500 B.C.E.)

A tyrant, in the ancient Greek sense, was a ruler who ignored legal niceties and simply seized power. He often did so with widespread popular support. A typical tyrant was an aristocrat who broke with his class and took control of a city by appealing to the masses of its poor and politically disenfranchised. He usually expelled his aristocratic opponents, distributed their land among his followers, and instituted economic programs that benefited the city at large.

A tyrant's authority was backed up by a personal bodyguard and troops of mercenary soldiers, but his rule was not necessarily oppressive. Tyrants preferred to concentrate on domestic development and avoid wars. (Aggression against neighboring states required the training of a citizen army that might turn on a tyrant.) Tyrants courted the masses by financing public works projects which were popular and which provided employment for the poor. They also promoted civic pride by sponsoring festivals and supporting the arts.

Despite the positive effect tyranny had on the evolution of some *poleis*, tyrannies faded away during the sixth century B.C.E. There was something about tyranny that was inconsistent with the forces that created the *polis*. The institutions of a *polis* were shaped by the responsibility all its citizens bore for its defense. Since they shared the traditional responsibilities of the military

The temple of Hera at Paestum in southern Italy (sixth century B.C.E.) is considered the finest surviving example of Doric architecture. [Hirmer Verlag, Munich]

aristocracy, they felt entitled to share the aristocratic prerogative of participation in government. The rule of a tyrant, no matter how beneficent, was unacceptable, for it was arbitrary and could not be held accountable. Tyranny did, however, contribute to the growth of popular government by breaking the monopoly aristocracies had on political power.

⤳ The Major States

There were many *poleis* and much diversity in their organization, but two—Sparta and Athens—were of such importance that they merit special attention.

Sparta

About 725 B.C.E., Sparta embarked on a path that made it Greece's most respected military power. It invaded Messenia, its western neighbor, to acquire more land to support its growing population. The conquest and enslavement of Messenia solved Sparta's economic problems, but created a difficulty of a different kind. The Spartans found themselves outnumbered ten to one by Helots, their slaves. A crisis was reached about 650 B.C.E. when a slave revolt nearly destroyed Sparta. The Spartans concluded that in order to survive they would have to live in a constant state of total military mobilization.

Spartan Society. The Spartan system subordinated natural feelings of devotion to self and family to the needs of the state. The state wanted all of its men to be superb soldiers, and it persuaded them to sacrifice privacy and comfort to physical conditioning, military training, and discipline. The Spartans allowed nothing to distract them from their goal of becoming the best warriors in the world.

The Spartan *polis* controlled the life of each of its members from birth. Only infants that officials of the state judged to be physically fit were raised. At the age of seven boys left their mothers to begin training at military camps. They learned to fight, to endure privation, to bear physical pain, and to live off the land. At twenty they joined the army in the field, and they lived in barracks until the age of thirty. They were allowed to marry, but not to live at home. Young Spartan husbands had to steal away from camp to visit their wives. When a man acquired full citizen rights at the age of thirty, he could maintain a home. But he took his meals at a public mess with other members of his military unit. His sparse diet included little meat or wine, and he eschewed all luxuries. His financial future was, however, secure, for he was supported by a grant from the state—a plot of land worked by Helots. A Spartan remained on active military duty until the age of sixty.

Sparta prepared its females as well as its males to serve the state. Female infants were examined for fitness in the same way as males, and young girls, like boys, were given athletic training. Because Spartan men concentrated on military affairs and were often absent from home, Spartan women had much greater freedom and responsibility than other Greek women.

Spartan Government. The Spartan constitution mixed elements of monarchy, oligarchy, and democracy. Sparta acknowledged two royal families; the functions of the kings who headed them were chiefly religious and military. The Spartan army was usually commanded by one of its kings when it was in the field, but kings did not govern Sparta. An oligarchic council composed of the kings and twenty-eight men (aged sixty or more and elected for life) devised policy and sat as a high court. All Spartan males over the age of thirty could take part in a democratic assembly that, in theory, had final authority. The assembly, however, could only consider proposals referred to it by the council. Since it voted by acclamation rather than counting ballots, it was limited to ratifying decisions already taken or deciding between alternative proposals.

The administration of Sparta's government was the duty of a board of five executives called *ephors*. The ephors were elected annually by the assembly. They controlled foreign policy, oversaw the generalship of the kings, presided at the assembly, and policed the Helots.

The Peloponnesian League. Suppression of the Helots required all the energy Sparta had, and the Spartans did not want to overextend themselves by conquering and assimilating potentially troublesome neighbors. They preferred to force these people into alliances that left them free internally but subservient to Sparta's foreign policy. Sparta eventually enrolled every southern Greek state except Argos in its Peloponnesian League and became the most powerful *polis* on the Greek mainland before the rise of Athens.

Athens

Athens evolved more slowly than Sparta. It had a large area (about 1,000 square miles) that absorbed population growth and slowed the consolidation of its villages as a *polis* until the seventh century B.C.E. Economic development was hampered by the fact that it was not situated on the trade routes most traveled during the eighth and seventh centuries B.C.E.

Aristocratic Rule. In the seventh century B.C.E. aristocratic families held the most and the best land around Athens. They also dominated government by controlling the tribes, clans, and brotherhoods (phratries) that structured Athenian society. The state was headed by the Areopagus, a council of nobles that annually elected nine magistrates, called archons. There was no written law.

Pressure for Change. An agrarian crisis that developed during the seventh century B.C.E. accelerated Athens' political evolution. Many Athenians depended on small family farms that grew wheat, the staple of the ancient diet. Years of consistent cultivation diminished the fertility of their fields and the size of their harvests, but few could afford to shift to more profitable crops. It required a lot of capital to bring a vineyard or olive grove into production. Poorer farmers survived by borrowing from wealthier neighbors—mortgaging future crops and, therefore, their own labor as surety for their loans. Slavery was often the result, and some Athenians were even sold abroad. The poor resented this and began to agitate for the abolition of debts and the redistribution of the land.

In 632 B.C.E., a nobleman named Cylon tried to establish a tyranny. He failed, but his attempt frightened Athens' aristocratic leaders into taking steps to head off future coups. In 621 B.C.E., they commissioned a man named Draco to codify and publish Athens' laws. The punishments Draco decreed were extremely harsh, for he wanted to discourage clans from launching blood feuds to avenge slights to their honor. The establishment of a common standard of justice for all Athenians helped dissuade individuals from taking things into their own hands.

Reforms of Solon. In the year 594 B.C.E., the Athenians instituted a more radical reform. They empowered a single archon (a man named Solon) to reorganize the *polis* as he saw fit. Solon attacked agrarian problems by canceling debts and forbidding loans secured by the person of the borrower. He freed people who had been enslaved for debt and brought home many Athenians who had been sold abroad. Instead of alienating the rich by redistributing their land to the poor, he tried to expand Athens' economy to create more opportunities for the poor. He forbade the export of wheat (which might create shortages and drive up the price of food for the common person), but not olive oil (one of Attica's cash crops). He facilitated trade by conforming Athenian weights and measures to standards used by Corinth, Euboea, and other commercial centers. And he developed industries by offering citizenship to foreign artisans who set up shop in Athens.

Solon also reformed Athenian political institutions. He divided Athens' citizens into four classes on the basis of wealth. Only members of the two richest classes qualified for archonships and membership in the council of the Areopagus. Men of the third class could serve as hoplites and be elected to a council of 400 chosen by all the citizens. Solon intended this council to serve as a check on the council of the Areopagus, and he gave it the power to decide what business was to be set before the assembly to which all adult male citizens belonged. The poorest class, the *thetes,* voted in this assembly, participated in the election of archons, and sat on a popular new court that heard appeals from other jurisdictions.

Pisistratus the Tyrant. The beneficial effects of Solon's reforms were slow to be felt, and political tensions continued to mount in Athens. On several occasions fighting was so bad that no archons could be elected. Twice (in 560 B.C.E. and 556 B.C.E.) an aristocratic military hero named Pisistratus tried and failed to establish a tyranny. In 546 B.C.E. his third attempt was successful. Pisistratus ruled Athens until his death in 527 B.C.E. Hippias, the son to whom he bequeathed his authority, continued the tyranny until a competitor drove him from the city in 510 B.C.E.

Like the tyrants of other Greek cities, Pisistratus dominated his subjects by courting them. He sponsored public works programs, urban development, and civic festivals. He employed poets and artists to add luster to his court. And he secured his power by hiding it behind the facade of Solon's constitution. All the councils, assemblies, and courts continued to meet, and all the magistrates were elected. Pisistratus merely saw to it that his supporters won the key offices and dominated the important meetings. The constitutional cloak he spread over his tyranny won him a reputation as a popular, gentle ruler, but it also gave his people more experience with (and a greater appetite for) self-government.

Spartan Intervention. Pisistratus' elder son, Hippias, began by imitating his father, but in 514 B.C.E. the murder of his brother, Hipparchus, made him fearful for his own safety. The harsh measures he imposed diminished popular support for his tyranny and created opportunities for his opponents. In 510 B.C.E. the Alcmaeonids, a noble family that had been exiled from Athens, persuaded the Spartans to help them overthrow Hippias.

Hippias fled, and the Spartans set a man named Isagoras over Athens. Isagoras planned to make Athens more like Sparta by returning its aristocrats to power. He purged the citizen lists to remove the commoners enfranchised by Solon and Pisistratus. This move was unpopular, and the Alcmaeonid leader, Clisthenes, knew how to turn it to personal advantage. He took the unprecedented step of mobilizing the masses against his political opponents. Isagoras responded by calling on his Spartan allies. This time, however, the Athenians resisted Spartan intervention in their affairs and helped Clisthenes drive out Isagoras.

Clisthenes, the Founder of Democracy. Clisthenes set about destroying the regional political machines that were the bases for the aristocracy's power. In 508 B.C.E., he divided Attica into small political units called *demes*. Demes were then grouped into the tribes that organized Athens' army and elected its government. Care was taken to make sure that each tribe was composed of demes scattered across Attica. This made it harder for wealthy aristocratic families to win control of tribes, for the new tribes contained many men who were strangers to them and not economically dependent on them.

Clisthenes increased Solon's council from 400 to 500 members. The council received foreign emissaries and managed some fiscal affairs, but its chief responsibility was to prepare legislative proposals for discussion by the assembly. Ultimate authority was vested in the assembly to which all adult male Athenians belonged. Debate was free, and any Athenian could submit legislation, offer amendments, or argue the merits of any question.

Thanks to Solon, Pisistratus, and Clisthenes, Athens entered the fifth century B.C.E. well down the path to prosperity and democracy. The city was ready to claim a place among Greece's leading *poleis.*

⌖ Life in Archaic Greece

Society

The features of a unique Greek society emerged at the end of the "dark ages." The vast majority of its people made their living from the land, but artisans and merchants acquired greater importance as contact with the non-Hellenic world increased.

Farmers. Ordinary country folk rarely leave any record of their thoughts or activities. But the poet Hesiod (ca. 700 B.C.E.), who claimed in his *Works and Days* to be a small farmer, described what life was like for members of his class in ancient Greece. Their common crops were barley, some wheat, grapes for wine, olives mainly for oil (used for cooking, lighting, and washing), green vegetables, beans, and fruit. Sheep and goats provided milk and cheese. Since land that was fertile enough to grow fodder for cattle was better used for growing grain, the only meat most people tasted was from animals sacrificed to gods at religious festivals.

Hesiod farmed with the help of oxen and mules and occasional hired laborers, but his life was one of continuous toil. The toughest season began with October's rains, the time for the first plowing. Plows were iron-tipped, but light and fragile. Even with the help of a team of animals it was difficult to break the sod. During autumn and winter, wood was cut and repairs made to buildings and equipment. Vines needed attention in late winter. Grain was harvested in May. At the height of summer's heat there was time for a little rest. But in September grapes had to be harvested and pressed, and then the round of yearly tasks began again. Hesiod says nothing about pleasures or entertainments, but the mere existence of his poetry testifies to the presence in Greece of a more dynamic rural population than we know of anywhere else in the ancient world.

Aristocrats. Wealthy aristocrats worked their extensive lands with hired laborers, sharecroppers, and slaves. This gave them leisure for other kinds of activities. The centerpiece of aristocratic social life was the "symposium," a men's drinking party. A symposium was more than a pursuit of inebriation. It began with prayers and libations to the gods. There were usually games such as dice or *kottabos* (a contest in which wine is flicked from cups at a target). Sometimes dancing girls or flute girls offered entertainment. Frequently guests amused themselves with songs, poetry, or philosophical discussion. These things were organized as contests and prizes were awarded, for aristocratic values put a premium on competition and the need to excel.

Athletic contests spread widely early in the sixth century. They usually included foot races, long jumps, discus and javelin throws, boxing, wrestling, and chariot races. Since the rich were the only ones who could afford horses, the chariot race was the special preserve of the nobility. Wrestling was also favored by the upper classes, and the *palaestra* where they practiced was an important gathering place. There was a great contrast between the drab lives of simple farmers and the pursuits of cultivated, leisured aristocrats.

Religion

Olympian Gods. Religion permeated every aspect of Greek culture. The Greeks were polytheists who honored a pantheon containing twelve major deities. Zeus, a sky god, resided on Mount Olympus and presided over a lively family of siblings and offspring. He had three sisters: Hera, who was also his wife; Hestia, goddess of the hearth; and Demeter, goddess of agriculture and marriage. His brother Poseidon was god of the seas and earthquakes. By various mates he had an assortment of children: Aphrodite, goddess of love and beauty; Apollo, god of the sun, music, poetry, and prophecy; Ares, god of strife; Artemis, goddess of the moon and the hunt; Athena, goddess of wisdom and the arts; Hephaestus, god of fire and metallurgy; and Hermes, a cunning messenger-god who was the patron of commerce.

Gods were believed, apart from their superhuman strength and immortality, to resemble mortals. Zeus, the defender of justice, presided over the cosmos, but he and the other gods were not omnipotent. They operated within limits set by the Fates, personifications of the inviolable order of the universe. Each *polis* chose one of the gods as its special guardian, but Olympian religion was Panhellenic. In the eighth and seventh centuries B.C.E. shrines sacred to all Greeks were established at Olympia (Zeus), Delphi (Apollo), Corinth (Poseidon), and Nemea (Zeus). Each sanctuary staged athletic games in honor of its god, and all Greeks were invited to attend. Sacred truces were declared to suspend all wars and provide all men with guarantees of safe conduct.

In the sixth century B.C.E., the shrine of Apollo at Delphi became famous for its oracle, the most important of several that the Greeks looked to for guidance. Delphian Apollo endorsed the pursuit of self-knowledge and self-control. "Know thyself" and "Nothing in excess" were Apollo's mottos. Arrogance or *hubris* brought on by excessive wealth or good fortune was believed to be the most dangerous of human failings. It created moral blindness and tempted the gods to take vengeance.

Immortality and Morality. In addition to the Olympians the Greeks worshiped countless lesser deities associated with local shrines. Some were human heroes, both real and legendary, whose deeds had won them divine status. But ordinary people had no expectation of immortality. Their religion was a matter of prayers and offerings beseeching divine help for this life.

The moral order the gods enforced was simple. Virtue consisted of paying one's debts, doing good to one's friends, and attacking one's enemies. Civic responsibility involved taking part in the cult of the state deities, performing public service, and fighting in the state's army.

The Cult of Dionysus and the Orphic Cult. The worship of the Olympian gods was a state religion that was not meant to address the concerns of private individuals. For their personal needs the Greeks employed rites of a different kind. The worship of Dionysus, a fertility deity associated with the grape vine, was very popular (particularly with women). Dionysus was a god of drunkenness and sexual abandon. His female devotees (the *maenads*) cavorted by night and were reputed, when possessed by their god, to tear to pieces and devour any creatures they encountered.

The cult of Orpheus, a mythical poet, offered the prospect of some form of life after death (perhaps a transmigration of souls). Orphic respect for life may have prohibited the killing of animals or the consumption of meat.

Poetry

Poetry reflected the great changes that swept through the Greek world in the sixth century B.C.E.. The era favored lyric poetry that was meant to be sung. The poems of Sappho of Lesbos, Anacreon of Teos, and Simonides of Cos were intimately personal—often describing the pleasure and agony of love. Alcaeus of Mytilene, an aristocrat driven from his city by a tyrant, wrote bitter invectives. But from a political point of view the most interesting poet of the century was Theognis of Megara. Theognis spoke for the aristocrats whose power over most *poleis* was declining. He insisted that only nobles could aspire to true virtue, for only nobles possessed the crucial sense of honor. A sense of honor could not be taught; it was innate, and noble families could lose it if they debased their lines by marrying commoners. Although the political privileges of the old nobility were reduced in most Greek states, traditional assumptions of aristocratic superiority survived and influenced important thinkers like Plato.

◆ The Persian Wars

The Greeks' era of freedom from interference from the outside world came to an end in the middle of the sixth century B.C.E. First, the Greek colonies, which had flourished on the coast of Asia Minor since the eleventh century B.C.E., came under the control of Croesus (ca. 560–546 B.C.E.), king of the Anatolian nation of Lydia. Then in 546 B.C.E. Lydia and its dependencies passed into the hands of the Persians.

The Persian Empire

The Persian Empire was created in a single generation by Cyrus the Great, founder of the Achaemenid dynasty. When Cyrus became the ruler of Persia in 559 B.C.E., it was a small kingdom well to the east of lower Mesopotamia. He steadily expanded his domain in all directions and ultimately reached Asia Minor where he defeated Croesus and occupied Lydia. Most of the Greek cities of Asia Minor resisted the Persians, but by 540 B.C.E. they had all been subdued.

The Ionian Rebellion

The Greeks of Ionia (on the west coast of Asia Minor) had been developing democratic governments, and they were restive under Persian rule. But the Persians were clever empire builders. They appointed Greek "tyrants" to govern Greek cities. Since these native leaders usually governed benignly and Persian tribute was not excessive, many Greeks were soon reconciled to life in Persia's empire. Neither the death of Cyrus in 530 B.C.E., nor the suicide of his successor Cambyses, nor the civil war that followed that event in 522–521 B.C.E. prompted the Greeks to revolt. In 521 B.C.E. when Darius became Great King (the Persian royal title), Ionia submitted to him as to his predecessors.

Aristagoras, an ambitious tyrant of Miletus, was responsible for stirring up trouble between Ionia and Persia. The Persians were angry with him for having persuaded them to undertake an unsuccessful campaign against the island of Naxos, and he was afraid they would punish him. He defended himself by persuading the Ionian cities to join him in a rebellion in 499 B.C.E. He won support by helping to overthrow unpopular fellow tyrants and by endorsing democratic constitutions for some cities. He also sought help from the mainland states. The Spartans declined to become involved. They had no ties with the Ionians and no national interest in the region. They also could not risk sending their army abroad and weakening their control over their slaves.

The Athenians were more sympathetic toward Aristagoras. They were related to the Ionians and had reasons of their own to fear the Persians. Hippias, the deposed tyrant of Athens, was an honored guest at Darius' court, and the

Great King supported Hippias' plans to restore his tyranny in Athens. The Persians also held both shores of the Hellespont, Athens' route to the grain fields surrounding the Black Sea. In light of all this, the Athenian assembly decided to send a fleet of twenty ships to help the rebels.

In 498 B.C.E. the Athenian and Ionian armies overwhelmed Sardis, the capital of Lydia and the seat of the Persian governor (the *satrap*). The sack of Sardis encouraged others to join the rebellion, but the Greeks did not follow up their victory. Athens withdrew, and the Persians gradually recovered the ground they had lost. In 495 B.C.E. they defeated the Ionian fleet at Lade, and a year later they leveled Miletus.

The War in Greece

In 490 B.C.E. the Persians launched an expedition to punish Athens, to restore Hippias, and to gain control of the Aegean Sea. They first landed their infantry and cavalry forces at Naxos and destroyed it as punishment for its resistance in 499 B.C.E. Then they conquered Eretria and deported its people, for the Eretrians had sent help to Miletus.

Despite the risk of suffering the same fate as the Eretrians, the Athenians refused to submit to Persia. They chose Miltiades, an Athenian with a personal grudge against the Persians, to lead them and marched out to Marathon (a plain north of Athens where the Persians were camped). Although the odds were against them, the Athenians defeated the Persians and forced them to retreat. Victory enhanced their pride in themselves and their confidence in the fledgling democracy they had recently established to govern their *polis*.

The Great Invasion. Internal troubles prevented the Persians from taking swift revenge for their loss at Marathon. Almost ten years elapsed before Darius' successor, Xerxes, turned his attention to the Greeks. In 481 B.C.E. he assembled an army of at least 150,000 men and a navy of more than 600 ships and set out to conquer the Aegean.

By then Athens had changed significantly. Themistocles, the city's leading politician, had begun to turn the *polis* into a naval power. During his archonship in 493 B.C.E., Athens built a fortified port at Piraeus. A decade later the Athenians used the income from a rich vein of silver discovered in the state mines to finance the construction of a fleet. By 480 B.C.E., Athens had over 200 ships. They proved to be the salvation of Greece.

Of the hundreds of Greek states, only thirty-one (led by Sparta, Athens, Corinth, and Aegina) were willing to commit to fighting the vast Persian army that gathered south of the Hellespont in the spring of 480 B.C.E. Xerxes' plan was to overwhelm the Greeks with superior numbers, but Themistocles perceived a weakness in this strategy. The Persian army had to stay in touch with the fleet that carried its supplies. If the Persian ships were destroyed, the army would have to retreat. Themistocles, therefore, argued that a naval engagement could win the war for the Greeks.

The Greek League, which was organized specifically to deal with the Persian invasion, met at Corinth as the Persians prepared to cross the Hellespont. Sparta was chosen to lead the Greeks, and the Greeks decided to take their stand at Thermopylae (the "hot gates"). The Persians had to march along the coast, and at Thermopylae the mountains came very close to the sea. It was conceivable that a small force might stop the Persians at this point by blocking the narrow strip of beach at the foot of the mountains. The Greek army with which the Spartan king, Leonidas, hoped to hold this spot numbered only about 9,000—of which 300 were Spartans.

The Greeks had some luck, for storms wrecked a large number of Persian ships before Xerxes attacked Thermopylae. For two days the Greeks stood their ground and butchered the troops he threw against them. On the third day, however, a traitor showed the Persians a trail through the mountains, and Xerxes sent out a company to ambush the Greeks from the rear. Leonidas sensed the hopelessness of the situation and dismissed his Greek allies. He and his 300 Spartans chose to stay and die fighting.

The way was now clear for the Persian army to invade Attica and burn Athens. If an inscription discovered in 1959 is authentic, Themistocles had foreseen this possibility and begun the evacuation of the city while the Greek army was still at Thermopylae.

The fate of Greece was decided by a sea battle fought in the narrow straits between Attica and the island of Salamis. The Spartans wanted the Athenian fleet to retreat to guard the coast of the Peloponnese, but Themistocles persuaded them to support his plan. If they refused, he threatened to abandon them and use the fleet to carry the Athenians to new homes in Italy. In the battle at Salamis the Persians lost more than half their ships. Xerxes then decided to return to Persia with part of the army, but he left a large contingent behind in Greece to continue the war.

While Mardonius, the general Xerxes left in charge, went into winter camp in central Greece, Pausanias, the Spartan regent, assembled the largest army the Greeks had ever fielded. In the summer of 479 B.C.E. it decisively defeated Mardonius' forces at a battle near Plataea in Boeotia.

At the same time, the Ionian Greeks persuaded Leotychidas, the Spartan king and commander of the Greek fleet, to take the offensive against a key Persian naval base at Mycale, on the coast of Asia Minor. Leotychidas routed the enemy, and the Persians fled the Aegean and Ionia. Greece was safe, but no one knew for how long.

The Hellenic civilization that has so powerfully influenced the modern West was itself influenced by the Bronze Age cultures of Minoan Crete and Mycenae. But these early Aegean states more closely resembled Egypt, Mesopotamia, and Palestine-Syria than the later Hellenic poleis. They were urbanized societies with systems of writing, centralized monarchies, large administrative bureaucracies, hierarchical social systems, professional standing armies, and systems of taxation. They resembled one another and changed little over time. The Hellenic civ-

ilization that slowly emerged from the rubble of the Mycenaean kingdoms was quite different.

The Mycenaean collapse inaugurated an era of cultural decline for the Greeks. Villages replaced their cities. Trade all but ended. Communication was curtailed. The art of writing was lost, and a "dark age" descended on the Aegean during which the Greeks were largely forgotten by the outside world. Between 1100 and 750 B.C.E., however, the Greeks laid foundations for a new civilization based on the polis, the Hellenic city-state.

Monarchy faded with the passing of the Mycenaean kingdoms, and several factors encouraged the development of republican governments in poleis. Because Greece was poor, distinctions of wealth between social classes were less dramatic than in other societies. Reliance on infantry—the hoplite phalanx—further narrowed the gap between aristocrat and commoner. A city that depended on its citizen-soldiers for its defense could hardly deny them some role in its government. Most poleis also had no need to impose regular taxation. They did not have to hire professional soldiers or administrators. These services were duties citizens were expected to volunteer to the state. There were, therefore, no professional bureaucracies to stifle individual initiatives and no castes of priests to enforce religious orthodoxy. A polis was a dynamic, secular, and remarkably free community that created the kind of environment in which speculative thinking (the basis of science) could thrive.

✧ Review Questions

1. Were there similarities between the Minoan and Mycenaean civilizations? How did they differ?

2. From what ancient sources do we derive our knowledge of Minoan and Mycenaean history? What is Linear B? What problems are involved in using it to reconstruct Bronze Age history? How reliable are the Homeric epics as sources of early Greek history?

3. What was involved in the ancient Greek concept of a *polis*? What role did geography play in the development of a *polis*? Why did the Greeks consider it a unique and valuable institution?

4. How did the fundamental political, social, and economic institutions of Athens and Sparta compare around 500 B.C.E.? Why did Sparta develop a unique form of government?

5. Through what stages did Athens pass between 600 and 500 B.C.E. as it evolved from an aristocratic state into a democracy? What did Draco, Solon, Pisistratus, and Clisthenes each contribute to the process?

6. Why did the Greeks and Persians go to war in 490 and 480 B.C.E.? What benefit would the Persians have derived from conquering Greece? Why were the Greeks able to defeat the Persians? What effect did victory have on them?

✧ Suggested Readings

A. ANDREWES, *The Greeks* (1967). A thoughtful general survey.

J. BOARDMAN, *The Greeks Overseas* (1964). A study of the relations between the Greeks and other peoples.

A. R. BURN, *The Lyric Age of Greece* (1960). A

discussion of early Greece that uses the evidence of poetry and archaeology to fill out the sparse historical record.

A. R. BURN, *Persia and the Greeks*, 2nd ed. (1984). A thorough narrative and analysis of the conflict between the Persians and the Greeks down to 479 B.C.E.

J. CHADWICK, *The Mycenaean World* (1976). A readable account, by a man who helped decipher Mycenaean writing.

R. DREWS, *The Coming of the Greeks* (1988). A fine study of the arrival of the Greeks as part of the movement of Indo-European peoples.

V. EHRENBERG, *The Greek State* (1964). A good handbook of constitutional history.

M. I. FINLEY, *World of Odysseus*, rev. ed. (1965). A fascinating attempt to reconstruct Homeric society.

W. G. FORREST, *A History of Sparta, 950–192 B.C.* (1968). A brief but shrewd account.

V. D. HANSON, *The Western Way of War* (1989). A brilliant and lively discussion of the rise and character of the hoplite phalanx and its influence on Greek society.

V. D. HANSON, *The Other Greeks* (1995). A revolutionary account of the invention of the family farm by the Greeks and the central role of agrarianism in shaping the Greek city-state.

J. M. HURWIT, *The Art and Culture of Early Greece* (1985). A fascinating study of the art of early Greece in its literary and cultural context.

D. KAGAN, *The Great Dialogue: A History of Greek Political Thought from Homer to Polybius* (1965). A discussion of the relationship between the Greek historical experience and political theory.

H. D. F. KITTO, *The Greeks* (1951). A personal and illuminating interpretation of Greek culture.

B. SNELL, *Discovery of the Mind* (1960). An important study of Greek intellectual development.

E. VERMEULE, *Greece in the Bronze Age* (1972). A study of the Mycenaean period.

3

Classical and Hellenistic Greece

Aftermath of Victory
The Delian League
The Rise of Cimon

The First Peloponnesian War: Athens Against Sparta
The Rise of Pericles
The Division of Greece

Classical Greece
The Athenian Empire
Athenian Democracy
The Women of Athens—Two Views
Slavery

The Great Peloponnesian War
Causes
Strategic Stalemate
The Fall of Athens

Competition for Leadership in the Fourth Century B.C.E.
The Hegemony of Sparta

The Hegemony of Thebes: The Second Athenian Empire

The Culture of Classical Greece
The Fifth Century B.C.E.
The Fourth Century B.C.E.
Philosophy and the Crisis of the Polis

The Hellenistic World
The Macedonian Conquest
Alexander the Great
The Successors

Hellenistic Culture
Philosophy
Literature
Architecture and Sculpture
Mathematics and Science

KEY TOPICS

- The Peloponnesian War and the struggle between Athens and Sparta
- Democracy and empire in fifth-century-B.C.E. Athens
- Culture and society in Classical Greece
- The struggle for dominance in Greece after the Peloponnesian War
- The Hellenistic world

The Greeks' victory over the Persians in 480–479 B.C.E. marked the start of an era of great achievement. Fear of another Persian incursion into the Aegean led the Greeks to contemplate some kind of cooperative defense. The Spartans refused to make commitments that would take them away from their homeland, but the Athenians were eager for opportunities to increase their influence. They negotiated a military alliance called the Delian League, which became the basis for an Athenian empire. Fear of Athens led other states to ally with Sparta, and the polarized Greek world erupted in civil war. In 338 B.C.E. Philip of Macedon imposed his will on the weakened and impoverished Greek states and brought the era of the polis to an end.

∽ Aftermath of Victory

The Delian League

The Spartans had led the Greeks to victory against the Persian invaders, but they were not prepared to take responsibility for defending the Greeks against the return of the Persians. Sparta could not risk inviting a revolt of its slaves by stationing its troops far from home for long periods. Also, the defense of the Aegean called for a naval power, not the Spartan army.

Athens was Greece's leading naval power, and, as an Ionion state, it had ties to the Greeks whom the Persians still threatened on the Aegean islands and coasts of Asia Minor. In the winter of 478–477 B.C.E., the Athenians joined other Greeks on the sacred island of Delos to swear oaths of mutual assistance in a continuing struggle with Persia (see Map 3-1). The purpose of this Delian League was to free Greeks still under Persian rule, to defend against a Persian return, and to obtain compensation from the Persians by raiding their lands.

The league was remarkably successful at driving back the Persians and also clearing the Aegean of pirates. In 467 B.C.E., it won a great victory over the Persians at the Eurymedon River in Asia Minor. Some cities then concluded that the league had served its purpose, and they tried to withdraw from it. But Athens forced them to continue their contributions. What had begun as a voluntary association of free states gradually became an empire dominated by Athens.

The Rise of Cimon

Themistocles fell from power at the end of the Persian Wars, and for two decades leadership of Athens was exercised by Cimon, son of Miltiades (the hero of Marathon). At home, Cimon defended a limited version of Clisthenes' democratic constitution. Abroad, he maintained pressure on Persia while seeking friendly relations with Sparta.

MAP 3-1 Classical Greece *Greece in the Classical period (ca. 480–338 B.C.E.) centered on the Aegean Sea. Although there were important Greek settlements in Italy, Sicily, and all around the Black Sea, the area shown in this general reference map embraced the vast majority of Greek states.*

∾ The First Peloponnesian War: Athens Against Sparta

The Rise of Pericles

In 465 B.C.E. the island of Thasos rebelled against the Delian League. During the two years it took to put down the revolt, Cimon was absent from Athens. When he returned, his political opponents tried to bring him down by charging him with taking bribes. He was acquitted, but a radically democratic faction led by a man named Ephialtes (and his young protege, Pericles) continued to attack Cimon for his pro-Spartan pro-aristocratic policies.

Significant Dates from Greek History: The Persian Wars to Alexander

478–477 B.C.E.	*Delian League founded*
462 B.C.E.	*Pericles rises to leadership*
449 B.C.E.	*Peace with Persia*
435 B.C.E.	*Civil war on Corcyra*
432 B.C.E.	*Sparta declares war on Athens*
421 B.C.E.	*Peace of Nicias*
415–413 B.C.E.	*Athens invades Sicily*
404 B.C.E.	*Athens surrenders to Sparta*
404–403 B.C.E.	*Thirty Tyrants rule at Athens*
401 B.C.E.	*Expedition of Greek mercenaries to Persia*
382 B.C.E.	*Sparta seizes Thebes*
378 B.C.E.	*Second Athenian Confederation founded*
371 B.C.E.	*Thebans defeat Sparta at Leuctra*
362 B.C.E.	*Battle of Mantinea (end of Theban hegemony)*
359–336 B.C.E.	*Reign of Philip II of Macedon*
338 B.C.E.	*Battle of Chaeronea (Philip conquers Greece)*
338 B.C.E.	*Founding of League of Corinth*
336–323 B.C.E.	*Reign of Alexander III of Macedon, the Great*
334 B.C.E.	*Alexander invades Asia*
333 B.C.E.	*Battle of Issus*
331 B.C.E.	*Battle of Gaugamela*
327 B.C.E.	*Alexander reaches Indus Valley*
323 B.C.E.	*Death of Alexander*

At the start of the Thasian rebellion, Thasos had asked Sparta to assist it by invading Athens. Sparta agreed, but an earthquake sparked a Helot revolt that kept the Spartan army tied up at home. Instead of attacking Athens, Sparta asked the Athenians for help. Cimon's fatal mistake was to talk the Athenians into sending it. The Spartans reconsidered the wisdom of letting an Athenian army into their land and ordered Cimon to retreat. The Athenians then turned on Cimon, exiled him (461 B.C.E.), and allied with Sparta's enemies. Ephialtes had been assassinated in 462 B.C.E., and Pericles had succeeded to his place as leader of the victorious democratic faction.

The Division of Greece

Since Sparta had been willing to help Thasos break up the Delian League, Pericles persuaded Athens to back the city of Megara when it withdrew from Sparta's Peloponnesian League. Athens was also interested in the strategic possibilities of Megara, as it guarded the route from Athens to the Peloponnesus. Sparta objected to this maneuver and hostilities flared into the First Peloponnesian War.

The Athenians were initially victorious, but about 455 B.C.E. they lost a fleet that they had sent to Egypt to stir up trouble for the Persians. Unhappy subjects of Athens' empire seized this opportunity to rebel, and Athens hastened to disentangle itself from other campaigns. Sparta agreed to a truce, and in 449 B.C.E. Athens made peace with Persia.

In 446 B.C.E., war again broke out between Sparta and Athens, but a year later Pericles ended it by negotiation. Sparta pledged to keep the peace for thirty years and to recognize the Athenian Empire, and Athens abandoned all its possessions on the Greek mainland outside of Attica. This effectively divided Greece into two power blocs: Sparta dominating the Greek mainland and Athens ruling the Aegean.

Classical Greece

The Athenian Empire

After the Egyptian disaster the Athenians moved the Delian League's treasury to Athens and began to keep one-sixtieth of its annual revenues for themselves. By 445 B.C.E. only Chios, Lesbos, and Samos were still providing their own ships for the league's navy. All the other states paid tribute. They resented doing so, for the fading of the Persian threat had removed the rationale for the league. Athenian prosperity and security, however, depended on the resources of the league, and the Athenians refused to allow it to dissolve. They turned the league into an empire, which was not universally unpopular. It had many friends among democratic factions in its subject cities, and steps were taken to persuade Athens' former allies to look on it not as an oppressor, but as a mother city to which they, like colonies, were bound by ties of good feeling and shared religion.

Athenian Democracy

Democratic Legislation. The Athenians found nothing inconsistent in strengthening their own democracy while pursuing a policy of imperial dominance abroad. The hoplite class became eligible for the archonship, and, in practice, the property qualification for holding this office was suspended. Pericles sponsored a law providing pay for jury members. This made it possible for the poor, who could not afford to take unpaid leave from their jobs, to serve. Pericles revived the custom of sending circuit judges into the countryside to make justice readily available to the rural poor. He also persuaded the electorate to limit citizenship to those who had two citizen parents. Democracy made citizenship a valuable commodity, and it was in the self-interest of the electorate to increase the significance of each vote by limiting the number of voters. All the Greek states denied participation in government to whole classes of persons (e.g., slaves, resident aliens, and women).

How Did the Democracy Work? Athenian democracy gave citizens extensive powers. Every decision of the state had to be approved by the popular assembly—by the voters themselves, not their representatives. Every judicial deci-

The Acropolis was both the religious and the civic center of Athens. In its final form it is the work of Pericles and his successors in the late fifth century B.C.E. This photograph shows the Parthenon and to its left the Erechtheum. [Meredith Pillon, Greek National Tourist Organization.]

sion was subject to appeal to a popular court composed of not fewer than 51 and as many as 1,501 citizens chosen from the Athenian population at large. Most officials were chosen by casting lots, and their class status was unimportant. Successful candidates for the chief offices—for example, those of the city's ten generals (who had both political and military authority) and the imperial treasurers—were usually wealthy aristocrats. But the voters could have, if they wanted, elected anyone. All public officials had to submit to examination before taking office. They could be called to account and removed from office during their tenure and at the end of their term were subject to a strict accounting for the uses they had made of their authority. Since there was no standing army and no police force (public or secret), the city's leaders had no way to coerce or intimidate voters.

Pericles was elected to the generalship fifteen years in a row and thirty times in all, not because he was a dictator but because he was a persuasive speaker and an incorruptible, respected leader. On occasions when he lost the people's confidence, they removed him from office.

After the defeat of the Athenian fleet in the Egyptian campaign and the failure of Athens' continental campaigns, Pericles, who had been something of an imperialist, endorsed a more conservative policy aimed at retaining the empire in the Aegean and living at peace with the Spartans. In 443 B.C.E., at the end of the First Peloponnesian War, he was at the height of his power as the guardian of Athens' imperial democracy.

The Women of Athens—Two Views

Subjection. Greek society, like most others throughout history, was dominated by men. But the position of women in democratic Athens has been the subject of much controversy. The bulk of the evidence suggests that women were excluded from most aspects of public life. They could not take any direct part in politics—that is, debate, vote, or hold office. In the private sphere they were always subject to the authority of male guardians: a father, a husband, or another male relative. They married young, usually between the ages of twelve and eighteen. Since men often did not marry until they were in their thirties, husbands probably treated wives like dependent children. Marriages were arranged—often without consulting the bride. Women were assigned dowries, but they had no control over their property. Divorce was difficult for a woman to obtain, for she had to find a male relative who was willing to take responsibility for her after the dissolution of her marriage.

The chief responsibility of a respectable Athenian woman of a citizen family was to produce male heirs for her husband's household (*oikos*). But if a woman's father died without leaving a male heir, she became an *epikleros*, the heiress to the family estate. Such a woman, if already married, was required by law to separate from her husband and wed one of her father's relatives. A son born of this union re-established the male line for her father's *oikos*.

Because citizenship was inherited, the legitimacy of children was important. Athenian males consorted freely with prostitutes, but citizen women were denied contact with any men but close relatives. Women spent their days confined to special women's quarters in their homes raising children, cooking, weaving, and managing their households. Occasionally they emerged in public to take part in the state religion. But for the most part, Athenian women were expected to be invisible. In a frequently quoted speech, Pericles declared that "the greatest glory of women is to be least talked about by men, whether for good or bad."

Power. Evidence from myths and especially from the works of the great Athenian dramatists suggests that the roles played by Athenian women may have been more complex than their legal status implies. The central characters of plays are often women. Clytemnestra in Aeschylus' tragedy *Agamemnon,* for example, arranges the murder of her husband, the king, and establishes her lover (whom she dominates) in his place. *Medea,* one of Euripides' tragedies, examines the contradictions in women's roles. Medea complains bitterly of the subjugation of women, but she is a powerful figure who determines the destiny of the men around her.

Slavery

The Greeks practiced various kinds of slavery. The most common forms of bondage were varieties of serfdom found in backward areas such as Crete, Thessaly, and Sparta. When the Spartans conquered territory, they reduced their new subjects to the status of Helots—slaves who belonged to the Spartan state and worked the land for Spartan masters. Default on a debt could lead to temporary bondage or sale into permanent slavery outside one's homeland. Solon put an end to this practice in Athens about 600 B.C.E.

Chattel slavery proper began to increase about 500 B.C.E. and remained important to Greek society thereafter. Most slaves were prisoners of war or persons abducted by pirates. Like other ancient cultures, the Greeks regarded foreigners as inferior, and most of the people they enslaved were foreigners. Greeks sometimes enslaved Greeks, but not to serve in their home territories.

Many shepherds were slaves, but most Greek farmers worked small holdings too poor to support more than one enslaved agricultural worker. The upper class had more land, but it was usually let to free tenant farmers. If it was worked by slaves (under an overseer who was often himself a slave), their numbers were modest. Wealthy men owned farms that were scattered about the *polis*, not consolidated as large plantations. They had no use for the hordes of slaves associated with plantation economies.

Slaves were used in greater numbers in industry, especially mining. They worked as craftsmen in almost every trade, and, like slaves on small farms, they labored alongside their masters. Slaves were also used as domestic servants, and publicly owned slaves served as prison attendants, clerks, and secretaries.

The numbers of slaves and their importance to ancient Greek society are debated issues. There are no reliable figures for the slave population or their percentage of the total population for any city except Athens. During the fifth and fourth centuries B.C.E. there may have been anywhere from 20,000 to 100,000 slaves in Athens. If the accurate number is the mean between these extremes—60,000—and the city had about 40,000 households, there were fewer than two slaves per family. Only a quarter to a third of free Athenians may have owned any slaves at all. This is comparable to the situation that existed in the American south prior to the Civil War, but unlike the south the Athenian economy did not depend on a single cash crop produced by slave labor. Greek slaves also did not differ from their masters in skin color, and slaves walked the streets of Athens with such ease as to offend class-conscious Athenians like Plato. The emancipation of slaves was rare in America, but common in Greece. On occasion the Athenians even contemplated the liberation of all their slaves.

✧ The Great Peloponnesian War

The Thirty Years' Peace that Sparta and Athens agreed to in 445 B.C.E. ended prematurely about 435 B.C.E. A dispute in a remote part of the Greek world developed into a war that shook the foundations of Greek civilization.

Causes

The spark that ignited the conflict was a quarrel between Corinth and Corcyra, an island at the entrance to the Adriatic Sea. The fight invited foreign intervention, for the Corcyraean fleet was second in size only to that of Athens. The Athenians feared that its capture by Corinth would upset the balance of power and threaten Athenian interests. When Athens decided to support Corcyra against Corinth, Corinth, a member of the Peloponnesian League, appealed to Sparta for help.

In the summer of 432 B.C.E., the Spartans hosted a conference to consider the grievances of their allies. The Peloponnesian League was persuaded by the Corinthians that Athens was an insatiably aggressive power, and it voted for war. In the spring of 431 B.C.E. Sparta marched into Attica.

Strategic Stalemate

The Spartan strategy was traditional: to invade the opponent's country, threaten his crops, and force him to defend them in a hoplite battle. Since the Spartans and their allies had the better army and outnumbered the Athenians by more than two to one, they were confident of victory.

Any ordinary *polis* would have yielded or been quickly defeated, but Athens had unique resources: the income from an empire, a vast reserve fund, and walls that created a fortified highway between the inland city and its port at Piraeus. So long as the Athenians had their enormous navy they could ride out a siege by supplying themselves from the sea. If they remained secure behind their walls and ignored the Spartan invasion, they could demonstrate to the world that the Spartan army had no power to hurt them. Meanwhile the Athenian fleet could raid the Peloponnesian coast to show that Sparta could not protect its allies. Pericles expected that this strategy would force the Peloponnesians to recognize the hopelessness of the situation and sue for peace.

The plan was intelligent, but difficult to implement. It required Athens' democratic assembly to exercise great self-control, and so long as Pericles provided inspired leadership, the city stayed the course. But in 429 B.C.E., in the wake of a devastating plague that swept the crowded city, Pericles died.

None of the politicians who followed him could hold the Athenians to a consistent course. Two factions appeared: one (led by a man named Nicias) wanted to continue the defensive strategy; the other (led by a certain Cleon) preferred to take the offensive. In 425 B.C.E. Athens captured 400 Spartans in a skirmish in the Peloponnese, and Sparta offered peace to get them back. But Cleon's party persuaded the Athenians to continue the war. After assaults on Megara and Boeotia failed in 424 B.C.E., the Athenian electorate's confidence in the aggressive policy was shaken. Meanwhile, however, Sparta's ablest general, Brasidas, had taken a small army to Thrace and captured Amphipolis, the most important Athenian colony in the region. (Thucydides, the commander of the Athenian fleet stationed in those waters, was exiled as punishment for the loss, and this gave him time to become the great historian of the war.) In 422 B.C.E. Cleon led an assault on Amphipolis, and both he and Brasidas died in battle. The deaths of the leaders of the aggressive factions in both cities paved the way in the spring of 421 B.C.E. for the Peace of Nicias, a treaty named for its chief negotiator.

The Fall of Athens

The agreement between Athens and Sparta was supposed to guarantee peace for fifty years, but neither side fulfilled all its commitments. Despite the precariousness of the situation, in 415 B.C.E. an ambitious young Athenian politician named Alcibiades persuaded the Athenians to send an army to intervene in the complicated affairs of Sicily. In 413 B.C.E. the entire expedition was destroyed, and Athens lost 200 ships and 4,500 men. Since the city's allies lost almost ten times as many, angry rebellions swept the Athenian empire. Persia, recognizing an opportunity to help the Greeks destroy themselves, immediately offered assistance to Sparta.

Remarkably, the Athenians found the strength to continue fighting. But their resources were no match for the aid their enemies received from Persia. In 405 B.C.E., when Athens' fleet was caught at Aegospotami and destroyed, the city could not afford to replace it. Lysander, the Spartan general who had obtained Persia's help, cut off Athens' food supply and starved the city into submission (404 B.C.E.). Athens was allowed to survive, but was stripped of its fleet and empire.

❧ Competition for Leadership in the Fourth Century B.C.E.

The Hegemony of Sparta

Sparta failed to take Athens' place as leader of the Greek world, and from 404 B.C.E. until 338 B.C.E. the Greeks squandered their resources fighting among themselves. Sparta's limited population, Helot problem, traditional conservatism, and indebtedness to Persia prevented it from developing a maritime empire to police the Aegean.

Sparta first disappointed its allies by ceding the Greek cities of Asia Minor to Persia as repayment for the Persian help it had received in the war with Athens. Lysander, the victorious Spartan commander, then made a mockery of Sparta's promise to free the Greeks from Athenian dominance by attempting to make them part of a new Spartan empire. To govern the cities he "liberated" from Athens, he installed boards of local oligarchs who were loyal to him. He deployed Spartan garrisons to back up his puppet governments and demanded tribute comparable to what Athens had collected. These policies alienated Thebes and Corinth, Sparta's most powerful allies, and upset conservative Spartans who were suspicious of foreign entanglements.

In 404 B.C.E., Lysander installed an oligarchic government in Athens that was so unpopular its members were dubbed the "Thirty Tyrants." Their democratic opponents fled to Thebes and Corinth, where they raised an army with which to retake the city. Sparta's cautious king, Pausanias, prevented an outbreak of fighting by recalling Lysander and allowing Athens to revert to democracy. So long as Athenian foreign policy remained under Spartan control, Sparta could afford to allow Athens to have any kind of government it wanted.

Persia was distracted from further intervention in Greek affairs by internal problems. In 405 B.C.E., when the emperor Darius II died, a young prince named Cyrus recruited a Greek mercenary army to contest the succession of his brother, Artaxerxes II. In 401 B.C.E., the Greeks defeated the Persians at Cunaxa in Mesopotamia, but Cyrus' death in that battle left them stranded without a leader or a purpose deep in hostile territory. They succeeded in fighting their way back to the Black Sea and safety, but the cities of Asia Minor that had supported Cyrus now faced the threat of Artaxerxes' revenge. In 396 B.C.E. the Spartans sent an army under the command of their king, Agesilaus, to defend them.

The Persians countered Agesilaus' strategy by offering aid to any Greek state willing to rebel against Sparta. By 395 B.C.E. Thebes had organized an alliance that included Argos, Corinth, and a resurgent Athens. The Corinthian War (395–387 B.C.E.) that followed ended Sparta's Asian adventure, and in 394 B.C.E. the Persian fleet destroyed Sparta's maritime empire. The Athenians seized the opportunity to rebuild their walls, enlarge their navy, and recover some of their foreign possessions.

The Persians believed that Athens was potentially a greater threat than Sparta and supported Sparta's ambitions so long as they were confined to the Greek mainland. Agesilaus broke up all alliances except Sparta's Peloponnesian League, and in 382 B.C.E. he seized Thebes in a surprise attack. By 379 B.C.E. the Thebans had regained their independence, and a Spartan attempt to occupy Athens had failed.

In 371 B.C.E. the Thebans, led by a great general named Epaminondas, defeated the Spartans at Leuctra. The Thebans freed the Helots, and helped them found a city of their own. This deprived Sparta of much of its farmland and its slave labor force. Hemmed in by hostile neighbors, Sparta ceased to be a major power.

The Hegemony of Thebes: The Second Athenian Empire

Thebes' victory over Sparta opened the way for Thebes to become the dominant power in Greece, and Epaminondas did win control of all the Greek states north of Athens and those of the Corinthian Gulf. Theban expansion, however, threatened many Greeks, and Athens was able to recruit help in opposing it. In 362 B.C.E. Epaminondas led an army into the Peloponnesus to confront Athens' allies. His men routed them at the battle of Mantinea, but he was killed. When no comparable leader appeared to take his place, the era of Theban dominance ended.

Sixteen years earlier (in 378 B.C.E.), an alliance known as the Second Athenian Confederation had been organized to guard against Spartan aggression in the Aegean. Although its constitution was designed to prevent Athens from exploiting the alliance as it had the Delian League, Athens soon alienated its confederates. The collapse of Sparta and Thebes and Persia's lack of aggressive behavior persuaded some of Athens' allies that the confederation should be dissolved, and they revolted. By 355 B.C.E., Athens had again lost most of its empire. Two centuries of almost continuous warfare ended with the Greek world in as chaotic a condition as it had been in the days before the founding of the Peloponnesian League.

✧ The Culture of Classical Greece

The Greeks' early victories in the Persian Wars inspired them with tremendous self-confidence and unleashed a flood of creative activity that was rarely, if ever, matched anywhere at any time. The result was the development of the "Classical Period" in the history of Western civilization. Ironically, the term *classical* often invokes the idea of calm and serenity, but the products of Greece's Classical Period reflect tension.

The Fifth Century B.C.E.

Two sources of tension shaped the work of Greek artists of the fifth century B.C.E. One was incompatibility between the soaring hopes of individuals and the limits the duties of citizenship in the *polis* put on private ambition. The other sprang from the conflict between the Greeks' pride in their accomplishments and their fear that the gods would intervene to punish excessive striving. The Greeks' faith in themselves had been strengthened by their victory over Persia, but they knew that they were not exempt from the kind of punishment Xerxes had received for his overreaching ambition. Attic tragedy flowered as a major literary form in the fifth century B.C.E. and pondered this problem just as Athens and Sparta were leading the Greeks to the brink of self-destructive war.

Attic Tragedy. Greek plays were written to be entered in competitions that were staged as festivals honoring the god Dionysus. Each poet who won a chance to compete submitted three tragedies (which might or might not have a common subject) and a concluding satyr play (a comic choral dialogue with Dionysus). An archon chose three competitors for each festival and assigned each of them three actors and a chorus. The actors were paid by the state, and the chorus was sponsored by a donation from a wealthy citizen. Most plays were performed in the temple of Dionysus, an amphitheater of 30,000 seats on the south side of the Acropolis. A jury of Athenians, chosen by lot, awarded prizes for the best author, actor, and sponsor.

Attic theater provided poets with an opportunity to challenge their fellow citizens to ponder vital issues of the day. On rare occasions the subject of a play might be a contemporary or historical event, but usually a playwright chose a tale from mythology that illuminated current affairs. The plays of Aeschylus and Sophocles, our earliest extant examples, deal with public issues of religion, politics, and ethics. The plays of Euripides, which were written a little later, show a greater interest in exploring the psychology of the individual.

Old Comedy. Comedies were added to the Dionysian festival early in the fifth century B.C.E. Cratinus, Eupolis, and Aristophanes (ca. 450–ca. 385 B.C.E.), the author of the only plays to survive complete, wrote humorously about serious political issues. They used scathing invective and satire to lampoon their contemporaries—men such as Pericles, Cleon, Socrates, and Euripides.

Architecture and Sculpture. Like the plays Pericles witnessed, the buildings the city erected during his lifetime reflect the creative tension that existed between civic responsibility and the transcendent genius of individual artists. In 448 B.C.E., Pericles used income from the Athenian Empire to inaugurate a great building program on the Acropolis. The plan included new temples to honor the city's gods and an imposing gateway for the sacred precinct. Pericles' intent was to represent visually the political power and intellectual greatness of Athens—to make Athens, in his words, "the school of Hellas."

The three orders of Greek architecture, Doric, Ionic, and Corinthian, have had an enduring impact on Western architecture.

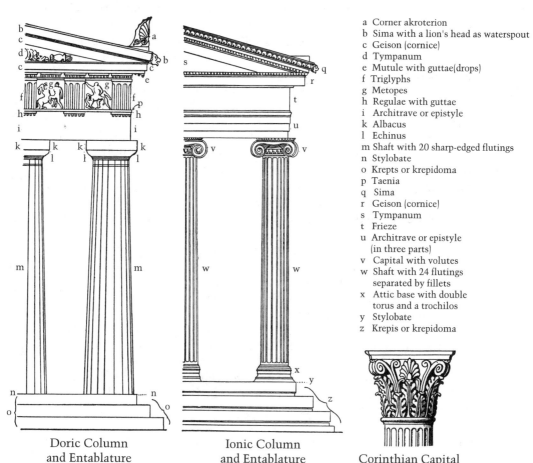

a Corner akroterion
b Sima with a lion's head as waterspout
c Geison (cornice)
d Tympanum
e Mutule with guttae(drops)
f Triglyphs
g Metopes
h Regulae with guttae
i Architrave or epistyle
k Albacus
l Echinus
m Shaft with 20 sharp-edged flutings
n Stylobate
o Krepts or krepidoma
p Taenia
q Sima
r Geison (cornice)
s Tympanum
t Frieze
u Architrave or epistyle (in three parts)
v Capital with volutes
w Shaft with 24 flutings separated by fillets
x Attic base with double torus and a trochilos
y Stylobate
z Krepis or krepidoma

Doric Column and Entablature

Ionic Column and Entablature

Corinthian Capital

Philosophy. The art of the fifth century B.C.E. attempted to define humanity and explore its place in the natural world order. Curiosity about such questions also prompted the invention of philosophy. Philosophy began in the sixth century B.C.E. when a thinker named Thales proposed a theory to explain how a world composed of changing phenomena could function as a stable, coherent whole. He suggested that the changes we see are nothing but alterations in the state of a single underlying universal substance. When attempts to identify this substance failed, later thinkers concluded that Thales had been naive in assuming that change and permanence could both exist in the same world.

Heraclitus argued that permanence was an illusion produced by our inability to perceive very slow change. Parmenides of Elea and his pupil Zeno countered that since the concept of change implied that something arose from nothing, change was a logical absurdity. Empedocles of Acragas proposed a compromise by suggesting that there were unchanging elements (fire, water, earth, and air) whose combinations changed. Similarly, Leucippus of Miletus and Democritus of Abdera imagined the world to be composed of innumerable tiny, solid, indivisible particles that move about in the void of space—clumping together to form the objects our senses perceive. These indestructible particles were called *atomoi* in Greek.

The atomists believed that "soul" or mind was composed of matter, and that physical laws could explain everything. Anaxagoras of Clazomenae, their older contemporary, accepted the existence of tiny fundamental particles he called "seeds," but claimed that these things were controlled by a rational force, *nous* ("mind"). What emerged was the debate between materialism and idealism that still continues.

These speculations were too abstract to interest many people, but the Sophists, a group of professional teachers who flourished in the mid-fifth century B.C.E., attracted much attention. They were paid to develop and teach a practical skill: rhetoric. The arts of rhetorical persuasion were much valued in democracies, where many issues were resolved through public debate.

Some Sophists claimed to teach wisdom and virtue. They refrained from speculations about the physical universe, but used reason to analyze human beliefs and institutions. In the process they identified a central problem of human social life: the conflict between nature and custom. The more traditional among them argued that laws were of divine origin and in accord with nature, but others argued that laws were merely conventions—arbitrary agreements among people. The most extreme Sophists maintained that law was contrary to nature—a device to reverse the natural order and enable the weak to dominate the strong. Critias, an Athenian oligarch, went so far as to say that the gods themselves had been invented to deter people from doing what they wanted to do. Such speculations undermined the concept of justice on which the *polis* was founded. A desire to refute them inspired the insights of the later giants of philosophy, Plato and Aristotle.

History. Herodotus—"the father of history," as he has been deservedly called—was born shortly before the outbreak of the Persian Wars. The account he wrote of those wars far exceeded attempts by earlier prose writers (in chronicles, genealogies, and geographical studies) to explain human actions. Although his *History* was completed about 425 B.C.E. and shows a few traces of Sophist influence, its spirit is that of an earlier time. Herodotus accepted, although not uncritically, information taken from legends and oracles, and he often explained events as the result of divine intervention. But his work is typical of its time in celebrating the crucial role of human intelligence in determining the course of human events. Nor was Herodotus unaware of the importance of institutions. He credited Greece's victory over Persia to the love of liberty the *polis* instilled in its citizens.

Thucydides, the historian of the Peloponnesian War, was born about 460 B.C.E. and died a few years after the end of the war he spent his life studying. His thought was influenced by the secular, human-centered, skeptical rationalism of the Sophists of the late fifth century B.C.E., and he shared the scientific attitudes that characterized the work of contemporaries like Hippocrates of Cos. (The Hippocratic school of medicine advocated careful observation and rational inference as strategies for diagnosing and treating disease.) Thucydides took great pains to achieve factual accuracy, and he searched his evidence for significant patterns of human behavior. He hoped that by discovering these patterns people would be able to foresee events. Since human nature was, he believed, essentially unchanging, similar circumstances ought to produce similar responses. But Thucydides admitted that the lessons of history were not always enough to guarantee success. He believed that an element of randomness—chance—helps to shape human destiny.

The Fourth Century B.C.E.

The Peloponnesian War marked the passing of the *polis* as an effective form of government. The Greeks of the fourth century B.C.E. may not fully have grasped this fact, but they did realize that their traditional way of life was threatened. Some tried to shore up the weakened structure of the *polis*; others looked for alternatives to it; and still others averted their gaze from the public arena altogether.

Drama. The poetry of the fourth century B.C.E. reveals the disillusionment some Greeks felt with the *polis*. Its subjects are no longer drawn from politics and public life, but from the private concerns of ordinary people—the family and the interior life of the individual. Old Comedy had focused on political issues and matters of public policy. Middle Comedy was devoted to a humorous-realistic depiction of daily life, to intrigue, and to mild satire of domestic situations. The role of the chorus, which in a way had represented the *polis* in the drama, was very much diminished. New Comedy pushed further in these directions. Menander (342–291 B.C.E.), its pioneer, wrote domestic tragicomedy: gentle satires of the foibles of ordinary people and tales of temporarily thwarted lovers—material such as is found in modern situation comedies.

Tragedy, which had been inspired by the robust political life of the *polis*, declined during the fourth century. No plays from the period have survived. The theatrical producers of the period may have sensed decline, for they began to revive the plays of the previous century. Euripides' tragedies, which had rarely won top honors when first produced, became increasingly popular. More than the other great playwrights of his age, Euripides had been interested in exploring the interior lives of individual human beings. Some of his late plays look like forerunners of New Comedy: *Helena, Andromeda,* and *Iphigenia in Tauris* are more like fairy tales, fantasy adventures, or love stories than tragedies.

Sculpture. The same movement away from the grand, the ideal, and the general and toward the ordinary, the real, and the individual is apparent in the evolution of Greek sculpture. To see this, one has only to compare the work of Polycleitus (ca. 450–440 B.C.E.) with that of Praxiteles (ca. 340–330 B.C.E.) or Lysippus (ca. 330 B.C.E.).

Philosophy and the Crisis of the *Polis*

Socrates. The life and teachings of Socrates (469–399 B.C.E.) reflect an early awareness of the crises that were developing for the *polis*. Socrates recognized the difficulties and criticized the shortcomings of the *polis,* and he did not seek an active political career. But he did not abandon the *polis* ideal. He fought as a soldier to defend it, obeyed its laws, and sought a sound rational foundation for its values.

Since Socrates wrote nothing, our knowledge of him depends on the reports of his disciples, Plato and Xenophon, and on the work of later commentators. As a young man, he supposedly took an interest in the theories about the physical world developed by the first philosophers, but his concern soon shifted to the interior world: the explication of the processes of human understanding and decision making. Unlike some Sophists, he believed in the existence of truth and the power of reason to search it out.

Socrates sought truth by cross-examining people who were reputed to have it, that is, those who knew something—craftsmen, poets, and politicians. His conversations with them always ended the same way. He demonstrated that, apart from technical information and skills, they had little knowledge of the fundamental principles of human behavior. It is not surprising that Athenians, whose opinions were challenged by his rigorous logical critiques, concluded that he was trying to undermine their confidence in the beliefs and values on which the *polis* was based. Socrates made more enemies by failing to conceal his contempt for democracy—a system of government that he believed empowered the ignorant to make important decisions about things of which they knew nothing.

In 399 B.C.E. Athens, its confidence shaken by the loss of the Peloponnesian War, decided that it could no longer tolerate Socrates. He was condemned to death on charges that implied that he was undercutting the traditions on which the survival of the *polis* depended. He was given a chance to escape, but Plato says that he refused because of his respect for the laws of the city. In taking this stand Socrates demonstrated that he was not a Sophist or an irresponsible skeptic. He accepted the *polis* and its laws as more than arbitrary human conventions that could be ignored whenever they proved inconvenient. What he had been unable to prove by rational argument, he witnessed to by powerful example.

The Cynics. Socrates had advocated concern with personal morality and the state of one's soul, disdain of worldly pleasure and wealth, and withdrawal from political life. After his death these ideas were developed as a program for a group of extremist philosophers called Cynics. Antisthenes (ca. 455–ca. 360 B.C.E.), a follower of Socrates, was the first, but the most famous was Diogenes of Sinope (ca. 400–ca. 325 B.C.E.), whom Plato described as Socrates gone mad.

Diogenes believed that happiness was achieved by satisfying natural needs in the simplest and most direct way. He dismissed all civilized constraints on the individual as nothing more than arbitrary social convention. Diogenes' way of life illustrated his contempt for the artifice of civilization and society. He begged for his bread, wore rags, lived in a tub, openly performed intimate acts of personal hygiene, and ridiculed religious observances.

Although the Cynics claimed to follow Socrates, they contradicted some of his beliefs. Socrates said that virtue was a matter of knowledge—that people do wrong only through ignorance of what is right. The Cynics, on the contrary, argued that wisdom and happiness derived from actions (a way of living), not from knowledge (philosophy). Where Socrates had criticized but ultimately defended the *polis*, the Cynics abandoned it. When Diogenes was asked about his citizenship, he answered that he was *kosmopolites*, "a citizen of the world."

Plato. Plato (429–347 B.C.E.), the most important of Socrates' associates, is the prime example of the pupil who becomes greater than his master. Plato was the first systematic philosopher—the first to lay out a consistent worldview that provided a context for all fundamental questions. He was also a brilliant writer. His twenty-six philosophical discussions—most cast in the form of dialogues— are artistic masterpieces that make the analysis of complicated philosophical ideas dramatic and entertaining.

Plato, like other members of his aristocratic Athenian family, planned a career in politics. But the excesses of the Thirty Tyrants and Socrates' execution discouraged him. He made two trips to Sicily, where he hoped that the tyrants of Syracuse (Dionysius I and II) would allow him to guide them in building a model state. When this project failed, he returned to Athens to found the Academy (386 B.C.E.), a center for research and a school for training statesmen and citizens. The Academy survived until a Christian government closed it in the sixth century C.E.

Like Socrates and unlike the radical Sophists, Plato believed in the *polis*. He thought that it was consistent with human nature and was an instrument for creating good people. But Socrates' insistence that virtue was a kind of knowledge led Plato to reject democracy as an ideal form of government for a *polis*. Justice, Plato said, consists in each man doing that to which his nature is best suited. The true knowledge on which virtue is based is beyond most people. It is *episteme*—science, a wisdom achieved by only a few highly trained and specially gifted individuals. Plato believed that these "philosopher kings" should be trusted with absolute political power, for only they were capable of subordinating private interests to the good of the community. Only they could restore harmony to the *polis* by eliminating the causes of strife: private property, the family, and everything that distracts individuals from the public good.

Concern for the redemption of the *polis* was central to Plato's philosophy. The survival of the *polis* depended on its ability to produce good citizens. Consequently, Plato had to define goodness. Because Plato believed that goodness was a kind of knowledge, this forced him to work out a theory of knowledge. And that led him into the realm of metaphysics. Thus Plato's purely logical and metaphysical work springs from his interest in politics. His search for a satisfactory foundation for the beleaguered *polis* culminated in the birth of systematic philosophy.

Aristotle. Aristotle (384–322 B.C.E.) was born at Stagirus in the Chalcidice, the son of the physician to the court of Macedon. As a youth he went to Athens to study at the Academy and remained there until Plato's death. He then conducted research in marine biology at Assos and at Mytilene in Asia Minor. In 342 B.C.E., he accepted an appointment as tutor to Alexander, son of King Philip of Macedon. In 336 B.C.E., he returned to Athens and founded his own school, the Lyceum or the *Peripatos*—a reference to a covered walkway on its grounds that led to Aristotle's disciples being called *Peripatetics.* After Alexander's death in 323 B.C.E., the Greeks turned against the Macedonians, and Aristotle found it wise to leave Athens. He died at Chalcis in Euboea a year later.

The program of the Lyceum was different from that of the Academy. Plato's students were preoccupied with mathematics; Aristotle was interested in gathering, ordering, and analyzing data relating to all fields of human knowledge. He and his students assembled collections of materials to support various scientific studies. The loose organization and style of much of Aristotle's prose suggests that we have his lecture notes, not his polished treatises. The range of subjects he taught is astonishing: logic, physics, astronomy, biology, ethics, rhetoric, literary criticism, and politics.

Aristotle began the study of every subject the same way. He gathered empirical evidence. Sometimes the evidence was physical; sometimes it was anecdotal—a garnering of common opinions. The evidence was then rationally analyzed to see if it could be consistently explained. Metaphysical principles ultimately emerged as Aristotle wrestled to resolve inconsistencies.

Like Plato, Aristotle viewed things teleologically; that is, he explained things in terms of their ultimate ends or purposes. Plato described these ends as universal ideas or forms—transcendent realities that shaped the world, but that were not part of human experience. Aristotle, however, inferred the purposes of most things from their behavior in the world. The most striking characteristic of his philosophy is its common sense. In his view, matter existed to achieve an end, and it evolved until it fully realized the form (the idea) that made it intelligible as what it was. Being was a constant process of moving from matter to form, from potentiality to actuality.

This metaphysical model is at the heart of Aristotle's thinking about the *polis*. He rejected the Sophists' claim that social life was a convention that frustrated the true nature of individuals. He believed that the *polis* was natural because it was necessary for the realization of human potential as a social being. Human survival and happiness depended on group life: family, village, and *polis*. The purpose of the *polis* was, therefore, not economic or military. It was moral. It made possible the good life.

Aristotle was less interested in theorizing about the perfect state than in designing the best state practically possible. To determine what this was, he assembled a collection of 158 constitutions. (Only the *Constitution of the Athenians* has come down to us.) He concluded that a *politeia*—not the best constitution but the one best suited to most states—was characterized by moderation. It empowered neither the rich nor the poor, but the middle class. A large middle class was essential for political stability, for this class was not tempted to the arrogance of the rich nor infected by the malice that resentment of their circumstances creates in the poor. Stable constitutions were also usually "mixed"—that is, they blended aspects of democracy and oligarchy.

All the political thinkers of the fourth century B.C.E. recognized that the *polis* was in danger, and all hoped to save it. All recognized the economic and social troubles that threatened it. But few made such realistic proposals for its reform as did Aristotle. It is ironic that the ablest defense of the *polis* came on the eve of its demise.

⤳ The Hellenistic World

The term *Hellenistic* was coined in the nineteenth century to describe the period in Greek history that began when a Macedonian dynasty conquered both Greece and the Persian Empire. This event brought elements of Greek and Middle Eastern culture together to create a new, more cosmopolitan civilization.

The Macedonian Conquest

The quarrels among the Greeks made them vulnerable to conquest by Macedon, the northernmost of the mainland Greek states. By Greek standards Macedon was a backward, semibarbaric land. It had no *poleis,* but was ruled by a king who, like Homer's Agamemnon, depended upon the cooperation of his nation's powerful aristocratic families. Hampered by constant wars with barbarian tribes on its northern frontier, internal strife, loose organization, and lack of money, Macedon played no great part in Greek affairs until the fourth century B.C.E.

Philip of Macedon. The Macedonian king who conquered Greece was Philip II (359–336 B.C.E.). As a youth, Philip had spent several years (367–364 B.C.E.) as a hostage in Thebes. There he learned much about Greek politics and warfare under the tutelage of Epaminondas, the general who defeated Sparta. Philip's talent and training made him the ablest king in Macedonian history. He solidified his hold on his throne, pacified the tribes on his frontiers, and challenged Athens' dominance of the northern Aegean. When conquest of Amphipolis gave him control of the gold and silver mines of Mount Pangaeus, he used this wealth to elevate the level of culture in Macedon. He founded new cities, won friends abroad, and turned his army into the world's finest fighting force.

The Macedonian Army. Philip's army was national, but more professional than the amateur armies of citizen-soldiers who fought for the individual *poleis*. Its infantry was recruited from Macedon's sturdy farming class and feisty hill people. Infantrymen were armed with thirteen-foot pikes instead of the hoplite's more common nine-foot weapon. This enabled them to spread out and form a more open, flexible phalanx than was customary. The Macedonian cavalry was recruited from the aristocracy. Its members, the "Companions," lived with the king and developed a special loyalty to him. Philip also employed mercenaries who knew the latest tactics and were familiar with the most sophisticated siege machinery. Altogether, he could field an army of about 40,000 men.

The Invasion of Greece. The Greeks themselves gave Philip the excuse he needed to intervene in their affairs. The people of Thessaly invited Philip to assist them in a war they had been fighting with the Phocians since 355 B.C.E. Philip won the war, treacherously occupied Thessaly, and marched on Thrace to take control of the northern Aegean coast and the Hellespont.

These actions threatened the vital interests of Athens, but although Athens had a formidable fleet of 300 ships, it was not the Athens of 350 B.C.E. or the Athens of Pericles. Its population was smaller than in the fifth century, and it had no empire from which to draw funds to support a major war. As a result, the Athenians were uncertain how to respond to Philip.

Eubulus, a financial official and conservative political leader, favored a cautious policy of cooperation with Philip in the hope that his aims were limited and posed no real threat to Athens. The leading opponent to appeasement of Macedon was Demosthenes (384–322 B.C.E.), one of the greatest orators in Greek history. He was convinced that Philip was a danger to Greece, and he spent most of his career urging the Athenians to fight. Other Athenian leaders, however, saw Philip as the savior of Greece. Isocrates (436–338 B.C.E.), the head of an important rhetorical and philosophical school in Athens, looked to Philip to provide the unity and leadership needed for a Panhellenic campaign against Persia. He and other orators believed that the conquest of Asia Minor would solve the economic, social, and political problems that had brought poverty and civil strife to Greece since the end of the Peloponnesian War.

In 349 B.C.E., Philip attacked several cities in northern and central Greece and firmly planted Macedonian power in those regions. The years between 346 B.C.E. and 340 B.C.E. were spent in diplomatic maneuvering until, at last, Philip attacked Perinthus and Byzantium, posts guarding the lifeline of Athenian commerce. When the Athenian fleet saved both, Philip marched into Greece. Demosthenes convinced Thebes to join Athens in opposing him. But in 338 B.C.E., a cavalry charge led by Philip's eighteen-year-old son, Alexander, defeated the allied forces at Chaeronea in Boeotia.

The Macedonian Government of Greece. The Macedonian settlement of Greek affairs was not as harsh as many had feared. Athens was spared from attack on condition that it accept Macedonian leadership, and Macedonian garrisons were stationed around Greece to guard against rebellions. In 338 B.C.E., Philip called the Greek states to Corinth and announced the formation of a federation: the League of Corinth. The constitution of the League promised autonomy, freedom from tribute and garrisons, and cooperation in suppressing piracy and civil war. This was a facade that enabled the Greeks to submit with dignity to Macedonian occupation. The defeat at Chaeronea had ended Greek freedom and the autonomy of the *polis*.

Philip chose Corinth as the seat of his new confederacy because it was at Corinth that the Greeks had gathered almost 150 years earlier to plan their strategy for the Persian Wars. It was there also, in 337 B.C.E., that Philip promised to restore the glory of Greece by renewing its war with Persia. This was a promise he failed to keep, for in the spring of 336 B.C.E., as he was about to launch this campaign, he was assassinated.

Alexander the Great

The Conquest of the Persian Empire. Alexander III (356–323 B.C.E.), who came to be known as "the Great," was only twenty when he ascended his father's throne, but he was determined to carry out his father's plan for invading Persia. The Persian Empire was vast and its resources enormous, but it was not an impossible target. Its size and the diversity of its subjects made it hard to control, and its rulers struggled constantly with threats to their far-flung frontiers and intrigues within their court. At the time of Philip II's death in 336 B.C.E., Persia's new king, Darius III, was inexperienced. But with a navy that dominated the sea, a huge army, and vast wealth, Darius was a formidable opponent.

In 334 B.C.E., when Alexander crossed the Hellespont into Asia, he had no navy and little money (see Map 3-2). His army consisted of about 30,000 infantry and 5,000 cavalry. He could not risk heading inland from the coast until he had neutralized the Persian navy at his back by taking all its ports, but he needed some quick victories over the Persians to inspire his men with confidence in him and to win the booty required to finance the war. Memnon, the commander of the Persian navy, proposed an excellent strategy for defeating the Greeks: retreat, scorch the earth, avoid all but guerrilla engagements, and deprive the enemy of supplies. Pride, however, led the Persians to reject his advice and give Alexander what he hoped for.

The Persians offered Alexander battle at the Granicus River on the coast of Asia Minor. Alexander led a cavalry charge across the river into the teeth of

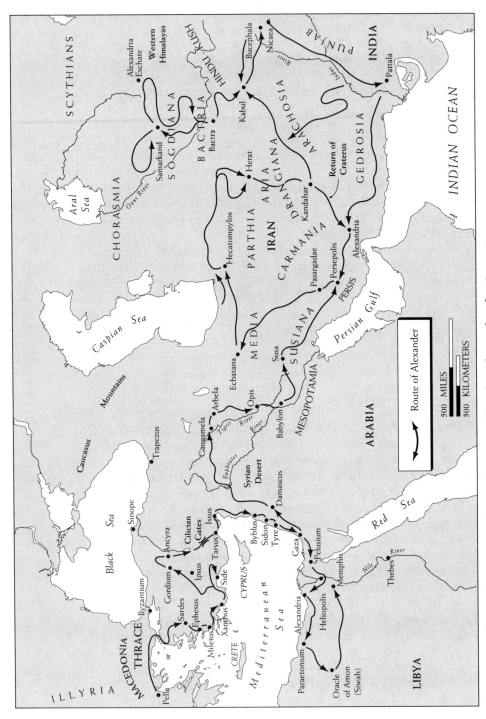

MAP 3-2 Alexander's Campaigns *The route taken by Alexander the Great in his conquest of the Persian Empire, 334–323 B.C.E.. Starting from the Macedonian capital at Pella, he reached the Indus Valley before being turned back by his own restive troops. He died of fever in Mesopotamia.*

This sculpture of Alexander the Great, king of Macedon and conqueror of the Persian Empire, was made in the second century B.C.E., and found at the ancient city of Magnesia in Asia Minor. Alexander's conquests spread Greek culture far from its homeland, laying the foundation of the Hellenistic world. [Erich Lessing/Art Resource, N.Y.]

the enemy and nearly lost his life. His courage, however, inspired his soldiers, and the victory opened all of Asia Minor to conquest by the Greeks.

In 333 B.C.E., Alexander marched out of Asia Minor into Syria to meet the main Persian army under Darius. At Issus, Alexander led a cavalry charge that broke the Persian line. But instead of pursuing Darius as he retreated inland, Alexander continued south along the coast, taking Persia's naval bases. When he arrived in Egypt, he was greeted as liberator and proclaimed pharaoh. Like all of Egypt's divine kings, he was proclaimed a son of Re, the god who, as head of the Egyptian pantheon, the Greeks equated with Zeus.

In the spring of 331 B.C.E., Alexander marched into Mesopotamia to meet an army Darius had assembled at Gaugamela (near the ancient Assyrian city of Nineveh). Once again the Persian line broke, and Darius was forced to flee. Alexander occupied Babylon, and in January of 330 B.C.E., he entered Persepolis, the Persian capital. Conquest of Persia's treasure cities ended Alexander's financial problems, and the gold he showered on his troops put vast sums of money into circulation—a development whose economic effects were felt for centuries.

Because the new regime could not be secure while Darius was at large, Alexander again set out to capture him. But the Persian nobles deprived the Greeks of that prize. Having lost faith in Darius, they killed him and proclaimed Bessus, one of his relatives, his successor. Alexander pursued Bessus into the east, captured him, and pushed on to the frontiers of India.

Near Samarkand, in the land of the Scythians, he founded the city of Alexandria Eschate ("Farthest Alexandria"), one of many cities Alexander created as part of a plan to secure the future of the empire. Alexander hoped to hold the empire he was winning by scattering Greeks through it and amalgamating its diverse peoples. To set an example, he married a princess (named Roxane) from a remote province called Bactria, and recruited 30,000 of her young countrymen to be trained for service in his army.

In 327 B.C.E., the Greeks crossed the Khyber Pass and entered the territory of modern Pakistan. Porus, the native king, was subdued, but Alexander still was not content. He ordered the army farther east to find the river called Ocean that Greek geographers believed encircled the world. At this point his exhausted men mutinied and demanded that he take them home for a rest. By the spring of 324 B.C.E., they were back at the Persian Gulf and celebrating, in true Macedonian style, with a drunken spree.

The Death of Alexander. Alexander, at age thirty-three, was filled with plans for the future, but in Babylon in June of 323 B.C.E., he succumbed to a fever and died. He quickly became the subject of myth, legend, romance, and controversy among historians. Some have seen him as a man of grand and noble vision who transcended the narrow limits of Greek and Macedonian ethnocentrism—seeking to create a great world state based on the common humanity all peoples share. Others have depicted him as a calculating despot, given to drunken brawls, brutality, and murder. The truth probably lies in between.

The Successors

Nobody was prepared for Alexander's sudden death, and he had no clear successor. He was one of history's greatest generals and a man of rare organizational talent, but even he would have had difficulty holding together the vast empire he had created. His nearest adult male relative, a weak-minded half-brother, could never have filled his shoes. Although Roxane, his queen, bore him a son soon after his death, an infant heir could not preserve such a legacy as Alexander had prepared for him. The Macedonian generals, therefore, divided up responsibility for ruling the empire until the boy came of age. But conflicting ambitions soon had them at each other's throats. In the battles that followed, all of the direct members of the Macedonian royal house were destroyed. The deaths of Roxane and her son in 310 B.C.E. removed the last restraints on the surviving governors, and in 306 B.C.E. and 305 B.C.E. they declared the lands they ruled independent kingdoms.

Three Macedonian dynasties emerged as heirs to major portions of Alexander's empire. Ptolemy I (367?–283 B.C.E.) claimed Egypt and founded its thirty-first dynasty. (Cleopatra, who died in 30 B.C.E., was the last of the Ptolemies.) Seleucus I (358?–280 B.C.E.) created the Seleucid dynasty that ruled Mesopotamia. And Antigonus I (382–301 B.C.E.) established the Antigonid family that reigned over Asia Minor and Macedon.

For about seventy-five years after Alexander's death the world economy expanded. The money that Alexander had loosed to circulate increased the level of economic activity. The opening of vast new territories to Greek trade, the increased demand for Greek products, the enhanced availability of goods, and the enlightened economic policies of the Hellenistic kings all helped the growth of commerce. Problems of overpopulation on the Greek mainland were also solved by opportunities to emigrate to new cities in the east.

The new prosperity was not evenly distributed. Urban Greeks, Macedonians, and Hellenized natives—the upper and middle classes—lived comfortable, even luxurious, lives, while the standard of living for rural laborers declined. The independent small farmers who had built the early *poleis* disappeared. Arable land was consolidated into large plantations, and farmers were reduced to the status of dependent peasants. During prosperous times their lot was bearable, but the costs of continuing wars and the effects of the inflation produced by the influx of Persian gold steadily eroded their position. Kings bore down heavily on the middle class, which shifted the burden to the peasants and the city laborers. These people responded by slowing their work and by striking. In Greece economic pressures brought clashes between rich and poor and demands for the abolition of debt and the redistribution of land. In places civil war returned.

These internal problems—and the strain of endemic warfare—increased the vulnerability of the Hellenistic kingdoms to invasion. By the middle of the second century B.C.E. they had all, except for Egypt, succumbed to conquest by the Italian city of Rome. The two centuries that separated Alexander from the Roman Empire had, however, not been unproductive. A powerful new phase in Greek civilization had begun to unfold.

✧ Hellenistic Culture

Alexander the Great's life marked a turning point in the history of Greek literature, philosophy, religion, and art. His empire and its successor kingdoms ended the role that the *polis* had played in shaping Greek culture. *Poleis* continued to exist throughout the Hellenistic period, but these communities were mere shadows of the vital *poleis* of the Hellenic era. Hellenistic cities were not free, sovereign states, but municipal towns submerged within great military empires.

As the freedoms central to the life of the *polis* faded, Greeks lost interest in pursuing political solutions for their problems. They abandoned public affairs and resorted to religion, philosophy, and magic for help in dealing with their private hopes and fears. The confident humanism of the fifth century B.C.E. gave way to a kind of resignation to fate, a recognition of helplessness before forces too great for humans to manage.

Philosophy

Athens survived as the center of philosophical studies during the Hellenistic era. Plato's Academy and Aristotle's Lyceum continued to operate, and they were joined by new schools advocating the popular new philosophies of Epicureanism and Stoicism.

The Lyceum abandoned the scientific interests of its founder and became a center for literary and historical studies. The Academy was even more radically transformed. It endorsed Skepticism, a critique of the fallacies and weaknesses of all schools of philosophy that led to the conclusion that nothing could be known. Skeptics urged their students, in lieu of better options, to accept conventional morality and not to try to change the world. The Cynics drew a more radical conclusion from the inevitability of human ignorance. They denounced convention and advocated a life in accordance with nature's crude impulses.

Neither of these views appealed much to the middle-class city dwellers of the third century B.C.E. They were searching for the kind of dignity and meaning that the *polis* had provided for the lives of their ancestors.

The Epicureans. Like many thinkers of his day, Epicurus of Athens (342–271 B.C.E.) doubted that human beings could obtain knowledge. The atomists (Democritus and Leucippus) convinced him that the world was nothing more than a swirl of atoms continually falling through a void. Knowledge was, therefore, only a stream of impressions that atoms left on human sense organs. Since Epicurus believed that the atoms did not obey permanent laws of motion, but swerved in arbitrary, unpredictable ways, he concluded that our experience of their movements could not help us discover truth or certainty.

Epicurus concluded from this that philosophers ought not to seek knowledge of the world, but insights that would promote human happiness. For instance, Epicurus believed that philosophy could free people from the fear of death. When people understood that death was merely the dispersal of the atoms of body and soul, they realized that nothing of themselves survived to suffer pain or loss. The gods, too, were no threat, for they were material beings who took no interest in human affairs.

The proper pursuit of humankind was pleasure in the sense of *ataraxia*, a state of being undisturbed, without trouble, pain, or responsibility. The happiest people were those who withdrew from the world, avoided business concerns, and stayed free of the duties of family and public life. Epicurus' ideal was the genteel, disciplined selfishness of intellectual men of means. It was a dream not calculated to be widely attractive.

The Stoics. Soon after Epicurus began teaching in Athens, Zeno of Citium (335–263 B.C.E.) established the Stoic school—named for the *Stoa Poikile,* the

Painted Portico in the Athenian *agora* (marketplace) where Zeno taught his disciples. Zeno and his successors owed much, by way of the Cynics, to Socrates and to Eastern thinkers.

Like the Epicureans, the Stoics sought the happiness of the individual, but Stoic philosophy relied more on religious images. Stoics believed that human fulfillment lay in living in harmony with nature, and Stoics claimed that nature was a manifestation of divine *logos*—an eternal principle of reason. Every human being had a spark of the divine "fire" of reason, and at death this returned to its source in the eternal spirit. Like other living beings, the whole world was periodically destroyed (in a great conflagration) and born anew.

Stoics held that humans experienced happiness when they lived virtuous lives. A sense of fulfillment was produced by living in accordance with natural law. This required one to understand which things in life were good and evil and which were morally "indifferent." Things like prudence, justice, courage, and temperance were good. Things like folly, injustice, and cowardice were evil. Some things—like life, health, pleasure, beauty, strength, and wealth—were morally neutral, for by themselves they did not produce either happiness or misery. Misery was the result of passion, a disease of the soul that arose from attaching the self to the wrong things. Happy people achieved *apatheia*, freedom from passion.

The Stoics saw the world as a single *polis* in which all people were equally children of god. Despite the fact that politics invited preoccupation with things that were morally indifferent, many Stoics led active public lives. Their aim was to live in accordance with the divine will. Thus they fatalistically accepted their places in life and sought to play out the roles in which they found themselves while cultivating a form of apathy. This fit well with the reality of post-Alexandrian societies in which docile submission was more important than active participation.

Literature

Alexandria became the center of literary production in the third and second centuries B.C.E. Its intellectuals, unlike the creative thinkers who were citizens of a *polis*, were more preoccupied with the past than with current affairs. (They knew they had little influence over these.) The Ptolemies supported a "museum," a great research institute that collected Greek literature of every kind for scholars to edit and interpret. Some of this work was dry and petty, but without it much of what survives today from the ancient era would have been lost.

Architecture and Sculpture

Hellenistic kings could afford conspicuous displays of royal patronage to artists and architects as well as scholars. Many new cities were built or rebuilt—usually laid out on the efficient grid plan introduced in the fifth century B.C.E. by Hippodamus of Miletus. Famous artists traveled the world, fulfilling commissions and creating a kind of uniform international style. It favored a sentimen-

This is a Roman copy of one of the master-pieces of Hellenistic sculpture, the Lao-coön. *According to legend, Laocoön was a priest who warned the Trojans not to take the Greeks' wooden horse within their city. This sculpture depicts his punishment. Great serpents sent by the goddess Athena, who was on the side of the Greeks, devoured Lao-coön and his sons be-fore the horrified peo-ple of Troy. [Robert Miller]*

tal, emotional realism rather than the idealism popular during the age of the *polis*.

Mathematics and Science

The most spectacular and remarkable intellectual achievements of the Hellenistic age were in mathematics and science. The scholars of Alexandria amassed the greater part of the scientific knowledge available to the Western world until the scientific revolution of the sixteenth and seventeenth centuries C.E.

Euclid's *Elements* (written early in the third century B.C.E.) remained the textbook of plane and solid geometry until recent times. Archimedes of Syracuse (ca. 287–212 B.C.E.) explored the principles of the lever in mechanics and invented hydrostatics. Heraclides of Pontus (ca. 390–310 B.C.E.) advanced a heliocentric theory of the universe that was fully developed by Aristarchus of Samos (ca. 310–230 B.C.E.). Unfortunately, however, since Hellenistic technology could not provide data to confirm this theory, it did not take hold. A geocentric model advanced by Hipparchus of Nicaea (born ca. 190 B.C.E.) and refined by Ptolemy of Alexandria (second century C.E.) acquired currency and remained dominant until the work of Copernicus in the sixteenth century C.E. The scholars of the age knew that the earth was round, and Eratosthenes of Cyrene (ca. 275–195 B.C.E.) calculated its circumference within about 200 miles. His maps were more accurate than those that were standard in the Middle Ages.

The achievements of Greece's Classical Age were unparalleled. To a great degree they sprang from the unique political experiences provided by the poleis, *the independent city-states. Democratic imperial Athens nurtured the greatest artists and intellectuals. The freedoms Athens gave its citizens bred respect for the human individual and curiosity about human potential. Philosophy, science, drama, and history evolved to explore this potential, and a naturalistic style of art developed to celebrate the human form.*

The Classical Period ended when the polis *was replaced by the great empires of the Hellenistic Age. Hellenistic civilization spread, assimilated influences from other cultures, and became a cosmopolitan phenomenon. By bringing diverse peoples together it prepared the way for Rome's empire.*

✑ Review Questions

1. How was the Delian League transformed into an Athenian empire during the fifth century B.C.E.? Did Athens' empire offer any advantages to its subjects? Why was there such resistance to Athenian efforts to unify the Greek world in the fifth and fourth centuries B.C.E.?

2. Why did Athens and Sparta come to blows in the Great Peloponnesian War? What was each side's strategy for victory? Why did Sparta win the war?

3. In what ways were the tensions that characterized Greek life in the Classical Period reflected in its art, literature, and philosophy? How does Hellenistic art differ from that of the Classical Period?

4. Between 431 and 362 B.C.E., Athens, Sparta, and Thebes each tried to impose hegemony over the city-states of Greece, but none succeeded except for short periods of time. Why did each state fail? What does your analysis tell you about what it takes to create a successful government?

5. How and why did Philip II conquer Greece between 359 and 338 B.C.E.? How was he able to turn Macedon into a formidable military and political power? Why was Athens unable to defend itself against Macedon? Did Philip's success result from Macedon's strength or from the weakness of the Greek city-states?

6. What were the major consequences of Alexander's early death? What were Alexander's achievements? Was he a conscious promoter of Greek civilization or only an egomaniac devoted to conquest?

✎ Suggested Readings

J. BUCKLER, *The Theban Hegemony, 371–362 B.C.* (1980). A study of Thebes at the height of its power.

W. BURKERT, *Greek Religion* (1985). A fine general study.

W. R. CONNOR, *The New Politicians of Fifth-Century Athens* (1971). A study on changes in political style and their significance for Athenian society.

J. M. COOK, *The Persian Empire* (1983). A solid history that makes good use of archaeological evidence.

J. R. ELLIS, *Philip II and Macedonian Imperialism* (1976). A study of the career of the founder of Macedonian power.

J. FERGUSON, *The Heritage of Hellenism* (1973). A good survey.

P. GREEN, *From Alexander to Actium* (1990). A brilliant new synthesis of the Hellenistic period.

C. D. HAMILTON, *Agesilaus and the Failure of Spartan Hegemony* (1991). An excellent biography of the king who was the central figure in Sparta during its domination in the fourth century B.C.E.

R. JUST, *Women in Athenian Law and Life* (1988). A good study of the place of women in Athenian life.

D. KAGAN, *Pericles of Athens and the Birth of Athenian Democracy* (1991). An account of the life and times of the great Athenian statesman.

D. KAGAN, *The Outbreak of the Peloponnesian War* (1969). A study of the period from the foundation of the Delian League to the coming of the Peloponnesian War that argues that war could have been avoided.

H. D. F. KITTO, *Greek Tragedy* (1966). A good introduction.

J. LEAR, *Aristotle: The Desire to Understand* (1988). A brilliant yet comprehensible introduction to the work of the philosopher.

A. A. LONG, *Hellenistic Philosophy: Stoics, Epicureans, Skeptics* (1974). A solid study.

R. MEIGGS, *The Athenian Empire* (1972). A fine study of the rise and fall of the empire, making excellent use of inscriptions.

M. I. ROSTOVTZEFF, *Social and Economic History of the Hellenistic World*, 3 vols. (1941). A masterpiece of synthesis by a great historian.

B. S. STRAUSS, *Athens After the Peloponnesian War* (1987). An excellent discussion of Athens' postwar recovery and of the nature of Athenian society and politics in the fourth century B.C.E.

W. W. TARN, *Alexander the Great*, 2 vols. (1948). The first volume is a narrative account; the second, a series of detailed studies.

G. VLASTOS, *The Philosophy of Socrates* (1971). A splendid collection of essays illuminating the problems presented by this remarkable man.

F. W. WALBANK, *The Hellenistic World* (1981). A solid history.

4

Rome: From Republic to Empire

KEY TOPICS

- The emergence of the Roman Republic
- The development of the republican constitution
- Roman expansion and imperialism
- The character of Roman society in the republican era
- The fall of the republic

The Romans, who started with nothing but a small village in central Italy, achieved remarkable things. They united the peoples of the Western world and maintained the longest period of peace in Western history.

By adapting and spreading aspects of Greek culture through their empire, the Romans created a universal Graeco-Roman tradition that remains at the heart of Western civilization to this day.

⌇ Prehistoric Italy

Italy's cultural evolution began slowly. The Paleolithic era lingered in Italy until 2500 B.C.E., and Italy did not feel the effects of the Bronze Age until 1500 B.C.E. About 1000 B.C.E., the Umbrians, Sabines, Samnites, and Latins—the peoples whose Italic languages gave the peninsula its name—began to immigrate from the east. The newcomers pioneered Italy's Iron Age. By 800 B.C.E., they had occupied the highland pastures of the Apennines, the mountain range that runs the length of Italy, and had begun to challenge earlier settlers for control of the western coastal plains (see Map 4-1).

⌇ The Etruscans

About 800 B.C.E., a mysterious people whose language was not Italic settled in Etruria (Tuscany) on a plain west of the Apennines between the Arno and Tiber rivers. Although the background of the Etruscan people is unknown, aspects of their civilization suggest an eastern origin. They had a powerful influence on the development of Rome.

Government

Etruscan communities were independent, self-governing city-states loosely linked in a religious confederation. Aristocratic landowners soon banished kings from most cities and set up governments run by councils and annually elected magistrates. The Etruscans were the militarized ruling class of their nation. They subjugated the peoples they conquered in Italy and took to the sea as traders and pirates. They competed with the other maritime powers of the western Mediterranean, the Carthaginians of north Africa and Italy's Greek colonists.

Dominion

In the seventh and sixth centuries B.C.E., the Etruscans extended their power north to Italy's Po Valley and overseas to the islands of Corsica and Elba. They also moved south into Latium (a region that included the small town of Rome) and Campania (a plain that the Greeks of Naples had begun to colonize). These

Significant Dates from Rome's Republican Era

509 B.C.E.	*Republic founded*
392 B.C.E.	*Fall of Veii; Etruscans defeated*
387 B.C.E.	*Gauls burn Rome*
338 B.C.E.	*Latin League defeated*
295 B.C.E.	*Samnites defeated*
287 B.C.E.	*Plebeian Assembly wins power to legislate*
275 B.C.E.	*Pyrrhus evacuates Italy*
264–241 B.C.E.	*First Punic War*
218–202 B.C.E.	*Second Punic War*
215–205 B.C.E.	*First Macedonian War*
200–197 B.C.E.	*Second Macedonian War*
189 B.C.E.	*Antiochus defeated; Asia Minor conquered*
172–168 B.C.E.	*Third Macedonian War*
149–146 B.C.E.	*Third Punic War*
133 B.C.E.	*Tribunate of Tiberius Gracchus*
123–122 B.C.E.	*Tribunates of Gaius Gracchus*
111–105 B.C.E.	*Jugurthine War and Marius*
90–88 B.C.E.	*War against the Italian allies*
88 B.C.E.	*Sulla's march on Rome*
60 B.C.E.	*Formation of First Triumvirate*
58–50 B.C.E.	*Caesar conquers Gaul*
49–48 B.C.E.	*Civil war between Caesar and Pompey*
46–44 B.C.E.	*Caesar's dictatorship*
43 B.C.E.	*Formation of Second Triumvirate*
31 B.C.E.	*Octavian's victory over Antony at Actium*

conquests were the work of independent Etruscan chieftains who rarely supported each other. As a result, they were short-lived.

Etruscan power peaked before 500 B.C.E. By 400 B.C.E., Celts from Gaul (modern France) had driven the Etruscans from the Po Valley, an area the Romans later called Cisalpine Gaul (i.e., "This side of the Alps" Gaul). Gradually the cities of Etruria lost their independence. Their language ceased to be a living tongue, but their culture was not forgotten. It had a profound effect on Rome.

Roman religion shows the clearest evidence of Etruscan influence. The Etruscans believed that innumerable supernatural beings had the power to intervene in human affairs. Since Romans were convinced that human survival depended on understanding and placating these spirits (many of whom were evil), they preserved the Etruscan rites for divining the wills and interpreting the omens of the gods.

⌁ Royal Rome

The Latin peoples who settled Rome may have been attracted by its location. Rome was established fifteen miles from the sea at the point where the Tiber

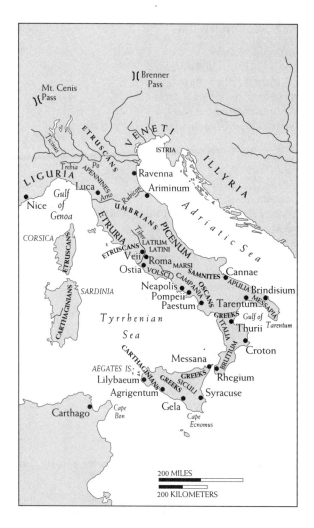

MAP 4-1 Ancient Italy
This map of ancient Italy and its neighbors before the expansion of Rome shows major cities and towns as well as a number of geographical regions and the locations of some of the Italic and non-Italic peoples.

River emerges from the foothills of the Apennines. Roads converged here, for just southwest of Rome's Capitoline Hill an island made the Tiber fordable. Rome's site attracted attention, therefore, as a center for Italy's inland communication and trade.

Government

Rome's potential was not realized until the sixth century B.C.E., when Etruscan kings established themselves in Rome and conquered most of Latium. Although one family monopolized the royal office, kingship was technically elective. The Roman Senate, an aristocratic council, had to approve a candidate for the throne, and only the assembly of the Roman people could bestow on him his unique power—the *imperium*, the right to enforce commands by fines, ar-

Busts of a Roman couple from the period of the republic. Although some people have identified the individuals as Cato the Younger and his daughter Porcia, no solid evidence confirms this claim. [Scala/Art Resource, N.Y.]

rests, and corporal or capital punishment. The king was Rome's chief priest, high judge, and supreme military commander.

According to legend, Rome's Senate originated when Romulus, Rome's founder, chose 100 of Rome's leading men to advise him. The early Senate had no formal executive or legislative authority. It met only when the king convened it to ask for advice. In practice, however, the Senate was very influential. It was composed of the most powerful men in the state, and a king could not safely ignore them.

The curiate assembly, an organization to which all citizens belonged, was the third organ of government. It met only when summoned by the king, and he set its agenda and decided who could address it. Its job was to listen and approve. Romans voted, not as individuals, but as members of groups. Citizens were registered in thirty groups, and each group had a single vote which was cast according to the will of its majority.

The Family

Family organizations were the basic units of Roman society. The head of a family was its "king" in the sense of holding *imperium* over it. Like the king who presided over the state cult, a father supervised his family's most important religious rites, the daily worship of its ancestors. Like the king, a father had the power to execute his dependents (even his adult children) or sell them into slavery. The male head of a household had less power over his wife, for she was protected by the family of her birth. She could not be divorced unless convicted of certain serious offenses by a court of her male blood relatives. A Roman wife was greatly respected as the administrator of her husband's household.

Clientage

The head of a wealthy family could extend its influence by providing patronage to dependents called clients. Roman clientage was a formal, legally recognized institution. A patron provided a client with physical and legal protection and, often, with economic assistance. A client might subsist on daily handouts, receive a grant of land, become a tenant farmer, or labor on his patron's estate. In return a client fought for his patron, voted as his patron ordered, and did any jobs that were requested of him. Ambitious members of the upper classes might even become clients of great families with powerful political machines in order to further their careers.

Patricians and Plebeians

From the start of Rome's history, Roman families were divided into two hereditary classes. The "patricians" were the upper class that monopolized power. Only they could serve as priests, sit in the Senate, or hold office. The lower "plebeian" class may originally have consisted of small farmers, laborers, and artisans who were clients of the patricians. But wealth alone did not define the classes. Some plebeians were rich, and incompetence and bad luck sometimes impoverished patricians.

∿ The Republic

According to Roman tradition, in 509 B.C.E. an atrocity committed by a member of the royal family sparked a revolt that drove the last Etruscan king from the city. The patricians chose not to appoint another king but to establish a republic.

Constitution

The Consuls. The Roman Republic had a very conservative unwritten constitution that transferred many of the duties and trappings of monarchy to republican magistrates. Two patricians were annually elected consuls and vested with *imperium.* Like the former kings, they led the army, oversaw the state religion, and sat as judges. They even used the traditional symbols of royalty—purple robes, ivory chairs, and *lictors* (guards who accompanied them, bearing the bundles of rods wrapped around an axe that signified their power to discipline and execute). A consul was, however, not a king. He remained in office for only a year, and he had an equal, a colleague who could prevent him from taking independent action. Consular *imperium* was also limited. Consuls could execute citizens who were serving with the army outside the city, but in Rome citizens had the right to appeal all cases involving capital punishment to the popular assembly.

     The checks on the consular office discouraged initiative, swift action, and change. This was what a conservative, aristocratic republic wanted. But since a divided command could create serious problems for an army in the field, the Romans usually sent only one consul into battle or assigned consuls sole command on alternate days. If this did not work, the consuls could, with the advice of the Senate, step down and appoint a single dictator. His term of office was limited to six months, but his *imperium* was valid everywhere and unlimited by any right of appeal.

These devices worked well enough for a small city whose wars were short skirmishes fought near home. But as Rome's wars grew longer and more difficult, adaptations had to be made. In 325 B.C.E. proconsulships were invented to extend the terms of consuls serving in the field. This maintained continuity of command during a long war, but it ran the risk of allowing ambitious men to monopolize political authority.

Consuls were assisted by financial officers called *quaestors,* and a need for more military commanders led to the introduction of other aides called *praetors.* A praetor's primary function was judicial, but he could also be granted a general's *imperium* and have his term of service in the field extended beyond a year. In the second half of the fifth century B.C.E., the consuls' responsibility for enrolling and keeping track of citizens was delegated to new officials, two *censors.* Since they determined the status and the tax liability of each citizen, they had to be men of unimpeachable reputation. They were usually senior senators who viewed the censorship as the pinnacle of their careers. By the fourth century B.C.E. censors had the right to expel from the Senate members whose conduct disgraced Senatorial dignity.

The Senate and the Assembly. The Senate was the only deliberative body continuously in session in the Roman Republic. Senators were prominent patricians, often leaders of clans and patrons with many clients. The Senate controlled the state's finances and foreign policy, and its advice was not lightly ignored by magistrates or by popular assemblies.

The centuriate assembly—the name for the Roman army when it was convened to deliberate rather than fight—was the early republic's most important popular assembly. It elected the consuls and several other magistrates, voted on bills the Senate put before it, made decisions of war and peace, and served as a court of appeal for citizens convicted of serious offenses. The centuriate assembly was named for the "centuries" in which its members voted. A century was, in theory, a unit of 100 soldiers who fought with the same kind of equipment. Because each man bought his own equipment, centuries grouped citizens into classes according to wealth. Each century cast a single vote, and votes were tallied beginning with the richest centuries, those of the cavalry.

The Struggle of the Orders. Plebeians were barred from all political and religious offices in the early days of the republic. They could not serve as judges. They did not even know the law, for the law was an oral tradition maintained by patrician magistrates. When Rome acquired new land by conquest, patricians were situated to reward themselves most generously. They dominated the assemblies and the Senate. And they refused to sanction marriages outside their caste that would have permitted at least the most wealthy plebeian families to share their privileges.

The plebeians responded to the intransigence of the patricians by launching the "struggle of the orders," a fight for political, legal, and social equality that lasted for 200 years. Plebeians had a strong position from which to negotiate with the patricians, for plebeians made up a large part of the republic's army. According to tradition, the plebeians discovered early in the republic's history how to better their situation. They simply withdrew from the city and refused to fight until the patricians granted them a concession.

The plebeians made progress one step at a time. They won the right to form a political organization of their own, the plebeian tribal assembly, and to elect "tribunes," officials with the power to protect plebeians from abuse by patrician magistrates. Tribunes could veto any action of a magistrate or any bill in a Roman assembly or the Senate. The protection of plebeian rights required that Rome's laws be fixed and published, and in 450 B.C.E. the first attempt to codify Rome's harsh customs yielded something called the Twelve Tables. In 445 B.C.E. plebeians won the right to marry patricians, but they were still barred from many public offices. It was not until 367 B.C.E. that one of the consuls was allowed to be of plebeian rank. Gradually other offices, even the dictatorship and the censorship, were opened to them, and in 300 B.C.E. they were admitted to the most important priesthoods. In 287 B.C.E. the plebeians completed their triumph by securing passage of a law that made decisions of the plebeian assembly binding on all Romans.

The plebeians' victory did not make Rome a democracy. It simply cleared the way for wealthy plebeian families to enter politics and share the privileges of the patrician aristocracy. The *nobiles,* a small group of rich and powerful families of both patrician and plebeian rank, monopolized the republic's highest offices. Since there was no secret ballot, the numerous clients of the wealthy *nobiles* could easily be intimidated into voting as their patrons ordered. This permitted the great families to build political machines and maintain their holds on offices. From 233 to 133 B.C.E. twenty-six families produced 80 percent of the consuls; ten of those families accounted for almost 50 percent of the successful candidates. Since the politically dominant families were all represented in the Senate, the Senate became the republic's chief deliberative body. The product of the struggle of the orders was, therefore, a republican constitution dominated by a senatorial aristocracy. Most Romans accepted it, for it led Rome well in the wars that won Rome an empire.

The Conquest of Italy

Not long after the birth of the republic in 509 B.C.E., a coalition of Romans, Latins, and Greeks defeated the Etruscans and drove them out of Latium. Rome's neighbor, the Etruscan city of Veii, continued to be a problem until 392 B.C.E. when Rome destroyed Veii and doubled its size by annexing Veii's territory.

Romans used both inducements and threats to come to terms with their foes. Friendly alliances with former enemies recruited their soldiers into Rome's army. If land belonging to a defeated people was annexed, the army again increased. Distribution of newly won land to poor Romans brought them the income they needed to equip themselves for military service. This gave the Roman poor a stake in their government and reconciled them to the aristocratic regime. The long siege of Veii, which kept soldiers from working their farms, prompted the Romans to begin paying men for military service. This, too, was popular with the poor and improved the quality of the army.

Gallic Invasion of Italy and Roman Reaction. Early in the fourth century B.C.E. Rome suffered a dramatic setback. In 387 B.C.E. the Gauls marched south from the Po Valley, defeated the Roman army, and burned Rome. The Romans had to pay the Gauls to evacuate the city. Rome quickly recovered from this humiliation, but in 340 B.C.E. the city's Latin neighbors, the Latin League, tried to block its expansion. In 338 B.C.E. Rome defeated and dissolved the League. The terms Rome offered set a precedent for its eventual reorganization of Italy.

Roman Policy Toward the Conquered. The Romans did not destroy any of the Latin cities, nor did they treat them all alike. Some were given full Roman citizenship. Others were granted municipal privileges: internal self-government, the right to intermarry and trade with Romans—but not to take part in Roman politics unless they moved to Rome and applied for citizenship. The treaties by which other states became allies of Rome differed from city to city. Some were given the private rights of intermarriage and commerce with Romans; some were not. (Allied states were always forbidden to exercise these rights with one another.) Some states, but not all, were allowed local autonomy. Land was taken from some, but not from others. All the allies supplied troops to Rome's army under Roman officers, but they did not pay taxes to Rome.

The Romans planted colonies of veteran soldiers on some of the land they annexed. The colonists retained Roman citizenship and served as a kind of permanent garrison to deter rebellion. A network of military roads was built to connect the colonies with Rome and guarantee that a Roman army could swiftly reinforce an embattled colony to put down an uprising.

The Roman settlement of Latium reveals the strategy that the Romans developed to extend their dominance. Rome used diplomacy and military actions to separate enemies. It cultivated a reputation for harsh, speedy punishment of rebels. But it was also generous to those who submitted, and the status given a newly conquered city was not a permanent sentence. Loyal allies could improve their prospects—even achieve full Roman citizenship. This policy gave Rome's allies a stake in Rome's future and a sense of being colleagues rather than subjects. Consequently, most of Rome's allies remained loyal even when put to severe tests.

Defeat of the Samnites. After the struggle with the Latin League, Rome's next challenge was a series of wars with the tough mountain people of the southern

Apennines, the Samnites. Some of Rome's allies joined the Samnites—as did various Etruscans and Gauls. But most of the allies remained loyal, and by 280 B.C.E. Rome's victories over these assorted opponents had won the city mastery of central Italy.

Rome's newly expanded territory came into direct contact with the Greek cities of southern Italy. Roman intervention in a quarrel between two of these cities led to a war with a Greek mercenary (Pyrrhus, king of Epirus) who was probably the best general of the day. Pyrrhus defeated the Romans twice but suffered so many casualties that he decided that he could not afford to see the war through to its conclusion. Judging his "Pyrrhic" victory not worth the cost, he withdrew, and his Greek employers had to join the Roman confederation. By 265 B.C.E. Rome ruled all of Italy south of the Po River, an area of 47,200 square miles. Victory over Pyrrhus also brought Rome international recognition as a power in the Hellenistic world.

Rome and Carthage

Late in the ninth century B.C.E. the Phoenician city of Tyre had planted a colony called Carthage ("New City") on the coast of northern Africa near modern Tunis (see Map 4-2). In the sixth century B.C.E. the conquest of Tyre by the Assyrians liberated the Carthaginians to develop the opportunities offered by their strategic location. The city had an excellent harbor and commanded rich lands that it worked with slave labor.

In the sixth century B.C.E. Carthage's domain expanded westward along the coast of northern Africa past Gibraltar and eastward into Libya. Parts of southern Spain, Sardinia, Corsica, Malta, the Balearic Islands, and western Sicily were also brought into the Carthaginian Empire. Their native peoples served in the Carthaginian army and navy and paid tribute to Carthage. Carthage also claimed exclusive rights to trade in the western Mediterranean.

Rome and Carthage became entangled when Hiero, tyrant of Syracuse, attacked the Sicilian city of Messana. Messana was strategically important, for it commanded the straits between Italy and Sicily. A band of Italian mercenaries who called themselves Mamertines ("Sons of Mars") had seized the city, and Hiero wanted to evict them. The Mamertines asked Carthage for help in fending him off, and Carthage agreed. But the Mamertines then tried to check Carthage by also inviting the Romans to send them aid. Rome realized that if it did not intervene, it was ceding control of the straits and of Sicily to Carthage. Consequently, in 264 B.C.E. the assembly voted to send an army to Messana. Since the Roman term for the Carthaginians was *Poeni* or *Puni* (Latin for "Phoenician"), the ensuing conflict came to be known as the Punic War.

The First Punic War (264–241 B.C.E.). The Romans made no progress against Carthage until they built a fleet to blockade the Carthaginian ports at the western end of Sicily. In 241 B.C.E., after a long war of attrition, Carthage capitulated. It surrendered Sicily and the islands between Italy and Sicily to Rome and agreed to pay a war indemnity. In 238 B.C.E., while Carthage struggled to put

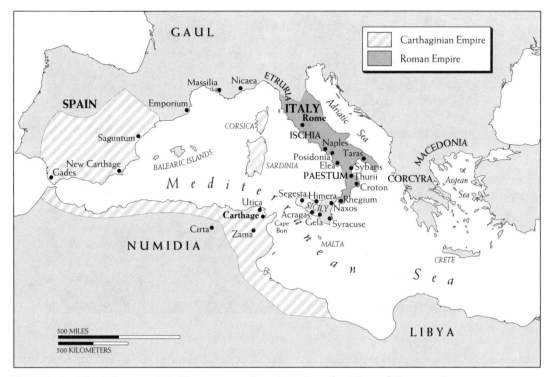

MAP 4-2   The Western Mediterranean Area During the Rise of Rome *This map covers the theater of conflict between the growing Roman dominions and those of Carthage in the third century B.C.E. The Carthaginian Empire stretched westward from the city (in modern Tunisia) along the North African coast and into southern Spain.*

down a revolt led by her unpaid mercenary soldiers, Rome seized Sardinia and Corsica and demanded an additional indemnity. This was a provocative action that was to cost Rome a second war with Carthage.

It is hard to understand why Rome sought more territory, for the administration of lands outside of Italy was difficult. Rome simply turned these lands over to military governors. Since Rome had no way of overseeing the behavior of magistrates outside the city, it was hard to guarantee that they would not abuse their offices. Sicily, Sardinia, and Corsica became the first provinces in a Roman empire, for the Romans did not feel that it was possible to continue their traditional policy of extending citizenship or alliances beyond the borders of Italy. The residents of the provinces were neither Roman citizens nor allies; they were subjects who paid tribute in lieu of serving in the army. Rome collected this tribute by "farming" out the right to gather money in the provinces to the highest bidder. Provincial governments soon became a source of corruption that undermined the machinery of the Roman Republic.

While Rome struggled to adjust to its new situation, Hamilcar Barca, the

A Roman warship. Rome became a naval power late in its history, in the course of the First Punic War. Roman sailors initially lacked the skill and experience in sea warfare of their Carthaginian opponents, who could maneuver their oared ships to ram the enemy. To compensate for this disadvantage, the Romans sought to make a sea battle more like an encounter on land by devising ways to grapple enemy ships and board them with armed troops. In time, they also mastered the skillful use of the ram. This picture shows a Roman ship, propelled by oars, with both ram and soldiers, ready for either kind of fight. [Vatican Museum]

Carthaginian governor of Spain (237–229 B.C.E.), put Carthage on the road to recovery. His plan was to build a Punic empire in Spain that would make up for the lands Carthage had lost to Rome. Hasdrubal, Hamilcar's son-in-law and successor, continued his policies with such success that he alarmed the Romans. They imposed a treaty in which he promised not to expand north of Spain's Ebro River. He doubtless assumed that if Carthage accepted the Ebro as its northern frontier, the Romans would grant Carthage a free hand in the south. He was wrong. Within a few years the Romans had violated, at least in spirit, the Ebro treaty by accepting an offer of an alliance from the people of Saguntum, a town 100 miles south of the Ebro.

The Second Punic War (218–202 B.C.E.). Hasdrubal was assassinated in 221 B.C.E., and the army chose Hannibal, the twenty-five-year-old son of Hamilcar Barca, to succeed him. Hannibal quickly consolidated and extended the Punic empire in Spain. At first, he avoided any action against Saguntum, but the Saguntines, confident of Rome's protection, began to stir up trouble for him.

When Hannibal besieged and captured the town, the Romans sent an ultimatum to Carthage demanding Hannibal's surrender. Carthage refused, and Rome declared war (218 B.C.E.).

Rome had repeatedly provoked Carthage, but had taken no steps to prevent Carthage from rebuilding its empire—and made no plans to defend itself against a Punic attack. Hannibal exacted a high price for these blunders. In the fall of 218 B.C.E. he crossed the Alps into Italy with an army to which the Gauls were eager to contribute. Hannibal defeated the Romans at the Ticinus River and crushed the joint consular armies at the Trebia River. In 217 B.C.E. he outmaneuvered and trapped another army at Lake Trasimene. He could not take Rome, however, unless he could persuade its allies to defect. Despite his efforts to court them, most of the allies remained firm.

Sobered by their defeats, the Romans suspended consular government and chose a dictator: Quintus Fabius Maximus. Since time and supplies were on Rome's side, his strategy was to avoid pitched battles and wear Hannibal's army down by harassing its flanks. In 216 B.C.E. Hannibal attacked a grain depot at Cannae in Apulia to tempt the Romans into an open fight. They took the bait and suffered the worst defeat in their history. Hannibal slaughtered 80,000 Roman soldiers.

Rome's prestige was shattered. Most of the allies in southern Italy—and the crucial port of Syracuse in Sicily—went over to Hannibal. For the next decade no Roman army dared confront Hannibal directly. But Hannibal had neither the numbers nor the supplies to blockade walled cities, nor did he have the equipment to storm them. If the Romans refused to fight, there was little he could do to bring the war to an end.

The Romans devised a plan to defeat Hannibal outside of Italy. Publius Cornelius Scipio (237–183 B.C.E.), whose Carthaginian victories earned him the title Africanus, set out to conquer Spain and prevent it from sending reinforcements to Hannibal. Scipio was not yet twenty-five, but he was almost as talented a general as Hannibal. Within a few years he had taken Spain and won the Senate's permission to open a front in Africa. In 204 B.C.E. Scipio landed in Africa, defeated the Carthaginians, and forced them to order Hannibal to withdraw from Italy. Hannibal had won every battle but lost the war. His fatal error was to underestimate the determination of Rome and the loyalty of its allies. When Hannibal returned to Carthage, hostilities flared up again. In 202 B.C.E. he and Scipio met at the battle of Zama, and the day was decided by Scipio's generalship and the desertion of Hannibal's mercenaries. Rome, now the undisputed ruler of the western Mediterranean, reduced Carthage to the status of a dependent ally.

The Republic's Conquest of the Hellenistic World

The East. By the middle of the third century B.C.E. the three great Hellenistic kingdoms that dominated the eastern Mediterranean had achieved equilibrium. The balance of power among them was threatened, however, by the efforts of Philip V of Macedon (221–179 B.C.E.) and Antiochus III, the Seleucid ruler (223–187 B.C.E.), to expand their domains. Philip had allied himself with Carthage during the Second Punic War—provoking Rome to stir up a conflict in the Aegean called the First Macedonian War (215–205 B.C.E.). Once the Second Punic War was over, Rome determined to make sure that Macedon did not succeed Carthage as a threat to Italy. In 200 B.C.E. the Romans challenged Philip by ordering him to cease preying on the Greek cities. Two years later the Romans demanded that Philip withdraw from Greece entirely. Philip refused, and Rome declared the Second Macedonian War. In 197 B.C.E. Flamininus, a gifted young Roman general, defeated Philip at Cynoscephalae in Thessaly, and the following year (196 B.C.E.) Flamininus surprised the Greeks by restoring the autonomy of the city-states and pulling Rome's troops out of Greece.

Philip's retreat offered Antiochus an opportunity to advance. On the pretext of freeing the Greeks from Roman domination, he invaded the Greek mainland. The Romans quickly drove him from Greece, and in 189 B.C.E., they crushed his army at Magnesia in Asia Minor. The peace of Apamia in the next year deprived Antiochus of his war-elephants and his navy and imposed a huge indemnity on him. Again, the Romans annexed no territory, but they treated Greece and Asia Minor as protectorates in whose affairs they could freely intervene. This benign policy was to change as the influence of Cato, a conservative and ruthlessly businesslike censor, increased in Rome.

In 179 B.C.E. Perseus succeeded Philip V as king of Macedon. His popularity with democratic, revolutionary elements in the Greek cities convinced the Romans that he was a threat to the stability of the Aegean. The result was the Third Macedonian War (172–168 B.C.E.) and a harsher Roman policy. Macedon was divided into four separate republics whose citizens were forbidden to intermarry or do business with each other, and leaders of anti-Roman factions in the Greek cities were punished severely. Aemilius Paullus, the Roman general who defeated Perseus, brought so much booty home that Rome abolished some taxes on its citizens. Romans discovered that foreign campaigns could be profitable for the state, its soldiers, and its generals.

The West. Rome's worst abuses of power were directed not against the Greeks, but against the people of the Iberian Peninsula whom the Romans considered barbarians. In 154 B.C.E. the natives of Iberia launched a fierce guerrilla campaign against their oppressors. By the time Scipio Aemilianus brought the war to a conclusion in 134 B.C.E. by taking the city of Numantia, Rome was having difficulty finding soldiers willing to go to Spain.

Carthage fared much worse. Carthage scrupulously observed the terms of its treaty with Rome and posed no threat to Rome, but fear and hatred of Carthage were deeply ingrained in some Romans. Cato is said to have ended all his speeches in the Senate with the same sentence: "Besides, I think that Carthage must be destroyed." The Romans finally took advantage of a technical breach of the peace to declare war on Carthage, and in 146 B.C.E. Scipio Aemilianus destroyed the city. A province of Africa was then added to the five existing Roman provinces: Sicily, Sardinia-Corsica, Macedonia, Hither Spain, and Further Spain.

⌁ Civilization in the Early Roman Republic

The Roman attitude toward the Greeks ranged from admiration for their culture to contempt for their political squabbling and money grubbing. Conservatives like Cato spoke contemptuously of the Greeks, but, as Roman life was transformed by association with the Greeks, even he learned Greek. The education of the Roman upper classes became bilingual, and young Roman nobles studied Greek rhetoric, literature, and sometimes philosophy. Greek refined the Latin language, and Greek models—such as Livius Andronicus's third-century B.C.E. translation of the Odyssey—prompted the birth of Latin literature.

Religion

The Romans identified their ancestral gods with the Greek deities and worked Greek mythology into their own traditions. But Roman religious practice was little affected until new Eastern influences were felt in the third century B.C.E. In 205 B.C.E. the Senate approved the public worship of Cybele, the Great Mother goddess from Phrygia. But since Cybele's cult involved rites that shocked and outraged conservative Romans, the Senate soon reversed itself. For similar reasons, it banned the worship of Dionysus (Bacchus) in 186 B.C.E., and in 139 B.C.E. the Senate drove from Rome Babylonian astrologers whom it believed to be an unhealthy influence.

Education

In the early centuries of the Roman Republic, education was entirely the responsibility of the family—a father teaching his sons at home. (Daughters may not have been schooled in those days, but they were at a later period in Rome's history.) The curriculum was designed to provide males with vocational skills, to elevate their moral standards, and to inspire them with respect for Roman tradition. Boys were taught to read, write, calculate, and farm. They memorized the laws of the Twelve Tables, practiced religious rites, learned the legends of early Roman history—particularly those involving their ancestors—and trained for military service.

Hellenized Education. Contact with the Greeks of southern Italy in the third century B.C.E. produced momentous changes in Roman education. Greek teachers introduced the Romans to the study of language, literature, and philosophy—and to what the Romans called *humanitas,* the broad training and critical habits of mind that are the characteristics of a liberal education.

Since Rome did not yet have a literature of its own, elementary education involved learning Greek as a preparation for the advanced study of rhetoric (the art of speaking and writing well). Philosophy was at the heart of Greek education, but the practical Romans preferred rhetoric. It was of great use in legal disputes and political life.

This carved relief from the second century C.E. shows a schoolmaster and his pupils. The one at the right is arriving late. [Alinari/Art Resource, N.Y.]

Some important Romans were powerful advocates of Greek literature and philosophy. Scipio Aemilianus, the man who destroyed Carthage, was a patron of important Greek intellectuals—particularly the historian Polybius and the philosopher Panaetius. Conservative Romans, like Cato the Elder, feared that Greek learning would weaken Roman moral fiber. On occasion the Senate was persuaded to expel philosophers and teachers of rhetoric from Rome, but Rome could not return to its simple agrarian past. If Romans were to deal with the sophisticated world of the Hellenistic Greeks which they had come to dominate, they needed the new education.

In the late republic, Roman education, though still entirely private, became more formal and organized. From the ages of seven to twelve, boys went to elementary school accompanied by a Greek slave called a *paedagogus* (hence our term "pedagogue"). He looked after them and helped them learn Greek by conversing with them. Boys learned to read, to write—using a wax tablet and a stylus—and to do simple arithmetic with the aid of an abacus and pebbles (*calculi*). From twelve to sixteen, boys studied Greek and Latin literature with a *grammaticus*. He gave them a liberal education involving dialectic, arithmetic, geometry, astronomy, music, and some elements of rhetoric. Some boys pursued advanced study in rhetoric. A few, like the great orator Cicero, undertook what we might call postgraduate study by traveling abroad to work with the great teachers of the Greek world.

Education for Women. Though the evidence is limited, it is certain that girls of the upper classes received an education equivalent at least to the early stages of a boy's education. They were probably taught at home by tutors and not sent out to school as was increasingly common for their brothers in the late republican period. Young women did not study with philosophers and rhetoricians, for they were usually married by the age at which a man began his higher education. Still, some women found ways to continue their studies, and some became prose writers and poets. By the first century C.E. there were women in aristocratic circles who were famous or—as conservative males saw it—infamous for their learning.

Slavery

The Romans, like most ancient peoples, had always had slaves. But the simple family-farmers of early Rome owned few. Slavery became fundamental to the Roman way of life only during the second century B.C.E. in the wake of Rome's conquests. Between 264 B.C.E. and 133 B.C.E. the Romans enslaved some 250,000 prisoners of war. Slaves could marry, and their children increased the slave population.

In Rome as in Greece, domestic slaves and those engaged in crafts and commerce were allowed to earn money with which to purchase their freedom. The freeing of slaves was very common among the Romans. After a time, a considerable portion of the Roman population consisted of people who had been slaves or whose ancestors had been slaves. It was not uncommon to see a freedman son or grandson of a slave become wealthy and the slave himself or his son become a Roman citizen. By importing slaves from all over the Mediterranean world and freeing them, the Romans transformed the ethnic composition of their population.

Rome's unique contribution to slavery was the invention of an agricultural system employing vast numbers of unfree workers. At the end of the republic there were 2 million to 3 million slaves in Italy, about 35 percent to 40 percent of the total population. Most belonged to great slave gangs working vast plantations called *latifundia*. These estates produced capital-intensive cash crops (wool, wine, olive oil, cattle) rather than the grain that small farmers raised. The lives of agricultural workers were harder than those of other kinds of slaves, for *latifundia* were designed to produce maximum profits. Slaves, who were simply a means to that end, were fed cheaply, treated like machines, and discarded when they were no longer productive.

Harsh treatment spawned slave rebellions of a kind unknown in other ancient societies. A rebellion in Sicily in 134 B.C.E. kept that island in turmoil for over two years. In 73 B.C.E. a gladiator named Spartacus raised an army of 70,000 fugitive slaves from the Italian countryside and repeatedly defeated the Roman legions. When the Romans finally subdued him, they crucified 6,000 of his men along the road from Capua to Rome.

Roman Imperialism: The Late Republic

Rome had no plan for building an empire. Territories were acquired as a result of wars that the Romans believed were either defensive or preventive. Roman foreign policy was designed to provide security for Rome on Rome's terms, not

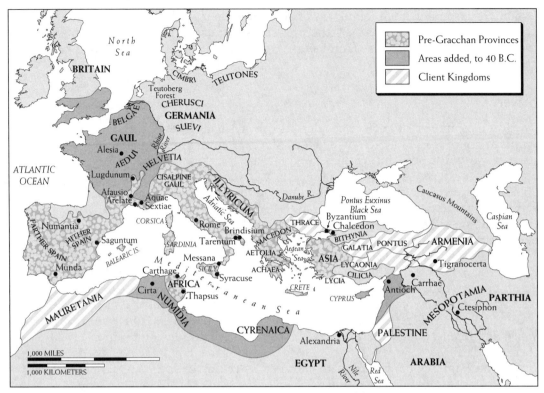

MAP 4-3 Roman Dominions of the Late Republic *The Roman Republic's conquest of Mediterranean lands—and beyond—until the death of Julius Caesar is shown here. Areas conquered before Tiberius Gracchus (ca. 133 B.C.E.) are distinguished from later ones and from client areas owing allegiance to Rome.*

to acquire land. Since these terms were often unacceptable to other nations, conflicts arose; and, intentionally or not, Rome expanded (see Map 4-3).

The empire undercut the very republic it was built to protect. The constitution of the republic had been designed for a city-state. It could be adapted to rule Italy, but not to handle the responsibility of governing an empire beyond the seas.

The Aftermath of Conquest

Before the Punic Wars most Italians owned their own farms and were largely self-sufficient. Some families had larger holdings than others, but they grew the same crops (grain) and used free laborers rather than slaves. The Punic Wars changed this. For fourteen years Hannibal marauded through Italy, doing terrible damage to its farmland. Many veterans returned from the wars to find that they did not have enough capital to get their devastated farms back into production. Some moved to Rome seeking work as day laborers. Most stayed in the country and became tenant farmers or hired hands. The land they abandoned was gathered into large parcels by the wealthy who had the capital to convert it to crops profitable on a world market (olives, grapes, and cattle). The upper classes had plenty of capital to invest, for the political offices they monopolized enabled them to win the governorships that allowed them to exploit Rome's new provinces. The economy that evolved with the empire separated the people of Rome and Italy more sharply into rich and poor, landed and landless, privileged and deprived. The result was an increasingly tense situation that threatened the survival of the republic.

The Gracchi

By the middle of the second century B.C.E., perceptive Roman nobles were aware that institutions fundamental to the republic were collapsing. The decline of the peasant farmer was shrinking the class from which Rome drew its soldiers, and the patron-client organizations that had structured Roman society were weakening. Patrons found it hard to control clients once the latter were no longer tied to the land. The introduction of the secret ballot in the 130s B.C.E. further weakened the traditional ties of clientage.

Tiberius Gracchus. In 133 B.C.E. Tiberius Gracchus, a tribune, tried to solve these problems by proposing a program of land reform. He suggested reclaiming public land that was being held illegally. Current holders of this land were to be allowed to retain as many as 300 acres in clear title as private property, but the state would take the rest and redistribute it, at low rents and in small lots, to the poor. Those who received farms were not to be allowed to sell them.

There was much opposition to Tiberius's proposal. Many wealthy senators would be hurt by its passage. Others worried about the precedent set by any interference with property rights. Still others feared the political gains that Tiberius would make if the beneficiaries of his legislation were properly grateful to its drafter.

When Tiberius put his land reform bill before the tribal assembly, one of his fellow tribunes, M. Octavius, vetoed it. This left Tiberius with the choice of dropping the matter or attempting a maneuver that would undercut the checks and balances of Rome's constitution. Tiberius opted for the later. He persuaded the assembly to remove the veto blocking discussion of his proposal by removing Octavius from office. At this point many of Tiberius's powerful senatorial allies deserted him. If the assembly could pass laws after they had been opposed by the Senate and vetoed by a tribune, then Rome would no longer be an oligarchical republic, but a democracy.

Tiberius gave up hope of conciliating the Senate and passed a second bill that was harsher than the first he had proposed—and, therefore, more appealing to the masses. It contained a scheme for funding a commission to carry out land redistribution. King Attalus of Pergamum had just died and left his kingdom to Rome. Tiberius's suggestion that this revenue be used to finance implementation of land reform was a second assault on the constitution: a challenge to the Senate's control of finances and foreign affairs.

Tiberius knew that he would be in great personal danger once he lost the protection of his tribunal office, so he announced his candidacy for a second successive term. This was another blow to tradition, and his opponents feared that he might hold office indefinitely and rule Rome as a demagogic tyrant. At the elections a riot broke out, and a mob of senators and their clients killed Tiberius and some 300 of his followers. The Senate had beaten back the threat to its rule, but at the price of the first internal bloodshed in Rome's political history.

The tribunate of Tiberius Gracchus permanently changed the thinking of Roman politicians. Heretofore Roman politics had been a struggle among great families for honor and reputation. Fundamental issues were rarely at stake. Tiberius's revolutionary proposals and the senatorial resort to bloodshed created a new situation. Tiberius, despite his failure, had shown how the tribunate could be used to challenge senatorial dominance. He had demonstrated that a man could acquire power, not by courting the aristocracy, but by appealing directly to the people with a popular issue. Politicians who took this route came to be known as *populares.* Those who supported the traditional role of the Senate were the *optimates* ("the best men").

These groups were not political parties with formal programs and party discipline, but they were more than vehicles for the political ambitions of unorthodox office seekers. They forced the Roman people to wrestle with fundamental issues of government. Some of their leaders were interested only in advancing their own careers, and others were sincere advocates of principled positions. Most, no doubt, had mixed motives.

Gaius Gracchus. In 123 B.C.E., ten years after the death of Tiberius, his brother Gaius Gracchus became a tribune. Gaius kept himself in power by putting together packages of legislation that appealed to different groups. He revived efforts to redistribute public land; when supplies of land proved insufficient, he proposed new colonies; and he put through a law stabilizing the price of grain in Rome. Gaius also weakened the rich by pitting the republic's two wealthiest classes (the senatorial and the equestrian) against each other. The equestrians—the men who could afford to equip themselves for the most expensive form of military service (the cavalry)—were businessmen with interests in the provinces. In 129 B.C.E., Gaius allowed them, but not senators, to serve on the courts that tried provincial governors. This prevented senators from sitting in judgment on themselves, but it did not improve the administration of the provinces. No senator dared interfere with the equestrian tax collectors in his province lest he find himself dragged before their court.

In 122 B.C.E., Gaius celebrated reelection to the tribunate—which was now legal—by proposing that Rome's Italian allies be given citizens' rights. The allies had not received a fair share of the profits from the empire they had helped Rome win, and their resentment was threatening Italy's stability. Ordinary Romans, however, did not want to dilute the power of their votes by creating more citizens. This issue cost Gaius support, and he lost the election of 121 B.C.E. The Senate then trumped up a charge against him and killed him and some 3,000 of his followers. Once again, the senatorial oligarchy triumphed over the *populares*, but the struggle was by no means over. Gaius's death simply taught the *populares* that they would have to resort to violence to oppose the Senate's violence. Marius, an officer who rose to prominence in the Jugurthine War, showed them the way.

Marius and Sulla

In 111 B.C.E. a group of Italian businessmen who were working in Numidia, a client kingdom in Africa, were caught and killed in the crossfire of a dispute over succession to the throne. The Roman electorate promptly declared war against Jugurtha, the perpetrator of this insult to their nation's honor. When the war dragged on longer than expected, rumors circulated that Rome's generals were being bought off.

In 107 B.C.E. the assembly elected C. Marius (157–86 B.C.E.) to a consulship and (usurping the Senate's right to control foreign policy) commissioned him to end the Jugurthine War. Marius was a *novus homo*, a "new man" who was the first of his family to hold a consulship and who was not, therefore, a member of the old Roman aristocracy.

Marius quickly defeated Jugurtha, and the grateful Romans elected him to a second consulship to deal with another problem. In 105 B.C.E., two barbaric tribes, the Cimbri and the Teutones, had crushed a Roman army in the Rhone Valley. The long struggle to contain them kept Marius in office for five consecutive terms.

Marius won battles because he persuaded Rome to make changes that allowed him to put large armies in the field. He convinced the assembly to drop the property qualification for military service. This was a popular idea for it opened the way to a career for impoverished citizens like those whom the Gracchi had tried to help. Marius's reforms built a strong army, but they also altered the balance of power in Roman politics. Marius's soldiers were semiprofessional clients of their general. They were dependent on him for their pay and for the grants of land on which they retired as veterans. Since they thought of themselves as his men more than the state's, he was able to use them to frighten the Senate into giving him whatever he needed to keep them happy.

Marius's example inspired imitation, and competitors soon challenged him. The most successful was L. Cornelius Sulla (138–78 B.C.E.), an impoverished aristocrat who had served under Marius in the Jugurthine War. Sulla made his mark in a campaign that Gaius Gracchus had tried to prevent: a war between Rome and its Italian allies. In 90 B.C.E. the allies gave up hope of receiving fair treatment from Rome and established a separate confederation with its own capital and coinage. Rome tried to undercut this by offering citizenship to cities that remained loyal and to rebels who laid down their arms. Despite this, hard fighting was needed to put down the uprising. By 88 B.C.E. the war was over, and all the Italians became Roman citizens.

Sulla's performance in the war brought him the consulship for 88 B.C.E. and command of a war against Mithridates, a native king who was leading an uprising in Asia Minor. Marius, at the age of seventy, suddenly emerged from obscurity to demand this assignment for himself. When the assembly acquiesced, Sulla loosed the army he had been recruiting against Rome. Marius had used the army as a kind of political party, but now a Roman general used it to directly threaten his fellow citizens. Sulla regained his command. But when he left for the East, Marius and the consul Cinna occupied Rome with their armies. Marius died soon after his election to a seventh consulship in 86 B.C.E., and Cinna became the leader of Marius's party. In 83 B.C.E. Sulla, who had forced Mithridates to retreat and agree to a truce, returned to Rome. He drove Marius's followers from Italy and assumed dictatorial powers.

His first step was to wipe out his opponents. He posted lists of names of men whom he "proscribed" as enemies of the state. Proscribed men could be executed by anyone who found them, and their executioners could claim rewards from the state. Sulla confiscated their property and awarded it to his own men. As many as 100,000 Romans may have died in Sulla's purge.

Sulla could have made himself the permanent ruler of Rome, but he saw himself as the republic's savior, not its enemy. His intent was to restructure and restore traditional senatorial government. The Senate's political privileges were reaffirmed, and the powers of the office of tribune, which the Gracchi had used to attack senatorial rule, were severely curtailed. In 79 B.C.E. Sulla declared his work complete and retired from public life. The example of what he had done long outlived the political arrangements he had made. It led to a civil war that destroyed the republic.

✧ Fall of the Republic

Pompey, Crassus, Caesar, and Cicero

Within a year of Sulla's death in 78 B.C.E. the Senate had to begin making exceptions to the very rules Sulla had designed to safeguard the Senate's power. The Senate discovered that the only way to deal with emergencies was to create "special" commands that were free of the constitutional limitations within which ordinary magistrates had to work. The most important of these commands went to a young general named Pompey (106–48 B.C.E.) who had never been elected to any office.

Pompey spent several years subduing a Marian army that had occupied Spain. In 73 B.C.E. the Senate appointed him and Marcus Licinius Crassus, a wealthy senator, to put down a slave rebellion led by a gladiator called Spartacus. Crassus and Pompey used their influence to repeal most of Sulla's constitution, and this opened the way for ambitious generals and demagogic tribunes to work together and undercut the Senate by appealing directly to the people.

In 67 B.C.E. a special law aimed at the suppression of piracy gave Pompey *imperium* for three years over the entire Mediterranean and its coast inland for fifty miles. In three months Pompey cleared the seas of pirates. The assembly then authorized Pompey to deal with a new war that had broken out with Mithridates. Pompey defeated Mithridates, drove him to suicide, and pushed Rome's frontier to the Euphrates River.

When Pompey returned to Rome in 62 B.C.E., he had more power than any Roman in history. The Senate had reason to fear that he might emulate Sulla and establish a dictatorship. Crassus had most to fear. Although rich and influential, he did not have the kind of military backing Pompey enjoyed. He, therefore, sought alliances with popular political leaders. The ablest of these was Gaius Julius Caesar (100–44 B.C.E.), a descendant of an old but obscure patrician family. Despite noble lineage, Caesar was connected to the popular party. His aunt had been Marius's wife, and he had married Cinna's daughter Cornelia. Caesar's rhetorical skill made him a valuable ally for Crassus, for he could rally the people to the cause of the *populares*. Each man needed the help of the other to win major military commands which they could use to build armies to compete with Pompey's.

Cicero (106–43 B.C.E.), a "new man" from Marius's home town of Arpinum, marshalled the opposition to Crassus and Caesar. Although he was an outsider to the senatorial aristocracy, he was no fan of the *populares*. He hoped to create a "harmony of the orders" between the Senate and the equestrians that would consolidate the power of the propertied classes. The Senate supported him primarily to block a bid for office made by an extremist named Catiline.

Cicero defeated Catiline for the consulship in 63 B.C.E., but Catiline refused to accept the verdict and hatched a plot to take over the state. News of it leaked to Cicero, who speedily suppressed the plot and thereby annoyed Pompey.

Formation of the First Triumvirate

Toward the end of 62 B.C.E. Pompey landed at Brundisium. He had delayed his return, hoping to find Italy facing some crisis that would justify his keeping his army. But Cicero's quick suppression of Catiline deprived him of a pretext, and Pompey had to disband his army to avoid the appearance of treason.

Pompey had achieved amazing things for Rome, and he expected the Senate to show its gratitude by deferring to him. He wanted the Senate to approve the treaties he had negotiated in the East and to give him land for his veterans. The Senate should have prudently granted his requests, which were reasonable. But it chose instead to try to curtail his power and influence. This forced him to ally with his natural enemies, Crassus and Caesar. They joined him in an informal political arrangement called the First Triumvirate. By working together they were able to control the republic.

Julius Caesar and His Government of Rome

With the aid of his colleagues, Caesar was elected to the consulship for 59 B.C.E., and he used the office to make sure that each of the triumvirs got what he wanted. Pompey obtained land for his veterans and confirmation of his treaties. Crassus won tax concessions for the equestrians who were his chief supporters. Caesar got a special military command that gave him a chance to rival Pompey. When Caesar's consulship ended, the triumvirs secured their gains by arranging for the election of friendly consuls and by forcing their enemies to leave Rome.

Caesar's special command gave him authority, for five years, over Cisalpine Gaul in the Po Valley and Narbonese Gaul on the other side of the Alps. From these provinces, he set about conquering the rest of Gaul. In 56 B.C.E. he bought himself additional time by persuading Crassus and Pompey to renew the triumvirate. By 50 B.C.E. Caesar had completed the conquest of Gaul and acquired the wealth, fame, and military power he needed to compete against Pompey.

The Triumvirate had dissolved in 53 B.C.E. when Crassus died leading an army into Parthia, the successor to the Persian Empire. Pompey saw no reason to sit by while Caesar's star continued to rise. In the late 50s B.C.E. the Senate appointed Pompey sole consul, for it concluded that Pompey was less of a threat than Caesar—and it hoped to help Pompey bring Caesar down.

Caesar searched for some way to retain an office that would allow him to keep his army, but the Senate refused to extend his term in Gaul. In January of 49 B.C.E. it ordered him to lay down his command. Caesar knew that this meant exile or death. Preferring treason, he ordered his legions to cross the Rubicon River, the boundary of his province, and march on Rome. A civil war ensued that Caesar won in 45 B.C.E.

Caesar made few changes in Rome's government. In theory, the Senate continued to play its role. But Caesar increased its size and packed it with his supporters. His monopoly of military power made a sham of senatorial decrees. In 46 B.C.E. Caesar was appointed dictator for ten years, and a year later his term was extended for life. His enemies concluded that he was aiming at monarchy, and they began to plot his destruction. Gaius Cassius Longinus and Marcus Junius Brutus recruited some sixty senators who helped them assassinate Caesar at a meeting of the Senate on March 15, 44 B.C.E. The assassins expected that once Caesar was dead the republic would automatically flourish. Instead, civil war returned, and it raged for thirteen more years. The assassins had not saved the republic, but doomed it.

The Second Triumvirate and the Emergence of Octavian

Caesar had designated his eighteen-year-old grandnephew Gaius Octavian (63 B.C.E.–14 C.E.) his heir. The Senate hoped to use the sickly, inexperienced young man to block Mark Antony, the second-in-command to whom Caesar's men had spontaneously turned for leadership. But Octavian broke with the Senate, marched on Rome, assumed the consulship for 43 B.C.E., and declared war on Caesar's assassins. Mark Antony and another of Caesar's officers, M. Aemilius Lepidus, joined him in the Second Triumvirate, a legally established shared dictatorship charged, ostensibly, with the restoration of the republic.

In 42 B.C.E. the triumvirs defeated Brutus and Cassius at Philippi in Macedonia. Each of the victors rewarded himself with a command. The weakest member, Lepidus, was given Africa. Octavian took the West—and the troubles that went with it (a war with one of Pompey's sons, the settlement of some 100,000 veterans, and the restoration of order in Italy). Antony received the most promising assignment: command of the East. This gave him a chance to invade Parthia and build an army large enough to sweep aside his fellow triumvirs.

In 36 B.C.E. Antony attacked Parthia, and the result was disastrous. His soldiers' faith in him was further undercut when Octavian mounted a propaganda campaign that convinced them that Antony had fallen under the spell of Egypt's queen, Cleopatra. By 32 B.C.E. all pretense of cooperation came to an end. Lepidus had already been shoved aside, and at Actium in western Greece in 31 B.C.E. Octavian defeated Antony.

The suicides of Antony and Cleopatra ended the civil war and left Octavian, at the age of thirty-two, absolute master of the Mediterranean world. His power was enormous, but so was the task that faced him. To restore peace, prosperity, and stability to Rome he needed to create a form of government that could handle the empire without violating the republican traditions to which the Romans were passionately attached.

The Roman Republic, at its start, resembled the early Greek poleis, but Rome long remained a nation of simple farmers and herdsmen. As Rome organized itself for war, the traditional distinctions between Rome's patrician and plebeian castes became less important than the wealth that determined how well a man could equip himself for battle. The republic needed a strong army, for it was engaged in virtually continuous warfare in defense of its lands and allies. Rome created something unique: an empire ruled by a republic, not by a king or bureaucracy. Rome acquired and managed its territory as a state guided by an aristocratic Senate and governed by magistrates elected annually by its citizens.

The temptations and responsibilities of governing an empire proved too much for the republican constitution. As trade increased, a class of merchants and financiers (the equestrians) grew strong enough to inject their commercial interests into Roman politics. Masses of slaves captured in war undermined the small farmers who had been the backbone of the Roman state and its army. Many impoverished citizens moved to Rome and survived by selling their only asset, their vote. Rome's armies of self-supporting farmers were then replaced by volunteer armies of landless men who made careers of being soldiers. They expected to be paid for their service with gifts of land or money and gave the generals who rewarded them the power to ignore constitutional restraints. When their leaders began to jostle among themselves for the upper hand, a long civil war sent the republic down the path to destruction. Despite itself, Rome drifted toward a form of monarchical government similar to those of the ancient states of Egypt and Mesopotamia.

✧ Review Questions

1. In what ways did the institutions of family and clientage and the establishment of patrician and plebeian classes contribute to the stability of the early Roman Republic? How important was education to the success of the republic? How essential was the institution of slavery?

2. What was "the struggle of the orders"? What methods did plebeians use to get what they wanted? How was Roman society different after the struggle ended?

3. Until 265 B.C.E., what were the motives for and the stages in the expansion of Roman territory? How was Rome able to conquer and to control Italy? How did Rome's desires for security, wealth, power, and fame shape its relations with Greece and Asia Minor in the second century B.C.E.?

4. Why did Romans and Carthaginians clash in the First and Second Punic wars? Could the wars have been avoided? How did Rome profit from its victory over Carthage? What problems did the victory create for Rome?

5. What social, economic, and political problems did Italy have in the second century B.C.E.? How did Tiberius and Gaius Gracchus propose to solve them? What questions about Roman society did the Gracchan reform program raise? Why did it fail?

6. What were the problems that plagued the Roman Republic in the last century B.C.E.? What caused these problems, and how did the Romans try to solve them? To what extent were ambitious, power-hungry generals responsible for the destruction of the republic?

✧ Suggested Readings

F. E. ADCOCK, *The Roman Art of War Under the Republic* (1940).

E. BADIAN, *Roman Imperialism in the Late Republic*, 2nd ed. (1968).

A. H. BERNSTEIN, *Tiberius Sempronius Gracchus: Tradition and Apostasy* (1978). A new interpretation of Tiberius's place in Roman politics.

J. BOARDMAN, J. GRIFFIN, AND O. MURRAY, *The Oxford History of the Roman World* (1990). An encyclopedic approach to the varieties of the Roman experience.

T. CORNELL AND J. MATTHEWS, *Atlas of the Roman World* (1982). Much more than the title indicates, this book presents a comprehensive view of the Roman world in its physical and cultural setting.

M. GELZER, *Caesar: Politician and Statesman*, trans. by P. Needham (1968). The best biography of Caesar.

L. P. HOMO, *Primitive Italy and the Beginning of Roman Imperialism* (1967). A study of early Roman relations with the peoples of Italy.

J. F. LAZENBY, *Hannibal's War* (1978). An excellent military history of the Second Punic War.

F. B. MARSH, *A History of the Roman World from 146 to 30 B.C.*, 3rd ed., rev. by H. H. Scullard (1963). An excellent narrative account.

M. PALLOTTINO, *The Etruscans*, 6th ed. (1974). Makes especially good use of archaeological evidence.

H. H. SCULLARD, *A History of the Roman World 753–146 B.C.*, 4th ed. (1980). An unusually fine narrative history with useful critical notes.

H. H. SCULLARD, *From the Gracchi to Nero*, 5th ed. (1982). A work of the same character and quality.

L. R. TAYLOR, *Party Policies in the Age of Caesar* (1949). A fascinating analysis of Roman political practices.

B. H. WARMINGTON, *Carthage* (1960). A good survey.

G. WILLIAMS, *The Nature of Roman Poetry* (1970). An unusually graceful and perceptive literary study.

5

The Roman Empire

KEY TOPICS

- The Augustan constitution
- The organization and government of the Roman Empire
- Culture and civilization from the late republic through the imperial period
- The early history of Christianity
- The decline and fall of Rome

The victory of Octavian over Mark Antony at Actium ended a century of civil strife that had begun with the murder of Tiberius Gracchus. Octavian (subsequently known as Augustus) brought peace to Rome by establishing a monarchy hidden behind a republican facade. The unification of the Mediterranean world improved its government and facilitated economic expansion. The spread of

101

Latin and Greek as the empire's official languages promoted growth of a common "classical" culture. This classical tradition had a great influence on the development of Christianity, which appeared in the first century C.E. as one of the empire's many competing Eastern cults.

In the third century C.E. Rome's institutions began to fail. Some emperors resorted to drastic measures to try to restore order. The result was growing centralization and militarization of an increasingly authoritarian government. A wave of barbarian attacks in the second half of the fifth century finally initiated the empire's collapse.

✥ The Augustan Principate

The memory of Julius Caesar's fate was fresh in Octavian's mind in 31 B.C.E. as he pondered what to do with the empire he had won. Octavian had gained control of all of Rome's armies, and he had loyal, capable assistants. The confiscation of Egypt's treasury brought him ample capital. He had the means to be the strong ruler who could end the civil war and restore order, but he knew that it would be dangerous to appear to threaten the republican traditions to which the Romans were so passionately devoted.

Slowly Octavian pieced together a constitution that was acceptable to the Romans and capable of running an empire. It inaugurated a long era of stability and order called the *pax Romana* ("Roman peace"). Despite republican trappings and an apparent sharing of authority with the Senate, it was a monarchy. All real power, both civil and military, lay with the ruler. Octavian disguised this fact by referring to himself simply as *princeps* ("first citizen") or *imperator* ("commander-in-chief"), but these titles soon acquired connotations of royalty that accurately reflected the power of his office.

During the civil war Octavian's legal authority derived from the triumvirate, a temporary dictatorship set up to restore the republic. After his victory in the civil war terminated the triumvirate, Octavian governed by holding consecutive consulships. This was an unpopular violation of Roman tradition, and he sought an alternative to it. On January 13, 27 B.C.E., at a dramatic Senate meeting, he resigned most of his offices—except for the governorships of Spain, Gaul, and Syria—and returned command of the other provinces to the Senate. This was less risky than it seems, for Octavian's provinces were the border lands that contained twenty of Rome's twenty-six legions. The Senate, however, declared this to be the restoration of the republic and thanked Octavian by granting him the surname "Augustus" ("revered"). (Historians use this title to indicate Octavian's role as founder of Rome's first truly imperial government, the "Principate.") In 23 B.C.E. Octavian Augustus made another republican gesture. He resigned the consulship. Henceforth his authority rested on two special powers: proconsular *imperium maius* (supreme military command) and the political privileges of an honorary tribune.

Significant Dates from the Imperial Era

The Julio-Claudian Dynasty

27 B.C.E.–14 C.E.	*Augustus*
[ca. 4 B.C.E.–30 C.E.	*Jesus of Nazareth]*
14–37 C.E.	*Tiberius*
37–41 C.E.	*Gaius (Caligula)*
41–54 C.E.	*Claudius*
54–68 C.E.	*Nero*
69 C.E.	*Year of the Four Emperors*

The Flavian Dynasty

69–79 C.E.	*Vespasian*
[ca. 70–100 C.E.	*Gospels written]*
79–81 C.E.	*Titus*
81–96 C.E.	*Domitian*

The "Good Emperors"

96–98 C.E.	*Nerva*
98–117 C.E.	*Trajan*
117–138 C.E.	*Hadrian*
138–161 C.E.	*Antoninus Pius*
161–180 C.E.	*Marcus Aurelius*

Selected Late Emperors

180–192 C.E.	*Commodus*
193–211 C.E.	*Septimius Severus*
222–235 C.E.	*Alexander Severus*
249–251 C.E.	*Decius*
253–260 C.E.	*Valerian*
253–268 C.E.	*Gallienus*
268–270 C.E.	*Claudius II Gothicus*
270–275 C.E.	*Aurelian*
284–305 C.E.	*Diocletian*
306–337 C.E.	*Constantine*
[311 C.E.	*Edict of Toleration]*
337–361 C.E.	*Constantius II*
361–363 C.E.	*Julian the Apostate*
364–375 C.E.	*Valentinian*
364–378 C.E.	*Valens*
379–395 C.E.	*Theodosius*

Administration

The Romans were willing to go along with Augustus, for they benefited from his administration. He weeded out inefficient and corrupt magistrates. He blocked ambitious politicians and generals who might otherwise have disturbed the peace. He eased tension among classes and between Romans and provincials. And he fostered rapid economic development.

This statue of Emperor Augustus (r. 27 B.C.E.–14 C.E.), now in the Vatican, stood in the villa of Augustus's wife Livia. The figures on the elaborate breastplate are all of symbolic significance. At the top, for example, Dawn in her chariot brings in a new day under the protective mantle of the sky god; in the center, Tiberius, Augustus's future successor, accepts the return of captured Roman army standards from a barbarian prince, and at the bottom, Mother Earth offers a horn of plenty. [Charitable Foundation, Leonard von Matt]

The Senate took over most of the political functions of the assemblies, but it became a less parochial institution. Augustus manipulated elections to offices and saw to it that promising young men, whatever their origin, had opportunities to serve the state. Those who did well were rewarded with appointments to the Senate. This allowed equestrians and Italians who had no connection with the old Roman aristocracy to earn Senate membership, and it ensured that the Senate was composed of talented, experienced statesmen.

Augustus was careful to court the politically volatile residents of Rome. He founded the city's first public fire department and police force. He organized grain distribution for the poor and set up an office to oversee the municipal water supply. The empire's rapidly expanding economy enabled him to fund a vast, popular program of public works.

The provinces, too, benefited from Augustus's union of political and military power. For the first time, Rome had a central government that was able to oversee the conduct of the men who administered its provinces. Good governors were appointed. Those who abused their power were disciplined, and the provincials themselves were granted a greater degree of political autonomy.

The Army and Defense

Augustus professionalized the military and reduced its numbers to about 300,000 men—a force barely adequate to hold the frontiers. The legions were recruited from Italians, but auxiliary companies admitted provincials. The term of enlistment was twenty years. Pay was good, with occasional bonuses and the promise of a pension on retirement. Armies were permanently based in the provinces where they were likely to be needed, and their presence helped introduce native peoples to Roman culture. Soldiers married local women and settled new towns. Eventually, as provincials qualified for Roman citizenship, they developed a commitment to the empire that strengthened its defenses.

Augustus's chief military problem was the defense of the empire's northern frontier. Since very little Roman territory protected Italy from invasion by the barbarians who wandered about Germany, Augustus wanted to expand the empire eastward to a new shorter and more defensible border. But in 9 C.E., when a German tribal leader called Herrmann (or Arminius, in Latin) ambushed and destroyed three Roman legions, the aged Augustus was forced to abandon the campaign.

Religion and Morality

Augustus tried to repair the damage that a century of strife had done to Rome's fundamental institutions. He devised a program to restore traditional values of family and religion. He passed laws to curb adultery and divorce and encourage early marriage and large families. His own austere behavior set a personal example for his subjects, and he banished his only child (Julia) to punish her flagrant immorality.

Augustus restored the dignity of formal Roman religion. He built many temples, revived old cults, invigorated the priestly colleges, and banned the worship of some foreign gods. He did not accept divine honors during his lifetime, but, like his step-father, Julius Caesar, he was deified after his death.

⤳ Civilization of the Ciceronian and Augustan Ages

Roman civilization reached its pinnacle in the last century of the republic and during the principate of Augustus. Hellenistic Greek influences were strong, but the spirit and sometimes the form of Roman art and literature were unique.

The Late Republic

Cicero. Cicero (106–43 B.C.E.) was the most important literary figure of the late republic. He wrote treatises on rhetoric, ethics, and politics, and developed Latin as an instrument for philosophical disputation. But it is the orations he delivered in the law courts and in the Senate and his private letters, which survive in large numbers, that are his most interesting works. They provide us with better insight into his thinking than we have for any other figure from antiquity.

Cicero's thinking was pragmatic and conservative. He believed that the world was governed by a divine natural law that human reason could comprehend and use to guide the development of civilized institutions. His respect for law, custom, and tradition as guarantors of stability and liberty led him to champion the Senate against *populares* leaders like Mark Antony. When the Second Triumvirate seized power and began its purges, it marked Cicero for execution.

History. Much of the work of the historians who wrote during the last century of the republic has been lost. A few pamphlets on the Jugurthine War and the Catilinarian conspiracy of 63 B.C.E. are all that survive from the pen of the man reputed to be the greatest historian of his generation: Sallust (86–35 B.C.E.). Julius Caesar wrote treatises on the Gallic and civil wars. They are military narratives that Caesar developed for use as political propaganda. Since their direct, simple, and vigorous style still makes them persuasive reading, they must have been most effective with their intended audience.

Law. Before the generation of the Gracchi, Roman law evolved case by case from juridical decisions. However, contact with foreign peoples and the influence of Greek ideas forced a change. The edicts of praetors began to expand the Roman legal code, and the decisions of the magistrates who dealt with foreigners spawned the idea of the *jus gentium*—the law of all peoples as opposed to the law that reflected only Roman practice. In the first century B.C.E. Greek thought promoted the concept of the *jus naturale*, a natural law that lay behind the customary laws of different nations. This law reflected the principles of divine reason that Cicero and the Stoics believed to be at work in the world.

Poetry. Two of Rome's greatest poets, Lucretius (ca. 99–ca. 55 B.C.E.) and Catullus (ca. 84–ca. 54 B.C.E.), were Cicero's contemporaries. Each represented a different aspect of Rome's poetic tradition. Hellenistic literary theory maintained that poets ought to be both entertainers and educators, and that was what Lucretius attempted in his epic poem, *De Rerum Natura* (*On the Nature of Things*). Lucretius hoped to save his generation from fear and superstition by converting it to the materialistic philosophies of Epicurus and Democritus. They had claimed that if living beings accepted that they were nothing more than temporary agglomerations of lumps of matter, they would cease to be anxious about death.

Catullus's poems were personal, even autobiographical, descriptions of the joys and pains of love. He hurled invective at important contemporaries like Julius Caesar, and he amused himself in witty poetic exchanges. But he offered no moral lessons. He celebrated himself—an affirmation of the importance of the individual that was one of the characteristics of Hellenistic art.

The Age of Augustus

The age of Augustus was the Golden Age of Roman literature. The great poets of the era relied on the patronage of the *princeps*, and their dependence on him limited their freedom of expression. But although their work served his political agenda, they were not mere propagandists. They were sincerely grateful for what he had done for Rome.

Vergil. The early works of Vergil (70–19 B.C.E.), the most important of the Augustan poets, were somewhat artificial pastoral idylls (the *Eclogues* or *Bucolics*). Maecenas, Augustus's chief cultural adviser, seems to have suggested the subject for Vergil's *Georgics,* a reworking of Hesiod's *Works and Days.* Vergil transformed the early Greek poet's praise of simple labor into a hymn to heroic human effort—the struggle to wrest civilization from the brutal world of nature. Vergil's celebration of the greatness of Italy's cults and institutions became the theme of his most important work, the *Aeneid.*

During the civil war, Augustus rallied the Romans to his side by persuading them that Mark Antony had succumbed to alien Eastern influences. Augustus had won the war by depicting himself as the guardian of Italy's culture. He was committed, therefore, to granting Italy special status within his empire. The *Aeneid* helped justify this. It explained Rome's origin and greatness by grounding its history in the founding myth of Hellenic civilization, the *Iliad's* account of the Trojan War. Vergil's hero, the Trojan prince Aeneas, is not motivated by Homeric lust for personal honor and excellence. He personifies Roman qualities: duty, responsibility, and patriotism—the civic virtues of men like Augustus, who maintained the peace and prosperity of the empire.

Horace. Horace (65–8 B.C.E.), the son of a freed man, was a highly skillful lyric poet. His *Satires* are genial and humorous. His *Odes,* which ingeniously adapt Latin to the forms of Greek verse, glorify the new Augustan order.

Ovid. Ovid (43 B.C.E.–18 C.E.), who wrote light love elegies, was the only one of the great poets to run spectacularly afoul of Augustus's program. His celebration of the loose sexual mores of certain sophisticated Roman aristocrats was not consistent with the serious, family-centered life Augustus was advocating, and Ovid's poetic textbook on the art of seduction, *Ars Amatoria,* confirmed Augustus's decision to exile the poet in 8 C.E. Ovid tried, but failed, to recover favor by switching to less sensitive themes. His *Fasti* was a poetic essay on Roman religious festivals, and his most popular work, the *Metamorphoses,* was a charming survey of Greek mythology.

History. Augustus's emphasis on tradition and his desire to increase Rome's reverence for its unique cultural traditions encouraged the writing of history. The most important of the Roman historians was Livy (59 B.C.E.–17 C.E.), although only a quarter of his monumental *History of Rome* survives. It treats the period from the legendary origins of Rome until 9 B.C.E. Livy based his history on secondary accounts and did little original research, but he was a gifted narrator. His sketches of historical figures have become perennially popular illustrations of good and bad behavior and the lessons of patriotism.

Architecture and Sculpture. Augustus embarked on a building program designed to make Rome worthy of its history. The Campus Martius and the Roman Forum were reconstructed. Augustus donated a new forum of his own to celebrate his victory in the civil war. A splendid temple to his patron god, Apollo, rose on Rome's Palatine Hill. Most of the new building conformed to the Greek classical style, which emphasized serenity and order. The same attributes are visible in the best surviving portrait sculpture of Augustus and his family: the reliefs carved for the Altar of Peace, which Augustus dedicated in 9 B.C.E.

❖ Imperial Rome 14–180 C.E.

The Emperors

Because Augustus was ostensibly only the "first citizen" of a restored republic, he had no public office to which he could openly appoint an heir. Tiberius (r. 14–37 C.E.), his step-son and immediate successor, at first tried to follow Augustus's example and hide the monarchical nature of his government. But as the Romans became accustomed to the new order, there was less reason to conceal its reality. The terms *imperator* and "Caesar" began to be used as titles for men whose connection with Julius Caesar's family brought them the military power that enabled them to run the Roman world.

Tiberius was followed by his nephew, Gaius Caligula (r. 37–41 C.E.). Caligula was succeeded by his uncle Claudius (r. 41–54 C.E.), and Claudius left the throne to his step-son Nero (r. 54–68 C.E.). Nero, who was not equal to the responsibility of his job, committed suicide when a rebellion in Gaul convinced him that he had lost control of the army. He was the last of the Julio-Claudians, the descendants of Augustus or of his wife Livia.

The year 69 C.E. saw four different emperors assume power in quick succession as different Roman armies marched on Rome. The victor, Vespasian (r. 69–79 C.E.), and his sons, Titus (r. 79–81 C.E.) and Domitian (r. 81–96 C.E.), compose the Flavian dynasty. Vespasian was the first emperor who had no connection with the old Roman nobility. He was a tough Italian soldier from the middle class. His sons inherited his excellent administrative talents, but Domitian may have succumbed to paranoia. His increasingly tyrannical behavior frightened his intimates into assassinating him.

Domitian had no close relative to succeed him, and those who killed him were not foolish enough to try to turn the clock back to the days of the republic. They appealed to the Senate to restore order by choosing a new emperor. The Senate elected one of its own, Nerva (r. 96–98 C.E.), the first of the "good emperors": Trajan (r. 98–117 C.E.), Hadrian (r. 117–138 C.E.), Antoninus Pius (r. 138–161 C.E.), and Marcus Aurelius (r. 161–180 C.E.). None of the first four men had a son to succeed him, so each followed an example set by Nerva—each adopted an heir. This system of succession was a fortunate historical accident, for it guaranteed that worthy men were promoted to power. It produced

Ruins of the Roman Forum. From the earliest days of the city, the Forum was the center of Roman life. Augustus had it rebuilt, and it was frequently rebuilt and refurbished by his successors, so most of the surviving buildings date to the imperial period. [The Bettmann Archive]

a century of peaceful, competent government that ended when Marcus Aurelius allowed his unworthy son, Commodus (r. 180–192 C.E.), to follow him to the throne.

The Administration of the Empire

Although some of the emperors tried to enlist the cooperation of the senatorial class—as counselors, judges, and department heads—in running the empire, the imperial government was largely staffed by professionals. These career bureaucrats were, in many ways, an improvement over the amateurs who had annually exchanged offices in the republic.

The provinces (see Map 5-1) especially benefited from imperial government. Once exploitation by governors was curbed, they discovered the economic advantages of being part of a huge empire. Rome strove to both unify the empire and respect local customs and differences. By 212 C.E. citizenship had been extended to almost every inhabitant of the empire. The spread of *Romanitas* ("Roman-ness") was more than nominal, for senators and even emperors began to be chosen from provincial families.

Local Municipalities. Administratively, the empire was structured as a federation of cities and towns. The typical city had about 20,000 inhabitants. Only three or four had a population of more than 75,000. Rome, however, certainly had more than 500,000 residents—perhaps more than a million. The central government dealt with city governments and had little contact with people who lived in the countryside. A municipal charter left much responsibility in the hands of local councils and magistrates. The holding of a magistracy or, at a later period, a seat on a municipal council, earned a man Roman citizenship.

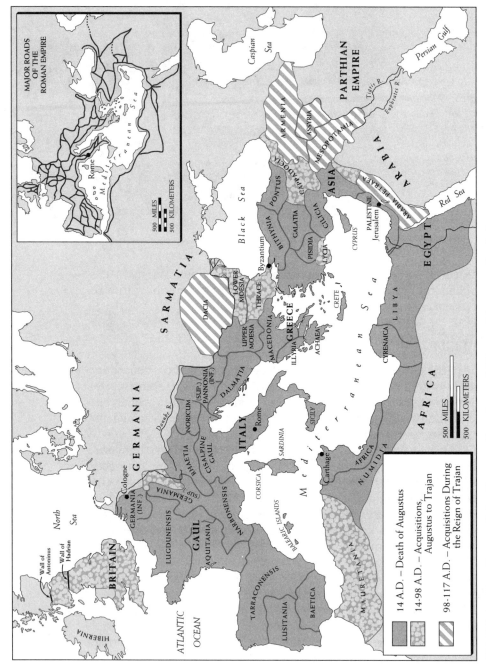

MAP 5-1 Provinces of the Roman Empire to 117 C.E. *The growth of the empire to its greatest extent is here shown in three stages—at the death of Augustus in 14 C.E., at the death of Nerva in 98 C.E., and at the death of Trajan in 117 C.E. The division into provinces is also indicated. The insert shows the main roads that tied the far-flung empire together.*

In this way the Romans brought the upper classes of the provinces into their own government, spread Roman law and culture, and won the loyalty of influential people.

Rome's policy of assimilation did not succeed everywhere. Jews, who on religious grounds refused to compromise with Rome, rebelled in 66–70, 115–117, and 132–135 C.E. and were savagely suppressed. Egypt's peasants were exploited with exceptional ruthlessness and not offered the opportunity to integrate.

The emperors took a broad view of their responsibility for the welfare of their subjects. Nerva conceived and Trajan introduced the *alimenta,* a program of public assistance aiding the children of indigent parents. More and more the emperors intervened when municipalities got into difficulties—sending imperial troubleshooters to deal with problems that were usually financial. As a result, the autonomy of the municipalities declined, and the central administration took on more and more functions. This caused the provincial aristocracy to lose interest in public service and to regard it as a burden rather than an opportunity. The price paid for increased efficiency was a loss of vitality by the empire's local governments.

Foreign Policy. Augustus's successors, for the most part, continued his conservative, defensive foreign policy. Trajan was the first to take the offensive. He crossed the Danube and mounted a campaign (101–106 C.E.) that added a new province to the empire: Dacia. His intent was probably to secure the empire by driving wedges into territory occupied by threatening barbarians. The same reasoning justified an invasion of the Parthian Empire in the East (113–117 C.E.), and Trajan initially succeeded in establishing three more eastern provinces: Armenia, Assyria, and Mesopotamia. His lines, however, were overextended, and rebellions forced him to retreat. He died on his way back to Rome.

Hadrian, Trajan's successor, developed a new policy for the defense of Rome's frontiers. Heretofore, the Romans had taken the initiative against the barbarians. Although they rarely sought new territory, they conducted frequent military maneuvers to chastise and pacify troublesome tribes. Hadrian hardened Rome's defenses, building a stone wall in the south of Scotland and a wooden one across the Rhine-Danube triangle. As Rome's defensive strategy grew rigid, initiative passed to the barbarians. Marcus Aurelius had to spend most of his reign fending off dangerous attacks in the East and on the Danube frontier.

***Agriculture: The Decline of Slave Labor and the Rise of* Coloni.** The defense of the empire's frontiers made enormous demands on its resources, but the effect was not immediately felt. Economic growth continued well into the reigns of the "good emperors." Internal peace and efficient administration benefited agriculture, as well as trade and industry, by making it easier to market products at a distance.

Small farms continued to exist, but more and more large estates, managed by absentee owners and growing cash crops, dominated agriculture. At first,

This is a reconstruction of a typical Roman apartment house found at Ostia, Rome's port. The ground floor contained shops, and the stories above it held many apartments. [Scala/Art Resource, N.Y.]

these estates were worked by slaves, but in the first century C.E. this began to change. Economic pressures forced many members of the lower classes to become *coloni* (tenant farmers), and *coloni* steadily replaced slaves as the mainstay of agricultural labor. *Coloni* were sharecroppers who paid rent in cash, in labor, or in kind. Ultimately, their movements were restricted, and they were tied to the land they worked. Thanks to the *coloni*, the economic importance of slavery declined in the second century, but slavery survived the fall of Rome's empire.

The Culture of the Early Empire

Literature. The years between the death of Augustus and the time of Marcus Aurelius (14–180 C.E.) are known as the Silver Age of Latin literature. In contrast to the hopeful, optimistic outlook of the Augustan authors, the writers of the Silver Age were gloomy and pessimistic. Their works are freighted with complaints and satires that reflect hostility to the growing power and personal excesses of the emperors.

The writers of the second century C.E. avoided commenting on contemporary affairs and events in recent history that might irritate their emperors. Historical writing about remote periods was safe, as were scholarly studies. But little poetry was produced. In the third century C.E., Greek romances became popular. They suggest that the readers of the age sought entertainment and escape from contemporary realities.

Architecture. Advances in engineering enabled Rome's architects to design new kinds of buildings—great public baths (like those of Diocletian and Caracalla), and huge free-standing amphitheaters (like the Flavian Colosseum). Romans continued the tradition of post-and-lintel construction pioneered by the Greeks, but supplemented it with the semicircular arch developed by the Etruscans. Romans were also the first to exploit fully a Hellenistic invention: concrete. The Pantheon, the only major Roman temple to survive intact, combines all these elements. They are also visible in multitudes of mundane but useful structures, like bridges and aqueducts.

Society. The Roman Empire was at its peak during the first two centuries C.E., but by the second century C.E. it was clear that difficult times lay ahead. The literature of the era expresses a desire to flee the present—to retreat from reality and public life to the remote past, to romance, and to private concerns.

The age's declining interest in public affairs correlates with a loss of vitality in the government of the empire's cities. In the first century C.E., members of the upper classes vied with one another for election to municipal office and for the honor of serving their communities. By the second century C.E., the emperors had to intervene to force unwilling citizens to accept public office. Reluctance to serve was understandable, for the central government had begun to hold local magistrates personally responsible for the revenues due from their towns. Men sometimes fled to avoid an office that might lead to their property being confiscated to make up for arrears in the collection of taxes.

The central government's extreme fiscal measures were a response to a declining economy. Initially, Rome had prospered from the end of civil war and the influx of wealth looted from the East, but the effects of this diminished in the first half of the second century C.E. For reasons that are unknown, population also seems to have declined. The cost of government, however, kept rising. An ever-increasing need for money compelled the emperors to raise taxes and to bring on inflation by debasing the coinage. These policies precipitated crises that finally overwhelmed the empire.

❧ The Rise of Christianity

Jesus of Nazareth

One of the most important developments of the imperial era was the rise of Christianity, the religion that came to dominate the West. The new faith originated in Judaea, a remote eastern province of the empire, in response to the life of an obscure Jew, Jesus of Nazareth. The Gospels tell us all we know about him. The earliest, by Mark, is dated about 70 C.E. (perhaps forty years after Jesus' death), and the latest, by John, about 100 C.E.. The Gospels were never intended to be read as objective historical narratives of a man's life. They were designed to proclaim the faith that Jesus was the Son of God who had come into the world to redeem humanity and to bring immortality to those who believed in him.

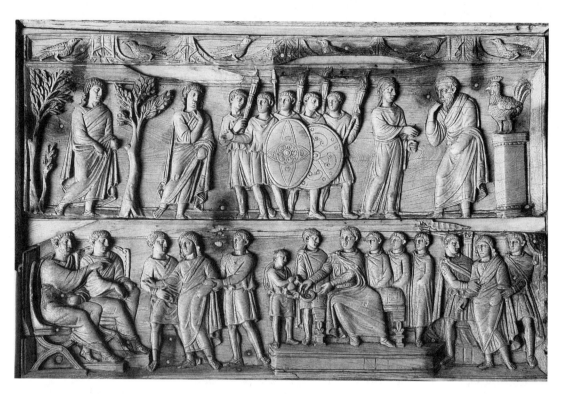

This early Christian art shows Christ arrested by soldiers on the night before his crucifixion. Note that Christ is portrayed clean-shaven and dressed in the toga of a Roman aristocrat. [Hirmer Verlag, Munich]

Jesus, who was born during Augustus's reign, was a most effective teacher in the tradition of the Hebrew prophets. Some of the prophets had predicted the coming of a Messiah, a redeemer who would help Israel triumph over its enemies and who would establish the kingdom of God on earth. Jesus modified this message—claiming that the Messiah would not establish an earthly kingdom but would end the world as human beings knew it at the Day of Judgment. God would then reward the righteous with immortality and happiness in heaven and condemn the wicked to eternal suffering in hell. While the faithful awaited the apocalyptic event, which they believed was imminent, Jesus advised them to forget worldly concerns, to trust in him, and to practice love, charity, and humility.

Jesus won a considerable following, but his criticism of the cultic practices associated with the temple at Jerusalem provoked the hostility of the Jewish religious authorities. The Roman governor of Judaea concluded that Jesus was a threat to peace and ordered his crucifixion (probably in 30 c.e.). Jesus' followers believed that he was resurrected on the third day after his death and that resurrection proved him to have been the Christ (*christos,* the Greek term for "Messiah").

Paul of Tarsus

The most important missionary at work in the generation that founded the Christian church was Paul (born Saul), a Roman citizen and native of the city of Tarsus in Asia Minor. Paul was at first a Pharisee, a member of a Jewish sect known for strict adherence to the Jewish law. And he was an ardent opponent of Christianity until his mysterious, precipitous conversion on the road to Damascus about 35 C.E.

To define themselves the early Christians had to define their relationship to Judaism. James, the brother of Jesus, led those who believed that the new faith was a version of Judaism and, therefore, that its members had to adhere to the Jewish law. The less conservative Hellenized Jews, like Paul, saw Christianity as a new universal religion. They feared that the imposition of the Jewish law—with its many technicalities, dietary prohibitions, and painful rite of circumcision—would be a tremendous and unnecessary deterrent to conversion. Paul had great success making converts among the gentiles, and the triumph of his point of view in the church greatly facilitated the work of its missionaries.

Paul inaugurated Christian theology. He believed that the followers of Jesus had to spread the gospel, the "good news" of God's gift of the Messiah. But he warned that faith in Jesus as the Christ was a necessary but not sufficient agent of salvation. Salvation was a gift of God's grace that could not be earned by an act of will or by good deeds.

Organization

Christianity had a unique appeal that enabled it to spread throughout the Roman Empire and beyond its borders. Christ's declaration of the spiritual importance of love and charity focused the Christian community's attention on the needs of the weak, the sick, and the unprotected. Consequently, early churches were characterized by a warmth and a human appeal that stood in marked contrast to the coldness and impersonality of the pagan cults. The Christian promise of salvation, which confirmed the importance of each individual human soul to God, also implied the spiritual equality of all believers, no matter what their social class or gender.

At first, Christianity appealed most to the uneducated urban poor, and its early rites were simple ceremonies congruent with the poverty of its people. Baptism by water brought converts into the community by cleansing them of original sin (the state of alienation from God into which they had been born). The central ritual of the church was a common meal (the *agape* or "love feast") followed by a *eucharist* ("thanksgiving"), a celebration of the Lord's Supper in which bread and wine were blessed and consumed. Prayers, hymns, and readings from the Gospels were also part of worship.

The church owed its success in part to the unique organization it evolved. At first, Christian groups had little formal structure, and Christianity was in danger of dissolving into a gaggle of tiny sects. But the need to support missionary preachers and to administer charities prompted churches to elect officers: *presbyters* ("elders") and *deacons* ("those who serve"). By the second century C.E., when converts had increased to the point where a city was likely to have many churches, an "overseer" (*episkopos,* "bishop") was chosen to coordinate their activities. Bishops then extended their authority over the Christian communities in outlying towns and the countryside. Bishops acting together in councils could resolve disputes and preserve the unity of the church, and it was soon accepted that the powers that Jesus had given his original disciples were passed on in the church from one generation of bishops to another (the doctrine of Apostolic Succession). It is unlikely that Christianity could have survived the travails of its early years without the strong government provided by its bishops.

The Persecution of Christians

The Roman authorities could not at first distinguish Christians from Jews and, therefore, gave Christians the same protection under the law as Jews. It soon became clear, however, that Christians were different in potentially dangerous ways. Christians and Jews both incurred suspicion by their hostility to aspects of Roman tradition. (Both, for instance, denied the existence of the pagan gods and refused to take part in the state cult of the emperor.) But while the Jews were not eager to spread their ancient faith, Christians were ardent missionaries, proclaiming an imminent end to the Roman world. They had a network of local associations spreading across the empire, and they were oddly secretive about the rituals they practiced.

Romans were traditionally suspicious of secret organizations—particularly those of a religious nature. Claudius expelled Christians from the city of Rome, and Nero made them scapegoats for the great fire that struck the city in 64 C.E. But for the most part the Roman government did not take the initiative in attacking Christians in the first two centuries. Most of the persecutions in this period were the work of mobs, not governmental officials. Christians alarmed their pagan neighbors by ridiculing the ancient cults on which the state had always depended for its security. When misfortunes befell communities, Christians were blamed for having angered the gods. Persecution was not all bad for the church. It weeded out weaklings, united the faithful, and created the martyrs who became the heroes of Christian legend.

The Emergence of Catholicism

The survival of the church was threatened as much by internal disputes as by external persecution. The simple beliefs held by the great majority of Christians were open to a wide range of interpretations and left many questions unanswered. As a result, differences of opinion about the content of orthodox ("correct") faith developed. Minorities who disagreed with the Catholic ("universal") majority were branded heretics ("takers" of unique positions) and driven out of the church.

The need to combat heretics compelled the orthodox to formulate their own views more clearly. By the end of the second century C.E., the church had agreed upon the core of a canon (a "standard" set of holy books): the Old Testament, the Gospels, and the Epistles of Paul. (It took at least two more centuries before consensus was reached on the rest of the Scriptures.) The church also drew up creeds, brief statements of faith to which true Christians were expected to adhere, and empowered its bishops to enforce conformity of opinion. Whatever the shortcomings of this development, it ensured the clarity of doctrine, unity of purpose, and discipline needed for the church's survival.

Rome as a Center of the Early Church

During this period, when the church's administrative structures were evolving, the bishop of the city of Rome began to lay claim to "primacy" (highest rank among bishops). Rome was, after all, the capital of the empire, and it had the largest number of Christians of any city. Rome also claimed to be the place where Peter and Paul, the two most important missionaries of the early church, were martyred. Peter, who was said to have been the first bishop of Rome, was an especially important figure. The Gospel of Matthew (16:18) claims that Peter was the first of the apostles to recognize Jesus as Messiah and that Jesus acknowledged Peter's faith by saying: "Thou art Peter [*Petros*, in Greek] and upon this rock [*petra*] I will build my church." Eventually the bishops of Rome would come to interpret this passage as granting Peter—and his episcopal successors in Rome—supremacy over the church.

❖ The Crisis of the Third Century

Barbarian Invasions

The pressure on Rome's frontiers, already serious in the time of Marcus Aurelius (d. 180 C.E.), reached massive proportions in the third century. The eastern frontiers were threatened by a new power arising in the lands that had belonged to the Persians and their successors, the Parthians. In 224 C.E. a new Iranian dynasty, the Sassanians, replaced the Parthians and began to make raids deep into Roman provinces. In 260 C.E., they captured and imprisoned the Roman emperor Valerian.

On the western and northern frontiers the pressure came from an ever-increasing number of semi-nomadic German tribes. Though they had been in contact with the Romans since the second century B.C.E., they had not been much affected by civilization. German males were hunters, fighters, and carousers. The limited farming Germans engaged in was done by women and slaves. Tribes were led by chiefs, usually elected from the princes of a royal family by an assembly of fighting men. A chief headed a fraternity (*comitatus*, in Latin) of warriors pledged by oath to his personal service. Eager for plunder, these career raiders were attracted by the delights they knew to exist in the civilized lands across the Rhine and Danube rivers.

The most aggressive of the Germans were the Goths. By the third century C.E., they had wandered from the coast of the Baltic Sea, their original home, into southern Russia. From there they launched attacks on Rome's Danube frontier, and, about 250 C.E., they overran the Balkan provinces. To meet the threats posed by the Goths and the Persian Sassanids, the Romans transferred soldiers from their western to their eastern armies. This weakened the defenses of the West and made it easier for the Franks and the Alemanni to cross the Rhine frontier.

Rome's internal weakness invited an unprecedented number of simultaneous attacks. A manpower shortage, brought on by a plague, had forced Marcus Aurelius to resort to the conscription of slaves, gladiators, barbarians, and brigands. By the second century C.E., the Roman army was made up mostly of Romanized provincials, and the training, discipline, and professionalism of Rome's forces had begun to decline.

Septimius Severus, who followed Marcus Aurelius's son Commodus to the throne (r. 193–211 C.E.), played a crucial role in the transformation of the character of the Roman army. Septimius was a military usurper who owed everything to the support of his soldiers, many of whom were peasants from the less civilized provinces. He was prepared to make Rome into an undisguised military dictatorship.

Economic Difficulties

The financial crisis exacerbated by the barbarian attacks also forced changes in Rome's military. Inflation had forced Commodus to raise the soldiers' pay, and the Severan emperors had to double it to keep up with prices. This increased the imperial budget by as much as 25 percent. To raise money, emperors resorted to new taxes, debased the coinage, and even sold the palace furniture. To attract men into the army, Septimius relaxed its discipline and made military service the path to social advancement.

The same developments that caused problems for the army did damage to other parts of society. As emperors devoted their attention to the defense of the empire's frontiers, they were less able to preserve internal order. Piracy, brigandage, and the neglect of roads and harbors all hampered trade—as did the debasement of the coinage and inflation. Taxation confiscated property that was badly needed as capital for commercial enterprises, and a shortage of workers reduced agricultural production.

More and more the government had to compel people to provide the food, supplies, money, and labor needed to sustain the armies. As the state began to demand that urban magistrates meet deficits in tax revenue out of their own pockets, the upper classes fled the cities. In the countryside, peasants abandoned farms made unprofitable by excessive taxation.

The Social Order

The new conditions led to changes in the social order. The senatorial and ruling classes were decimated by attacks from hostile emperors and by economic losses, and their ranks were filled by men coming up through the army. As a result, the state was increasingly militarized. Classes had been distinguished by dress since the days of the Republic, but in the third and fourth centuries C.E. the people's everyday clothing became a kind of uniform that precisely declared their status. Titles were assigned to ranks in society just as in the army. Septimius Severus drew a sharp line between the *honestiores* (senators, equestrians, the municipal aristocracy, and the soldiers) and the lower classes, the *humiliores*. The *honestiores* enjoyed legal privileges: lighter punishments for crimes, immunity from torture, and a right of appeal to the emperor. As time passed, it became more difficult to move from the lower order to the higher. Peasants were tied to their lands, artisans to their crafts, soldiers to the army, and merchants and shipowners to the service of the state. Freedom and private initiative declined as the state strengthened control over its citizens.

Civil Disorder

In 235 C.E. the death of Alexander Severus, the last member of the dynasty founded by Septimius Severus, brought on a half-century of internal anarchy that invited foreign invasion. The empire teetered on the brink of collapse as conspirators overthrew and replaced emperors in rapid succession. A few able men appeared. Claudius II Gothicus (r. 268–270 C.E.) and Aurelian (r. 270–275 C.E.) drove back the barbarians and restored some discipline. But the soldiers who succeeded Aurelian on the throne followed strategies for defending the empire that acknowledged that it was losing ground. They built walls around Rome, Athens, and other cities and drew back their best troops from the frontiers. Their armies were mobile infantry and heavy cavalry that functioned as a kind of expanded imperial bodyguard. They recruited their soldiers from the least civilized provinces and even from the German tribes. Military power made these men the empire's new aristocrats. They dominated its government and monopolized its throne. In effect, the Roman people succumbed to an army of foreign mercenaries they had hired to protect them.

∾ The Late Empire

The Fourth Century and Imperial Reorganization

At the start of the fourth century an effort was made to save the empire by extensively reorganizing it (see Map 5-2). The Emperor Diocletian (r. 284–305 C.E.), a native of the Balkan province of Illyria, was a man of undistinguished birth who rose through the ranks of the army. Recent history convinced him that the job of defending and governing the empire was too great for one man. Therefore, he set up a tetrarchy—a committee of four rulers, each of whom had responsibility for a different part of the empire. Diocletian administered the provinces of Thrace, Asia, and Egypt. He assigned Italy, Africa, and Spain to his friend, Maximian. Those two men were the senior members of the tetrarchy

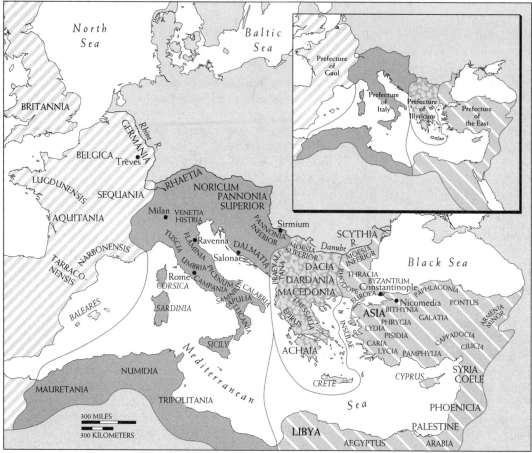

MAP 5-2   Divisions of the Roman Empire Under Diocletian *Diocletian divided the sprawling empire into four prefectures for more effective government and defense. The inset map shows their boundaries, and the larger map gives some details of regions and provinces. The major division between East and West was along the line running south between Pannonia and Moesia.*

and shared the title "Augustus." Their subordinates, the "Caesars," were Galerius, in charge of the Danube frontier and the Balkans, and Constantius, governor of Britain and Gaul.

The tetrarchy stabilized the empire by giving four powerful men a stake in the status quo and by providing for an orderly process of succession to the throne. The Augusti recognized the Caesars whom they appointed as their successors and enhanced their loyalty by dynastic marriages. The system was a return, in a way, to the precedent set by the "good emperors" of 96–180 C.E., who adopted their successors from the pool of ablest men.

Each tetrarch established a residence at a place convenient for frontier defense. No one chose Rome, for it was too remote from the centers of military activity. Maximian's base at Milan commanded the Alpine passes and functioned as the effective capital of Italy. Diocletian donated monumental baths to Rome, but he visited the city only once and resided at Nicomedia in Bithynia.

In 305 C.E. Diocletian retired and compelled Maximian to do the same, but the hope for a smooth succession faded when Constantius died and his son, Constantine, claimed his father's throne. Other pretenders followed his example, and by 310 C.E. there were five Augusti and no Caesars. Constantine (r. 306–337 C.E.), who began the confusion, was responsible for ending it. In 324 C.E., he defeated his last opponent and made himself sole emperor. He continued Diocletian's policies—with one exception. Where Diocletian had tried to stamp out Christianity, Constantine became the patron of the church.

Development of Autocracy. The mounting crises facing the government encouraged a drift toward total military mobilization. In the name of efficiency, the government stifled the individuality, freedom, and initiative of its citizens. Traditions of popular government were forgotten. More and more emperors ruled by decree, consulting only a few high officials whom they themselves appointed. They protected themselves from assassination by removing themselves from their people and becoming remote figures, unapproachable at the center of elaborate courts. Those who had audiences with them in their great palaces had to prostrate themselves and kiss the hems of their purple robes. The emperor's new title, *dominus* ("lord"), asserted a claim to an authority that derived not from the Roman people but from the gods.

Constantine built a new capital for the empire. He chose the district of Byzantium on the Bosporus as the location for "Constantinople" (modern Istanbul) because it was midway between the eastern and Danubian frontiers. The site was also easy to defend, for it was surrounded on three sides by water. Constantinople's dedication in 330 C.E. marked the start of a new empire that repudiated Rome's pagan and republican traditions and embraced Christian autocracy.

The Byzantine emperors of Constantinople secured their position by keeping the civilian and military bureaucracies separate. This reduced the chance that anyone might combine both kinds of power and mount a coup. An elaborate administrative hierarchy was set up to divide responsibility and prevent anyone from having very much authority. The entire system was kept under surveillance by a network of spies and secret police. The situation was an invitation to corruption and inefficiency.

The cost of a 400,000-man army, a vast civilian bureaucracy, an imperial court, and the splendid buildings the government erected was more than the empire's already weak economy could sustain. The fiscal experiments begun by Diocletian and continued by Constantine only made things worse. In 301 C.E., Diocletian had instituted price controls to deal with inflation, but his Edict of Maximum Prices, which set legal limits for the costs of goods and services, simply drove commerce underground. When the peasants who could not pay their taxes and the officials who could not collect them tried to escape, Diocletian used force to keep them in their places. Peasants, faced with enslavement by their government, often sought protection on a villa, the country estate of a powerful landowner. He protected them from the tax collectors, and they became his *coloni*. Their descendants increasingly became tied to these estates.

Division of the Empire. Constantine's death was followed by a struggle for succession among his sons. Constantius II (r. 337–361 C.E.), the victor, reunited the empire and bequeathed it to his cousin Julian (r. 361–363 C.E.). The new emperor, whom Christian historians dubbed "the Apostate," concluded that Constantine's pro-Christian policy had caused more strife within the empire than it had resolved, and he set about reviving Rome's traditional cults. His reign, however, was too short to permit his ideas to take root. When he died in battle against Persia, the pagan renaissance died with him.

By the time that Emperor Valentinian (r. 364–375 C.E.) came to the throne, there were so many trouble spots (see Map 5-3) that he concluded that he could not defend the empire alone. He appointed his brother Valens (r. 364–378 C.E.) as co-ruler. Valentinian resided at Milan and spent his reign fighting, defending the West against German tribes known as Franks and Alemanni.

Valens was posted to the East, where he was confronted by a different kind of threat from another group of Germans. In 376 C.E., the Visigoths asked permission to enter the empire to escape the Huns, a fierce tribe migrating out of central Asia. Valens acquiesced, but was unable to provide for the huge number of refugees who fled into the empire. In desperation the Goths began to plunder the Balkan provinces. Valens confronted the Goths at Adrianople in Thrace in 378 C.E., and he and his army were destroyed.

Theodosius (r. 379–395 C.E.), an able general, was then named co-ruler for the East. He pacified the Goths, enrolling many of them in his army. After the death of his colleague in the West, Theodosius united the empire for the last time.

The Rural West. The disintegration of the empire was encouraged not just by wars and politics, but by the divergence of the cultures of its eastern and western halves. The West, which had fewer and younger cities, was increasingly rural. The institution of the *villa,* a fortified country estate, reorganized its society. The *coloni* who lived on a villa served its owner in return for economic assistance and protection from both barbarian invaders and imperial officials. As the upper classes moved to the country and slipped from the control of the imperial authorities, the central government lost its ability to provide fundamental services like the maintenance and policing of roads. This hastened the decline of trade and communications, depressed the standard of living, and forced regions to become self-sufficient. By the fifth century C.E., the western empire had dissolved into isolated estates belonging to rural aristocrats who dominated a large class of dependent laborers. Only the Christian church kept alive a memory of imperial unity.

The Byzantine East. In the East the situation was quite different. The loss of the West enabled Constantinople to concentrate on its own affairs. A vital and

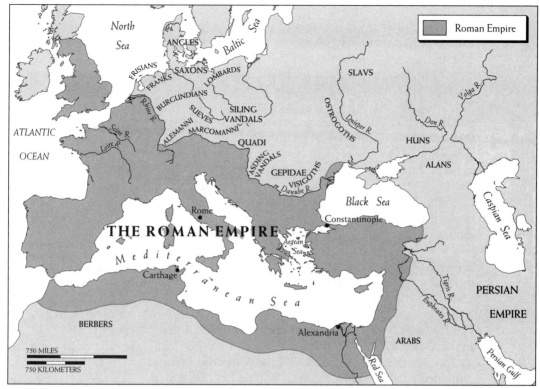

MAP 5-3 The Empire's Neighbors *In the fourth century the Roman Empire was nearly surrounded by ever more threatening neighbors. The map shows who these so-called barbarians were and where they lived before their armed contact with the Romans.*

flourishing hybrid of Christian and classical culture emerged, and the East entered the "Byzantine" phase in its civilization. Because of its defensible location and the relative health of its economy, Constantinople was able to divert most of the barbarians to the West. Eastern cities continued to prosper, and the East's central government retained its power. Christian emperors reigned in Constantinople until the Turks conquered the city in 1453. For a thousand years it saw itself as chief heir to the cultural legacy of ancient Greece and Rome.

The Triumph of Christianity

Christianity's rise to dominance over the empire was connected with the political and cultural developments that were causing it to be transformed in other ways. Pagan religions lost much of their appeal as the old Roman cities declined. People still took some comfort in traditional rites, but the deities worshiped in these cults seemed less and less effective as the problems of the fourth and fifth centuries mounted. Worshipers sought more powerful, personal gods who could offer them safety and prosperity in this world and immortality in the next. Consequently, new religions appeared and old ones were combined and interpreted in new ways.

Manichaeism, named for Mani, a Persian prophet who lived in the third century C.E., was an especially potent rival for early Christianity. The Manichaeans saw human history as a war between forces of light and darkness, good and evil. The human body was a material prison for the element of light that was the human soul. To achieve salvation, humans had to free the light by subduing the desires of the flesh. Manichaeans led ascetic lives, practiced a simple worship, and sustained a sophisticated religious organization. Their faith persisted into the Middle Ages.

Christianity drew much from the cults with which it competed for converts. But none had its universal appeal, and none was as great a threat as the ancient philosophies and the state religion.

Imperial Persecution. Until the middle of the third century, Rome's emperors generally ignored Christianity. But as the empire's problems increased and Christians became more numerous and visible, government policy changed. A growing sense of insecurity made rulers less willing to tolerate dissent.

Serious trouble erupted in 250, when the Emperor Decius (r. 249–251 C.E.) invoked the aid of the gods in his war against the Goths. He ordered all citizens to sacrifice to the state gods. True Christians could not obey, and Decius launched a major persecution to uphold his law. Valerian (r. 253–260 C.E.) continued the policy, partly in order to confiscate the wealth of rich Christians. His successors, however, were preoccupied by other more pressing matters, and persecution lapsed until the end of the century.

By Diocletian's day the number of Christians had grown still greater—as had hostility to Christians. Diocletian, who was struggling to hold the empire together, was not tolerant of unorthodox movements. In 303, he launched the most serious persecution Rome ever inflicted on the church. The policy was self-defeating. Christians were, by then, too familiar to seem threatening to most people, and the government's extreme actions horrified many pagans. The courageous demeanor of Christian martyrs also aroused sympathy and made new converts.

In 311, the Eastern emperor Galerius, who had been one of the most vigorous persecutors, was persuaded, perhaps by his Christian wife, to issue an edict of toleration permitting Christian worship. Constantine concurred, and his support began Christianity's rise to the status of the empire's sole legal religion.

Emergence of Christianity as the State Religion

Constantine's son supported the new religion, but the succession of Julian the Apostate posed a brief threat. Julian was a student of Neoplatonism, a religious philosophy devised by Plotinus (205–270 C.E.). It combined rational speculation and mysticism and was harshly critical of the church's lack of intellectual sophistication. Julian refrained from persecuting the church, but he withdrew its privileges, removed Christians from high offices, and introduced new forms of pagan worship. His reform lasted only as long as his brief reign.

In 394 C.E. Theodosius forbade the celebration of pagan cults, and Christianity became the official religion of the empire. Its victory ended some of the church's problems, but created others. As the church acquired prestige and influence, it began to attract converts for the wrong reasons and to lose its spiritual fervor. It also had to work out a relationship with the state. In the East the state was strong enough to subordinate the church. But in the West imperial power faded, and church leaders exercised remarkable independence.

Arianism and the Council of Nicaea. As Christianity matured, doctrinal disputes arose among Christians. These created factions that struggled for control of the state church, and the threat they posed to the social order forced governments to intervene to preserve the peace. Christians, as it turned out, could persecute Christians with as much zeal as pagan fanatics.

The most disruptive of the doctrinal controversies was the fight over Arianism, an explanation of Christ's role advanced by a priest named Arius of Alexandria (ca. 280–336 C.E.). Arius argued that Jesus was a unique being created by God the Father through whom the Father created all other beings. For Arius, Jesus was neither fully man nor fully God but something in between. In Arius's opinion, proponents of the doctrine of the Trinity, which asserts that God is a unity of three persons (Father, Son, and Holy Spirit), were indistinguishable from polytheists.

Arian theology had the advantage of seeming simple and rational. But Athanasius (ca. 293–373 C.E.), bishop of Alexandria, objected that the Arian view of Christ destroyed Christ's effectiveness as an agent of human salvation. Athanasius believed that only a fully human and fully divine Christ could have the power to turn humanity into divinity and thus bestow eternal life on his followers.

In 325 C.E., Constantine tried to resolve the issue by inviting all the Christian bishops to a meeting at Nicaea, not far from Constantinople. Athanasius's arguments prevailed and were enshrined in the council's Nicene Creed. Arianism, however, continued to spread. Some later emperors were Arians, and some of the most successful missionaries to the barbarians were Arians. Many of the German tribes that overran the empire were Arian Christians. In the end, Christianity did prove to be a unifying force, but it was also a source of new conflicts.

Arts and Letters in the Late Empire

The art and literature of the late empire reflect the confluence of pagan and Christian ideas and the changing tastes of the aristocracy. Much of the literature of the period is polemical, and much of its art is propagandist. The men who came to power as the empire declined were soldiers from the provinces whose roots were in the lower classes. By restoring and absorbing classical culture they hoped to stabilize their world and confirm their credentials as aristocrats.

Acquisition of classical culture by the newly arrived ruling class was facilitated in several ways. Works by great authors were reproduced in many copies and were transferred from inconvenient papyrus rolls to sturdier *codices* (with pages stitched together like modern books). Scholars also condensed long works into shorter versions and wrote commentaries to make them more intelligible. Grammars for the classical languages also had to be compiled, for various native tongues were replacing Latin and Greek in many of the provinces.

Christian Writers. Original works by pagan writers of the late empire were neither numerous nor especially distinguished. But the late empire saw a great outpouring of Christian writings. Christian "apologists" (authors who explained Christian practices to pagans) produced much poetry and prose. There were also sermons, hymns, and biblical commentaries designed for use by Christians.

The church was served by several important scholars in this period of its history. Jerome (348–420 C.E.), who was thoroughly trained in classical Latin literature and rhetoric as well as Hebrew, produced a Latin translation of the Bible. His Vulgate ("common use") became the standard text for the Roman Catholic Church. Eusebius of Caesarea (ca. 260 C.E.–ca. 340 C.E.) wrote an idealized biography of Constantine and an *Ecclesiastical History* that set forth a Christian view of history as a process whereby God's will is revealed. But it is the work of Augustine (354–430 C.E.), bishop of Hippo in North Africa, that best illustrates the complexity of the relationship between classical culture and Christian faith.

Augustine was born at Carthage and trained as a teacher of rhetoric. His father was a pagan, but his mother was a Christian and hers was ultimately the stronger influence. He had a difficult intellectual journey that carried him through Manichaeism, skepticism, and Neoplatonism before he was converted to Christianity. His skill in pagan rhetoric and his gifts as a philosopher made him peerless among his contemporaries as a defender of Christianity. Augustine reconciled Christianity and classical culture by arguing that faith was the starting point for and liberator of human reason. Reason is the means by which people understand what is revealed by faith.

Augustine's greatest works are his *Confessions*, an autobiography describing his path to faith, and *The City of God*, a response to the pagan charge that a sack of Rome by the Goths in 410 C.E. took place because Rome had abandoned its old gods. Augustine separated the destiny of the church from that of the Roman Empire. He contrasted the evil secular world, the "City of Man," with the spiritual realm represented by the church, the "City of God." The former was fated to be destroyed on the Day of Judgment, and there was no reason to expect that its conditions would improve before that. The fall of Rome was, therefore, neither surprising nor important. All states, even a Christian Rome, were part of the City of Man and were therefore corrupt and mortal. Only the City of God was immortal, and it, consisting of all the saints on earth and in heaven, was untouched by earthly calamities.

The Problem of the Decline and Fall of the Empire in the West

Whether important to Augustine or not, the massive barbarian invasions of the fifth century terminated imperial government in the West. Since that time, people have speculated about the causes of the collapse of the ancient world. Theories have been advanced that cite soil exhaustion, plague, climatic change, and even poisoning caused by lead water pipes. Some scholars blame the institution of slavery for Rome's failure to make advances in science and technology that might have solved its economic problems. Others target excessive governmental interference in the economic life of the empire, and still others point out the significance of the destruction of the urban middle class, the carrier of classical culture.

Although all these things may have contributed something, a simpler explanation for Rome's failure can be found. The growth of Rome's empire was fueled by conquests that provided the Romans with the means to continue to expand. Ultimately, there were not enough Romans to conquer and govern any more territory. When pressure from outsiders grew, the overextended Romans could not find the resources to advance once again to defeat yet another enemy, as they had in the past. Still, their tenacity and success in holding out for so long were remarkable. To blame the ancients for their failure to end slavery and bring on industrial and economic revolutions is no help, for no one has yet satisfactorily explained why those revolutions took place in the modern era. The real question may not be why did Rome fall, but how did it manage to last so long.

Augustus ended the civil wars that plagued the republic and created an era of unity, peace, order, and prosperity. As a result, he was regarded with almost religious awe and attained more military and political power than any Roman before him. At his death he was able to pass on the regime to his family, the Julio-Claudians, and for almost 200 years, with a few brief interruptions, the empire was prosperous, peaceful, and well-run.

But problems developed as the government assumed numerous responsibilities that promoted the growth of a large, expensive bureaucracy. The costs of government also grew as pressure on the frontiers from barbarian tribes forced Rome to maintain a great standing army. Higher taxes and bureaucratic control combined to stifle civic spirit and private enterprise.

Rome's rulers resorted to many devices for dealing with their problems. More and more, the emperors' rule and their safety depended on the loyalty of the army. When they courted the soldiers with gifts, the burden of taxes increased. The rich and powerful succeeded in avoiding many of their obligations, but this forced the government to bear down ever more heavily on vulnerable ordinary people. Ultimately, even extreme measures failed, and the Roman Empire fell. Something of its culture survived, however, to lay a foundation for the modern West.

Review Questions

1. How did Augustus alter Rome's constitution and government? How did his innovations solve the problems that had plagued the republic? Why were the Roman people willing to accept him as their head of state?

2. How was the Roman Empire organized? What enabled it to function smoothly? What role did the emperor play in the maintenance of political stability?

3. How did the literatures of Augustus's "Golden Age" and of the "Silver Age" of the first and second centuries C.E. differ? What contributions did the poetry of Vergil and Horace make to the stabilization of Augustus's imperial system of government?

4. Why were Christians at first persecuted by Roman authorities? What enabled them to acquire such enormous popularity by the fourth century C.E.?

5. What were the political, social, and economic problems that beset Rome in the third and fourth centuries C.E.? How did Diocletian and Constantine deal with them? Were these emperors effective in stemming the Roman empire's decline? What problems were they unable to solve?

6. What are the difficulties involved in explaining the fall of the Roman Empire? What sorts of theories have scholars advanced to explain Rome's decline and fall? Which explanations do you find most convincing? Why?

Suggested Readings

J. P. V. D. Balsdon, *Roman Women* (1962). A standard treatment.

T. Barnes, *The New Empire of Diocletian and Constantine* (1982). A study of the character of the late empire.

P. Brown, *The World of Late Antiquity*, A.D. 150–750 (1971). A brilliant and readable essay.

J. Burckhardt, *The Age of Constantine the Great* (1956). A classic work by the Swiss cultural historian.

C. M. Cochrane, *Christianity and Classical Culture* (1957). A study of intellectual change in the late empire.

S. Dill, *Roman Society in the Last Century of the Western Empire* (1958). A classic social history.

M. Grant, *The Fall of the Roman Empire* (1990). A lively, well-written account.

T. Rice Holmes, *Architect of the Roman Empire*, 2 vols. (1928–1931). An account of Augustus's career in detail.

A. H. M. Jones, *The Later Roman Empire*, 3 vols. (1964). A comprehensive study of the period.

H. Lietzmann, *History of the Early Church*, 2 vols. (1961). From the Protestant viewpoint.

R. Macmullen, *Enemies of the Roman Order* (1966). An original and revealing examination of opposition to the emperors.

R. Macmullen, *Corruption and the Decline of Rome* (1988). A study that examines the importance of changes in ethical ideas and behavior.

R. W. Mathison, *Roman Aristocrats in Barbarian Gaul: Strategies for Survival* (1993). An unusual slant on the late empire.

F. G. B. Millar, *The Roman Empire and Its Neighbors* (1968). An analysis of Roman foreign relations in the imperial period.

A. Momigliano (ed.), *The Conflict Between Paganism and Christianity* (1963). A valuable collection of essays.

M. I. Rostovtzeff, *Social and Economic History of the Roman Empire*, 2nd ed. (1957). A masterpiece whose main thesis has been much disputed.

R. Syme, *The Roman Revolution* (1960). A brilliant study of Augustus, his supporters, and their rise to power.

L. R. Taylor, *The Divinity of the Roman Empire* (1931). A study of the imperial cult.

6

The Early Middle Ages (476–1000): The Birth of Europe

KEY TOPICS

- How the fusion of Germanic and Roman cultures laid the foundation for a distinctively European society following the collapse of the Roman Empire
- The Byzantine and Islamic empires and their impact on the West
- The role of the church in Western society during the early Middle Ages
- Politics and economics in Europe under the Franks
- The characteristics of feudal society

The collapse of Roman civilization forced the peoples of the Mediterranean world to experiment with new ideas and institutions. In what had been the northern and western provinces of the Roman Empire, aspects of Greco-Roman and German cultures combined with Christianity to create a uniquely European way of life. In the East, two other "medieval" civilizations appeared: Byzantium and Islam.

Significant Dates from the Early Middle Ages

313	*Constantine legalizes Christianity*
325	*Council of Nicaea defines Christian doctrine*
410	*Visigoths sack the city of Rome*
476	*Last Roman emperor of the West is deposed*
529	*Benedictine monasticism originates*
533	*Justinian codifies Roman law*
622	*Muhammad's flight from Mecca (Hegira)*
732	*Charles Martel defeats Muslims at Poitiers*
751	*Pepin III "the Short" crowned king of the Franks*
755	*Pepin creates the Papal States*
768–814	*Charlemagne builds a European empire*
800	*Pope Leo III crowns Charlemagne emperor*
814–840	*Louis the Pious*
843	*Treaty of Verdun partitions the Carolingian Empire*

❧ On the Eve of the Frankish Ascendancy

The attempts made to save the Roman Empire in the late third century influenced how it fell. Diocletian (r. 284–305) dealt with simultaneous threats to the empire in the East and the West by sharing leadership with a colleague, Maximian. His division of the central government set the stage for the halves of the empire to evolve separately. Imperial rule gradually faded from the West, but in the East it grew increasingly autocratic.

Constantine the Great (r. 306–337) reunited the empire and, in 324, relocated its capital to Constantinople, a new city he built in Byzantium on the border between Europe and Asia Minor. This "new Rome" flourished as the old one declined. The city of Milan, which had direct communications with the Rhine and Danube frontiers, managed the defense of the western empire. In 402 Milan was judged too exposed to barbarian invasions, and the seat of western government was moved to Ravenna on the Adriatic coast. By the late fourth century, the West was in political disarray, the city of Rome was no longer of much political significance, and imperial power and prestige had shifted decisively to Constantinople.

Germanic Migrations

The German tribes did not burst on the West all of a sudden (see Map 6-1). Roman and Germanic cultures had commingled peacefully for centuries as Romans "imported" barbarian domestics, slaves, and soldiers. Some barbarians rose to command posts in Roman legions.

The arrival of the Visigoths (the "West Goths") in 376 marked the point

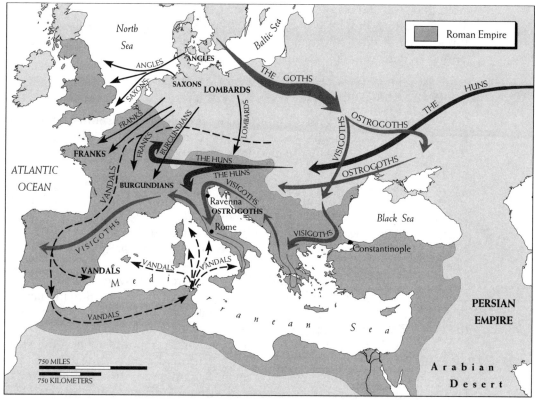

MAP 6-1   Barbarian Migrations into the West in the Fourth and Fifth Centuries *The intrusion of barbarians into the empire from the end of the fourth through the fifth centuries created a constantly shifting pattern of migration. The map shows the routes usually taken by the newcomers and the areas most affected.*

where the rate of barbarian migration began to overwhelm the western half of the empire. The Visigoths were pushed into the empire by the notoriously violent Huns of Mongolia. The eastern emperor Valens (r. 364–378) admitted the Visigoths to the empire in exchange for their promise to help defend its eastern frontier. They became the first *foederati*—the first allied alien nation resident within the empire.

The Visigoths entered the empire as impoverished refugees. Exploitation of their misery by Roman profiteers caused them to rebel, and in 378, at the battle of Adrianople, they destroyed Valens and his army. Constantinople defended itself by persuading the Visigoths to move west. The western government responded by withdrawing troops from the frontiers to guard Italy, and this cleared the way for other German tribes to cross those frontiers unopposed.

It may seem surprising that there was so little resistance in the West to the migration of the Germanic tribes. The largest tribe probably numbered no more than 100,000 people, a small group compared to the Roman population. But the western empire was badly overextended, divided by struggles among ambitious military commanders, and weakened physically by decades of famine, pestilence, and overtaxation.

Fall of the Roman Empire

In the early fifth century, Italy suffered a series of devastating blows. Rome was sacked by the Visigoths and their king Alaric (ca. 370–410) in 410. In 452 the Huns were led into Italy by the infamous Attila, and in 455 the Vandals sacked Rome.

By the mid-fifth century, power in western Europe had passed from Roman emperors to barbarian chieftains. In 476, the traditional date for the fall of the Roman Empire, the barbarian general Odovacer (ca. 434–493) deposed the West's nominal emperor, Romulus Augustulus, and ruled without an imperial figurehead. In 493, with encouragement by the eastern emperor Zeno (r. 474–491), Theodoric (ca. 454–526), king of the Ostrogoths (the "East Goths"), took Odovacer's place. By that time barbarians had thoroughly overrun the West. The Ostrogoths settled in Italy, the Franks in northern Gaul, the Burgundians in Provence, the Visigoths in southern Gaul and Spain, the Vandals in Africa and the western Mediterranean, and the Angles and Saxons in England.

Despite the rise of barbarian leaders, western Europe did not become a savage land. The Germans respected Roman culture and were willing to learn from the people they had conquered. Except in Britain and northern Gaul, Roman language, law, and government coexisted with the Germanic institutions. Only the Vandals and the Anglo-Saxons—and, after 466, the Visigoths—refused to profess at least titular obedience to the emperor in Constantinople.

Religion was a potential link between the Romans and their new rulers. The Visigoths, the Ostrogoths, and the Vandals had converted to Christianity before entering the West. Unfortunately, western Christians considered them heretics. Many of the missionaries to the Germans were followers of Arius, the heretical theologian who argued that Christ was a creature subordinate to God the Father, not an equal member of the holy Trinity. This problem was resolved about 500 when the Franks converted to the orthodox or catholic ("universal") form of Christianity endorsed by the bishops of Rome. The Franks then conquered and converted the other barbarians in western Europe.

Despite Rome's military defeat, Goths and Franks were more Romanized than Romans were Germanized. Latin language, orthodox Christianity (that which professed the creed written by the Council of Nicaea in 325), and Roman law triumphed in the West during the Middle Ages.

✧ The Byzantine Empire

As western Europe succumbed to the Germanic invasions, the eastern part of the old Roman Empire became a new medieval state, the Byzantine Empire of

Constantinople. From 324, when Constantinople was founded, to 1453, when it was occupied by the Ottoman Turks, the city was the seat of a Christian government. Its power waxed and waned, but it endured.

The Reign of Justinian

The Byzantine Empire reached a territorial and cultural peak during the reign of the emperor Justinian (r. 527–565). Although urban institutions were disappearing in the West, Justinian's domain boasted more than 1,500 cities. The largest (with perhaps 350,000 inhabitants) was Constantinople—the center of Western commerce and communications. The greater provincial cities of the empire had populations of about 50,000 and sustained thriving economies.

Justinian's most important counselor was his brilliant wife Theodora (d. 548). If the controversial *Secret History* by Procopius, Justinian's court historian, is to be believed, Theodora, the daughter of a bear trainer in the circus, began her career as a prostitute. Her background may have given her a toughness that was useful to her husband, for she guided him through crises that might have overwhelmed his government. She was particularly useful in dealing with the religious quarrels that troubled the peace of the empire. Whereas Justinian was a strictly orthodox Christian, Theodora used patronage to pacify a powerful faction of Christian heretics, the Monophysites. The Monophysites believed that Jesus had a single nature that was partially human and partially divine, while the orthodox church claimed that he had two: one fully human and the other fully divine. The Monophysites were strong enough to form a separate church in the eastern provinces of the empire. After Theodora's death, the imperial government made the mistake of trying to stamp them out. A few years later, when Persian and Arab armies invaded, the resentful Monophysites offered little resistance.

Law. Byzantine policy was to centralize government and enforce legal and doctrinal conformity throughout the empire: "one God, one empire, one religion." One of Justinian's major achievements was the codification of Roman law, the *Corpus Juris Civilis* (*Body of Civil Law*). It contained four parts. The *Code,* which appeared in 533, revised imperial edicts issued since the reign of Hadrian (117–138). The *Novellae* ("*New Things*") was composed of Justinian's decrees— which were added to by his successors. The *Digest* was a summary of the opinions of famous legal experts. The *Institutes* was a textbook for young lawyers. It spelled out the principles of law implied by the *Code* and the *Digest.* These works had little immediate effect on medieval common law, but from the Renaissance on they greatly influenced the development of law in Europe.

Religion. Like law, religion was used to promote the centralization of the Byzantine Empire. Christianity was proclaimed the official religion of the eastern empire in 380. The coronation of emperors became a Christian religious ceremony presided over by the "patriarch" (chief bishop) of Constantinople. And as the great churches of Constantinople, Alexandria, Antioch, and

Jerusalem acquired enormous wealth, they took on the functions of state welfare agencies.

Persecution and absorption into popular Christianity served to curtail pagan practices, but orthodox Christianity never succeeded in stamping out the heresies that continued to spring up in the empire. Large numbers of Jews also had to be accommodated. Under Roman law Jews had legal protection so long as they did not proselytize Christians, build new synagogues, or attempt to enter sensitive public offices or professions. Justinian pressured Jews to convert, and later emperors both ordered Jews to be baptized and granted tax breaks to those who voluntarily complied. Neither policy—persuasion nor coercion— was very successful.

Eastern Influences

Justinian tried, but failed, to conquer Italy and reestablish the old Roman Empire. His successors were much too preoccupied by developments in the East to devote any thought to the West. Under the emperor Heraclius (610–641), the Byzantine Empire took a decidedly Eastern turn. Heraclius spoke Greek, not Latin, and spent his entire reign struggling with Persians and Muslims. He fought the Persians to a draw but after 632 Islamic armies advanced relentlessly into his territory. They overran Asia Minor, and in 677 they besieged Constantinople for the first, but not last, time. Not until the reign of Leo III (717–740), founder of the Isaurian dynasty, were they driven back and Asia Minor recovered.

Leo's relations with western Christians worsened when he outlawed the use of images in Christian worship. Islamic theology equated image veneration with idolatry, and it may have had some influence on Leo and his successors. Be that as it may, western Christians were deeply affronted by the East's *iconoclasm*, for they had great affection for holy images of Jesus, Mary, and the saints. Leo's assumption that secular rulers have the right to legislate religious practices—a doctrine called *Caesaro-papism*—was also rejected by the Western church. The ban on images in the East was ultimately lifted in the late eighth century, but in the interim it worsened the divisions in Christendom and destroyed much religious art.

In 1071 the Byzantines were defeated in a battle at Manzikert, and the Muslim Seljuk Turks overran the eastern provinces of the empire. This was the beginning of a long slow decline for the eastern empire. In 1092 the Byzantine emperor Alexius I Comnenus (r. 1081–1118) appealed to the West for help, and three years later the West responded with the first of the great Crusades. The First Crusade enabled Constantinople to recover some territory, but a century later (1204) the Fourth Crusade overwhelmed Constantinople itself and did more damage to the city than all previous Muslim attackers.

Despite its vicissitudes, the Byzantine Empire maintained a protective barrier between Europe and its non-Christian enemies in the East until 1453. Byzantine civilization was also, for much of this time, more advanced than European civilization and the source of much of the classical learning that filtered through to the West.

Islam and the Islamic World

A new religion called Islam arose in Arabia in the sixth century in response to the work of the Prophet Muhammad. It sparked the creation of a third medieval civilization and a rapidly expanding empire that quickly became a threat to Byzantium's Greek emperors and Europe's German kings.

Muhammad's Religion

Muhammad (570–632) was orphaned at a young age and raised by relatives in modest circumstances. As a youth, Muhammad worked on caravans as a merchant's assistant. At the age of twenty-five, he married a wealthy Meccan widow and with her support became a kind of social activist. He opposed the materialism of Meccan society and some of his people's pagan practices. When he was about forty, he had a deep religious experience in which he received visitations from the angel Gabriel. Muhammad then began (and continued for the rest of his life) to recite what his followers believe literally to be God's words. Between 650 and 651, the revealed texts which God had chosen him to convey were collected in a sacred book, the Qur'an ("reciting"). At the heart of Muhammad's message was a call for all Arabs to submit to God's will as revealed through "the Prophet." The terms *Islam* (the religion) and *Muslim* (its followers) both imply "submission" or "surrender."

Muhammad did not claim that his message was new—only that it was final and definitive. What he taught was consistent with what a long line of Jewish prophets—from Noah to Jesus Christ—had taught. His special role was to be the last of the prophets that God would send. Islam, like Judaism, was a strictly monotheistic and theocentric religion, and it concurred with Judaism in rejecting Christianity's Trinitarian view of God and the concept of God's incarnation in the person of Jesus.

Muhammad's birthplace, the community of Mecca, was the location of the Ka'ba, one of Arabia's most holy shrines. The Ka'ba was a simple, rectangular building containing a sacred black stone and various other holy objects. Muhammad's attack on the idols of the Ka'ba was not only an offense to traditional Arab religion, it threatened to diminish Mecca's appeal as a center for trade. In 622, the Meccan authorities forced Muhammad and his followers to flee to Medina, 240 miles to the north. This event, the *Hegira* ("flight"), has been chosen as the pivot date for the Islamic calendar, for it marks the moment when Muhammad founded the first Muslim community.

Muhammad and his followers prospered in Medina by raiding caravans going to and from Mecca. Success brought him throngs of converts, and by 624 he was powerful enough to persuade Mecca to submit to his authority. He returned in triumph, cleansed the Ka'ba of its idols, and designated it the chief shrine for his new religion. Islam, like Christianity, eased life for its converts by making some compromises with their cherished pagan customs.

Muhammad stressed practice more than doctrine, and, as Islam matured, it evolved characteristic customs and values: (1) to be honest and modest in all dealings and behavior, (2) to be absolutely loyal to the Islamic community, (3) to abstain from pork and alcohol, (4) to pray facing Mecca five times a day, (5) to contribute to the support of the poor and needy, (6) to fast during daylight hours for one month each year, and (7) to make a pilgrimage to the Ka'ba at least once in a lifetime. Muslim men were allowed as many as four wives—provided they were able to treat them all justly and equally. A man could divorce a wife with a simple declaration of his intent. A wife could also initiate divorce, although the procedure was more complicated for her. She was expected to be totally loyal and devoted to her husband, and only her husband was to be allowed to see her face.

Islam made no rigid distinction between clergy and laity. It had no priesthood, but looked for leadership to a scholarly elite of laymen, the *ulema* ("persons with correct knowledge"). The authority of these men derived from their reputations for great piety and learning, and their opinions had the force of law in Muslim society. They also kept a critical eye on Muslim rulers to ensure that they adhered to the letter of the Qur'an.

Islamic Diversity

Islam was very successful in unifying the Arab tribes and various pagan peoples, for it appealed to the pride of groups that had been marginalized in a world dominated by Judaism and Christianity. Islam proclaimed Muhammad to be history's most important religious figure and his followers to be the people God chose to receive his most significant revelation.

Passionate faith in Muhammad did not prevent divisions from emerging within Islam. Factions contested who had the best right to the *caliphate*—the office held by the men who succeeded to Muhammad's leadership of the Muslim community. Doctrinal issues were also debated, as was the issue of the extent to which Islam was meant to be a religion only for Arabs.

The most radical positions were taken by the Kharijites. Their leaders seceded from the camp of the fourth caliph, Ali (r. 656–661), when, in their opinion, he sacrificed important principles for political advantage. (In 661, one of their members assassinated Ali.) The Kharijites were "Puritans" who excluded from Islam all but rigorously virtuous Muslims.

More influential were the Shi'a, or "partisans of Ali" (*Shi'at Ali*). The Shi'a regarded Ali and his descendants as the only rightful successors to Muhammad—not only by virtue of kinship, but also by the expressed will of the Prophet. To the Shi'a, Ali's assassination revealed the basic truth of a devout Muslim life: a true *imam* ("ruler") must expect to suffer unjustly even unto death. So too must his followers. A theology of martyrdom is the mark of Shi'a teaching, and the Shi'a are still an embattled minority within Islam.

A third group, which has been dominant for most of Islamic history, is the majority centrist Sunnis (followers of *sunna*, "tradition"). Sunnis emphasize loyalty to the fundamental principles of Islam more than the particular issues that cause the Kharijites and the Shi'a to exclude various people from the Muslim community.

Islamic Empires

Muhammad's first three successors—the caliphs Abu Bakr (r. 632–634), Umar (r. 634–644), and Uthman (r. 644–656)—won control of the southern and eastern rim of the Mediterranean. Islam's capital shifted from Mecca to the more centrally located Damascus, and by the eighth century the caliphs ruled an empire that stretched from Spain to India. In 750, the Abbasid family overthrew the Umayyad caliphs of Damascus and moved the seat of their government to Baghdad. Shortly thereafter, their huge domain began to break up into separate states, and rival caliphs contested their authority.

The Muslim conquests proceeded rapidly because their Byzantine and Persian opponents had exhausted themselves in a long war. The Muslims struck just as the Byzantine emperor Heraclius drove the Persians out of Egypt, Palestine, Syria, and Asia Minor. Before Heraclius died in 641, Arab armies had taken all of this, except for Asia Minor, from him. By 643 they had overrun what remained of the Persian Empire, and by the end of the century the last Byzantine outpost in North Africa had fallen to them.

Most of the inhabitants of the Byzantine lands the Muslims occupied were Christians, but many were also Semitic peoples with links to the Arabs. Heraclius's efforts to stamp out heresy and impose Greek orthodoxy on the Monophysite communities of Egypt and Syria led many of them to welcome the Islamic invaders as liberators from Byzantine oppression.

Islam won control of Christian territories in North Africa and Spain, but its thrust into the European heart of Christendom was rebuffed in 732 by Charles Martel, ruler of the Franks. His defeat of an Arab raiding party at Poitiers (in central France) marked the point at which the Muslim advance in the West began to be reversed. The Isaurian dynasty, which Leo III (r. 717–740) established in Constantinople, defended Asia Minor from Islamic aggression and blocked Muslim access to Europe from the east.

The Western Debt to Islamic Culture

The Christian West was very hostile to Islam, but it profited a great deal from contact with the Muslims. Arab cultures of the early medieval period were far superior to those of Christian Europe. Europe learned important technologies from the Muslims, and Muslim scholars made major works of Greek science and philosophy available to the West in Latin translation. As late as the sixteenth century, in addition to the works of the ancient world's Hippocrates and Galen, the basic gynecological and child-care manuals in use in the West were editions prepared by a Baghdad physician, Al-Razi, and by the philosophers

POLITICAL TRANSFORMATIONS

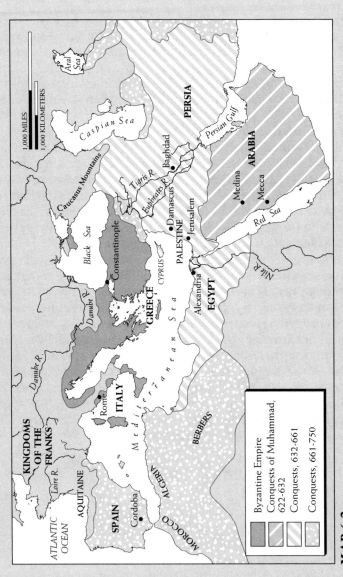

MAP 6-2

Muslim Conquests and Domination of the Mediterranean to About 750

In the eighth century, Muslim armies marched west across Africa to Spain and east through Persia and Khorasan to India. Muslim rule of this huge territory was tolerant by comparison to Byzantine and Persian conquerors. Arab Muslim immigration into Iraq and Iran was heavy, and native political elites in those regions quickly converted to Islam. In North Africa and Spain the growth of Muslim political authority was somewhat slower. The Muslim empire began to fragment in the eighth century, but, with the notable exception of Spain (from which Muslims were driven in the fifteenth century), most of the territory Islam initially conquered has remained Muslim.

While scholars have debated the religious significance of war for Muslims, it is clear that fighting for Islam was a fundamental Muslim duty and a key to the rapid growth of the medieval Islamic Empire. As the following excerpt from the Qur'an makes clear, the conquest of new lands and the maintenance of firm control over Islamic states were not understood to be acts of aggression.

Fight those in the way of God who fight you, but do not be aggressive: God does not like aggressors. And fight those wheresoever you find them, and expel them from the place they had turned you out from. Oppression is worse than killing. Do not fight them by the Holy Mosque unless they fight you there. If they [fight], then slay them: such is the requital for unbelievers. But if they desist, God is forgiving and kind.

Fight them until sedition comes to an end, and the Law of God [prevails]. If they desist, then cease to be hostile, except against those who oppress. (Qur'an 2:190–193)

Those who believe fight in the way of God; and those who do not, fight only for the powers of evil; so you should fight the allies of Satan. (Qur'an 4:74–76)

A Reader on Classical Islam, F. E. Peters (Princeton: Princeton University Press, 1994), p. 155.

La Mezquita, *the Great Mosque at Cordoba, Spain was begun in 786. The city was reconquered in 1236, and the mosque became a place of Christian worship, but its Islamic character remains clear. [Robert Frerck/Woodfin Camp & Associates]*

Avicenna (980–1037) and Averröes (1126–1198), Islam's great authorities on Aristotle. The works of multilingual Jewish scholars also helped create bridges between the Muslim and Christian worlds.

⤳ Western Society and the Developing Christian Church

Europe, overrun by barbarians from the north and east and threatened in the south by a vigorous and expansive Islam, declined during the fifth and sixth centuries. Trade waned, and the West lost the urban centers where exchanges of goods and ideas promoted cultural growth.

No help could be expected from the East. The Byzantine emperors of the seventh century were preoccupied with the Islamic threat to their domains and maintained little contact with Europe. As the Muslims conquered Mediterranean islands and ports and strangled Christian shipping, Europe's communications with the East declined even further. Forced by these developments to rely on their own resources, westerners drew on their Germanic and Greco-Roman heritages to create distinctive new cultures.

As western cities and governments declined, people sought employment and protection on the self-sufficient estates of the great landholders. Peasants made up 90 percent of the population of medieval Europe. Some were free and owned their own land. Some surrendered their land to a more powerful man in exchange for assistance and became *serfs*. Serfs were bound to the land they worked. They were not free to leave it, but, on the other hand, custom protected them from being separated from it and sold as slaves.

As trade declined, agricultural districts became insular and self-contained. Barter sufficed for exchanging goods among the great estates that were the basic political and economic units of medieval society. Producers adjusted their output to local need. And since there was no way to turn excess goods into profit, there was little incentive to experiment with more efficient techniques or expand production. This was the background for the evolution of the characteristic medieval institutions: an economic system called *manorialism* and a political system called *feudalism.*

The Christian church kept some of medieval Europe's fading urban centers alive. During the period of the late empire the church had modeled itself on Rome's imperial government and had located its administrative offices near the empire's centers of power—in cities. As the western empire crumbled and secular magistrates disappeared, many of their functions were transferred to bishops, the only Roman "officials" still available. The local *cathedral* (a church served by a bishop) became the center of urban life and its bishop the effective governor of his city. The church thus preserved some of the skills and procedures of Roman government.

The church was forced by Rome's decline and the loss of the state's protection to involve itself in politics. The struggle to survive the period of the German and Islamic invasions cost the church some of its spiritual integrity, but did not diminish its effectiveness as a civilizing and unifying force. Its rituals and creeds united people across barriers of social class, education, and gender, and its clergy—the best-educated minds in Europe—had knowledge that was invaluable to the German kings who were trying to reestablish order.

Monastic Culture

The early medieval church drew much of its strength from religious institutions called monasteries. The first monks were hermits who protested the relaxation of standards of Christian discipline that followed Constantine's popularization of Christianity in the fourth century. They fled to remote areas to find the freedom to practice the extreme ascetic disciplines that they believed were the mark of true Christian commitment. They became the new Christian heroes—successors to the martyrs that the Roman government now declined to persecute.

Saint Gregory the Great, shown in a monastic scriptorium, or study, receiving the divine word from a dove perched on his shoulder. Below him three monks are writing. The middle monk holds an inkwell in his left hand. [Kunsthistorisches Museum, Vienna]

Medieval Christians viewed monastic life—governed, as it was, by the biblical "counsels of perfection" (chastity, poverty, and obedience)—as humanity's highest calling. Monks and the secular clergy (whom popular opinion forced to adopt some monastic disciplines) met a more demanding spiritual standard than was expected of ordinary believers. Consequently, clergy appeared superior to laity, a belief that served the papacy well in struggles with secular rulers.

The hermit monasticism pioneered by men like Anthony of Egypt (ca. 251–356) soon evolved into communal monasticism. In the first quarter of the fourth century, Pachomius (ca. 286–346), another Egyptian recluse, set up a highly regimented community in which hundreds of monks lived in accordance with a strict penal code. Such monastic communities tried to become "cities of God," isolating themselves from the collapsing Roman Empire and its nominally Christian society. The form of monasticism that spread throughout the East, however, was that championed by Basil the Great (329–379). It put less stress on personal asceticism and urged monks to care for the needy outside their communities.

Athanasius (ca. 293–373) and Martin of Tours (ca. 315–ca. 399) introduced the West to the monastic practices that were evolving in the East. But, in 529, Benedict of Nursia (ca. 480–547) wrote a *Rule* (a constitution) for a monastery he established at Monte Cassino near Naples, Italy. It defined a uniquely Western style of monasticism that became standard throughout Europe. Benedict's *Rule* governed a monk's every activity, including sleep. It discouraged the kind of flamboyant asceticism that was popular in the East. Benedict insisted that monks have adequate food, some wine, serviceable clothing, and proper amounts of sleep and relaxation. Periods of time were set aside each day for prayer, communal worship, and study—as well as the manual labor by which monks supported themselves. The program was designed to create autonomous religious communities that were economically, spiritually, and intellectually self-sufficient. Benedictine monks did not turn their backs on the world. They were chiefly responsible for the missionary work that converted England and Germany to Christianity, and their discipline and devotion to hard work made them both an economic and a spiritual force wherever they went.

The Doctrine of Papal Primacy

Constantine and the eastern emperors treated the church like a department of state. They intervened in its theological debates and legislated its doctrine. The bishops of Rome, however, grew more independent as imperial power faded in the West. They proclaimed the doctrine of "papal primacy," an assertion of their right to undisputed leadership of an independent church.

Papal primacy was a response to the decline of imperial Rome and the increasing pretensions of Constantinople. In 381, when the ecumenical Council of Constantinople declared the bishop (patriarch) of Constantinople to be first in rank after the bishop of Rome, Pope Damasus I (366–384)[1] objected. He

---

[1] Papal dates give the years of each reign.

claimed that Rome had a unique "apostolic" primacy, for its bishops were heirs to the Apostle Peter and his unique legacy as the "rock" on which Jesus had said (Matthew 16:18) that the church was to be built. After the Council of Chalcedon (451) accorded the Byzantine patriarch the same primacy over the East that Rome traditionally had in the West, Pope Leo I (440–461) assumed the title *pontifex maximus* ("supreme priest") to assert his claim to supremacy over all bishops everywhere. At the end of the fifth century, Pope Gelasius I (492–496) further clarified the nature of papal authority by declaring it to be "more weighty" than that of the state—his reason being that the church was responsible for the means of salvation, the most serious human concern.

The Germanic and Islamic invasions prevented Constantinople from exercising much control over the popes and the Western church. When the Lombard tribes invaded Italy late in the sixth century, Pope Gregory I, "the Great" (590–604), ignored the imperial authorities and assumed the right to negotiate with the barbarians as the chief representative of the Italian people.

The Division of Christendom

By the time Gregory became pope, the patriarch of Constantinople was using the title "universal" patriarch—implying a claim to supremacy over Rome. Since he had no authority in the West, this was really an admission that separate churches were functioning in the Byzantine East and the Roman Catholic West.

The division of the church was apparent in language, doctrine, disciplinary codes, and liturgies. The Greek Byzantine church had a mystical, otherworldly orientation that contrasted with the more practical Christianity of the West's Latin church. Ecclesiastical organization in the East more closely paralleled the hierarchy of imperial government than did the structure of the Western church. But the power of the Byzantine patriarch over the clergy was limited by the power the emperor had over him. Where the Western church tried to impose monastic celibacy on all clergy, parish priests in the Eastern church (except for bishops) were allowed to marry. The Eastern church used leavened bread in the Eucharist; Rome mandated unleavened bread. The Byzantines rejected the Catholic doctrine of purgatory. They also permitted divorce, and, unlike the Catholics, performed their liturgies in the vernacular of the laity.

From time to time, Eastern and Western Christians differed markedly on doctrine. Where the Latin church looked to the Roman pope to define doctrine, the Greek church relied on the authority of the Bible and ecumenical councils. Disputes over the right to define doctrine became acute when the East mounted an assault on the veneration of holy images ("iconoclasm") and when the West added the word *filioque* ("also from the Son") to the Nicene Creed. (This was an attempt to subvert eastern compromises with Arianism by insisting that the Holy Spirit proceeded from the Father and the Son as equal partners in the Godhead.) The claims of Roman popes to a primacy of authority over the whole church were dismissed in the East, for eastern Christianity evolved not as a single organization, but as a communion of independent national churches. In the ninth century, when the crucial issue of authority over the universal church came to a head, Pope Nicholas I and Patriarch Photius excommunicated each other. In 1054, Pope Leo IX and Patriarch Michael Cerularius again officially divided the church by repeating the mutual condemnation.

Rome took a risk in quarreling with Constantinople, for popes looked to the eastern empire to defend them from barbarian invaders. But as help declined from that quarter and Christianity spread to the invaders, the popes sought new allies among the Germans. They correctly intuited that the Franks of northern Gaul were Europe's ascendant power and the church's most promising potential protectors. In 754, Pope Stephen II (752–757) took the dramatic step of throwing in his lot with the Germans. He persuaded Pepin III, ruler of the Franks, to defend Rome from the Lombards. This acknowledged the end of the old empire and the transfer of the West to new hands.

✧ The Kingdom of the Franks

Merovingians and Carolingians: From Clovis to Charlemagne

A warrior chieftain named Clovis (ca. 466?–511) founded the first Frankish dynasty, the Merovingian (named for Merovich, an early leader of a branch of the Franks.) Clovis and his successors united the Salian and Ripuarian Franks, subdued the Burgundians and Visigoths, won the support of the Gallo-Romans by converting to orthodox Christianity, and transformed Rome's Gaul into "France" (land of Franks).

Governing the Franks. The Merovingians struggled with the perennial problem of medieval politics: the competing claims of the "one" and the "many." As kings worked to centralize governments, powerful local magnates fought to preserve their regional autonomy. The result was a battle between forces that tried to unify society and those that promoted fragmentation.

The Merovingian kings hoped to pull their nation together by making pacts with the landed nobility and by relying for help in running their domain on a new kind of royal official, the *count*. Counts were appointed to manage lands to which they had no hereditary claim. Kings believed that counts would be easier to control than landed aristocrats, for the people the counts governed had no tradition of loyalty to their families. But as time passed, kings found it impossible to prevent counts from establishing hereditary claims to their offices and becoming as independent as the older nobility. The unification of the Frankish state was also impeded by Frankish inheritance customs, which gave all a king's legitimate male heirs a right to a share in his kingdom.

By the seventh century the Merovingian king was king in title only. Real executive authority had devolved on one of his officials, the "mayor of the palace." The family of Pepin I of Austrasia (d. 639) monopolized this post until 751, when, with the connivance of the pope, they shoved the Merovingians aside, expropriated the Frankish crown, and founded the Carolingian dynasty.

Pepin I's descendent, Pepin II (d. 714), had ruled the Frankish kingdom in fact but not in title, and bequeathed that anomalous situation to his illegitimate son, Charles "Martel" (Charles "the Hammer"). Martel (d. 741) created a great cavalry by bestowing lands as fiefs or benefices ("provisional" grants) on powerful noblemen on condition that they equip themselves to fight for him. His army proved its worth at Poitiers in 732, when it broke the momentum of the Muslim advance and secured the Pyrenees as the border of western Europe.

Much of the land that Martel distributed as fiefs to create his army came from the church. The church was dependent on the protection of the Franks, and it could do little to prevent the confiscation of property that was used to fund its own defense. Eventually, however, the church was partially compensated for its losses.

The land that Martel handed out forged an alliance between the Carolingians and the landed aristocracy. Where the Merovingians had tried to weaken the aristocrats by raising landless men to power, the Carolingians staffed their government almost entirely from the ranks of the landed nobility. By playing to strength rather than challenging it, the Carolingians secured their position—in the short run.

The Frankish Church. The church played a major role in the Frankish government, for its monasteries were the intellectual centers of Carolingian society. Already in Merovingian times the higher clergy were employed in tandem with counts as royal agents.

The Carolingians—particularly Charles Martel and his successors, Pepin III, "the Short" (d. 768), and Charlemagne (r. 768–814)—relied on Christian missionaries to pacify the barbarian lands which they conquered. Conversion to Nicene Christianity was an essential part of the process of assimilating new subjects. After the cavalry broke their bodies, the clergy won their hearts and minds. The missions of the church and state tended to be confused, however, when the king appointed Christian bishops to govern the lands they were converting.

An event from the career of Boniface (born Wynfrith, 680?–754), an Anglo-Saxon monk who was the most famous of the Carolingian missionaries, illustrates how deeply involved in politics the church became. In 751, Pope Zacharias (741–752) sanctioned Pepin the Short's bid for the Frankish throne. Pepin was proclaimed king by the nobility in council, and the last of the Merovingians—the puppet king Childeric III—was hustled off to a monastery. (Enforced celibacy guaranteed the extermination of his line.) Boniface may have anointed Pepin at his coronation. Since anointing was part of the ritual of priestly ordination, the rite was apparently intended to give the Carolingian monarchy a sacral character.

In 753 Pope Stephen II (752–757), Zacharias's successor, collected what the church wanted in exchange for its support. He visited Pepin's court to demand that the Franks defend Rome from the Lombards and confirm papal claims to central Italy. In 755 the Franks defeated the Lombards and turned over to the pope the lands surrounding Rome—including some to which the eastern emperor had title. This confirmed the pope's secular authority over a region known as the Papal States.

About this time (750–800) a document called the *Donation of Constantine* began to be circulated to support the church in its dealings with the Franks. It said that Constantine had given the papacy title to the western half of his empire—which implied that the papacy had the right to pass judgment on the legitimacy of western governments. The *Donation* was exposed as a forgery in the fifteenth century, but initially it gave the popes some leverage in dealing with their potentially overwhelming protectors. The Franks drew almost as slight a boundary between state and church as did the eastern emperors, and the church had to fight hard to avoid being subordinated to the Frankish monarchy.

The Reign of Charlemagne (768–814)

In 774 Charlemagne, the son of Pepin the Short, completed his father's work by conquering Italy's Lombards and assuming their crown. He devoted the rest of his reign to expanding the size of the kingdom he had inherited (see Map 6-3). The Saxons of northern Germany were brutally subdued and pacified by being scattered in small groups throughout Frankish lands. The Muslims were chased beyond the Pyrenees, and the Avars (a tribe related to the Huns) were practically annihilated—bringing the Danubian plains into the Frankish orbit. By the time of Charlemagne's death on January 28, 814, his kingdom embraced modern France, Belgium, Holland, Switzerland, almost the whole of western Germany, much of Italy, a portion of Spain, and the island of Corsica—an area about equal to the modern Common Market.

The New Empire. Charlemagne believed that his huge domain entitled him to an imperial title. To win support for assuming it, he tried to look as imperial as possible. Since eastern emperors ruled from a fixed capital, he constructed a palace city for himself at Aachen (Aix-la-Chapelle), and he turned to the church for help.

Charlemagne's imperial pretensions were confirmed on Christmas Day, 800, when Pope Leo III (795–816) crowned him emperor. The ceremony, which established a fateful link between German kings and Roman Italy, was in part an effort by the pope to gain some leverage over a powerful king. By arranging for the emperor to receive the crown from the hands of the pope, a precedent was set that was useful for the church in its future dealings with the state. At the time, however, the coronation in no way diminished Charlemagne's power over the church, and it strengthened him abroad by confronting the eastern emperors with a *fait accompli.* They reluctantly acknowledged his title once he disclaimed any ambition to move into their lands.

The New Emperor. Charlemagne stood a majestic six feet three and one-half inches tall. (His tomb was opened and exact measurements of his remains were made in 1861.) He was restless, informal, and gregarious—ever ready for a hunt or for a swim in Aachen's hot springs with his friends. He was widely known

MAP 6-3 The Empire of Charlemagne to 814 *Building on the successes of his predecessors, Charlemagne greatly increased the Frankish domains.*

for his practical jokes, lusty good humor, and warm hospitality. Aachen was a festive court to which visitors and gifts came from all over the world. In 802 the caliph of Baghdad, Harun-al-Rashid, even sent Charlemagne a white elephant, the transport of which was as great a wonder as the creature itself.

Charlemagne had five official wives (in succession), many mistresses and concubines, and numerous children. This connubial variety caused some political upheavals when Pepin, his oldest son by his first marriage, grew jealous of the attention he showed the sons of his second wife. Pepin joined some nobles in an ill-fated conspiracy against Charlemagne and spent the rest of his life confined to a monastery.

Problems of Government. Charlemagne relied on counts for help in governing his empire. There may have been as many as 250 deployed to strategic locations. A Carolingian count was usually a local magnate who had soldiers and who was persuaded by royal generosity to put them at the service of his king. He maintained a local army, collected tribute and dues, and administered justice—all in the name of the king.

A count presided over a district law court called the *mallus*. Its job was to hear testimony and to pass judgment based less on evidence than on the character or believability of each party to a quarrel. In situations where such testimony was insufficient, recourse was had to duels or to various tests or ordeals. A defendant's hand might be immersed in boiling water and his innocence determined by the way his wounds healed. Or a suspect might be bound with ropes and thrown into a river or pond that had been blessed by a priest. If the sacred water rejected him and he floated, he was assumed to be guilty. God was believed to render the verdict in an ordeal. Once guilt was determined, the *mallus* ordered monetary compensation to be paid to injured parties. This settled grievances that otherwise might have caused bloody vendettas.

Charlemagne never solved the problem of creating a loyal bureaucracy to govern his kingdom. The counts he appointed, like their Merovingian predecessors, tended to become little despots within their districts. Charlemagne issued *capitularies* (royal decrees) to establish policies he wanted his administrators to implement. He tried to exercise some oversight by sending envoys called *missi dominici* to inspect the counts and report back on their behavior. When the *missi*'s infrequent inspections had little impact, Charlemagne created provincial governors (prefects, dukes, and margraves) to keep permanent watch over the counts. They, however, proved no more trustworthy than the counts.

Charlemagne often appointed churchmen to government offices, for bishops, like counts, were considered royal servants. This, however, did little to improve the situation. The higher clergy shared the secular lifestyles and aspirations of the counts and were generally indistinguishable from the lay nobility. To be a Christian at this difficult period in the history of Europe was largely a matter of submitting to rituals (like baptism) and assenting to creeds. Both clergy and laity were too preoccupied with the struggle to survive to worry much about elevated ethical issues.

Alcuin and the Carolingian Renaissance. Charlemagne tried to improve the government of his empire by making an intensive effort to elevate the educations of the aristocratic boys who were destined for offices in the church and state.

Charlemagne's conquests brought him a great deal of wealth, and he used some of it to attract Europe's best scholars to Aachen—men like Theodulf of Orleans, Angilbert, Einhard (Charlemagne's biographer), and Alcuin of

York (735–804), a famous Anglo-Saxon educator who became director of the king's palace school. The school provided basic instruction in the seven liberal arts, with special concentration on grammar, logic, rhetoric, and simple mathematics.

The curriculum was designed to give bureaucrats the simple tools of their trade, but it accomplished more than that. It improved the accuracy of the Latin used in official documents, and it spread a new and much more legible style of handwriting throughout the empire. This Carolingian "minuscule" made reading far easier and more pleasurable than the Merovingian scripts. A modest renaissance or rebirth of interest in antiquity also took place at the palace school as its scholars collected and copied ancient manuscripts. Alcuin worked on the text of the Bible and made editions of the works of Gregory the Great and the Rule of Saint Benedict. Most scholarly projects aimed at concrete reforms. They helped establish uniformity in church law and liturgy, educate the clergy, and raise personal and professional standards for monks and priests.

The Carolingian Manor. Early medieval Europe's chief economic institution was a kind of communal farm called a *manor*. Medieval farmers often preferred to cluster in villages rather than to live on individual farms. This increased security and enabled them to share labor and expensive agricultural implements like plows and oxen. But instead of dividing harvests equally among all of a manor's workers, each family had its own strips of land on the manor and lived from what they produced.

The status of peasants was determined by the nature of their holdings. A freeman had allodial property—land free from the claims of an overlord. If he surrendered this to an overlord in exchange for protection, he became a serf. He received his land back from his lord with a new set of rights and obligations. Although the land was no longer his property, he had full use of it and could not be separated from it. His chief duty to his lord was to work his lord's *demesne,* the fields on the manor that produced the crops meant for the lord's table. Peasants who entered the service of a lord with little real property (perhaps only a few farm implements and animals) became unfree serfs. Such serfs were much more vulnerable to a lord's demands, often spending up to three days a week working their lord's fields. Truly impoverished peasants, those who had nothing to offer except their hands, had the lowest status and were the least protected from excessive demands.

By Charlemagne's day, a new type of plow was coming into use. It was heavy enough to break up the dense, waterlogged soils of northern Europe and open to cultivation lands that had defeated Roman farmers. Unlike the ancient "scratch" plow (a pointed stick), it cut deeply into the soil and had a moldboard that turned earth over to utilize more of its fertility.

Ancient farmers had maintained the fertility of their fields by using a two-field system of crop rotation—that is, by simply alternating fallow and planted fields annually. A fallow field was plowed to keep down weeds, but was not planted. The medieval three-field system left only one-third of a farm fallow in a given year. This decreased the amount of unproductive land that had to be plowed and used crop rotation to help maintain fertility. In fall, one field was planted with winter crops of wheat or rye that were harvested in early summer. In late spring, a second field was planted with summer crops of oats, barley, lentils, and legumes, which were harvested in August or September. The third field was left fallow.

Religion and the Clergy. Religion had an intrinsic appeal for the masses of ordinary men and women who were burdened, fearful, and had little hope of improving their lots this side of eternity. The privileged upper classes were no less pious. Charlemagne frequented the Church of Saint Mary in Aachen several times a day and decreed on his deathbed that all but a fraction of his great treasure be spent to endow masses and prayers for his soul.

The priests who served the people—the lower clergy—were poorly prepared to provide spiritual leadership. They were recruited from the ranks of the serfs and fared no better than other peasants. Lords owned the churches on their lands and often staffed them with their own serfs. The church expected a lord to liberate a serf who entered the clergy, but many "serf priests" said mass on Sunday and toiled as peasants during the rest of the week.

Because priests on most manors were no better educated than their congregations, religious instruction barely existed. For most people religion was more a matter of practice than doctrine. They baptized their children, attended mass, tried to learn the Lord's Prayer and the Apostles' Creed, and received the last rites when death approached. They were in awe of sacred relics and devoted to an army of saints who they hoped would intercede for them with their divine overlord in the court of heaven. Simple faith had little need for understanding.

Breakup of the Carolingian Kingdom

As Charlemagne aged, his empire became progressively ungovernable, for there was no way to prevent his nobles from doing what they wanted with the lands they held. In feudal society the intensity of one's loyalty to a lord depended on how far away that lord was. Local people obeyed local leaders more readily than distant kings. Charlemagne had to appoint powerful men if he hoped to keep the far-flung regions of his empire under control, but their power always diminished his. In the Carolingian as in the Merovingian kingdom, the noble tail increasingly wagged the royal dog.

Louis the Pious. The Carolingians did not give up easily. Charlemagne's successor was his only surviving son, Louis "the Pious" (r. 814–840). During Charlemagne's last years he shared his imperial title with Louis, for it symbolized the Carolingian hope of consolidating the kingdom by persuading its subjects to transcend regional and tribal loyalties. Unfortunately, Louis's fertility made this impossible. He had three sons by his first wife, and, according to Salic (Salian Frankish) law, each was entitled to a share of his kingdom. Louis tried to break with tradition by making his eldest son, Lothar (d. 855), co-regent and sole imperial heir (817). In 823, Louis's second wife bore him a fourth son, Charles "the Bald" (d. 877). In the interest of securing an inheritance for her boy, the queen incited her step-sons, Pepin and Louis "the German," to rebel. Supported by the pope, they joined forces and defeated their father in a battle near Colmar in 833.

The Treaty of Verdun and Its Aftermath. Pepin's death in 838 and his father's in 840 helped clear the field of contenders. In 843 the Treaty of Verdun divided the empire among the three remaining Carolingian princes. Lothar retained the meaningless imperial title and region called Lotharingia (Holland, Belgium, Switzerland, Alsace-Lorraine, and Italy). Charles the Bald got the equivalent of modern France, and Louis the German, Germany.

The Treaty of Verdun was only the start of the division of the Carolingian lands. When Lothar died in 855, his middle kingdom was split up among his three sons. This upset the balance of power and set the larger eastern and western Frankish kingdoms—Germany and France—loose to contest control of portions of Lothar's diminished legacy.

In Italy the decline of the Carolingian Empire created a political vacuum the popes tried to fill. But both popes and kings became pawns in the hands of the landed nobility. It is at this juncture in European history—the last quarter of the ninth and the first half of the tenth century—that one may speak accurately of a "dark age." Historical record keeping declined not only because the empire and papacy deteriorated politically, but because barbarian attacks on Europe were renewed. Successive waves of Normans ("North-men") or Vikings from Scandinavia, Magyars (Hungarians from the plains of Russia), and Muslims (from Sicily and Africa) simultaneously invaded Europe from different directions.

The Vikings were the most serious threat. Thanks to their unique skills as seamen, they were able to raid Europe's coasts and use its rivers to reach targets deep inland. Since they moved rapidly and randomly, there was little defense against them. The Franks built fortified towns and castles to serve as refuges. Sometimes they bought off the invaders with silver or grants of land. France even created a duchy of "Normandy" for the newcomers. Since there was little that the central governments of kings could do against myriad bands of raiders, communities looked to resident local strongmen for protection.

✧ Feudal Society

In the absence of effective central governments that were able to protect them, medieval people resorted to feudal arrangements. The weaker submitted to the stronger, and those who could guarantee security from rapine and starvation ruled.

Medieval feudalism emerged from a world dominated by warlords. Feudal society was held together by the oaths that individuals made—promises to provide subordinates with protection or maintenance in exchange for their service.

Men who pledged themselves as soldiers became vassals and formed a professional military class with its own code of knightly conduct. Networks of personal relationships among members of this class created regional military organizations. The leaders of these organizations, whether or not they had a legal right, assumed responsibility for governing the people who lived under their protection.

Origins

The roots of feudal government go back to the sixth and seventh centuries, when the weakness of the West's governments made it necessary for freemen who were unable to fend for themselves to seek alliances with more powerful neighbors. Freemen who entered into various kinds of contractual relations of dependence on superiors were known as *vassi* (vassals, "those who serve").

Owners of large estates tried to acquire as many vassals as they could afford to equip as soldiers for their private armies. Originally, such men were maintained as part of their lord's household. But as their numbers grew, this became impractical. Since the collapsing economy was taking money out of circulation, there was no way to pay vassals salaries. Hence, the custom developed of granting them *benefices* or *fiefs* (the right to use a piece of their lord's land to maintain themselves for his service). Vassals lived on their fiefs and were responsible for the peasants who farmed them.

Vassalage and the Fief

A vassal swore *fealty* to his lord. That meant that he promised to serve his lord and to refrain from actions contrary to his lord's interests. His chief obligation was military—duty as a mounted knight. Bargaining might take place over terms of service, but custom limited the number of days a lord could keep a vassal in the field. (In France in the eleventh century, forty days was standard.) In addition to military duty a vassal was expected to attend his lord's court when summoned and to render his lord financial assistance at times of special need: to ransom him from his enemies, to outfit him for a major military campaign, or to defray the costs of the festivities at the marriage of a daughter or the knighting of a son.

Louis the Pious extended vassalage beyond the lay nobility to the higher clergy. He required bishops and abbots to swear fealty and to accept their appointments on the same terms as royal benefices. He formally "invested" clerics with the rings and staffs that were the symbols of their spiritual offices. This practice was offensive to the church, for it implied the subservience of the church to the state. In the late tenth and eleventh centuries, reform-minded clergy rebelled against the ceremonies of vassalage and "lay investiture," but the reformers never suggested surrendering the grants of land that were the rewards for oaths of homage.

A lord's obligations to his vassals were very specific. He had to protect the vassal from physical harm, to stand as his advocate in court, and to provide for his maintenance by giving him a fief. In Carolingian times a fief varied in size from one or more small villas to several *mansi* (a unit of twenty-five to forty-eight acres). Royal vassals might receive fiefs ranging from 30 to 200 *mansi*. With prizes like this in the offing, vassalage was acceptable to the highest classes of Carolingian society. In the short run the policy marshalled the nobility behind the king, but in the long run the granting of fiefs undercut royal power. Kings found it difficult or impossible to reclaim land once it was granted to vassals. A vassal whom a king enriched sufficiently could then create vassals of his own. Since it was possible for a vassal to accept fiefs from more than one lord, all kinds of conflicts of interest might arise. The ninth century developed the concept of the "liege lord," the master to whom a vassal owed primary duty, but this did not halt progressive fragmentation of land and loyalty.

Kings were further weakened by the fact that the fiefs they granted tended to become the real property of their vassals. Although title to a fief remained with the lord who granted it, it was hard for him to prevent his vassal from passing the fief on to an heir. In the ninth century, hereditary possession became a legally recognized principle and laid the basis for claims to outright ownership. In this way, the nobility gradually appropriated much of the royal domain.

Lay society was illiterate. Consequently, the feudal era used symbols and ceremonies to seal the contracts involved in vassalage. A freeman became a vassal by a secular act of "commendation." In the mid-eighth century, a religious "oath of fealty" was added to increase the solemnity of the act. A vassal reinforced his promise of fidelity to a lord by swearing an oath with his hand on a sacred relic or a Bible. In the tenth and eleventh centuries, paying homage to the lord involved not only the swearing of such an oath but also the placement of the vassal's hands between his lord's hands and the sealing of the ritual with a kiss.

Despite feudalism's obvious vulnerability to abuse and confusion, it created social stability in early medieval Europe and helped restore political centralization during the High Middle Ages. The genius of feudal government lay in its adaptability. Contracts of different kinds could be made with almost anybody to serve almost any purpose. The foundations of the modern nation-state were laid in France and England as kings compromised with vassals and fine-tuned feudal arrangements to reconstruct centralized government.

Between 476 and 1000 the eastern and western halves of the old Roman Empire lost contact with each other and developed in different directions. Classical civilization faded, and three new medieval civilizations took its place. In the East the Byzantine Empire, with its capital at Constantinople, preserved classical literature, but used it to nourish a passionately Christian culture. Religion also pro- *vided the means for uniting the Arabs and sending them forth to conquer an empire that soon stretched from Spain to China. Islamic culture, as well as the Islamic state, reached its creative peak during the earlier medieval centuries while the West was still recovering from the barbarian invasions and the collapse of the ancient economy. In the West, cities diminished, and society became largely agrarian. Al-*

though the Latin church preserved some classical literature and some shreds of *Roman institutions, the West was slow to reclaim its classical heritage*

☙ Review Questions

1. What changes took place in the Frankish kingdom between its foundation and the end of Charlemagne's reign? Why did his empire break apart?

2. How and why was the history of the eastern half of the former Roman Empire so different from that of its western half? Did Justinian strengthen or weaken the Byzantine Empire? How does his reign compare to Charlemagne's?

3. What were the tenets of Islam? How were the Muslims able to build an empire so quickly? What contributions did the Muslims make to the development of western Europe?

4. How and why did feudal society begin? What were the essential features of feudalism? Could modern society "slip back" into a feudal pattern?

☙ Suggested Readings

G. BARRACLOUGH, *The Crucible of Europe: The Ninth and Tenth Centuries* (1976). Sweeping survey of political history.

H. CHADWICK, *The Early Church* (1967). Among the best treatments of early Christianity.

K. F. DREW (ed.), *The Barbarian Invasions: Catalyst of a New Order* (1970). Collection of essays that focuses the issues.

H. FICHTENAU, *The Carolingian Empire: The Age of Charlemagne*, trans. by Peter Munz (1964). Strongest on political history of the era.

F. L. GANSHOF, *Feudalism*, trans. by Philip Grierson (1964). The most profound brief analysis of the subject.

R. HODGES AND D. WHITEHOUSE, *Mohammed, Charlemagne and the Origins of Europe* (1982). For the social and economic history of early medieval Europe.

A. HOURANI, *A History of the Arab Peoples* (1991). A comprehensive text that includes an excellent overview of the origins and early history of Islam.

C. MANGO, *Byzantium: The Empire of New Rome* (1980). Perhaps the most readable account.

M. MCCORMICK, "Byzantium and the West, A.D. 700–900," in *The Cambridge Medieval History*, vol. 2: *The Early Medieval West 700–900* (1993). Up-to-date framing of events and political developments.

H. PIRENNE, *A History of Europe, I: From the End of the Roman World in the West to the Beginnings of the Western States*, trans. by Bernhard Maill (1958). Comprehensive survey, with now-controversial views on the demise of Western trade and cities in the early Middle Ages.

S. RUNCIMAN, *Byzantine Civilization* (1970). Succinct, comprehensive account by a master.

R. W. SOUTHERN, *The Making of the Middle Ages* (1973). Originally published in 1953, but still a fresh account by an imaginative historian.

S. WEMPLE, *Women in Frankish Society: Marriage and the Cloister, 500–900* (1981). What marriage and the cloister meant to women in these early centuries.

L. WHITE, JR., *Medieval Technology and Social Change* (1962). Often-fascinating account of the way primitive technology changed life.

7

The High Middle Ages (1000–1300): The Ascendancy of the Church and the Rise of States

KEY TOPICS

✦ Germany's Saxon dynasty and the Holy Roman Empire

✦ A movement to reform the church and free it from political domination by kings and emperors

✦ The emergence of strong national monarchies in England and France

✦ The fragmentation of Germany, the conclusion of a struggle for supremacy between the Hohenstaufen dynasty and the papacy

The High Middle Ages (1000–1300) was a period of political expansion and consolidation and of intellectual flowering and synthesis. With respect to the develop- *ment of Western institutions, this may have been a more creative era than the Italian Renaissance or the German Reformation.*

The borders of western Europe were secured against foreign invaders, and Europeans, who had long been the prey of foreign powers, mounted a military and economic offensive against the East. The rulers of England and France established nuclei for nation-states by adapting feudal principles of government to the creation of centralized political realms. Parliaments and popular assemblies emerged in some places to enable the propertied classes to influence the development of the new monarchies. Germany and Italy—the Holy Roman Empire—were the great exceptions to the trend toward political consolidation. They remained fragmented until modern times.

The High Middle Ages also saw the establishment of the distinctive Western custom of separating church and state. By asserting monarchical authority over the church, the popes prevented it from being split up by and absorbed into Europe's emerging states. The cost to the papacy was the charge that it was diverting the church from its spiritual mission into the murky world of politics.

✑ Otto I and the Revival of the Empire

Unifying Germany

In 918 the duke of Saxony, Henry I ("the Fowler," d. 936), founded the Saxon dynasty—Germany's first non-Frankish monarchy. Henry reversed the process of political fragmentation that had set in with the decline of the Carolingian Empire. He consolidated the duchies of Swabia, Bavaria, Saxony, Franconia, and Lotharingia and checked the invasions of the Hungarians and the Danes.

The German state that Henry bequeathed to his son Otto I, ("the Great," r. 936–973), was the strongest kingdom in Europe. In 951 Otto invaded Italy and proclaimed himself its king. In 955 he defeated the Hungarians at Lechfeld. This secured German borders against barbarian attack and established the frontiers of western Europe.

Embracing the Church

Otto secured the power of the throne by refusing to allow Germany's dukes to turn their duchies (like lesser fiefs) into hereditary properties. He also diminished the role powerful lay lords played in his government by appointing bishops and abbots of monasteries to administer his lands and be his agents. Clergy were more likely than laymen to be sympathetic to his plans to restore imperial authority, and, unlike laymen, they could not marry and pass on to their sons the lands they held from the king. The church—sensing no conflict between its spiritual and political duties—eagerly embraced the wealth and power Otto pressed on it.

In 961 Otto rescued Pope John XII (955–964) from a scuffle with the Italian nobility, and on February 2, 962, the pope bestowed the lapsed imperial title on Germany's king. Otto's intervention in Italian politics increased his power over the church. Otto appointed the higher clergy and declared himself

910	*Monastery of Cluny founded*
955	*Otto I defeats the Hungarians*
1059	*Papal elections by the College of Cardinals*
1066	*Norman Conquest of England*
1075–1122	*Investiture Controversy*
1095–1099	*First Crusade captures Jerusalem*
1144	*Islamic armies reconquer Edessa*
1152	*Hohenstaufen dynasty founded*
1154	*Plantagenet dynasty founded*
1187	*Jerusalem reconquered by Saladin*
1189–1192	*Third Crusade (Richard the Lion-Hearted)*
1202	*Fourth Crusade (Constantinople)*
1209	*Albigensian Crusade*
1214	*Battle of Bouvines*
1215	*Fourth Lateran Council; Magna Carta*
1257	*Imperial electoral college established*

special "protector" of the Papal States. When Pope John belatedly recognized the royal web in which he had become entangled, he joined a plot against the new emperor. Otto promptly ordered an ecclesiastical synod to depose John and to decree that no pope take office without first swearing allegiance to the emperor. Otto's popes ruled at his pleasure.

The Italian interests that Otto bequeathed to his successors—Otto II (r. 973–983) and Otto III (r. 983–1002)—distracted them from events in Germany, and they allowed their German base to disintegrate. It had been unwise to dream of empire before monarchy was firmly in place. As the fledgling empire began to crumble in the first quarter of the eleventh century, the papacy seized the opportunity to reassert its independence.

⌁ The Reviving Catholic Church

The Cluny Reform Movement

In the tenth century a campaign designed to reform the church by liberating the clergy from the control of the feudal nobility was launched by a monastery in east-central France. Since the last days of the Roman Empire, monks—the least worldly of the clergy—had been the church's most popular advocates. Their educations were the best available, the relics and rituals they maintained were believed to have magical potency, and the religious ideals embodied in their way of life set the standard for Christian society.

In 910 William the Pious, duke of Aquitaine, founded a new monastery at Cluny that was pledged to maintaining the strictest observance of the Benedictine Rule and to restoring the purest liturgical practices. The Cluniac re-

A portion of the Romanesque abbey church of Cluny, reconstructed between 1080 and 1225. In the twelfth century it was Europe's largest church (555 feet long). [Adros Studio]

formers claimed that the church could not reach its full spiritual potential so long as laymen had the power to appoint and dominate clerics. The lords who endowed the Cluniac houses gave them complete independence, and the abbots who ran them were sincere churchmen who enforced the strictest religious discipline.

Cluniac ideals spread from the monastery to the parish, for the reformers argued that the "secular clergy" (those serving the *saeculum,* the "world") ought to adopt the ascetic lifestyle of the "regular" clergy (those living by a *regula,* a monastic "rule"). They also insisted that bishops be freed from the authority of feudal governments and made accountable only to an independent papacy.

Men trained at Cluny were dispatched to reform monasteries throughout France and Italy. Thanks to aggressive abbots, like Saint Odo (926–946), Cluny acquired nearly 1,500 dependent cloisters and took the lead in various social reform movements. In the late ninth and early tenth centuries, Cluny inspired the "Peace of God" movement. This was an attempt to ease the suffering caused by the endemic warfare that plagued medieval society. It threatened excommunication for all soldiers who attacked members of non-combatant groups—women, peasants, merchants, and clergy. A "Truce of God" was subsequently proclaimed. It prohibited combat during part of each week (Wednesday night to Monday morning) and in all holy seasons.

During the reign of Emperor Henry III (r. 1039–1056), Cluniac reformers won high offices in the church. Pope Leo IX (1049–1054) appointed them to key administrative posts in Rome, and they encouraged him to suppress *simony* (the selling of church offices) and to enforce celibacy among parish priests. The papacy itself, however, continued to be dominated by powerful laymen. Leo IX was himself appointed by Henry III. In the course of his reign, Henry deposed three popes who were pawns of the Roman aristocracy.

When Henry died, he left the empire to an underage son, Henry IV (r. 1056–1106). Reform-minded popes took advantage of the weakness of the boy king's regents to assert their independence. Pope Stephen IX (1057–1058) reigned without seeking imperial confirmation of his title, and in 1059 Pope Nicholas II (1059–1061) decreed that a body of high church officials (the college of cardinals) would henceforth choose the popes. The procedures that were developed—and which are still followed—were designed to prevent the Italian nobles and the German kings from interfering in papal elections. The reformers made the papacy an independent, self-perpetuating ecclesiastical monarchy.

The Investiture Struggle: Gregory VII and Henry IV

The German monarchy did not react to the church's new policies until the reign of Pope Gregory VII (1073–1085), a fierce advocate of Cluny's reforms. In 1075 Gregory condemned "lay investiture," the appointment of a clergyman to a church office by a layman. The pope's decree attacked the foundations of imperial government. Since the days of Otto I, German kings had preferred to use bishops rather than lay nobles to administer state lands. If the king lost the right to appoint men to ecclesiastical office, he lost the power to choose some of the most important agents of his government. By prohibiting lay investiture the pope proclaimed the spiritual nature of the episcopacy, but he failed to recognize that the church's religious offices had long since become entwined with the secular offices of the state.

Henry opposed Gregory's action on the grounds that it violated a well-founded tradition on which imperial authority rested. But the pope had important allies. The German nobles were eager for opportunities to undercut their king, for his strength threatened their independence. When German bishops loyal to Henry assembled at Worms in January 1076 to repudiate Gregory, Gregory excommunicated Henry and absolved his subjects from their oaths of allegiance to him. This gave the German magnates an excuse to rebel against Henry and forced Henry to come to terms with Gregory. Henry crossed the Alps in mid-winter to reach Gregory's castle at Canossa. There he reportedly stood barefoot in the snow for three days until the pope agreed to absolve him.

The pope only appeared to win, for Henry's absolution deprived his nobles

A twelfth-century German manuscript portrays the struggle between Emperor Henry IV and Pope Gregory VII. In the top panel, Henry installs the puppet pope Clement III and drives Gregory from Rome. Below, Gregory dies in exile. The artist was a monk, his sympathies were with Gregory, not Henry. [Thuringer Universitäts- und Landesbibliothek, Jena]

of their excuse for continuing their rebellion. The king regrouped his forces and regained much of his power. In March 1080, Gregory excommunicated Henry once again, but this time the German nobles refused to rise to the bait. Four years later Henry drove Gregory into exile and placed his own man, Clement III, on the papal throne.

The investiture controversy ended in 1122 with a compromise spelled out by the Concordat of Worms. Emperor Henry V (r. 1106–1125) agreed to cease investing bishops with the ring and staff that symbolized spiritual office. In return, Pope Calixtus II (1119–1124) recognized the emperor's right to be present at episcopal consecrations and to preside at the ceremonies that bestowed fiefs on bishops. The old church–state "back scratching" continued, but now on a basis that made the church at least look like an independent organization. The pope's attempts to weaken the emperor did little to promote freedom for the church. As the power of emperors declined, Germany's feudal nobles grew stronger and better able to impose their wills on the clergy.

The First Crusades

What the Cluny reform was to the clergy the Crusades to the Holy Land were to the laity: an outlet for the religious zeal and self-confidence that invigorated Europe in the High Middle Ages.

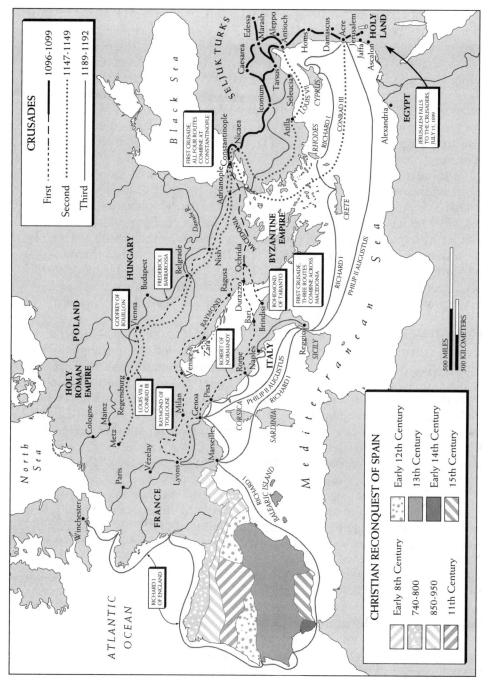

MAP 7-1 The Early Crusades *Routes taken by several leaders of the Crusades during the first century of the movement are shown.*

Late in the eleventh century, Alexius I Comnenus, emperor of Constantinople, appealed to the Christian West for help against the Seljuk Turks. At the council of Clermont in 1095, Pope Urban II answered this appeal by proclaiming the First Crusade (see Map 7-1). The Crusade was popular with different people for different reasons. By calling the Crusade, the pope was able to show that he truly was the West's spiritual leader and to gain leverage in dealing with the Eastern church. The departure of large numbers of warring nobles eased the task of maintaining the peace in Europe, and hordes of restless young knights were enthralled by the opportunity to enrich themselves from foreign conquests. Many were the younger sons of noblemen who, in an age of growing population and limited land, had few prospects of obtaining fiefs at home.

Although motives were mixed, the First Crusade owed more to genuine piety than the mercenary ventures organized by the later Crusaders. Popes recruited Crusaders by promising those who died in battle a plenary indulgence—a complete remission of punishment for their unrepented mortal sins and from all suffering in purgatory. The Crusaders were driven by the passions of a Holy War, a struggle against a hated infidel who had seized control of the most sacred Christian shrines. The Crusade was also the ultimate pilgrimage to the Holy Land. The desire to be part of it even affected those who did not go East. They crusaded at home by launching the first massacres of Europe's Jews.

The First Victory. Three great armies—perhaps 100,000 men—gathered in France, Germany, and Italy. In 1097 they converged on Constantinople by different routes. They were not the disciplined professional force the East had hoped to enlist. The Eastern emperor was suspicious of their motives, and the common people whom they pillaged hardly considered them Christian brothers. Nonetheless, these fanatical Crusaders accomplished what no Eastern army had ever done. They defeated one Seljuk army after another and on July 15, 1099, captured Jerusalem. The Crusaders' success was due to the superior military technology the West had evolved and to the inability of the Muslim states to cooperate in mounting an effective resistance.

The Crusaders set up governments in Jerusalem, Edessa, and Antioch. Godfrey of Bouillon (and after him his brother Baldwin) was chosen to rule a new kingdom of Jerusalem. The pretentious claims of the "Crusader States" ignored the fact that they were little more than precarious European outposts in a Muslim world. This became clear as the Muslims rallied and took the offensive against the "savages" who had invaded their lands. The Crusaders erected castles and hunkered down in a state of perpetual siege. The once fierce warriors became international businessmen promoting trade between East and West. Some, like the Knights Templars, built huge fortunes. The Templars were an order of soldier-monks devoted to protecting pilgrims to the Holy Land. Their services to travelers led them into the profitable fields of banking and money-lending and made their monastic order one of Europe's greatest commercial institutions.

The Ultimate Defeat. After forty years the Latin hold on the East began to weaken. Edessa fell to Islamic armies in 1144, and Bernard of Clairvaux (1091–1153), Christendom's most influential monastic leader, called for a Second Crusade. It was a dismal failure.

In October 1187 Saladin (r. 1138–1193), king of Egypt and Syria, conquered Jerusalem, and Europe responded with a Third Crusade (1189–1192). It enlisted the most powerful western rulers: Emperor Frederick Barbarossa; Richard the Lion-Hearted, king of England; and Philip Augustus, king of France. Despite its resources, the Third Crusade degenerated into a tragicomedy. Frederick Barbarossa drowned while fording a stream in Asia Minor. Richard the Lion-Hearted and Philip Augustus reached the outskirts of Jerusalem, but their intense personal rivalry doomed their campaign. Philip Augustus quickly returned to France to prey on Richard's continental possessions. When this forced Richard finally to head home, he was captured by the Emperor Henry VI. (Richard's brother-in-law, Henry "the Lion," duke of Saxony, was the emperor's mortal enemy.) England's bill for its king's Eastern adventure was greatly increased by the ransom Germany demanded for his release.

The Crusades failed to achieve their political and religious objectives. The Holy Land remained under Muslim control into the modern era. Economically and culturally, however, the Crusades were more constructive. They stimulated trade between the East and the West, and the merchants of Venice, Pisa, and Genoa, who followed the Crusaders, succeeded at sea where the Crusades failed on land at challenging Islamic domination. Wherever trading centers sprang up, cultural as well as economic exchanges were made.

The Pontificate of Innocent III (1198–1216)

The pope who inaugurated the Crusades hoped that they would unite Europe behind the leader of its church. The papal dream of establishing some kind of supremacy over the nations that were emerging in Europe during the High Middle Ages reached its apogee during the reign of Pope Innocent III.

The New Papal Monarchy. Under Innocent, the papacy became a great secular power with a treasury and a bureaucracy equal to that of any king. Innocent increased ecclesiastical taxation—both in amount and in effectiveness of collection. A tax known as Peter's pence was imposed on all but the poorest laymen. The clergy paid the pope an income tax of 2.5 percent—as well as *annates* (the forfeiture to the papacy of the first year's income from a new benefice) and fees for the bestowal of things like the *pallium* (the stole that was the archbishop's symbol of office). Innocent also reserved to the pope the right to grant absolution for many kinds of sins and religious crimes. The penalties imposed were frequently monetary payments to the papacy.

Crusades in France and the East. Innocent did not shrink from using the Crusade, the church's weapon against Islam, to suppress dissent in Europe. Protests were raised against the church as it became increasingly secular and material-istic, and the papacy accused some of its critics of heresy. Heresy was often the laity's response to clerical greed and negligence.

In 1209 Innocent launched a Crusade to exterminate the Albigensians (residents of Albi in France), also known as the Cathars ("pure ones"). These people advocated a simple, pious way of life modeled on the New Testament's description of Jesus and his apostles. But they rejected important Christian doc-trines. They were dualists. They denied that the wrathful deity of the Old Tes-tament who created the sinful material world was the same god as the heav-enly Father to whom Jesus prayed. Their belief that the flesh was the source of sin and a threat to the spirit led them to reject the Christian claim that God was incarnate in Jesus—and to assert that the true church was an invisible, spir-itual entity and not the worldly institution headed by the pope. The more rad-ical Cathars recommended celibacy, contraception, or abortion to prevent more immortal souls from being captured and imprisoned in sinful matter. (The Catholic Church's positions on social issues like contraception and abortion were shaped in this environment.) Paradoxically, the Cathars' dualism might also be used to justify moral laxity. If the flesh and the spirit are fundamentally different and separate realities, it matters little what the former does.

Since the Albigensian lands were wealthy, knights from northern France were eager to enlist in the pope's Crusade. The church gave them an excuse to seize their neighbors' lands. After a succession of massacres and a special cam-paign that King Louis VIII of France headed in 1226 utterly devastated the pros-perous Albigensian districts, Pope Gregory IX (1227–1241) sent in the Inquisi-tion to root out any heretics who remained. An *inquisition* was a formal ecclesiastical tribunal set up to detect and punish heresy. Bishops had used in-quisitions in their dioceses since the mid-twelfth century, but Innocent III cre-ated a centralized court of inquisition that dispatched papal legates to preside at trials and executions throughout Europe.

Innocent also called the fourth of the Crusades intended for the Holy Land. In 1202 some 30,000 Crusaders gathered in Venice, planning to sail for Egypt. Many were poor soldiers of fortune who were unable to pay the price the Vene-tians demanded for their transport. Venice persuaded them to work off their passage by conquering Zara, a Christian city that was one of Venice's commer-cial rivals. To the shock of Pope Innocent III, the Crusaders obliged and then al-lowed Venice to seduce them into storming the most important Christian city in the East: Constantinople.

Although the assault on Constantinople in 1204 was an embarrassment to the pope, the papacy came to terms with the Venetians and shared the spoils. One of Innocent's confidants was appointed patriarch of Constantinople and or-dered to win the Greeks and the Slavs to the Roman church. Westerners re-tained control of Constantinople until 1261, when the Genoese, who envied Venice's coup, helped the exiled Eastern emperor, Michael Paleologus, recap-ture the city. The half-century of occupation did nothing to reunite the church or improve relations between East and West.

The Fourth Lateran Council. At the Fourth Lateran Council, which met in 1215, Innocent defined crucial disciplines and doctrines that the church was to enforce throughout Europe. Most significant for the development of Catholicism was the council's endorsement of the doctrine of transubstantiation as the church's explanation of the miracle of the Eucharist. *Transubstantiation* is the belief that at the moment of priestly consecration the bread and wine of the Lord's Supper become the body and blood of Christ. This idea was consistent with the popular piety of the twelfth century. But since the power to perform this miracle was reserved to priests, it also helped Innocent achieve his goal of enhancing the power of the clergy over the laity. This was also the effect of the council's formalization of the sacrament of Penance and its order to every adult Christian to confess and take communion at least once a year—usually at Easter.

Franciscans and Dominicans. The interest the laity took in religious devotion was particularly intense at the turn of the twelfth century. It won recruits for new movements that preached a life of poverty in imitation of Christ. This idea was not necessarily heretical, but it could promote criticism of the church that caused groups like the Waldensians, Beguines, and Beghards to fall under suspicion of heresy.

By licensing two new religious orders—the Franciscans and the Dominicans—Innocent fought fire with fire. Unlike the regular monks, these orders of *friars* ("brothers") were *mendicants* ("beggars"). Refusing to accept land and endowments, they stayed in the world, preaching and caring for the poor and supporting themselves by begging and working. Their saintly behavior did much to refute the heretics who argued that Christian unworldliness was incompatible with obedience to the orthodox church. The *tertiaries*, or "Third Orders," created by these groups provided refuges for pious laypersons whose desire to live according to high religious ideals might otherwise have led them into heresies.

The Franciscan Order was founded in 1210 by Saint Francis of Assisi (1182–1226), the son of a rich cloth merchant. The Dominican Order, the Order of Preachers, was founded in 1216 by Saint Dominic (1170–1221), a well-educated Spanish cleric. Since both orders reported directly to the pope and not to any local bishops, they provided the central government of the church with an army of dedicated servants who could be dispatched on special missions.

Pope Gregory IX (1227–1241) canonized Saint Francis only two years after Francis's death. But the pope also turned the Franciscans from the path their founder had charted for them. The pope declared that a nomadic life of strict poverty and extreme asceticism was both impractical and unbiblical. Most Franciscans accepted the pope's modification of their order's rule, but a radical branch, the Spiritual Franciscans, resisted and drifted into heresy.

The Dominicans were dedicated to combating heresy. They preached, staffed the offices of the Inquisition, and taught at universities. The man who most furthered their mission was the great theologian, Thomas Aquinas

(d. 1274). His synthesis of faith and reason has been embraced by the Catholic Church as the definitive statement of its beliefs.

◇ England and France: Hastings (1066) to Bouvines (1214)

While Germany and Italy were engaged in struggles between popes and emperors, new dynasties were establishing themselves in England and France. They laid the foundations for medieval Europe's strongest nations.

The old Roman province of Britain became England ("Anglo-land") as Germans from the tribes of the Angles and Saxons took it over at the start of the Middle Ages. When the last of the their kings, Edward the Confessor, died childless in 1066, the English throne was claimed by his distant relative, Duke William of Normandy (d. 1087). The Anglo-Saxon assembly—which, in accordance with the ancient traditions of the German tribes, had the right to enthrone kings—preferred a native son, Harold Godwinsson. William invaded England, and at Hastings on October 14, 1066, he destroyed Harold and decimated the Anglo-Saxon nobility.

William the Conqueror

By judiciously combining continental feudalism and Anglo-Saxon custom, William constructed the most effective monarchy in Europe. To discover what the country he had conquered was worth, he carried out a county-by-county survey of its people, animals, and implements. The results, which were compiled as the *Domesday Book* (1080–1086), offer a uniquely detailed description of a medieval kingdom. William compelled every man of property to become his vassal and to hold all land in fief from the king. The Norman nobles who replaced the Anglo-Saxon magnates had no following among their new subjects. They realized, therefore, that they needed the help of a strong leader, and they rarely challenged their king. William's government was further strengthened by unique Anglo-Saxon tax and court systems, and the king honored the Anglo-Saxon tradition of *parleying*—that is, of holding conferences with people who had vested interests in royal policies. By consulting with his nobles on affairs of state, William kept England on track toward the creation of the parliamentary traditions that have shaped the constitutions of so many modern states.

Henry II

The English monarchy continued strong under William's sons and heirs, William Rufus (r. 1087–1100) and Henry I (r. 1100–1135). When Henry died without a male heir, a civil war erupted that threatened to undo the Conqueror's work. But a compromise between the factions resulted in the accession of Henry II (r. 1154–1189), son of the duke of Anjou and Matilda, daughter

William the Conqueror on horseback urging his troops into combat with the English at the Battle of Hastings (October 14, 1066). From the Bayeux Tapestry, about 1073–1083. [Giraudon/Art Resource, N.Y.]

of Henry I. Henry II established the Plantagenet dynasty, the family name of the Angevin (or Anjouan) kings who ruled England until the death of Richard III in 1485. Henry, by his own rights of inheritance and those of his wife, Eleanor of Aquitaine (ca. 1122–1204), controlled much more of France than did the king of France. Henry also conquered a part of Ireland and made the king of Scotland take an oath of homage to him. The French king, Louis VII, who had good reason to fear these developments, tried to contain the English. French efforts to drive them from the continent were ultimately successful—but not until the mid-fifteenth century and the end of the Hundred Years' War.

Eleanor of Aquitaine and Court Culture

Eleanor of Aquitaine had been married to King Louis VII of France before she wed King Henry II of England in 1152, and she was a powerful influence on the politics and culture of both nations. Women of Eleanor's generation were beginning to venture into the masculine fields of politics and business, and she blazed the way. She insisted on accompanying her first husband on the Second Crusade, and she stirred up so much trouble for her second that from 1179 until his death in 1189 he kept her under house arrest.

After marrying Henry, Eleanor established a court in Angers, the chief town of Anjou, that became a center of patronage for musicians and poets. The troubadour Bernart de Ventadorn composed many of the popular love songs of the period in her honor. From 1154 to 1170, the queen resided in England, but then she separated from Henry and moved to Poitiers to live with her daughter Marie, the countess of Champagne. Poitiers popularized a new fad among the aristocracy: "courtly love." The troubadours who elaborated the rules of the game composed erotic stories to satirize physical passion. They contrasted carnal love with "courteous" love, a spiritual passion for a lady that ennobled her lover. Chrétien de Troyes's stories of King Arthur and the Knights of the Round Table—and of Sir Lancelot's tragic, illicit love for Arthur's wife, Guinevere—are the most famous products of the movement.

Popular Rebellion and Magna Carta

Henry II was a strong king who believed in autocratic monarchy. He insisted that the church operate within parameters set by the state, and he spelled these out in 1164 in the *Constitutions of Clarendon*. The Constitutions limited the right to appeal cases from England to the papal court, subjected clergy to the king's courts, and gave the king control over the election of bishops. The archbishop of Canterbury, Thomas à Becket (1118?–1170), who was once Henry's compliant chancellor, fled England rather than accept the Constitutions. He was induced to return in 1170, but his continued opposition to the king prompted some of Henry's men to assassinate him. The church leapt at the opportunity to canonize Becket (1172) and to use his martyrdom to bolster its case for freedom from state control.

Henry was followed on the throne by two of his sons: Richard the Lion-Hearted (r. 1189–1199) and John (r. 1199–1216). Neither was a success. Richard imposed ruinous taxation to fund the disastrous Third Crusade and died fighting to recover lands the French had taken from him while he was in the East. In 1209 Pope Innocent III excommunicated his successor, John, in a dispute over the appointment of an archbishop for Canterbury. To extricate himself from a mess of his own making and to win support for a war with France, John surrendered to the pope and declared his kingdom a papal fief. John's efforts to restore his father's Angevin empire foundered, however, when the French defeated him at Bouvines in 1214. England's disillusioned barons then rebelled and forced their king to accept limitations on royal authority.

A document known simply as the *Magna Carta* (the "Great Charter") spelled out the terms that John and his subjects agreed to in 1215. Among other things, the king promised not to arrest and hold people without giving his reasons, and he acknowledged the necessity of consulting with representatives of the propertied classes before imposing new taxes. Magna Carta was designed to put some constraints on monarchy without fatally weakening it. In the short run, it had little effect, for John's successors largely ignored it. But Magna Carta helped keep alive the traditions that undergird modern English law.

Philip II Augustus

In England during the High Middle Ages, the propertied classes had to fight a strong monarchy to secure their rights. In France the shoe was on the other foot. There, weak kings were confronted by powerful subjects who opposed the growth of monarchy.

In 987, when the Carolingian line came to an end in France, the French nobles chose Hugh Capet, count of Paris, to be king. Although his descendants managed to hang on to the title—and to create a "Capetian" dynasty—for the next two centuries the great feudal princes were France's real rulers. The early Capetian kings even had a struggle to control their own royal domain, the area around Paris and the Île-de-France to the northeast. By the time Philip II (1180–1223) came to the throne, the Capetians had secured hereditary rights to the crown and made Paris the center of French government and culture. Only then was it possible for them to begin to impose their will on their vassals.

In a way the Norman conquest of England in 1066 helped the Capetian kings to unify France and build a true national monarchy. As the Plantagenet dynasty extended its control over French territory, the Capetians were able to enlist support from powerful nobles who considered the English king the greater threat to their independence. The Capetians also won the help of the wealthy merchant class that was beginning to appear in France's reviving cities.

The king of England was at a disadvantage in dealing with the king of France, for, as duke of Normandy, he was a vassal of the French king. A skillful politician like Philip II Augustus was able to exploit the ambiguity of this relationship. By accusing his English rival of violating the duties of vassalage, Philip could enlist his other vassals in campaigns to repossess the English king's French fiefs. During the reigns of Richard the Lion-Hearted and John, France's armies seized all the territories the English had occupied in France (with the exception of part of Aquitaine).

King John of England enlisted the help of the German emperor Otto IV (r. 1198–1215) against France in what became Europe's first multinational war. France won decisively at the battle at Bouvines in Flanders on July 27, 1214. The victory helped the French king to unite his people, and it greatly weakened his opponents. Otto IV fell from power, and John's subjects welcomed him home with the rebellion that culminated in Magna Carta.

∽ France in the Thirteenth Century: The Reign of Louis IX

The growth of Capetian royal power under Philip Augustus seemed to receive divine confirmation during the reign of his grandson Louis IX (r. 1226–1270). Louis embodied the medieval view of the perfect ruler, and he was canonized shortly after his death. The saintly king was an ascetic whose ethics were far superior to those of his royal and papal contemporaries. But he was also what his generation expected a king to be, a decisive leader and an enthusiastic soldier.

Generosity Abroad

Some of Louis's decisions suggest naiveté or an overly scrupulous conscience. Although he could have driven the English off the continent, he refused to take advantage of King Henry III's weakness. In 1259 he negotiated a generous compromise (the Treaty of Paris) to end the long-simmering dispute between England and France. Had he ruthlessly confiscated English territories in France, he might have prevented the resumption of hostilities between the two nations and spared Europe the bloodshed of the Hundred Years' War.

Louis remained officially aloof while the papacy fought with Frederick II, an emperor from Germany's Hohenstaufen dynasty. But after Frederick's death, Louis's brother, Charles of Anjou, entered the fray on the pope's side, exterminated Frederick's dynasty, and seized its lands in Italy and Sicily. The pope rewarded him by crowning him king of Sicily.

Order and Excellence at Home

Louis's greatest achievement was to improve the government of France. He used the efficient bureaucracy that his predecessors had developed to exploit their subjects to provide his people with more secure order and justice. He sent out auditors (*enquêteurs*) to monitor royal officials—especially the *baillis* and *prévôts* whom Philip Augustus had appointed to run the government's grassroots offices. He abolished private warfare among the nobles and serfdom on the lands of the royal domain. He gave his subjects the judicial right of appeal from local to higher courts, and he made the tax system more equitable. The services the French people received from their king generated enthusiasm for the monarchy and for the nationhood it symbolized.

Developments of other kinds helped to shape a French national identity during Louis's reign. His was the golden age of Scholasticism—a time when thinkers like Thomas Aquinas and the Franciscan scholar Bonaventure made the University of Paris Europe's intellectual center. France became the showcase for monastic reform, chivalry, and the new Gothic style in art and architecture that had been pioneered by Suger, abbot of St. Denis and advisor to Louis IX's great-grandfather, Louis VII. France began to set the cultural standard for Europe, a pattern that continued into the modern era.

Louis's virtues reflected medieval ideals of kingship. He was something of a religious fanatic. He supported the work of the Inquisition, and he personally led the last two of the great Crusades for the Holy Land. Both were failures, but Louis's death of a fever during the second of his holy wars only enhanced his reputation as a saintly king. His successors pointed to him to confirm their claim that God had bestowed a divine right to rule on the Capetians.

❧ The Hohenstaufen Empire (1152–1272)

During the twelfth and thirteenth centuries, while stable governments were developing in both England and France, something quite different happened within the Holy Roman Empire (Germany, Burgundy, and northern Italy). There (see Map 7-2), disunity and feuding created a legacy of political fragmentation that endured into modern times.

MAP 7-2 Germany and Italy in the Middle Ages
The Holy Roman Empire embraced hundreds of independent territories that the emperor ruled only in name. The papacy controlled the area around Rome and tried to enforce its will on Romagna. Under the Hohenstaufens (mid-twelfth to mid-thirteenth centuries), German rulers briefly extended their power to southern Italy and Sicily.

Frederick I Barbarossa

The Investiture Controversy, in which the popes had challenged the right of emperors to appoint the higher clergy, had weakened Germany's kings and strengthened its barons. The church was unable to prevent the German princes from dominating episcopal appointments and appropriating their rich endowments.

Imperial authority revived with the accession to the throne of Frederick I Barbarossa (r. 1152–1190), founder of the Hohenstaufen dynasty. Frederick had some help in laying a strong foundation for a new empire. Disaffection with the incessant squabbling of the feudal princes was widespread, and there was growing resentment of the theocratic pretensions of the papacy. At the University of Bologna a scholar named Irnerius (d. 1125) was also reviving the study of Roman law (Justinian's *Code*). Frederick found this useful, for Roman law promoted the centralization of states and provided a secular foundation for imperial power that minimized the significance of papal coronation.

From Frederick's base of operation in Switzerland, the bridge between Germany and Italy, he conducted a relatively successful campaign to regain control over the German nobility. In 1180 his strongest rival, Henry the Lion (d. 1195), duke of Saxony, fell from power and was exiled to Normandy. Although Frederick was not strong enough to intervene in the internal affairs of Germany's great duchies, he was vigilant in enforcing his rights as their feudal overlord. This kept memories of royal authority alive until the king was strong enough to risk a showdown with his greater vassals.

Italy proved to be the major obstacle to realization of Frederick's imperial dreams. In 1155 Frederick restored Rome to Pope Adrian IV (1154–1159) after a religious revolutionary, Arnold of Brescia (d. 1155), had wrested control of the city from the papacy. Frederick's reward was a papal coronation which he believed gave him title to Italy. Although the imperial Diet of Roncaglia in 1158 officially sanctioned Frederick's claim to Italy, the Italian people, particularly those of Lombardy, refused to accept the governors he appointed.

Just as this challenge to royal authority was being mounted, one of Europe's most skilled lawyers, Cardinal Roland, was elected Pope Alexander III (1159–1181). Frederick soon found himself at war with the pope, the city of Milan, and the kingdom of Sicily. In 1167, the combined forces of the northern Italian cities drove him back into Germany, and a decade later (1176) an Italian army soundly defeated him at Legnano. In the Peace of Constance in 1183 Frederick recognized the claims of the Lombard cities to rights of self-rule.

Henry VI and the Sicilian Connection

Frederick's reign ended with stalemate in Germany and defeat in Italy. But in the last years of his life, he discovered a new opportunity for his dynasty. The Norman ruler of the kingdom of Sicily, William II (r. 1166–1189), asked Frederick for help in launching a campaign for the conquest of Constantinople. In 1186 an alliance was sealed by a marriage between Frederick's son, the future Henry VI (r. 1190–1197), and Constance, heiress to Sicily.

Sicily was a fatal acquisition for the Hohenstaufen kings, for it tempted them to sacrifice their territorial base in northern Europe for projects in Italy. It also stirred up greater resistance to them in Italy. By encircling Rome the Hohenstaufens convinced the papacy that the church's survival hinged on the empire's destruction.

When Henry VI came to the throne in 1190, he faced a multitude of enemies: a hostile papacy; independent German princes; and an England whose adventurous king, Richard the Lion-Hearted, was encouraged to plot against Henry by the exiled duke of Saxony, Henry the Lion. In 1194, Constance bore her husband a son, the future Frederick II. To strengthen his dynasty, Henry campaigned vigorously for recognition of the boy's hereditary right to the imperial throne. The German princes were reluctant to abandon the custom of electing emperors, and the encircled papacy was determined to prevent anything that might secure Hohenstaufen power.

Otto IV and the Welf Interregnum

After Henry's premature death in September 1197, his widow tried to save her young son's Sicilian legacy by arranging for him to become a ward of the papacy. The boy's uncle, Philip of Swabia, claimed the title of German king, but the Welf family, which opposed the Hohenstaufens, backed a rival—Otto of Brunswick, the son of the troublesome Henry the Lion. Richard of England supported Otto; the French supported the Hohenstaufens; and the papacy switched its allegiance back and forth to prevent anyone from surrounding Rome. The result was anarchy and civil war.

Otto outlasted Philip and won general recognition in Germany and coronation as emperor by Pope Innocent III (1198–1215). Within four months of his coronation (October 1209), the wind suddenly changed. Otto attacked Sicily, and this convinced Innocent that he was a threat to Rome. The pope excommunicated him and raised up a rival for his throne.

Frederick II

Pope Innocent's ward, the Hohenstaufen prince Frederick, was now of age, and unlike Otto he had a hereditary claim to the throne. In December 1212, the pope, Philip Augustus of France, and Otto's German enemies arranged for Frederick to be crowned king of the Romans in Mainz. When Philip Augustus defeated the armies of Otto and John of England at the battle of Bouvines in 1214, the way was cleared for Frederick II to mount the imperial throne in Charlemagne's city of Aachen (1215). The young ruler's allies probably expected him to be their puppet, but he quickly demonstrated an independent streak.

Frederick, who had grown up in Sicily, disliked Germany. He spent only nine of the thirty-eight years of his reign in Germany, and he wanted only one thing from the German princes: the imperial title for himself and his sons. To secure it, he was willing to grant Germany's feudal nobility absolute authority over their domains. Frederick's lack of interest in building a centralized monarchy for Germany halted the development of the nation and condemned it to six centuries of chaotic disunity.

Frederick's policy with respect to the papacy was equally disastrous. The popes excommunicated Frederick four times and came to view him as the Antichrist, the biblical beast of the Apocalypse whose persecution of the faithful signaled the end of the world. Although Frederick abandoned Germany, he was determined to win control over Lombardy, unite it with his Sicilian kingdom, and surround Rome. This the popes were determined to prevent.

The popes won the fight with the Hohenstaufens, but their victory was Pyrrhic. The contest led Pope Innocent IV (1243–1254) to immerse the church more deeply in European politics than ever before. Wholesale secularization increased criticism of the church by religious reformers and by the patriotic champions of national monarchies. Innocent organized and led the German princes against Frederick, and German and Italian resistance kept Frederick on the defensive throughout his last years.

When Frederick died in 1250, the German monarchy died with him. The German nobility repudiated the idea of hereditary succession to the throne, and in 1257 the barons formed an electoral college that claimed the right to bestow the title "king of the Romans." This ensured that the kings they created would be their puppets.

Manfred, Frederick's illegitimate son, fought hard to save something of the Hohenstaufen legacy, but he was defeated in 1266. In 1286 Charles of Anjou, the adventurous brother of the saintly Louis IX, destroyed the last of the Hohenstaufens (Frederick's grandson Conradin). Germany temporarily ceased to meddle in Italy's affairs, but this did not free Italy from the threat of outside interference. France and, to a lesser extent, England aspired to the role Germany had tried to play in Italy.

⌁ Medieval Russia

According to legend, Vladimir (972–1015), prince of Kiev (early Russia's greatest city), decided to modernize his people by converting them to one of the world's great religions. He invited delegations from Muslims, Roman Catholics, Jews, and Greek Orthodox Christians to come to his court to make cases for their faiths. After viewing what each had to offer, Vladimir chose the Greek option. Given Kiev's proximity to Constantinople and Russia's commercial ties with the Byzantine Empire, his decision must have been a foregone conclusion.

Politics and Society

Vladimir's successor, Yaroslav the Wise (1016–1054), turned Kiev into a magnificent political and cultural center that rivaled Constantinople. After his death, however, rivalry among the Russian princes split their people into three groups: the Great Russians, the White Russians, and the Little Russians (Ukrainians). Kiev was reduced to being simply one principality among many.

The governments of the Russian states combined monarchy (a prince), aristocracy (a council of noblemen), and democracy (a popular assembly of all adult males). The broadest social division was between freemen and slaves. Freemen included clergy, army officers, boyars (wealthy landowners), townsmen, and peasants. Slaves were mostly prisoners of war. There was also a large semi-free group composed of debtors who were working off their obligations.

Mongol Rule (1243–1480)

In the thirteenth century, Mongol (or Tatar) armies swept over China, much of the Islamic world, and Russia. Ghengis Khan's forces (1155–1227) invaded Russia in 1223, and Kiev fell to the Mongol general Batu Khan in 1240. When the Mongols divided their empire, a group called the Golden Horde (a name derived from the Tatar words for the color of Batu Khan's tent) exacted tribute from the Russian cities. The Golden Horde established its seat at Sarai on the lower Volga and ruled the steppe region of what is now southern Russia. Its agents were stationed in all the principal Russian towns to oversee taxation and the conscription of soldiers.

Mongol rule distanced the Russians from Western culture. Russian women who married Mongols were influenced by Islam, the religion adopted by the Golden Horde. They began to wear veils and to lead secluded lives. But the Mongols interfered little with the political institutions and religion of their Russian subjects, and the peace they maintained and the trade contacts they established brought Russia economic benefits.

Russian Liberation

The princes of Moscow assisted the Mongols with the collection of tribute and grew wealthy in the service of their masters. When Mongol rule began to weaken, the princes added to the territory Moscow controlled. In pursuit of a policy called "the gathering of the Russian Land," they expanded the principality of Moscow by purchase, colonization, and conquest.

In 1380 Grand Duke Dimitri of Moscow (1350–1389) defeated Tatar forces at Kulikov Meadow. His victory precipitated the decline of Mongol hegemony. Another century passed before Ivan III ("the Great," d. 1505) brought all of northern Russia under Moscow's control and ended Mongol rule (1480). By the last quarter of the fourteenth century, Moscow had become the political and religious center of Russia. In 1453, when Constantinople fell to the Turks, Moscow took on a new role. It proclaimed itself the "third Rome" and the guardian of Orthodox civilization.

With borders that were finally secured at the start of the High Middle Ages, western Europe began to develop its characteristic cultural and political institutions. The map of Europe as it appears today began to take shape. England and France built centralized monarchies that unified them as modern nation-states. Germany and

Italy, however, failed to overcome the forces of feudal fragmentation.

The dream of creating a Holy Roman Empire tempted German rulers into Italy, where they made enemies of the popes and the rising commercial cities. The result was an unprecedented contest between church and state that promoted the growth of a powerful papal monarchy. The church's involvement with politics alienated kings, secularized the papacy, and increased the church's vulnerability to attack on the grounds that it was failing in its spiritual mission.

✦ Review Questions

1. How did the Saxon king Otto I rebuild the German Empire?

2. What were the main reasons for the Cluny reform movement? How do you account for its success? What was the impact of the reform on the subsequent history of the medieval church?

3. In the dispute between Pope Gregory VII and King Henry IV over the issue of lay investiture, what were the causes of the controversy, the actions of the contending parties, and the outcome of the struggle?

4. What developments in western and eastern Europe promoted the crusading movement? What impact did the Crusaders have on the West's politics, religion, and economics?

5. If France and England could coalesce into reasonably strong states, why was Germany not able to do the same?

✦ Suggested Readings

J. W. BALDWIN, *The Government of Philip Augustus* (1986). An important scholarly work.

G. BARRACLOUGH, *The Origins of Modern Germany* (1946). Dated but penetrating political narrative setting modern Germany in the perspective of the Middle Ages.

G. BARRACLOUGH, *The Medieval Papacy* (1968). Brief survey with pictures.

H. E. J. COWDREY, *Popes, Monks, and Crusaders* (1984). Re-creation of the atmosphere that gave birth to the Crusades.

J. C. HOLT, *Magna Carta*, 2nd ed. (1992). The famous document and its interpretation by succeeding generations.

E. H. KANTOROWICZ, *The King's Two Bodies* (1957). Controversial analysis of political concepts in the High Middle Ages.

H. LEYSER, *Hermits and the New Monasticism: A Study of Religious Communities in Western Europe, 1000–1150* (1984). The new power and influence of reformed monasticism.

H. E. MAYER, *The Crusades*, trans. by John Gilligham (1972). Extremely detailed; the best one-volume account.

J. B. MORRALL, *Political Thought in Medieval Times* (1962). Readable and illuminating account.

C. PETIT-DUTAILLIS, *The Feudal Monarchy in France and England from the Tenth to the Thirteenth Century*, trans. by E. D. Hunt (1964). Political narrative in great detail.

I. SPECTOR, *Russia: A New History* (1935). Admirable simplicity.

G. VERNADSKY, *A History of Russia*, I–IV (1946–1963). A graspable magisterial survey.

8

The High Middle Ages(1000–1300): People, Towns, and Universities

The Traditional Order of Life
Nobles
Clergy
Peasants

Towns and Townspeople
The Chartering of Towns
The Rise of Merchants
Challenging the Old Lords
New Models of Government
Towns and Kings

Jews in Christian Society

Schools and Universities
University of Bologna
Cathedral Schools
University of Paris
The Curriculum

Women and Children in Medieval Society
The Lives of Children

KEY TOPICS

- The major groups composing medieval society
- The rise of towns and a new merchant class
- The founding of universities and educational curriculum
- How women and children fared in the Middle Ages

From the tenth to the twelfth centuries, the effects of increasing political stability were felt in Europe. Agricultural production increased, population exploded, and trade and urban life revived. Crusades promoted contacts with foreign lands that stimulated both economic and cultural development. A new merchant class, the ancestors of modern capitalists, appeared to serve the West's growing markets, and an urban proletariat developed.

Guided by Muslim intellectuals, Western scholars began again to study classical literature. Schools and universities opened. Literacy increased among the laity, and the twelfth century witnessed a true renaissance. The creative vigor of the new European civilization was proclaimed by the awesome Gothic churches that were the supreme products of its art and science.

177

✣ The Traditional Order of Life

Medieval political theorists identified three services that were essential for society's functioning and assigned each to a separate class: protection (the knights and landed nobility), prayer (clergy), and production (peasants and village artisans). The revival of towns in the eleventh century created a fourth class: traders and merchants. They were thought of as a "middle" class, for they combined features of both the laboring and the propertied classes. Like the peasantry, they were economically productive, but they did not work the land. Like the nobility and clergy, they were rich, but they were not integrated into the institutions of feudal government. Their appearance unbalanced the old social order and ultimately caused it to collapse.

Nobles

As medieval society evolved, a landed aristocracy with special social and legal status emerged from the ranks of the feudal vassals and warrior knights. In the late Middle Ages the aristocratic class was composed of a higher and lower nobility. The higher were the great landowners and territorial magnates; the lower were petty knights with fiefs, newly rich merchants who bought country estates, and wealthy farmers whose prosperity raised them from serfdom. Land ownership was important, for it was the special mark of the nobility that they lived off the labor of others. Nobles were lords of manors. They neither tilled the soil nor engaged in commerce—activities considered beneath the dignity of aristocrats.

Warriors. In the eighth century, European warfare changed dramatically. The appearance of the stirrup enabled cavalry to rout the infantry that had dominated ancient battlefields. The stirrup gave a rider a firm mount so that he could charge an enemy and strike a blow without lofting himself off his horse. Cavalry equipment and training was expensive, so lords divided their lands up to create fiefs to support the vassals who staffed their armies. Arms thus became the nobleman's profession and war the justification for his way of life.

The code by which the nobility lived exalted strength, honor, and aggression. Nobles welcomed war as an opportunity to increase their fortunes by plunder and their reputations by acts of courage. Peace threatened them with economic stagnation and boredom. Peasants and townspeople, on the other hand, needed peace in order to prosper. Consequently, the interests of the classes conflicted, and the nobility looked down on the commoners as cowards.

The quasi-sacramental dubbing ceremony, which created a knight, marked a man's entrance into the noble class. A candidate for knighthood took a bath of ritual purification, confessed, communed, and maintained a night-long prayer vigil. A priest then blessed his standard, lance, and sword and girded him with the weapons he was to use in the defense of the church and the service of his lord. *Dubbing* (i.e., striking) on the shoulders with a sword by a senior knight raised the candidate to a state as sacred in his sphere as clerical ordination made the priest in his.

In the twelfth century, knighthood was legally restricted to men of high birth. The closing of the ranks of the nobility was a reaction to the growing wealth and power of the social-climbing commercial classes. Kings, however, maintained some social mobility by reserving the right to bestow knighthood on anyone. The sale of titles to wealthy merchants was an important source of royal revenue.

Way of Life. When not warring, noblemen honed their military skills at hunts and tournaments. Their passion for hunting was so great that they forbade commoners to take game from the forests. Peasants greatly resented being deprived of a source of free food, and anger at the nobility's hunting monopoly contributed to peasant uprisings in the late medieval period.

Tournaments sowed seeds of social disruption of a different kind. Mock battles, intended as military training, tended to get out of hand—resulting in serious bloodshed and animosity among the combatants. The church opposed tournaments as occasions for pagan revelry and senseless violence, and kings and princes finally agreed that they were a danger to public order. Henry II of England proscribed tournaments in the twelfth century, but they continued in France until the mid-sixteenth century.

During the twelfth century, distinctive standards for conduct at court ("courtesy") began to be imposed on vassals who were called to attend their lords. Thanks to the influence of powerful women like Henry II's queen, Eleanor of Aquitaine, knowledge of court etiquette became almost as important for a nobleman as battlefield expertise.

Knights were expected to be literate gentlemen, capable of praising ladies in lyric poetry. The poetry of courtly love was sprinkled with frank eroticism, and courtly poets wrote rapturously of women married to other men. But the love that ennobled a knight was usually not assumed to be the kind consummated by sexual intercourse. Court poets warned that illicit carnal love led to suffering, and the courtly love movement may actually have been an attempt to curtail the notorious philandering of the noble classes.

Social Divisions. The noble class was composed of many different kinds of noblemen, and some were superior to others. Status within the nobility was a function of how much authority one had over others; a chief with many vassals obviously far outranked the small country nobleman who was lord over none but himself.

In the late Middle Ages there were shifts in wealth and power that sent the landed nobility into a decline from which it never recovered. Climatic changes depressed the agricultural economy that was the source of its wealth, and famines and plagues caused massive demographic dislocations. Changing military tactics rendered noble cavalry nearly obsolete. And wealthy towns helped kings curtail the power of the nobles in local government. After the fourteenth century, possession of land and wealth counted far more than family tree as a qualification for entrance into the highest social class.

Clergy

Unlike the nobility and the peasantry, the rank of clergy was acquired by training and ordination, not by birth. Consequently, people of talent could climb the clerical hierarchy, and the church provided a ladder of social mobility for gifted individuals.

Secular and Regular Clerics. There were two clerical vocations: secular and regular. The secular clergy lived and worked among the laity in the world (the *saeculum*). The most prestigious among them were wealthy cardinals, archbishops, and bishops who were recruited almost exclusively from noble families. Below them in rank were the urban priests, the cathedral canons, and the court clerks. At the bottom of the clerical hierarchy was the great mass of poor parish priests, who were neither financially nor intellectually superior to the lay people they served. Until the eleventh century, parish priests routinely lived with women in a relationship akin to marriage, and they stretched their meager incomes by "moonlighting" as teachers, artisans, and farmers. This practice was accepted and even admired by their parishioners.

Regular clergy were monks and nuns (women were not, strictly speaking, entitled to clerical status) who lived under the rule (*regula*) of a cloister. By retreating from the world and adopting rigorous ascetic disciplines, monks and nuns emulated the suffering of Christ and practiced what their contemporaries believed to be the ideal Christian way of life. This made them respected, influential persons. The regular clergy were never completely cut off from the secular world. They maintained contact with the laity through charitable activities (such as feeding the destitute and tending the sick), as instructors in monastic schools, and as supplemental preachers and confessors in parish churches. Some monks of great learning and rhetorical skill rose to prominence as secretaries and private confessors to kings and queens. Nunneries produced famous female scholars, and monasticism inspired many of the religious and social reform movements of the medieval era.

The Benedictine rule had been adopted by most Western monasteries by the end of the Carolingian era, but during the High Middle Ages numerous new orders appeared. Saint Benedict had emphasized hard work and self-sufficiency more than rigorous ascetic discipline. Thanks to generations of bequests and careful husbandry of resources, many Benedictine houses, like the famous Cluny, grew wealthy and self-preoccupied—devoting much of their time to creating ever more elaborate liturgies for their elegantly appointed sanctuaries. The new orders rejected Benedictine "luxury." They modeled their rules on the example of poverty and self-sacrifice set by Christ and the apostles in the New Testament.

The Carthusians, who were founded in 1084, were the strictest of the new orders. Carthusian monks lived in isolation, fasted three days a week, observed long periods of silence, and disciplined their flesh by acts of self-flagellation.

The Cistercians, who were founded in 1098 at Cîteaux in Burgundy, claimed to restore what they believed was the original intent of the Benedictine rule before it was corrupted by materialistic influences. They stressed cultivation of the inner life and the spiritual goals of monasticism. To avoid contamination by the secular world, they located their houses in remote areas where there were few worldly comforts.

The monastic ideal was so popular in the eleventh century that many secular clergy (and some lay persons) chose to live as Canons Regular. These people stayed in the world to serve the laity, but lived according to a rule that was credited to Saint Augustine. They merged the spiritual disciplines of the cloister with traditional pastoral duties. Early in the thirteenth century, the desire to combine the virtues of the secular and regular clerical professions inspired another innovation: the mendicant friars (the Dominicans and Franciscans). And during the late thirteenth and fourteenth centuries, laymen and laywomen set up satellite convents known as *Begard* (male) or *Beguine* (female) houses. These were religious communes formed by people who worked in the world but lived together under a quasi-monastic rule. The church was uncomfortable with them, for their religious enthusiasm sometimes blossomed into heresy. The Franciscans and Dominicans assumed responsibility for many of these establishments.

Prominence of the Clergy. The clergy were far more numerous in medieval than in modern society. Estimates suggest that 1.5 percent of fourteenth-century Europe was in clerical garb. The clergy as a whole, like the nobility, lived on the labor of others. Their income came from tithes, church taxes, and endowments. The church was a major landowner that collected huge sums in rents and fees. Monastic communities and high prelates acquired great fortunes and immense secular power.

Respect for clergy as members of society's "first estate" derived in large part from their role as mediators between God and humankind. When the priest celebrated the Eucharist, he brought the very Son of God down to earth in tangible form. The priest alone had the power to extend God's forgiveness to sinners or to block their access to it by imposing excommunication—cutting a sinner off from the sacraments that were the only avenue to salvation.

Since the priest was the agent of an authority far superior to any earthly magistrate, it was considered inappropriate for him to be subservient to the laymen who ran the state. Clergy, therefore, had special privileges and immunities. They were not to be taxed by secular governments without approval from the church. Clerical crimes were under the jurisdiction of special ecclesiastical courts, not the secular courts. The churches and monasteries where clergy worked were also deemed to be outside the legal jurisdiction of the state. People who took refuge in them received asylum and could not be apprehended by officials of secular governments.

By the late Middle Ages lay people came increasingly to resent the special privileges of the clergy. The anti-clerical sentiments that developed during the medieval era contributed to the success of the Reformation of the sixteenth century. The Protestant theologians insisted that clergy and laity had equal spiritual standing before God.

Peasants

The largest and lowest class in medieval society was the one on whose labor the welfare of all the others depended: the agrarian peasantry. Many peasants lived and worked on manors, the primitive cells of rural social life. When the Frankish tribes moved into Europe at the start of the Middle Ages, individuals divided up the lands belonging to farming villages. They became the lords of these estates or "manors," and those who lived on them became their property. A manor was a kind of rural plantation supporting a lord.

The Duties of Tenancy. The lord was given a manor to support him as a soldier, not a farmer. The peasants who lived on his land worked it for him. They were free to divide the labor as they wished, and any products they raised above and beyond what they owed their lord they could keep for themselves. No set rules governed the size of manors—nor how many a lord could have.

There were both servile and free manors. The tenants of free manors were descendants of freemen (*coloni*)—the owners of land they had swapped for a guarantee of protection by their lord. Tenancy obligations on free manors were limited, for their residents had some leverage in negotiating terms. Tenants of servile manors were, by comparison, far more vulnerable to the whims of their landlords. Time, however, tended to obscure differences between the two types of manors. Free, self-governing peasant communities that acknowledged no lords also survived in many regions.

The lord was the supreme authority on his manor. Cultivation of his *demesne*, the plots of land producing his income, took precedence over those of his tenants. He could impress his tenants into labor gangs for special projects or lead them out as foot soldiers when he went to war. He owned and leased to his peasants some of the instruments and facilities they used to raise and process food. His income was fattened by petty taxes and monopolies called *banalities:* the requirement, for instance, that all his tenants grind their grain in his mill or bake their bread in his oven. The lord also collected an inheritance tax—usually the best animal from a deceased serf's estate. A serf who wished to travel or to marry outside his manor also had to obtain—usually by purchase—his lord's permission.

The Life of a Serf. Burdened as a serf's life was, it was superior to chattel slavery. Serfs had their own dwellings and modest strips of land. They managed their own labor. They were permitted to market surpluses for their own profit. They were free to choose spouses from the local village community. Their marriages were protected by the church. They could pass on property to their children. And they could not be sold away from their land.

Serfs seldom ventured far beyond the villages where they were born. Since the church was the only show in town, life on the manor was organized around religion. But poverty of religious instruction meant that beliefs and practices were by no means unambiguously Christian. Although there were social and economic distinctions among the peasants, common dependence on the soil forced them to work together to survive. The ratio of seed to grain yield was poor; about two bushels of seed were required to produce six to ten bushels of grain in good times. There was rarely an abundance of bread and ale, the staple peasant foods. Two crops on which the modern West depends, potatoes and corn (maize), were unknown in Europe until the sixteenth century. Pork was the major source of animal protein, for pigs, unlike cattle, could forage for themselves in the forests. Excess plow teams were also slaughtered when winter set in. Survival hinged on the grain crops. When they failed or fell short, famine threatened.

Changes in the Manor. As the medieval era waned, the manor and serfdom gave way to the free single-family farm. Many things contributed to the change. Technological advances such as the collar harness (ca. 800), the horseshoe (ca. 900), and the three-field system of crop rotation improved agricultural productivity. To meet the demand of the new markets created by the towns that sprang up during the High Middle Ages, peasants brought more fields into production. They used the surplus income they produced to buy their freedom from the obligation of labor services. As the towns revived trade and brought back a money-based economy, lords found it more profitable to lease their holdings to tenant farmers than to work them with serfs. Although tenants thereby gained greater personal freedom, they were not necessarily better off materially. In hard times serfs might expect assistance from their lords, for their lords viewed them as valuable personal resources. But independent, rent-paying workers were expected to take care of themselves.

As the medieval economy expanded and costs of living rose, the landed aristocracy found it hard to make ends meet. The incomes they drew from their manors were fixed by tradition. In the mid-fourteenth century the nobles in England and France tried to increase taxes on the peasants and limit their freedom of movement. The result was often a mass revolt. Although such uprisings were brutally crushed, they revealed that traditional medieval society was breaking up.

✧ Towns and Townspeople

In the eleventh and twelfth centuries, only about 5 percent of western Europe's population lived in towns. Most urban communities were small. Of Germany's 3,000 towns, 2,800 had populations under 1,000. Only 15 exceeded 10,000, and the largest (Cologne) had a mere 30,000. London was the only English city greater than 10,000. Paris was bigger than London, but not by much. Europe's most populous towns were in Italy. Florence and Milan approached 100,000.

The Chartering of Towns

Despite their comparatively small size, towns were where the action was. In the beginning, they tended to be dominated by the feudal lords who granted the land on which they were built, but most acquired political independence. The charter that a lord issued to the residents of a town gave them much greater freedom than rural workers enjoyed. Freedom was a requirement of life for men and women who lived by invention and audacious commercial enterprise, and lords and bishops were willing to grant it to them in exchange for the products that they made available in their markets.

The oases of freedom from lordship that developed in towns hastened the disintegration of feudal society by providing serfs with options. A serf who fled a manor could find refuge in a town. It offered a chance for a better life, for skill and industry could lift a craftsperson into a higher social class. The mere threat of migration of serfs to towns forced lords to offer them more favorable terms of tenure to keep them on the land. The growth of towns improved the lot of all peasants—both those who stayed in the countryside and those who left.

The Rise of Merchants

The first merchants were probably enterprising serfs or outcasts who found no place in the feudal system. Only men who had nothing to lose and everything to gain would have been tempted by the enormous risks and dangers of foreign trade. They traveled together in armed caravans and convoys, buying goods and products as cheaply as possible at the source, and selling them elsewhere for all they could get. The greed and daring of these rough-hewn men, more than anything else, created our modern urban lifestyle.

Merchants were considered an oddity, for they did not fit into the three classes that theoretically constituted feudal society (the nobility, the clergy, and the peasantry). As late as the fifteenth century, nobles were still snubbing the urban "patriciate" (the hereditary ruling class that arose in some cities). Over time, however, the powerful grew to respect the merchants as much as the weak aspired to imitate them, for wherever merchants went, they left a trail of wealth behind.

Challenging the Old Lords

As the traders established themselves in towns and grew in wealth and numbers, they organized to challenge the feudal authorities. They wanted to end the tolls and tariffs demanded by the myriad of nobles through whose domains their caravans traveled. Wherever merchants settled, they opposed whatever tolls, tariffs, and petty restrictions might hamper the flow of goods. Merchant *guilds* (unions, or protective associations) sprang up in the eleventh century, and they were followed in the twelfth by guilds of craftsmen. These groups worked together to change what the feudal classes had assumed to be a natural and static social order.

Townspeople wanted simple, uniform laws that were valid over large areas. They objected to the fortress mentality that led feudal lords to split up the countryside into tiny jurisdictions. City-dwellers set up independent communes to wrest control of their towns from the nobles, and they began to try to overcome the political fragmentation created by feudalism. Both the church and the king were eager, for reasons of their own, to join the townspeople in a fight to weaken local magnates.

New Models of Government

By 1100 the old urban nobility and the new *burgher* upper class had merged in many cities. The wealthiest citizens cooperated to create town councils that became the chief organ of municipal government. Small artisans and craftsmen developed their own protective associations or guilds and won political recognition on these town councils. Townspeople thought of themselves as citizens with basic rights, not as subjects liable to a master's whim. The urban poor certainly knew economic hardship and political exploitation, but so long as there was some social mobility, they had a stake in the system and the reason to support it.

Social Tensions. Despite democratic tendencies, class distinctions were prominent in towns. The wealthiest urban groups aped the lifestyle of the old landed nobility. They acquired coats of arms, castles, and country estates. Once businesses had set up lines of communication and worked out banking procedures for moving funds around, their managers left most traveling to underlings. Investors could settle down on country manors and still run companies. The departure from town of social-climbing entrepreneurs was an economic loss for the communities that had given these people their starts.

A need to be socially distinguished and distinct was not confined to the rich. Towns tried to restrain competition by defining grades of luxury in dress and residence for each social group and vocation. Overly conspicuous consumption was a kind of indecent exposure punishable by "sumptuary" laws—regulations restricting the types and amount of clothing one might wear or the decoration of one's home. These rules were meant to maintain order by keeping everyone clearly and peacefully in place.

The need for laws to limit competition among classes suggests that medieval towns were not internally harmonious social units. They were collections of self-centered groups, each seeking to advance its own interests. Conflict between haves and have-nots was inevitable. The poorest workers in the export trades (usually the weavers and woolcombers) were distinct from the economically better off and socially ascending independent artisans and small shopkeepers. These latter had differences with the merchants who brought competitive foreign goods into the city. Theoretically, poor men could work their way up this hierarchy from its lower social and vocational levels. Some lucky ones succeeded, but until they did they were excluded from the city council. Only property-owning families of long standing had full rights of citizenship.

Urban self-government, in other words, tended to become inbred and aristocratic.

Artisans formed guilds to gain the clout needed to win a direct voice in government. Guilds empowered the more successful among them, but curtailed the social mobility of poor laborers. The guilds' representatives on city councils worked to monopolize the local market for their members by discouraging imports. They protected the health of that market by ensuring that those who served it produced acceptable products at fair prices. But guilds also discouraged improvements in techniques of production that might give some persons advantages over others, and they refused to license new producers. This infuriated the journeymen who trained in guild shops, for it prevented them from setting up in business for themselves. They became politically disenfranchised workers who had no hope of advancement—a true urban proletariat. The protectionism practiced by guild-dominated urban governments ultimately depressed the economy for everyone.

Towns and Kings

A natural alliance developed between the governments of towns and the centralized nation-states that medieval kings labored to build. Towns supplied royal governments with experienced bureaucrats and lawyers who knew Roman law, the tool for designing kingdoms and empires. Towns provided the money that kings needed to hire professional armies and free themselves from dependence on the feudal nobility. Towns, in short, had the human, financial, and technological resources to empower kings.

Towns wanted strong monarchs, for national governments provided the best support for commerce. A powerful king could control the local despots whose tolls and petty wars disrupted trade. Unlike a local magnate, kings also tended to keep their distance and allow towns to exercise autonomy. Kings could provide security for large areas, create standardized currencies to ease buying and selling, and simplify the payment of dues and taxes.

The relationship between kings and towns fluctuated with the fate of monarchy in various nations. In France, where the Capetian dynasty flourished, towns were integrated into royal government. In England, towns supported the barons against unpopular kings like John, but cooperated with more effective monarchs in subduing the nobility. In Germany, where the feudal magnates triumphed over their kings, towns came under the control of territorial princes. Italy offered towns unique opportunities. Italy had no native royal family for towns to support against its nobles, and a shared opposition to the political ambitions of German kings and Roman popes encouraged Italy's town dwellers and nobles to work together. As the two classes fused, town governments extended their authority into the countryside and revived the ancient institution of the city-state.

Between the eleventh and fourteenth centuries, towns enjoyed considerable autonomy and once again became the centers of Western civilization. But when true nations began to appear in the fourteenth century, both towns and the church tended to come under the control of kings. By the seventeenth century, few had escaped integration into the larger purposes of the "state."

Jews in Christian Society

The Jews who survived in medieval Europe tended to congregate in towns. Since they could not take Christian oaths of homage, they were excluded from feudal land tenure and forced to earn their livings from trade. For reasons of protection and to be able to practice their religion, they gathered together in tight communities. The church forbade them to employ Christians, and efforts to keep the two peoples apart promoted mutual suspicion. Ignorance of Jewish practices, resentment of the wealth acquired by some Jews, and a popular tendency to hold the Jews responsible for Christ's crucifixion, fueled baseless rumors of Jewish plots against Christian society. These sparked periodic mob violence against Jews and decisions by church and state authorities to exile them or penalize them in some way.

✥ Schools and Universities

In the twelfth century, European scholars discovered Aristotle's treatises on logic, the writings of Euclid and Ptolemy, Roman law, and the basic works of Greek physicians and Arab mathematicians. Islamic scholars living in Spain were chiefly responsible for the translations and commentaries that made these ancient texts accessible to westerners. The result was a cultural renaissance and the invention of a new center of intellectual activity, the university.

University of Bologna

When the term university was first used, all it implied was a corporation of individuals who "united" for mutual protection. Schools attracted students and teachers from great distances, and many were foreigners who had no civil rights in the towns where they worked. Unless they organized to protect themselves—like the members of an urban trade guild—they could be exploited by the townspeople on whom they were dependent for food and lodging.

The first of the great medieval universities was chartered in Bologna, Italy, by Emperor Frederick Barbarossa in 1158. Bologna, which became a model for schools in Italy, Spain, and southern France, was organized by its students. They "unionized" to guarantee fair rents and prices and high-quality teaching from their masters. They hired their teachers, set pay scales, and assigned lecture topics. Masters who did not live up to student expectations were boycotted, and price-gouging by townspeople was countered by threats to take the university and its profitable business to another town.

Bologna was most famous for the courses in law it offered advanced students. In the late eleventh century, Western scholars discovered the *Corpus Juris Civilis*, the collection of ancient Roman law made by the Byzantine emperor

Justinian in the sixth century. In the early twelfth century, Irnerius of Bologna began to use the Roman law to create commentaries (glosses) on current laws. Around 1140, another resident of Bologna, a monk named Gratian, wrote the standard legal text in church (canon) law, the *Concordance of Discordant Canons* (or, simply, the *Decretum*).

Masters, as well as students, formed protective associations, and their guilds dominated the universities of northern Europe (among which Paris was pre-eminent). Masters' guilds had a monopoly on teaching, and their tests for admission set standards for certification of teachers. The licenses to teach (*licentia docendi*) medieval guilds awarded were the predecessors of the modern academic degree.

Cathedral Schools

The basic course of study at all medieval universities was the liberal arts program. It consisted of the *trivium* (grammar, rhetoric, and logic) and the *quadrivium* (arithmetic, geometry, astronomy, and music). This amounted to instruction in reading, writing, and computation. Students usually entered the university between the ages of twelve and fifteen. Since all books and all instruction were in Latin, they were expected to arrive knowing how to read and speak that language. The first four years of their course of study were devoted to the *trivium*—the polishing of their Latin. This earned them a bachelor of arts degree. A master's degree entailed an additional three or four years of work on the *quadrivium*, the study of classical texts dealing with mathematics, natural science, and philosophy. Doctoral degrees were available in a few fields like law, medicine, and theology. It could take twenty or more years to earn the degree in theology at the University of Paris.

The liberal arts curriculum evolved in the cathedral and monastery schools that trained clergy. In the early Middle Ages these were the only schools that existed, and the clergy were the only literate class. But by the late eleventh century, students who had no interest in clerical vocations, but who needed Latin and related intellectual disciplines for careers as notaries or merchants, began to frequent the church's schools. In 1179 a papal decree ordered cathedrals to provide teachers gratis for laity who wanted to learn. By the thirteenth century, the demand for literate men to staff the growing urban and territorial governments and expanding merchant firms gave rise to schools offering secular vocational education.

University of Paris

The University of Paris, which provided the model for the schools of northern Europe, was founded in part on the cathedral school of Notre Dame. King Philip Augustus and Pope Innocent III chartered Paris in 1200 and gave its students protections and privileges denied ordinary citizens. Only in self-defense might a citizen strike a student. All citizens were obligated to testify against anyone seen abusing a student. And university laws required teachers to be carefully

The architecture of the early Middle Ages is known as Romanesque because it is closely related to the style of the late Roman Empire. It is characterized by thick stone walls and rounded arches that support the roof. The few windows are often very small, mere slits, giving Romanesque buildings a fortresslike appearance. Shown here is the Abbey of Germigny-des-Pres in northern France. [Giraudon/Art Resource, N.Y.]

Beginning in the mid-twelfth century, the Gothic style evolved from Romanesque architecture. The word gothic at first meant "barbaric," and was applied to the new style by its critics. Its most distinctive visible features are its ribbed, criss-crossing vaulting; its pointed rather than rounded arches; and its prominent exterior "flying" buttresses. The vaulting, the flying buttresses, and the increased height they made possible gave prominence to the strong vertical aspect of Gothic buildings. The buttresses, by shifting much of the structural weight of the buildings off the walls, also made possible wide expanses of windows—hence the extensive use of stained glass and the characteristic colored light that often floods Gothic cathedrals. Use of the windows to show stories from the Bible, saints' lives, and local events was similar to earlier use of mosaics. Shown here is an example of French Gothic, Reims Cathedral, where the kings of France were crowned. [Scala/Art Resource, N.Y.]

examined before being licensed to teach Parisian students. The law recognized students as a valuable and a vulnerable resource.

Paris originated the college or house system. The first colleges were charitable hospices providing room and board for poor students who would not otherwise be able to afford to study. The university soon discovered that these institutions were useful for overseeing students, and it encouraged all students to enroll in them. The most famous of the Parisian colleges was the Sorbonne, which was founded around 1257 by a royal chaplain named Robert de Sorbon. Early universities had been highly mobile institutions that used rented or borrowed space. But the buildings provided by endowed colleges rooted a university to a particular spot. This reduced the university's leverage in negotiating with townspeople, for it could no longer threaten to move to another place.

The Curriculum

The education provided by cathedral and monastery schools was limited to grammar, rhetoric, and some elementary geometry and astronomy. The standard texts were the Latin grammars of Donatus and Priscian, Saint Augustine's *On Christian Doctrine,* Cassiodorus's *On Divine and Secular Learning,* Boethius's treatises on arithmetic and music, and a few of Aristotle's logical works. The books that entered Europe from Muslim lands in the early twelfth century vastly expanded libraries and made possible the more elaborate curricula of universities. The most revolutionary of the new texts were works by Aristotle which had previously been unknown in Europe. They were in general circulation by the mid-thirteenth century, and they shaped the dominant intellectual movement of the day: Scholasticism.

In the High Middle Ages scholars assumed that truth was not something one had to go out and find for oneself. It was already enshrined in the works of the great authorities of the past—men like Aristotle and the fathers of the church. It had only to be apprehended and absorbed. Teachers did not encourage students to strive independently for undiscovered truth. They taught them rather to use logic and dialectic to organize and harmonize the accepted truths of tradition. Dialectic, the art of discovering a truth by finding the contradictions in arguments against it, reigned supreme in all disciplines. Instead of observing phenomena for themselves, students read the traditional authorities in their fields, made short summaries of their teaching, disputed interpretations by elaborating arguments pro and con, and then took positions based on logical cogency.

Because printing with movable type did not yet exist, only a few expensive, hand-copied books were available. Few students could afford texts for quiet, private study. Most had to learn from discussions, lectures, and debates. They memorized the information with which they worked, and they were required to think on their feet. Rhetorical skill, the ability to make an eloquent defense of the points one had clarified by logic and dialectic, was the goal of an education. To win debates, students had to become walking encyclopedias filled with information they could regurgitate as needed.

The Summa. The *summa,* a summary of all that was known about a particular subject, was the characteristic intellectual product of the High Middle Ages. The *summa*'s chief purpose was to heap up clarified truth by reconciling apparent contradictions among authorities.

Medieval scholars labored to produce universal summaries for all disciplines, but the most influential were those that appeared in theology, the "queen of the sciences." About 1122 Peter Abelard (1079–1142) published *Sic et Non,* a book that facilitated scholastic debate by juxtaposing seemingly contradictory statements from the works of sacred authorities. A few years later (1155–1157), Peter Lombard (1100–1169) worked this material into his *Four Books of Sentences,* the standard theological textbook of the Middle Ages. About 1265 Thomas Aquinas entered the field with the *Summa Theologica.* It was, in the opinion of Catholic theologians, the epitome of what the *summa* aspired to be: the last word.

Critics of Scholasticism. Even in its heyday, Scholasticism had opponents. Some complained that the regimen of the schools was heartless and potentially damaging to Christian faith. The *dictatores,* the professional grammarians and rhetoricians who taught good writing and speaking rather than the highly abstract dialectic of Scholasticism, urged students to go directly to sources (in their original languages) and draw their own conclusions. Their point of view was championed by the humanists of the sixteenth-century Renaissance, and it still informs modern liberal arts curricula.

The church, too, was not completely at ease with Scholasticism. Scholastic thinkers relied heavily on Aristotelian logic to develop their arguments, and there were obvious conflicts between Christian doctrine and ideas that Aristotle defended. For example, since logic cannot account for why there is something rather than nothing or deal with an infinite regression of causes, Aristotle claimed that the world was not created but eternal. Christianity, however, affirmed the Jewish concept of creation found in the book of Genesis. Aristotle also taught that since logic was the same in all minds, intellect or mind was ultimately the same in all people. This obliterated individuality and threatened Christian teaching about personal responsibility and immortality.

Some of the early Scholastics were inclined to question Christian doctrines that could not be reconciled with Aristotle's teachings. Berengar of Tours (d. 1088), for example, concluded that the church's claim that the bread and wine of the Eucharist became the body and blood of Christ was logically indefensible. Peter Abelard attempted a reinterpretation of the Trinity that preserved a premise of Aristotle's logic; namely, that three could not be one and one could not be three. The boldness of the new logicians shocked conservatives, who concluded that the love of learning at the universities had clearly got in the way of the love of God.

A century of suspicion that Aristotle was undermining Christian theology culminated in 1277, when the bishop of Paris condemned 219 philosophical propositions. The condemnation was a warning to scholars who were more interested in secular philosophy than in Christian truth, and it chilled the relationship between learning and religion. Thinkers ceased to look for ways to reconcile reason and revelation. William of Ockham (d. 1349), for instance, denied that theological truths could be dealt with as if they were of the same order as the truths that came from empirical experience of natural phenomena. Knowledge of God, he insisted, was available only through biblical revelation.

✑ Women and Children in Medieval Society

The concept of femininity developed by medieval scholars was at odds with the lives of the real women of the era. Christian theologians concluded from the evidence contained in Greco-Roman medical, philosophical, and legal texts—and the Bible—that women were physically, mentally, and morally inferior to men. The Bible clearly taught that a female was a "weaker vessel" who required protection and guidance from a male. Wives were to submit to their husbands and accept corrective beatings from them. The celibate Christian clergy felt that women were debased by marriage and that virgins and chaste widows were more to be honored than wives.

Contrary forces were shaping the roles women played in medieval society. The church reinforced many traditional negative assumptions about women, but it condemned bawdy literature that denigrated women and insisted on the female's spiritual equality with the male. The learned churchman Peter Lombard argued, for instance, that God took Eve from Adam's side because he wanted woman neither to rule over nor to be enslaved by man. She was to stand with him—his companion and partner in a marriage characterized by mutual aid and trust. In chivalric romances, in courtly love literature, and in the cult of the Virgin Mary that swept Europe in the twelfth and thirteenth centuries, female traits of gentleness, compassion, and grace were exalted over the rougher male virtues. In these traditions, women were put on pedestals and praised as superior to men in the delicate arts of self-control and civilized life.

Germanic traditions tended to moderate Roman customs. They gave medieval women basic rights that prevented their being treated as mere chattel. Roman women in their teens married men much older than themselves, but German women married later in life and took husbands of their own age. In German lands a groom provided a dowry for his bride to hold as her own property, and all the Germanic law codes granted women economic freedom. They could inherit, administer, dispose of, and confer on their children family property and personal possessions. They could also prosecute men in court for bodily injury and rape.

In the ninth century, the Carolingians, who had tolerated polygyny, concubinage, and divorce, were influenced by Christianity to make monogamous marriage official policy. The result was both a gain and a loss for women. On the one hand, the choice of a wife became a very serious matter, and wives gained greater dignity and legal security. But on the other hand, a woman's burden as household manager and bearer of children greatly increased. Where previously several women may have shared the tasks of running a nobleman's estate and providing heirs to continue his line, now all these duties rested on the shoulders of one woman. After the ninth century, mortality rates for Frankish women rose and their longevity decreased.

The demands placed on wives explain the cloister's appeal as a refuge for women, but few women were able to choose the celibate life. (There may, for instance, have been no more than 3,500 nuns in all of England at the end of the Middle Ages.) Entrance into a nunnery was contingent on a woman's ability to bring the house a sizable donation (a "dowry"). Only a few upper-class women could afford the price of admission. Those who did could acquire educations, rise to positions of leadership, and enjoy economic and political power beyond the reach of their sisters in secular life.

Most medieval women were neither aristocratic housewives nor nuns. They were laboring family women who were as prominent and as creative a part of a community's work force as its men. They could not attend the universities and were excluded from the learned professions of scholarship, medicine, and law. They were, however, admitted to the blue-collar trades. Between the ages of ten and fifteen, girls, like boys, held apprenticeships, and many learned to be skilled workers. When they married, they might continue their trades, operating bake shops or dress shops next to a husband's business, or they might become assistants and partners in a husband's line of work. Women held virtually every job from butcher to goldsmith, and they were especially prominent in the food and clothing industries and in domestic service. Women, as well as men, earned membership in guilds and were accorded the rank of "master," but they often found their opportunities to be more restricted than a man's. Women's wages for comparable work averaged 25 percent less than men's. Townswomen had opportunities to go to school and acquire literacy in the vernacular. Peasant women, who tilled the fields, had no such chance for self-improvement.

The Lives of Children

With children, as with women in the Middle Ages, image diverged from life's realities. In medieval art children are rarely portrayed as different from adults, and some historians have questioned whether people in the Middle Ages thought of childhood as a distinct period of life requiring special treatment. The same historians have also noted that infant and child mortality was extremely high, and they have speculated that a parent could not have risked becoming emotionally attached to a child who had a 30 to 50 percent chance of dying before the age of five.

The practice of infanticide, which continued despite its condemnation by the church, suggests that children were held in low esteem in ancient and early medieval society. The Romans regulated family size by exposing unwanted children, but showered attention and affection on the offspring they chose to raise. The Germans, on the other hand, had large families, but tended to neglect their children. Among the German tribes one paid a much lower *wergild*, or compensatory fine, for injury to a child than for injury to an adult.

It is possible that instead of distancing parents from children, high rates of infant and child mortality increased attachment to offspring. Evidence of special attention being paid to children is found in the great variety of children's toys and child-rearing equipment (e.g., walkers and potty chairs) that existed in the Middle Ages. Medieval medical authorities also offered advice on postnatal care and childhood diseases—cautioning against abuse and recommending moderation in discipline. The church urged parents to love children as Mary loved Jesus. And evidence from medieval art and literature suggests that when infants and children died in the Middle Ages, parents grieved as pitiably then as now.

Childhood was brief in the Middle Ages, for very young children shared adult responsibilities. Peasant children joined their parents in the fields as soon as they could physically manage the labor. The urban working class sent children as young as eight away from home to begin apprenticeships. The church allowed boys to marry at fourteen and girls at twelve. The pressure put on children to mature and learn may have been a sign of concern for them, for no parental responsibility was deemed greater than that of equipping a child for useful employment.

The economic expansion of the High Middle Ages revived urban life in Europe. As cities grew, new social groups—most notably the merchant-artisan classes—rose to prominence. They successfully challenged the old feudal nobility and brought European communities the blessings and problems of nascent capitalism. The seeds of social conflict and class struggle were sown, but a potentially significant alliance was also struck between the urban classes and the kings who were struggling to reverse the fragmenting influences of feudalism. Together they defeated feudalism and began to consolidate Europe's nations.

The new wealth of towns provided patronage for education and culture. The first universities appeared in the eleventh century and, with them, a new way of thinking (Scholasticism) and a revival of art and science. The creativity of the era testifies to the vitality of the rising "middle" class and its determination to reshape the social and political institutions of the Western world.

✧ Review Questions

1. How did the responsibilities of the nobility differ from those of the clergy and peasantry during the High Middle Ages? In what ways did each social class contribute to the stability of society?

2. What led to the revival of trade and the growth of towns in the twelfth century? What political and social conditions were essential for a revival of trade?

How did towns change medieval society?

3. What were the strengths and weaknesses of the educations provided by medieval universities? How would you evaluate the standard curriculum?

4. How would you define Scholasticism? What was the Scholastic program and method of study? Who were the main

critics of Scholasticism? What were their complaints?

5. Do Germanic law and Roman law reflect different understandings of the position of women in society? How did options and responsibilities differ for women in each of the social classes? What are the theories concerning the concept of childhood in the Middle Ages?

∾ Suggested Readings

E. AMT (ed.), *Women's Lives in Medieval Europe: A Sourcebook* (1993). Outstanding collection of sources.

P. ARIÈS, *Centuries of Childhood: A Social History of Family Life* (1962). Pioneer effort on the subject.

J. W. BALDWIN, *The Scholastic Culture of the Middle Ages: 1000–1300* (1971). Best brief synthesis available.

M. BLOCH, *French Rural History*, trans. by J. Sondheimer (1966). A classic by a great modern historian.

B. A. HANAWALT, *The Ties That Bound: Peasant Families in Medieval England* (1986). Elucidating demographic and economic study of rural life.

C. H. HASKINS, *The Renaissance of the Twelfth Century* (1927). Still the standard account.

C. H. HASKINS, *The Rise of Universities* (1972). A short, minor classic.

D. HERLIHY, *Medieval Households* (1985). Bread-and-butter account of household structure in antiquity and the Middle Ages.

G. KÜNSTLER, *Romanesque Art in Europe* (1973). Standard survey.

E. MÂLE, *The Gothic Image: Religious Art in France in the Thirteenth Century* (1913). An enduring classic.

K. MERTES, *The English Noble Household, 1250–1600* (1988). Good background for the debate over the structure and quality of English family life.

A. MURRAY, *Reason and Society in the Middle Ages* (1978). A view of the Middle Ages as an age of reason as well as of faith.

E. PANOFSKY, *Gothic Architecture and Scholasticism* (1951). A controversial classic.

H. PIRENNE, *Medieval Cities: Their Origins and the Revival of Trade*, trans. by Frank D. Halsey (1970). A minor classic.

H. RASHDALL, *The Universities of Europe in the Middle Ages*, vols. 1–3 (1936). Dated but still extremely useful for documents of the period.

S. SHAHAR, *The Fourth Estate: A History of Women in the Middle Ages* (1983). A comprehensive survey, making clear the great variety of women's work.

B. STOCK, *The Implications of Literacy* (1983). How the ability to read changed medieval society.

9

The Late Middle Ages (1300–1527): Centuries of Crisis

Political and Social Breakdown

The Hundred Years' War and the Rise of National Sentiment
Progress of the War

The Black Death

Preconditions and Causes
Social and Economic Consequences

Ecclesiastical Breakdown and Revival: The Late Medieval Church

The Thirteenth-Century Papacy

Boniface VIII and Philip the Fair
The Avignon Papacy (1309–1377)

The Great Schism and the Conciliar Movement

Urban VI and Clement VII
Conciliar Theory of Church Government

KEY TOPICS

- The Hundred Years' War between England and France
- The effects of the bubonic plague on population and society
- The growing power of secular rulers over the papacy
- Schism, heresy, and reform of the church

During the late Middle Ages, the West endured so many calamities that European civilization seemed in imminent danger of collapse. From 1337 to 1453, France and England waged an increasingly bloody conflict. Between 1348 and 1350, the first wave of the bubonic plague swept over Europe, carrying off a third of its population. In 1378 a quarrel between competing candidates for the papacy inaugurated a schism that endured for thirty-seven years. And in 1453, the Turks overran Constantinople and charged up the Danube valley toward the heart of Europe.

These crises were accompanied by intellectual developments that undercut assumptions about God, mankind, and the social order that had given comfort to earlier generations. Feudal institutions, which had been assumed to be divinely ordained, were assaulted by kings who aspired to absolute monarchy. Claims to absolute authority were challenged by political theorists who argued that subjects could hold rulers accountable for their actions.

∽ Political and Social Breakdown

The Hundred Years' War and the Rise of National Sentiment

Late medieval rulers practiced the art of feudal government, but on a grander scale and with greater sophistication than their predecessors. The Norman kings of England and the Capetian kings of France centralized royal power by fine-tuning feudal relationships and carefully negotiating alliances with powerful factions within their domains: the feudal nobility, the church, and the towns. These strategies fostered a sense of "national" consciousness that equipped both kingdoms for war on an unprecedented scale.

The Causes of the War. The Hundred Years' War began in May 1337 as a fight over the right of succession to the French throne. In 1328 Charles IV of France died without male issue. This extinguished the senior branch of the Capetian royal house. Edward III (r. 1327–1377), king of England, claimed France's throne by right of his mother, Charles IV's sister. But the French barons had no intention of turning themselves over to England's king. They pledged their allegiance to a cadet branch of the Capetian house: to Charles IV's cousin, Philip VI, duke of Valois (1328–1350). Philip inaugurated the Valois dynasty that ruled France into the sixteenth century.

England and France had long been on a collision course, and the English king's assertion of a claim to the French throne was more a justification than a cause for war. Since the days of the Norman conquest, the king of England had held fiefs on the continent as a vassal of the king of France. English possession of French land hampered attempts by the French kings to centralize the government of their nation. England and France also had competing economic interests in Flanders and on the high seas. The Hundred Years' War was, in light of its many causes, a struggle for national identity as much as for territory.

French Weakness. France should have had no difficulty in winning the war. It had three times the population of England, far greater resources, and the advantage of fighting on its own soil. Yet, until 1415, the major battles were stunning victories for the English.

Internal disunity prevented France from marshalling all its forces against the English, and powerful feudal traditions slowed France's adaptation to new military strategies employed by the English. England's infantry was more disciplined than France's, and English archers wielded a formidable weapon, the longbow. It was capable of firing six arrows a minute and could pierce the armor of a knight at 200 yards.

Progress of the War

The Conflict During the Reign of Edward III. In the first of the three stages (see Map 9-1) into which the war can be divided, Edward stirred up rebellions

Significant Dates from the Period of the Late Middle Ages

1309–1377	*Avignon Papacy*
1340	*Sluys: First Major Battle of Hundred Years' War*
1346	*Battle of Crécy and seizure of Calais*
1348	*Black Death strikes*
1356	*Battle of Poitiers*
1358	Jacquerie *disrupts France*
1360	*Peace of Brétigny*
1378–1417	*Great Schism*
1381	*English Peasants' Revolt*
1414–1417	*Council of Constance*
1415	*Battle of Agincourt*
1420	*Treaty of Troyes*
1431	*Joan of Arc executed as a heretic*
1431–1449	*Council of Basel*
1453	*End of Hundred Years' War*

against France in the cities of Flanders by placing an embargo on the English wool that fed Flemish mills. In 1340 the Flemish cities decided that their economic interests lay with England and acknowledged Edward's claim to be king of France and, therefore, overlord of Flanders. On June 23 of that same year, Edward defeated the French fleet in the Bay of Sluys, the first battle of the war.

In 1346 Edward attacked Normandy. After a series of easy victories that culminated at the battle of Crécy, he seized the port of Calais. Exhaustion and the onset of the Black Death forced a truce in late 1347. There was no further action until 1356, when the English won their greatest victory. Near Poitiers, they routed France's feudal nobles and captured the French king, John II, "the Good" (1350–1364). The loss of king and vassals led to a breakdown of government in France.

Power in France shifted momentarily to the *Estates General*, a body (resembling England's Parliament) that represented the propertied classes. The powerful merchants of Paris, led by Étienne Marcel, demanded rights similar to those granted the English privileged classes by Magna Carta. But unlike the English Parliament, which represented the interests of a comparatively unified island people, the French Estates General was too divided to be an instrument for effective government. It took time for the leaders of the far-flung regions of a large nation like France to come to know and trust each other.

The French privileged classes were able to avoid taxation by foisting the costs of the war onto the backs of the peasants. Beginning in 1358, the desperate peasants rose up in bloody rebellions called the *Jacquerie* (from "Jacques Bonhomme," a peasant caricature). The nobility restored order by matching the rebels atrocity for atrocity.

On May 9, 1360, England compelled France to accept terms spelled out in

MAP 9-1 The Hundred Years' War *The Hundred Years' War went on intermittently from the late 1330s until 1453. These maps show the remarkable English territorial gains up to the point when Joan of Arc suddenly and decisively turned the tide of battle in favor of the French in 1429.*

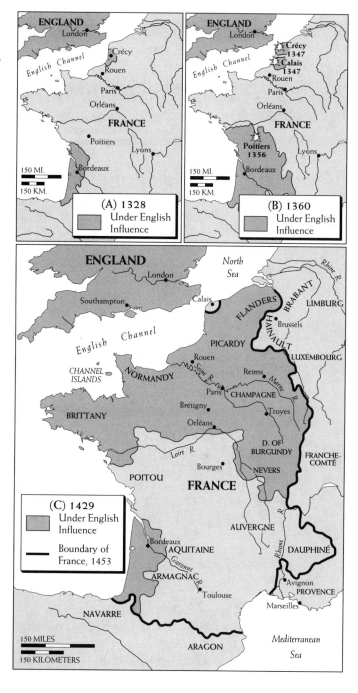

the Peace of Brétigny. Edward renounced his claim to the French throne, but he demanded an end to his vassalage to the king of France and confirmation of his sovereignty over the lands he held in France (including Gascony, Guyenne, Poitou, and Calais). France was also required to pay a ransom of 3 million gold crowns for King John the Good. The treaty was completely unrealistic, and sober observers on both sides knew that the peace it brought could not last long. Within a few years France had reopened hostilities, and by the time of Edward's death in 1377, the English possessed only a few coastal enclaves and the territory around Bordeaux.

French Defeat and the Treaty of Troyes. After Edward's death, domestic problems caused England to lose interest in war with France. During the reign of Edward's grandson and successor, Richard II (r. 1377–1399), England experienced its own version of the *Jacquerie*. In June 1381, John Ball, a secular priest, and Wat Tyler, a journeyman, led a mob of peasants and artisans in an assault on London. The revolt was quickly put down, but it left scars that took decades to heal.

Richard's autocratic behavior turned his nobles against him, and he was replaced on the throne by his cousin, Henry IV. Henry spent his reign confirming his hold on England. His son and heir, Henry V (r. 1413–1422), revived the war with France as a strategy for uniting his people behind their king.

Henry's moment was well chosen, for antagonistic factions had split the French nobility. When Henry V invaded Normandy, the duke of Burgundy's party refused to assist its enemies, the Armagnacs, in defending France. After Henry routed the Armagnacs at Agincourt on October 25, 1415, the Burgundians came to terms with the Armagnacs. But their fragile alliance was shattered in September 1419, when the duke of Burgundy was assassinated by an Armagnac. Burgundy's son and heir decided to avenge his father's death by helping the English invade Armagnac territory.

With Burgundian assistance Henry V took Paris, captured the French king (Charles VI), and married his daughter. In 1420 the Treaty of Troyes disinherited the French king's son and proclaimed Henry V heir to the French throne. When Henry and Charles died within months of one another in 1422, Henry's infant son, Henry VI, was declared king of both France and England.

Joan of Arc and the War's Conclusion. Charles VI's son, the future Charles VII, escaped the English and asserted his right to his father's throne. But the success of the campaign that won him that prize owed less to him than to a remarkable young woman called Joan of Arc (1412–1431). Joan was a peasant from Domrémy who informed Charles VII, in March 1429, that God had commissioned her to deliver Orléans from the English armies that besieged it. The king was skeptical, but he was willing to try anything to reverse French fortunes.

Circumstances worked to Joan's advantage. The siege of Orléans had gone on for six months, and the exhausted English troops were at the point of withdrawal when Joan arrived with a fresh French army. The English retreat from Orléans was followed by a succession of victories popularly attributed to Joan.

A contemporary portrait of Joan of Arc (1412–1431) in the National Archives in Paris. [Giraudon/Art Resource, N.Y.]

She deserved credit, but not for military leadership. Joan's talent lay in inspiring her men with self-confidence and a sense of commitment to a nation. Within a few months of the liberation of Orléans, Charles VII had recovered the city of Rheims and been anointed king in its cathedral—the traditional place for French coronations.

Charles showed little gratitude to his unconventional female ally. When the Burgundians captured Joan in May 1430, Charles abandoned her. The Burgundians and the English, hoping to demoralize their opponents by discrediting Joan, accused her of heresy and turned her over to the Inquisition. After ten weeks of interrogation, the "Maid of Orléans" was executed as a relapsed heretic (May 30, 1431). Twenty-five years later (1456), Charles reopened her trial and had her cleared of all charges. But it was not until 1920 that she became Saint Joan.

Once France was united behind its king, the English had no hope of clinging to their continental possessions. In 1435 the duke of Burgundy recognized the inevitable and came to terms with Charles. By the time the war ended in 1453, the English held only a little territory around the port of Calais.

Once separated, England and France had to adjust to their new situation. The war had awakened French nationalism and hastened France's transition from a feudal monarchy to a powerfully centralized state. The loss of England's continental empire, on the other hand, disillusioned the English people with their government and set them on the path to a civil war that ended the medieval phase in the history of their monarchy.

The Black Death

Preconditions and Causes

European society in the late Middle Ages was still thoroughly agrarian. Nine-tenths of the population worked the land. The three-field system of seasonal planting and crop rotation had increased food production, but population growth kept pace with the food supply. The number of people living in Europe doubled between 1000 and 1300—until there were more mouths than could be fed. The average European probably faced extreme hunger at least once during a life span that averaged only thirty-five years.

Between 1315 and 1317, crop failures contributed to the worst famines of the Middle Ages. Starvation undermined health and increased vulnerability to a virulent bubonic plague that struck in 1348. This "Black Death" (so called because of the way it discolored the bodies of its victims) followed the trade routes from Asia into Europe. Appearing first in Sicily, it entered Europe through the ports of Venice, Genoa, and Pisa. Some places, like Bohemia, which lay outside the major trade routes, were virtually unaffected, but by the early fifteenth century the plague may have reduced the population of western Europe by two-fifths.

The plague bacilli were injected into an individual's bloodstream by flea bites. Pneumonic infection—from a victim's sneezing—was also possible. Medieval physicians had no understanding of these processes and could offer no explanation, defense, or cure. Consequently, the plague inspired deep pessimism, panicky superstition, and an obsession with death and dying. Amulets and folk remedies abounded. Some people recommended a temperate, disciplined regimen. Others hastened to enjoy as many of life's pleasures as possible before it was too late. Troops of flagellants, religious fanatics who whipped themselves in ritual penance, paraded through the countryside stirring up mass panic. Sometimes unpopular minorities, like the Jews, were accused of spreading the disease and were murdered.

Social and Economic Consequences

Farms Decline. The plague was most virulent in places where people lived close together. Whole villages and urban districts were sometimes wiped out. As the number of laborers decreased, the wages of those who survived increased. This tempted serfs to abandon farming and seek more rewarding jobs in towns. Agricultural prices fell because of lowered demand, and the price of luxury and manufactured goods—the work of scarce, skilled artisans—rose. These economic developments hurt the nobility. Without workers, the value of their estates declined. To keep workers on their manors, landowners had to offer them better deals. As a result, incomes from rents declined steadily after the plague.

The church was insulated from some of the problems that afflicted the nobility. As a great landholder, it suffered economic losses. But these were offset by an increased demand for masses for the dead and by a flood of gifts and bequests.

To recoup their losses, some landowners converted arable land to sheep pasture. (Herding required far fewer expensive laborers than the cultivation of grain.) The nobility also used their monopoly of political power to reverse their declining fortunes. They passed laws ordering peasants to stay on the land and freezing wages at low levels. Resentment of such legislation helped fuel the French *Jacquerie* and the English Peasants' Revolt.

Cities Rebound. Although the plague hit urban populations especially hard, cities ultimately prospered from its effects. Cities carefully controlled immigration and limited competition in their markets. The omnipresence of death whetted the appetite for pleasure and for the luxuries produced by cities. Initially the demand for manufactured goods could not be met, for craft guilds purposely kept the numbers of masters and apprentices low. The first wave of plague drastically reduced the already restricted supply of artisans, and this caused the prices of manufactured and luxury items to rise to new heights. As high prices for manufactured goods caused wealth to pour into cities, reduced demand for agricultural products (caused by the fall in the numbers of consumers) lowered the cost of living for urban dwellers and the value of investments in farm land. The forces that enriched townspeople impoverished the landed nobility. This enabled cities to extend their influence into the countryside, and the rural gentry began to be absorbed into the ranks of the urban patriciate.

The rapidly changing economic conditions created by the plague were not an unmixed blessing for towns. They increased some of the tensions that had long seethed within urban communities. The merchant classes found it difficult to maintain their traditional dominance over the prospering artisans' guilds. The guilds used their increasing political clout to enact restrictive legislation designed to protect local industries. Master artisans kept demand for their products high by limiting the number of shops licensed to share their market. This frustrated many journeymen who were eager to set up in business for themselves, and it created strife within the guilds.

⬦ Ecclesiastical Breakdown and Revival: The Late Medieval Church

Kings took full advantage of the rising power of the towns and the declining status of the feudal nobility to centralize governments and economies. The church, which might have resisted the royal drift toward nationalism, faltered just as the new monarchies began to flex their muscles. The plague had weakened the church by killing large numbers of clergy, but the church owed its most serious problems to its own leaders.

The Thirteenth-Century Papacy

In the latter half of the thirteenth century the papacy appeared to be in a strong position. Frederick II had been vanquished. Imperial pressure on Rome had been removed. The saintly French king, Louis IX, was an enthusiastic supporter of the church. The Eastern orthodox clergy even accepted reunion with Rome in 1274 in an attempt to persuade the West to send Constantinople help against the Turks.

But as early as the reign of Pope Innocent III (1198–1216), when papal power reached its height, there were signs of trouble. By creating a centralized papal monarchy with a clearly political mission, Innocent had increased the church's secular power, but diminished its spiritual authority. The thirteenth-century papacy became a powerful political institution. It legislated its own laws and enforced them in its own courts. It presided over an efficient international bureaucracy and was preoccupied with finances and the pursuit of secular influence. The papacy thought more in terms of its own needs than those of the church at large.

Many observers noted how far the papacy had departed from the simplicity and other-worldliness of the New Testament apostolic community. In the minds of some, a crucial distinction began to be made between the papal monarchy and the "true" church of faithful Christians.

Political Fragmentation. The papacy was undermined by its own success. The demise of imperial power meant that popes could no longer appeal for support as leaders of Italian resistance to German kings. As external threats from Germany retreated, political intrigues swept the Italian states, and the papacy became just another prize up for grabs.

Pope Gregory X (1271–1276) tried to guarantee the freedom of papal elections by ordering the cardinals to be sequestered when choosing successors to the papal throne. He hoped that physical isolation would prevent outsiders from promoting political candidates, but the college of cardinals was already too politicized for this to have much effect. Infighting was so great that from 1292 to 1294 the college was unable to elect a pope. In frustration, the cardinals finally chose a compromise candidate—a saintly but inept Calabrian hermit, Celestine V. Celestine shocked Europe by abdicating under suspicious circumstances after only a few weeks in office. His death, which soon followed, led to rumors that he had been murdered to guarantee that his successor had a clear title to office. The new pope, Boniface VIII (1294–1303), was as worldly wise as Celestine had been naively innocent.

Boniface VIII and Philip the Fair

Boniface won the papacy just as England and France were forming nation-states. France's Philip IV, "the Fair" (r. 1285–1314), was a ruthless politician who taught Boniface that the pope's inheritance from Innocent III was not the reality, but only the illusion, of power. Papal monarchy was no match for a king at the helm of one of Europe's new nations.

The Royal Challenge to Papal Authority. If Edward I (r. 1272–1307) of England had been able to resolve problems with Scotland, the Hundred Years' War might have been underway by the time Boniface became pope. France and England were both mobilizing resources for a war they considered inevitable, and their preparations created a problem for Boniface. Both states were levying extraordinary taxes on their clergy. Since Pope Innocent III had decreed in 1215 that rulers had no right to tax the clergy without papal approval, Boniface had to take a strong stand in defense of papal prerogatives. On February 5, 1296, he issued a bull (*Clericis Laicos*) forbidding lay taxation of the clergy.

Edward I retaliated by denying the clergy the protection of the state's laws and courts, and Philip the Fair cunningly deprived the papacy of the bulk of its income by forbidding the exportation of money from France to Rome. Boniface, who had no choice but to come to terms, issued a second bull that conceded the right of a king to tax clergy "during an emergency." To smooth things over, he also agreed to canonize Philip's grandfather, Louis IX.

For much of his reign Boniface was besieged by powerful enemies in Italy. The Colonnas—rivals of Boniface's family, the Gaetani—joined the Spiritual Franciscans in a campaign to invalidate Boniface's election. They alleged that Boniface had forced his predecessor (Celestine V) from office, murdered him, and won the papacy by bribing the cardinals. Boniface fought back, and his fortunes slowly improved. In 1300 Rome celebrated a Jubilee, an occasion on which pilgrims to the city received unique spiritual benefits. Tens of thousands flocked to Rome in what the papacy took to be a show of support.

This emboldened Boniface to reassert the papacy's claim to leadership in international politics. He infuriated Edward by supporting the Scots against the English. But his most serious confrontation was with Philip. Philip had arrested Boniface's Parisian legate, Bishop Bernard Saisset of Pamiers, and convicted him in the royal courts of heresy and treason. Philip demanded that Boniface recognize the legitimacy of the proceedings, but to do so would have been to relinquish the pope's jurisdiction over the French clergy. Boniface demanded Saisset's unconditional release and revoked his previous concessions on the matter of clerical taxation. In December 1301, Boniface sent Philip another bull: *Ausculta Fili* (*Listen, My Son*). It pointedly informed the king that "God has set popes over kings and kingdoms."

Philip responded with a ruthless anti-papal campaign that forced Boniface to justify the papacy's claim that it and not the state should control the churches within a nation's boundaries. On November 18, 1302, the bull *Unam Sanctam* declared that the temporal authority of kings was "subject" to the spiritual power of the church. Philip viewed this as a declaration of war.

Guillaume de Nogaret, Philip's chief minister, denounced Boniface to the French clergy and led an army into Italy to take the pope prisoner. In mid-August of 1303, Nogaret surprised Boniface in his retreat at Anagni. The pope was badly beaten and nearly killed before the people of Anagni rescued him. He returned to Rome, but the ordeal was too much for an aged man. He died in October 1303.

Boniface's successor, Benedict XI (1303–1304), excommunicated Nogaret, but he was in no position to retaliate against the French government. His successor, Clement V (1305–1314), a Frenchman and former archbishop of Bordeaux, utterly capitulated. He lifted Nogaret's excommunication and explained that *Unam Sanctam* was not intended to diminish royal authority in any way. He also gave in to Philip's demand that the Crusading order, the Knights Templars, be condemned for heresy and dissolved—so that the Philip could confiscate its wealth. France's victory seemed complete in 1309, when Clement, pleading safety and convenience, moved the papal court to Avignon. Avignon was an independent city situated on land that belonged to the pope, but it was in the southeast corner of territory that was culturally French. The papacy was to remain in Avignon for almost seventy years (until 1377), and no pope was ever again seriously to threaten a king.

The Avignon Papacy (1309–1377)

The Avignon popes were in appearance, although not always in fact, dominated by the French king, and during Clement V's pontificate Frenchmen flooded into the college of cardinals. Cut off from their Roman estates, the popes at Avignon had to find new sources of income. Their ingenuity and success quickly earned them unfortunate reputations as greedy materialists. Clement V expanded papal taxes on the clergy. Clement VI (1342–1352) began selling *indulgences* (releases from penance for sin). The doctrine of purgatory—a place of punishment where souls ultimately destined for heaven atoned for venial sins—developed as part of this campaign. By the fifteenth century, the church was urging the living to buy reduced sentences in purgatory for deceased loved ones.

Pope John XXII. By the time Pope John XXII (1316–1334) ascended the throne, the popes were well enough established in Avignon to re-enter the field of international politics. The result was a quarrel with the German emperor, Louis IV, that inspired an important debate about the nature of legitimate authority.

John backed a candidate who lost the imperial election of 1314 to Louis, and he obstinately—and without legal justification—refused to confirm Louis's title. Louis retaliated by accusing John of heresy and declaring him deposed in favor of an antipope. Two outstanding pamphleteers made the case for the king: William of Ockham, whom John excommunicated in 1328, and Marsilius of Padua (ca. 1290–1342), whose teaching John declared heretical in 1327.

William of Ockham (d. 1349) was a brilliant logician and critic of the "realist" philosophers who claimed that general terms, like "church," corresponded to transcendent realities that actually existed. Ockham, a "nominalist," insisted that such words were only names the human mind gave to abstract ideas it invented. This position led Ockham to conclude that the real

The Palace of the Popes in Avignon, France. In 1311, Pope Clement V made the city his permanent residence, and the popes remained there until 1377 [Fritz Henle/Photo Researchers, Inc.]

church was the historical human community, not some supernatural entity. The pope was only one of its members, and, as such, had no special powers that made him infallible. The church was best guided not by popes, he believed, but by scripture and by councils representing all Christians.

In *Defender of Peace* (1324), Marsilius of Padua argued that clergy were limited to purely spiritual functions and had no right to coerce laity. The spiritual crimes over which the pope had jurisdiction would be punished in the next life, not in this one. An exception might be made if a secular ruler declared a divine law also a law of the state, for God had given the state exclusive authority to maintain secular order by force. A true pope lived according to the strictest apostolic ideals and presumed to lead only by spiritual example.

National Opposition to the Avignon Papacy. John's successor, Benedict XII (1334–1342), began construction of a great palace at Avignon, and his high-living French successor, Clement VI (1342–1352), presided over a splendid, worldly court. The cardinals became lobbyists for various secular patrons, and Avignon's fiscal tentacles spread farther and farther afield.

Secular governments responded by passing legislation restricting papal jurisdiction and taxation. The English had no intention of supporting a papacy that they believed was the puppet of their French enemy. The French monarchy insisted upon its "Gallican liberties," a well-founded tradition that granted the king control of ecclesiastical appointments and taxation. German and Swiss cities also took the initiative to limit and even to overturn traditional clerical privileges and immunities.

John Wycliffe and John Huss. Discontent with the worldly clergy and politicized papacy was expressed not only in government legislation, but in popular lay religious movements. The most significant were the Lollards in England and the Hussites in Bohemia. The Lollards drew their ideas from the writings of John Wycliffe (d. 1384)—as did John Huss (d. 1415), the martyr of the Hussite movement. Neither man would have approved, however, of all that his alleged followers did in his name.

Wycliffe was an Oxford theologian and a major intellectual spokesman for the rights of royalty against the secular pretensions of popes. Wycliffe strongly supported the actions English kings took from 1350 on to reduce the power of the Avignon papacy over the church in England. Wycliffe, like the Franciscans, believed that clergy "ought to be content with food and clothing." His arguments for clerical poverty provided justification for confiscations of ecclesiastical property by the state.

Wycliffe maintained that since all authority came from God, only leaders who lived pious lives could lay claim to legitimacy. He believed that faithful laypeople had the right to pass judgment on corrupt ecclesiastics and undertake the reform of the church. The argument could also be used to justify resistance to secular rulers whose immoral lives proved that they held no mandate from God. Wycliffe anticipated some positions that Protestants would eventually take—challenging papal infallibility, the dogma of transubstantiation that gave the priesthood power over the laity, and policies that restricted the laity's access to the Scriptures.

The Lollards, English advocates of Wycliffe's teaching, preached in the vernacular, disseminated translations of Holy Scripture, and championed clerical poverty. So long as they restricted their attention to religious matters, the English government tolerated them. But after the Peasants' Revolt of 1381 popularized egalitarian notions that were linked to Wycliffe's works, the state decided that Lollardy was subversive. In 1401 it was declared a capital offense.

Heresy was not so easily dealt with in Bohemia, where government was weak. The University of Prague, founded in 1348, became the center for a Czech nationalistic movement opposing German encroachments on Bohemia. John Huss, the leader of the movement, became rector of the university in 1403. He hoped that reformed religion would promote Czech national identity.

The Czech reformers advocated vernacular translations of the Bible and rejected practices they labeled superstitions (particularly some customs associated with the Eucharist). Like the Lollards, they doubted that a priest guilty of mortal sin could perform a valid sacrament. They repudiated the Catholic rubric that reserved the cup at communion to the priest. By offering both the wine and the bread to the laity, they removed any suggestion that the clergy were spiritually superior to the people. Hussites also rejected the doctrine of transubstantiation and asserted that bread and wine remained bread and wine after priestly consecration.

Wycliffe's teaching was partly responsible for the Hussite movement. After Anne of Bohemia married King Richard II of England in 1381, Czech students enrolled at Oxford and sent copies of Wycliffe's works home. Huss was the leader of the Wycliffe faction at the University of Prague.

Huss was excommunicated in 1410, and in 1414 he successfully petitioned for a hearing before an international church council that was assembling at Constance, Switzerland. Although he was guaranteed safe conduct by Emperor Sigismund, he was imprisoned and executed for heresy on July 6, 1415. The reaction in Bohemia to his execution and that of his colleague, Jerome of Prague, a few months later was fierce. The Taborites, a militant branch of the Hussites, took up arms under John Ziska and declared their intention to transform Bohemia into a religious and social paradise. Within a decade, they had won control of the Bohemian church.

☞ The Great Schism and the Conciliar Movement

Urban VI and Clement VII

In January 1377, Pope Gregory XI (1370–1378) yielded to international pressure and announced that the papacy would leave Avignon and return to Rome. Europe rejoiced—prematurely, as it turned out—at the end of the church's "Babylonian Captivity" (a reference to the exile of the ancient Israelites from their homeland).

Gregory died soon after returning to Rome, and the cardinals elected an Italian archbishop, Pope Urban VI (1378–1389). When Urban announced his intention to reform the Curia (the church's central administration), the cardinals, most of whom were French, sensed a challenge to their power and insisted on returning the papacy to their base of operation in Avignon. Five months after Urban's enthronement, a group of thirteen cardinals announced that Urban's election was invalid because it had been forced on them by the Roman mob. They then proceeded to elect a "true" pope, Clement VII (1378–1397), a cousin of the French king. Urban denied their allegations and appointed new cardinals to replace them in his college.

Europe, confronted with two papal courts, distributed its support along political lines: England and its allies (the Holy Roman Empire, Hungary, Bohemia, and Poland) acknowledged Urban VI, whereas France and those in its orbit (Naples, Scotland, Castile, and Aragon) supported Clement VII. (The Roman Catholic Church has subsequently decided that the Roman line of popes was the legitimate one.)

Since the schism threatened the survival of the church in its traditional form, responsible leaders hoped to end it quickly. The easiest solution would have been for one or both of the popes to resign for the good of all, but neither was willing to sacrifice himself. In 1409, thirty-one years after the schism began, cardinals from both sides attempted to resolve the problem by deposing both popes and electing a new one. To their consternation, neither Rome nor Avignon accepted their action, and Christendom acquired a third pope (headquartered in Pisa).

Conciliar Theory of Church Government

Europe's leaders, seeing no other option, began to listen to scholars who argued that an ecumenical church council was needed to end the schism. There were problems: Only a pope could call a legitimate council, and none of the popes wanted to summon a council that might depose him. Also, since a pope's authority derived directly from God and not from his people, it was not at all certain that a council could depose a pope.

To make their argument for a council, the conciliarists had to examine medieval assumptions about the nature of authority. This led them to develop a rationale for popular government. The conciliarists defined the church as the whole body of the faithful and argued that, therefore, ultimate authority rested with all the people. Since popes were chosen to care for the people's church, they were accountable to the people and served at the people's pleasure.

The Council of Constance (1414–1417). Emperor Sigismund finally prevailed on John XXIII, the Pisan pope, to summon a council to meet in the Swiss city of Constance in 1414. Deprived of all support, the competing popes either came to terms or were abandoned. The cardinals at the council then chose a new pope whom everyone agreed to acknowledge, Martin V (1417–1431). Before the council disbanded, it passed a resolution (*Sacrosancta*) that stated that the council was the true government of the church and supreme over popes. Provisions were also made for councils to meet at regular intervals.

Conciliar power peaked at the Council of Basel (1431–1449). Basel presumed to negotiate church doctrine with the heretic Hussites of Bohemia. In November 1433, it granted the Bohemians jurisdiction over their church (similar to that held by the French and the English), a unique liturgy, and an exalted role for the laity.

The pope believed that this action trespassed on his jurisdiction, and in 1438 he upstaged the council by negotiating reunion with the Eastern church. The agreement signed in Florence in 1439 was short-lived, but at the time it enhanced papal prestige. When Basel responded by threatening the pope with deposition, the kings of Europe, fearing a return to schism, withdrew their support for the conciliar movement. A decade later the papal bull *Execrabilis* (1460) condemned conciliarism. The movement had, however, achieved something. It had planted the thought that the role of the leader of an institution was to care for the well-being of its members. This idea had wide-ranging ramifications for the state as well as the church.

War, plague, and schism convulsed Europe in the late Middle Ages. Even God's house became a shambles as competing popes fought over it, and leading intellectuals acknowledged the limits of human reason. As the leadership of traditional institutions failed, ordinary men and women took things into their own hands. But there was more to the age than loss, doubt, and desperation. The fourteenth century saw the birth of humanism, an explosion of lay education, and artistic and cultural movements that heralded Italy's great Renaissance.

◇ Review Questions

1. What were the underlying and precipitating causes of the Hundred Years' War? What advantages did each side have? Why were the French finally able to drive the English almost entirely out of France?

2. What were the causes of the Black Death, and why did it spread so quickly throughout western Europe? What were its effects on European society?

3. What was at issue in the struggle between Pope Boniface VIII and King Philip the Fair? How had political conditions changed since the reign of Pope Innocent III?

4. What changes took place in the church and in its relationship to secular society between 1200 and 1450? How did it respond to political threats from increasingly powerful monarchs? How great an influence did the church have on secular events?

5. What is meant by the term Avignon Papacy? How did this period in the church's history shape the development of the papacy? What caused the Great Schism? How was it resolved? Why was the Conciliar Movement a threat to the papacy?

6. Why did kings in the late thirteenth and early fourteenth centuries have more power over the church than it had over them? What did kings hope to achieve through their struggles with the church?

◇ Suggested Readings

J. HUIZINGA, *The Waning of the Middle Ages: A Study of the Forms of Life, Thought, and Art in France and the Netherlands in the Dawn of the Renaissance (1924)*. A classic study of "mentality" at the End of the Middle Ages. Exaggerated, but engrossing.

G. LEFF, *Heresy in the Later Middle Ages*, vols. 1–2 (1967). Magisterial survey of all the major heretical movements.

W. H. MCNEILL, *Plagues and Peoples* (1976). The Black Death in a broader context.

F. OAKLEY, *The Western Church in the Later Middle Ages* (1979). Eloquent, sympathetic survey.

E. PERROY, *The Hundred Years' War*, trans. by W. B. Wells (1965). Still the most comprehensive one-volume account.

Y. RENOVARD, *The Avignon Papacy 1305–1403*, trans. by D. Bethell (1970). The standard narrative account.

B. TIERNEY, *Foundations of the Conciliar Theory* (1955). Important study showing the origins of conciliar theory in canon law.

W. ULLMANN, *Origins of the Great Schism* (1948). A basic study by a controversial interpreter of medieval political thought.

10

Renaissance and Discovery

KEY TOPICS

> ⬥ The politics, culture, and art of the Italian Renaissance
> ⬥ Political struggle and foreign intervention in Italy
> ⬥ The powerful new monarchies of northern Europe
> ⬥ The thought and culture of the northern Renaissance

The late medieval period was an era of creative breaking up. The social order that had persisted in Europe for a thousand years failed, but Europe did not decline. It merely changed direction.

By the late fifteenth century, Europe's population was recovering from the losses inflicted by the plagues, famines, and wars of the fourteenth century. In

many places, able rulers were establishing stable, centralized governments. The city-states of Italy were doing especially well. Italy's strategic location permitted it to dominate world trade, which still centered on the Mediterranean. The great wealth trade brought Italy's rulers and merchants allowed them to become patrons of government, education, and the

212

arts. The result was a cultural renaissance led by Italians.

Renaissance Humanists revived the study of Greek and Latin and recovered the classical literary heritage. They reformed education and, thanks to the invention of the printing press, became the first scholars able to reach out to the general public. In their eagerness to educate ordinary men and women, they championed the development of vernacular languages as vehicles for art and serious thought.

During the late fifteenth and sixteenth centuries, powerful nations arose in western Europe and inaugurated an era of unprecedented territorial expansion. The colonies they planted around the world yielded a flood of gold and exotic new products that transformed the Western way of life.

✧ The Renaissance in Italy (1375–1527)

The Renaissance was a time of transition from the medieval to the modern world. Medieval Europe, especially before the twelfth century, was a fragmented feudal society with a marginal agrarian economy. Intellectually, it was dominated by the church. Renaissance Europe, especially after the fourteenth century, was characterized by growing national consciousness and political centralization, an urban economy based on commerce and capitalism, and an increasingly secular culture. These changes appeared first in Italy.

The Italian City-State

Italy had always had a cultural advantage over the rest of Europe, for its location made it the link between East and West. Trade with the Middle East, which continued uninterrupted throughout the Middle Ages, supported a vibrant urban culture in Italy. During the thirteenth and fourteenth centuries, Italy's cities extended their influence into the countryside and became great city-states (see Map 10-1).

The growth of Italy's cities and urban culture was promoted by the endemic warfare between Guelf (pro-papal) and Ghibelline (pro-imperial) political factions. Either the pope or the emperor might have brought the cities under control if either had been free to concentrate on the task. Instead, each tried to weaken the other, and the merchant oligarchies that governed the cities were the winners. Free from dominance by kings or territorial princes, the Italian cities expanded into the surrounding countryside and assimilated the rural nobility. The five greatest were the duchy of Milan, the republics of Florence and Venice, the Papal States, and the kingdom of Naples.

Social Class and Conflict. Social strife and competition for power were intense within Italy's city-states. By the fifteenth century, most had concluded that they could preserve order only by turning themselves over to despots. Venice was a notable exception; it remained an oligarchic republic controlled by a

MAP 10-1 Renaissance Italy *The city-states of Renaissance Italy were self-contained principalities whose internal strife was monitored by despots and whose external aggression was controlled by treaty.*

small group of merchant families. Florence, on the other hand, was fairly typical of the forces that contended within Italian urban governments.

There were four politically active groups in Florence: the old rich (the *grandi*, the nobles and merchants who were traditional leaders), an emergent newly rich merchant class (capitalists and bankers known as the *popolo grosso* or "fat people"), the middle-burgher ranks (guildmasters, shop owners, and professionals), and the *popolo minuto* (the "little people" of the lower middle classes). In 1457 about 30,000 Florentines, one-third of the population, were listed as paupers.

In 1378 the economic dislocation of the Black Death prompted the Ciompi Revolt, a great uprising of the poor in Florence. Stability was not restored until Cosimo dé Medici (1389–1464) took over in 1434. Cosimo dé Medici, in addition to being the richest man in Florence, was an astute statesman. He controlled the city from behind the scenes, skillfully manipulating the constitu-

Significant Dates from the Italian Renaissance (1375–1527)

1434	*Medici rule established in Florence*
1454–1455	*Treaty of Lodi*
1494	*Charles VIII of France invades Italy*
1495	*League of Venice*
1499	*Louis XII invades Italy*
1500	*The Borgias conquer Romagna*
1512–1513	*The Holy League defeats the French*
1515	*Francis I invades Italy*
1527	*Sack of Rome by imperial soldiers*

tion and influencing elections. Florence was governed by a council of six (later, eight) men, the *Signoria,* elected from the most powerful guilds. Through informal, cordial relations with the electoral committee, Cosimo saw to it that the members of the *Signoria* were his men. His grandson, Lorenzo the Magnificent (1449–1492), had absolute control of Florence. After 1478, when the pope and a rival Florentine family (the Pazzi) assassinated Lorenzo's brother, Lorenzo ruled with a firm hand. But he was careful to court popular support.

Despotism was less subtle elsewhere. When internal fighting and foreign intrigue got so bad that city governments were paralyzed, warring factions agreed to the appointment of a *podestà.* He was a neutral outsider, a hired strongman who was empowered to do whatever was necessary to maintain law and order and foster a good climate for business. Because a despot could not depend on everyone's cooperation, he policed and protected his town with a mercenary army hired from military brokers called *condottieri.*

The *podestà's* job was hazardous. He could be dismissed by the oligarchy that hired him or assassinated by those whom he offended. The potential spoils of such a career were, however, tempting, for a *podestà* might establish a dynasty. The Visconti family that came to power in Milan in 1278 and the Sforza family that followed them in 1450 both had such roots.

No matter what kind of government it had, a disciplined Italian city provided a congenial climate for intellectual and artistic pursuits. Despots promoted Renaissance culture as enthusiastically as republicans, and spiritually minded popes were no less generous than worldly vicars of Christ.

Humanism

The Florentine Leonardo Bruni (1374–1444) was the first to describe the scholarship of the Renaissance as the study of *humanitas* ("humanity"). Modern authorities do not agree on how to define the term. For some, Humanism is an un-Christian philosophy that exalts human dignity, individualism, and secular values. There were, however, Christian Humanists who defended faith from attack by extreme rationalists. Humanism, for many, may have been less a philosophical position than an educational program emphasizing rhetoric and sound scholarship. It championed the study of Latin and Greek classics and Christian church fathers as an end in itself and as a guide to reforming society. The first Humanists were orators and poets. Some taught at universities, but many worked as secretaries, speech writers, and diplomats at princely and papal courts.

The Humanists were not the first Europeans to take an interest in the study of classical and Christian antiquities. There had been a Carolingian renaissance in the ninth century. Another was led by the cathedral school of Chartres in the twelfth century. The University of Paris in the thirteenth century was transformed by the study of Aristotle, and the works of Saint Augustine reinvigorated intellectual life in the fourteenth century. These earlier scholarly revivals pale, however, in comparison with Italy's late medieval Renaissance.

Humanists did not use the same techniques of debate as those on which the medieval Scholastics relied. Instead of summarizing and reconciling the views of respected commentators on a topic, they went directly to original sources. Avidly searching out neglected manuscripts, Italian Humanists recovered all that remained of Greek and Latin literature and made it generally available to all scholars. They so assimilated the classics and so identified with the ancients that they came to think of the previous centuries as a hiatus, a dark "middle age" separating ancient civilization from its rebirth in their day.

Petrarch, Dante, and Boccaccio. Francesco Petrarch (1304–1374), "the father of Humanism," aspired to write like one of the giants of Roman literature. His *Letters to the Ancient Dead* was an imagined correspondence with Cicero, Livy, Vergil, and Horace. His epic poem *Africa* (a tribute to the Roman general Scipio Africanus) continued Vergil's *Aenead*. His biographies of famous Romans, *Lives of Illustrious Men*, paid homage to Plutarch. But Petrarch's most popular work was both original and not in a classical language: a collection of highly introspective Italian love sonnets which he addressed to a married woman named Laura. He admired her as a courtly lover—from a safe distance.

Classical and Christian values coexist in Petrarch's work. He rejected Scholastic learning as sterile and useless, but published tracts refuting Aristotelian arguments that undercut faith in personal immortality. His imagined dialogues with Saint Augustine bear witness to his acceptance of many other traditional medieval Christian beliefs.

Petrarch had a far more secular point of view than his famous near-contemporary, Dante Alighieri (1265–1321). Dante's *Vita Nuova* and *Divine Comedy* rank with Petrarch's sonnets as cornerstones of Italian vernacular literature. They are also moving testimonies to medieval piety. Petrarch's student, Giovanni Boccaccio (1313–1375), created bridges of another kind between medieval literature and Humanism. His *Decameron* consists of 100 often bawdy tales, many retold from medieval sources.

Educational Reforms and Goals. Humanists were activists who treated the magnificent manuscript collections they assembled as if books were potent medicines for the ills of society. The goal of their studies was to discover the good and to practice virtue. Humanist learning was intended to ennoble people by fitting them for the free use of their gifts of mind and body.

Traditional methods of education had to be reformed to nurture the kind of well-rounded people the Humanists wanted to produce. The rediscovery in 1416 of the complete text of Quintilian's *Education of the Orator* provided Humanists with a classical guide for the revision of curricula. Mentors, such as Vittorino da Feltre (d. 1446), articulated the goals and methods of the reform. Vittorino required his students to master difficult works by Pliny, Ptolemy, Terence, Plautus, Livy, and Plutarch, and to undergo vigorous physical training.

Humanist learning was not confined to the classroom. Baldassare Castiglione's (1478–1529) influential *Book of the Courtier* was written as a practical guide for the nobility at the court of Urbino. It urged them to combine the study of ancient languages and history with the practice of athletic, military, and musical skills. In addition to these accomplishments, a courtier was to have good manners and an exemplary moral character.

Women, most notably Christine de Pisan (1363?–1434), helped shape and profit from educational reform. Christine's father was physician and astrologer to the court of King Charles V of France. At the French court she received as fine an education as any man and became an expert in classical, French, and Italian languages and literature. Married at fifteen and widowed with three children at twenty-seven, she turned to writing lyric poetry to support herself. Her works were soon being read at all the European courts. Her most famous book, *The City of Ladies*, chronicles the accomplishments of the great women of history.

The Florentine "Academy." The revival of the study of ancient Greek literature, particularly the works of Plato, was the most important of the Renaissance's renewed contacts with the past. Interest in Greek led Florence, in 1397, to invite a Byzantine scholar, Manuel Chrysoloras, to immigrate and open a school. The Council of Ferrara-Florence, which met in 1439 to negotiate the reunion of the Eastern and Western churches, brought more Greek scholars and manuscripts to Italy. Their numbers increased greatly when Turks overwhelmed the city of Constantinople in 1453.

Medieval Scholastics were preoccupied with Aristotle's logic and science, but Renaissance thinkers were enthralled by Plato's poetry and mysticism. Platonism's appeal lay in its flattering view of human nature and its apparent congruence with Christianity. Platonism posited the existence of a realm of eternal ideas that were the prototypes for the imperfect, perishable things of the world in which humans lived. Plato argued that the presence in the human mind of an innate knowledge of mathematical truths and moral standards proved that a part of a human being was rooted in the eternal.

To encourage the study of Plato and the Neoplatonic philosophers Cosimo dé Medici (1389–1464) funded a Platonic Academy, a gathering of influential Florentine Humanists headed first by Marsilio Ficino (1433–1499) and later by Pico della Mirandola (1463–1494). From Florence Plato's work circulated throughout the West to promote a new, more optimistic view of human nature. Pico's *Oration on the Dignity of Man* succinctly articulated the Renaissance's faith in human potential. Published in Rome in December 1486, the *Oration* was a preface to a collection of 900 theses proposed for a public debate on all of life's important issues. It lauded human beings as the only creatures in the world possessed of the freedom to become whatever they wanted—angels or pigs.

Civic Humanism. Although some Humanists were clubbish snobs—an intellectual elite with narrow, antiquarian interests—others preached a "civil Humanism," an education that promoted virtue and equipped one for public service. They entered politics, produced art and literature to celebrate the cities where they lived, promoted the use of vernacular languages so that ordinary people could profit from their work, and wrote histories of contemporary events.

The Humanists' careful study of classical languages equipped them to carry out scientific, critical analyses of important historical documents. Some Humanists, like Lorenzo Valla (1406–1457), author of the standard Renaissance text on Latin philology (*Elegances of the Latin Language*), made discoveries that shook the foundations of medieval institutions. Valla demonstrated that the *Donation of Constantine,* a document which the church had cited since the eighth century to bolster its claim to secular power, was a fraud. Valla pointed out that the *Donation* was filled with anachronistic terms (e.g., fief) and references that would have been meaningless to a man of Constantine's day. Valla also publicized errors in the Latin Vulgate, the version of the Bible authorized for use in the Western church. Intentionally or unintentionally, Humanism provided ammunition for critics of traditional medieval organizations.

Renaissance Art

In Renaissance Italy—and in Reformation Europe—the interests of the laity triumphed over those of the clergy. As people began to value the secular world, secular learning, and purely human pursuits as ends in themselves, medieval Christian attitudes adjusted to accommodate a more this-worldly spirit. This development owed something to the crises within the papacy that cost the late medieval church much of its power and prestige. It was also encouraged by the rise of patriotic nationalism, the creation of governmental bureaucracies staffed by laypersons rather than clerics, and the rapid growth of lay education during the fourteenth and fifteenth centuries.

The new perspective on life can be perceived in the painting and sculpture of the "High" or mature Renaissance (the late fifteenth and early sixteenth centuries). Whereas medieval art was abstract and formulaic, Renaissance art focused on describing the natural world and communicating human emotions. It displayed a rational (chiefly mathematical) order, a symmetry and proportionality that reflected a Humanistic faith in the harmony and intelligibility of the universe.

Florentine women doing needlework, spinning, and weaving. These activities took up much of a woman's time and contributed to the elegance of dress for which Florentine men and women were famed. [Alinari/Art Resource]

During the fifteenth century, artists developed new technical skills. Slow-drying oil-based paints were invented, and new methods of drafting were devised. *Chiaroscuro*, the use of shading, and linear perspective, the adjustment of the size of figures to create the illusion of depth, permitted artists to paint a more natural world. Whereas flat Byzantine and Gothic paintings were intended to be read like pages in a book, Renaissance paintings were windows on a three-dimensional world filled with life.

Giotto (1266–1336), the father of Renaissance painting, was the first to intuit what could be done with the new techniques. Though still filled with religious seriousness, his work was less abstract and more naturalistic than that of a medieval painter. The Black Death of 1340 slowed the development of art, but ideas like Giotto's emerged again in the fifteenth century in the work of the painter Masaccio (1401–1428) and the sculptor Donatello (1386–1466). The heights were reached by the great masters of the High Renaissance: Leonardo da Vinci (1452–1519), Raphael (1483–1520), and Michelangelo Buonarroti (1475–1564).

Leonardo came closer than anyone to achieving the Renaissance ideal of universal competence. He was one of the greatest painters of all time—as is demonstrated by his famous portrait of Mona Lisa. Kings and dukes employed him as a military engineer. As an early advocate of scientific experimentation, he defied the church by dissecting corpses to study human anatomy. He also did significant descriptive work in botany. Leonardo's sketch books were filled with designs for such modern machines as airplanes and submarines. He had so many ideas that it was difficult for him to concentrate long on any one of them.

Raphael, an unusually sensitive man, was loved for both his work and his kindly personality. He is best known for his tender depictions of madonnas. Art historians consider his fresco *The School of Athens*, a group portrait of the great Western philosophers, a perfect example of Renaissance technique.

Michelangelo was a more melancholy genius, but he also excelled in several fields. His David, an eighteen-foot-high sculpture of a biblical hero in the guise of a Greek god, splendidly illustrates the Renaissance artist's devotion to harmony, symmetry, and proportion—and to the glorification of the human form. Four different popes commissioned works from Michelangelo. The most famous are the frescoes that Pope Julius II (1503–1513) ordered for the Vatican's Sistine Chapel. They originally covered 10,000 square feet and featured 343 figures—most of which Michelangelo executed himself with minimal help from his assistants. It took him four years to complete the extraordinarily original images that have become the best-known icons of the Christian faith.

Michelangelo lived to be nearly ninety, and his later works illustrate the passing of the High Renaissance and the advent of a new style known as Mannerism. Mannerism was a reaction against the simplicity and symmetry of High Renaissance art. It made room for the strange, even the abnormal, and gave free reign to the subjectivity of the artist. The name reflects a tendency by artists to employ "mannered" or "affected" techniques—distortions that expressed individual perceptions and feelings. The Venetian Tintoretto (d. 1594) and the Spanish El Greco (d. 1614) represent Mannerism at its best.

Slavery in the Renaissance

The vision of innate human nobility that inspired the Renaissance was marred by what modern observers would consider a major blind spot. Slavery flourished in Italy as extravagantly as art and culture. The slave market developed as early as the twelfth century when Spaniards began to sell Muslim war captives to wealthy Italians. Many of these slaves were employed as domestic servants, but collective plantation slavery also appeared in the eastern Mediterranean during the High Middle Ages. Venetian sugar cane plantations were models for later west Mediterranean and New World slavery.

The demand for slaves soared after the Black Death (1348–1350) reduced the supply of laborers throughout western Europe. A strong young slave cost the equivalent of the wages paid a free servant over several years. But given the prospect of a lifetime of free service, slaves were considered good bargains. Owners could also dispose of them like any other pieces of property. Slaves of all races were imported from Africa, the Balkans, Constantinople, Cyprus, Crete, and the lands surrounding the Black Sea. Most well-to-do Italian households had slaves, and even clergy kept them.

As in ancient Greece and Rome, slaves of the Renaissance era were often integrated into households like family members. Some female slaves became mothers of their masters' children, and quite a few of these children were adopted and raised as legitimate heirs. It was clearly in the self-interest of owners to protect their investments by keeping slaves healthy and happy, but slaves remained an uprooted and resentful people—a threat to social stability.

This portrait of Katharina, by Albrecht Dürer, provides evidence of African slavery in Europe during the sixteenth century. Katharina was in the service of one Jao Bradao, a Portuguese economic minister living in Antwerp, then the financial center of Europe. Dürer became friends with Bradao during his stay in the Low Countries in the winter of 1520–1521. [Bildarchiv Foto Marburg/Art Resource, N.Y.]

✦ Italy's Political Decline: French Invasions (1494–1527)

The Treaty of Lodi

The protection of Italy from foreign invasion depended on the ability of its independent city-states to cooperate. During the last half of the fifteenth century, the Treaty of Lodi (1454–1455) brought Milan and Naples, traditional enemies, into alliance with Florence against Venice and the Papal States. This created a balance of power within Italy and a united front against external enemies.

The peace established by the Treaty of Lodi ended in 1494 when Naples, Florence, and Pope Alexander VI prepared to attack Milan. Ludovico il Moro, the despot of Milan, asked France for help. He urged the French to revive their claim to Naples, which they had ruled from 1266 to 1435. He did not pause to consider that France also had a claim on Milan.

Charles VIII's March Through Italy

Charles VIII (r. 1483–1498) was an eager youth in his twenties, and he responded to Ludovico's call with lightning speed. It took him only five months to cross the Alps (August 1495) and march through Florentine territory and the Papal States to Naples. Piero dé Medici, ruler of Florence, tried to placate him by handing over Pisa and other Florentine possessions. This angered his people, and the radical preacher Girolamo Savonarola (1452–1498) persuaded them to rebel and drive him into exile. Savonarola told the Florentines that France's invasion was God's punishment for their sins, and they paid Charles a large ransom to spare the city. Savonarola remained in power for four years. The Florentines then tired of his puritanical tyranny and pro-French policy and executed him (May 1498).

Charles's lightning march through Italy alarmed Ferdinand of Aragon, who believed that a French-Italian axis constituted a threat to his homeland. Ferdinand proposed an alliance (the League of Venice) to unite Aragon, Venice, the Papal States, and the Emperor Maximilian I against the French. When Milan, which regretted inviting the French into Italy, joined the League, Charles was forced to retreat.

Pope Alexander VI and the Borgia Family

Louis XII (r. 1498–1515), Charles's successor, was able to return to Italy, for he made an ally of Pope Alexander VI (1492–1503). Alexander was a member of the infamous Borgia family and probably the church's most corrupt pope.

Alexander's goal was to use the power of the papacy to recover Romagna, a district on the Adriatic coast northeast of Rome that had broken free from the Papal States during the Avignon papacy. His intent was to turn it over to his children, Cesare and Lucrezia, as a hereditary duchy. Venice's opposition to this plan led the pope to break with the League of Venice and ally with France. The dissolution of the league allowed the French to reconquer Milan, and the pope claimed as his reward the hand of the sister of the king of Navarre for his son and the promise of French military aid in Romagna. In 1500 Louis and Ferdinand of Aragon divided up Naples while the pope and Cesare completed the conquest of Romagna.

Pope Julius II

When Cardinal Giuliano della Rovere became Pope Julius II (1503–1513), he suppressed the Borgias and restored Romagna to Rome's control. Julius, the "warrior pope," brought the Renaissance papacy to a peak of military prowess and diplomatic intrigue. Once he had driven the Venetians out of Romagna (1509) and fully secured the Papal States, he set about ridding Italy of his former allies, the French. Julius, Ferdinand of Aragon, and Venice formed a second Holy League in October 1511. Emperor Maximilian I and the Swiss joined them, and by 1512 the French were in full retreat.

The French were nothing if not persistent. Louis's successor, Francis I (r. 1515–1547), led yet another assault on Italy. The Holy League weakened after French armies massacred its Swiss allies at Marignano in September 1515, but the Habsburg emperor then took up the cause. Four Habsburg-Valois wars finally ended in defeat for France.

Francis was more successful in dealing with the pope. The Concordat of Bologna (August 1516) gave the French king control over the French clergy in exchange for France's recognition of the pope's supremacy over church councils and his right to collect certain fees from clergy in France. This virtually nationalized the French Catholic church and, thereby, undercut any appeal the Reformation might have had for France's kings.

Niccolò Machiavelli

As the armies of France, Spain, and Germany made a shambles of Italy, Niccolò Machiavelli (1469–1527), a Florentine scholar, struggled to make sense of the tragedy befalling his homeland. The lesson it taught him was that political ends—the maintenance of peace and order—are justified by any means.

Machiavelli's Humanist education had included a close, if somewhat romanticized, study of the history of ancient Rome. He was impressed by the apparent ability of the Romans to act decisively and heroically for the good of their country, and he lamented the absence of such traits among his compatriots. He believed that if the Italians could cease their internal feuding and unite in defense of their nation, they could drive out the invaders. Machiavelli was devoted to republican ideals, but the realities of political life in Italy convinced him that only a strongman could rescue the Italians from the consequences of their own short-sightedness. The salvation of Italy required a cunning dictator who was willing to use "Machiavellian" techniques to manipulate his people.

Machiavelli may have intended *The Prince*, which he wrote in 1513, to be a satire on politics, not a serious justification for despotism. But he seems to have been in earnest when he advised rulers to consider fraud and brutality necessary means to the higher end of unifying Italy.

Machiavelli hoped that the Medici family might produce the leader Italy needed. In 1513 its members controlled both the papacy—Leo X (1513–1521)—and the powerful territorial state of Florence. *The Prince* was dedicated to Lorenzo dé Medici, duke of Urbino and grandson of Lorenzo the Magnificent. The Medicis, however, failed to rise to the challenge Machiavelli set them. In the year he died (1527), a second Medici pope, Clement VII (1523–1534), watched helplessly as Rome was sacked by the army of Emperor Charles V.

✧ Revival of Monarchy in Northern Europe

The feudal monarchies of the High Middle Ages divided the powers of government between kings and their vassals. The nobility and the towns—through representative assemblies such as the English Parliament, the French Estates General, and the Spanish *Cortes*—tried to thwart the growth of royal authority. But by 1450, territorial magnates in many parts of Europe were being brought under the control of centralized national monarchies.

Towns were the crucial factor in this political transition. With the help of townspeople, kings could escape the limitations feudalism imposed on them. Townspeople took the place of the nobility as royal officials, and helped kings reclaim the powers of taxation, war making, and law enforcement that under the feudal system were the prerogatives of semiautonomous vassals. As the vassals ceded these functions to a centralized government, the regions they had ruled combined to form a true nation. Unlike the nobility, who were identified with certain districts, the careers of professional civil servants—the Spanish *corregidores*, the English justices of the peace, and the French bailiffs—depended on advancing national, not regional, issues.

As kings acquired the bureaucratic machinery needed to enforce their decrees, they were able to bypass feudal councils and representative assemblies. Ferdinand and Isabella of Spain rarely called the *Cortes* into session. The French Estates General did not meet from 1484 to 1560. And after 1485, when England's Parliament granted Henry VII (r. 1485–1509) the right to collect the customs revenues he needed to cover the costs of government, the king summoned no more parliaments.

By the fifteenth century, monarchies had also begun to create standing national armies that ended the nobles' traditional military monopoly. Changing technologies—such as artillery—enhanced the importance of the common man's infantry and diminished the significance of the noble cavalry. Professional soldiers—even foreign mercenaries—who fought for pay and booty were far more efficient than feudal vassals who fought for honor's sake.

Since the strength of infantry is dependent upon numbers, monarchs wanted large armies. Professional soldiers, however, tended to mutiny if payrolls were not met. Fifteenth and sixteenth century governments had, therefore, to find new sources of income to meet the rising costs of warfare. Efforts to expand royal revenues were hampered by the upper classes' determined resistance to taxation. The nobles believed that their king should live as they did, from the income of personal estates. They considered taxation demeaning. In light of their opposition, kings usually found it easier to levy taxes on those who were least able to resist and least able to pay.

Monarchs had several sources of income. As feudal lords, they collected rents from the royal domain. They could levy national taxes on basic food and clothing. (France, for instance, had a tax on salt, and Spain had a 10 percent sales tax.) Rulers could also, with the approval of parliamentary bodies that did not represent the lower classes, levy direct taxes on the peasantry. (France's king relied heavily on such a tax: the *taille*.) Some governments sold public offices and issued high-interest bonds, and rather than taxing the nobility, they turned to them and to bankers for loans. A king's most powerful subjects were often also his creditors.

France

Charles VII (r. 1422–1461) was a king made great by those who served him. His ministers created a permanent professional army, which—thanks to the inspiration of Joan of Arc—drove the English out of France. An enterprising merchant banker, Jacques Coeur, devised policies to strengthen France's economy, diplomatic corps, and national administration. These tools helped the ruthless Louis XI (r. 1461–1483), Charles's son, make France a great power.

The rise of France in the fifteenth century depended on the defeat of two opponents: the king of England, and the duke of Burgundy. The Hundred Years' War cost England its continental possessions. But Burgundy, England's sometime ally in that war, emerged in the mid-fifteenth century as Europe's strongest state. Burgundy's duke, Charles the Bold, hoped to pull together his scattered family domains to create a new "middle" kingdom between France and Germany. It required a coalition of continental powers to stop him.

When Charles the Bold died in battle in 1477, the dream of a Burgundian empire died with him. Louis XI and the Habsburg emperor, Maximilian I, divided up Burgundy's lands. The Habsburgs got the better parts, but the dissolution of Burgundy freed Louis XI to concentrate on France's internal affairs. Louis harnessed France's nobility, fostered its trade and industry, and ended his reign with a kingdom almost twice the size of that with which he had started.

Louis's successors failed to build on the excellent foundation he laid. Their invasions of Italy in the 1490s and the long series of losing wars with the Habsburgs that resulted left France, by the mid-sixteenth century, almost as divided internally as it had been during the Hundred Years' War.

Spain

In 1469 the marriage of Isabella of Castile (r. 1474–1504) and Ferdinand of Aragon (r. 1479–1516) greatly accelerated the process of creating a unified Spanish monarchy. Castile was the richer and more populous of the two states, having about 5 million inhabitants to Aragon's 1 million. Castile also had a lucrative, centrally managed sheep-farming industry managed by a state-backed agency called the *Mesta*. Although both kingdoms shared a dynasty (Ferdinand and Isabella's family), each retained its own government agencies, laws, armies, coinage, taxation, and cultural traditions.

Together, Ferdinand and Isabella were able to do what neither could do alone: bring the nobility under control, secure the borders of their realms, launch wars of conquest, and enforce a common Christian faith among all their subjects. In 1492 they conquered the last Muslim state on the Iberian peninsula, Granada. Naples became a Spanish possession in 1504, and by 1512 Ferdinand had acquired the kingdom of Navarre.

Ferdinand and Isabella relied on the *Hermandad,* a league of cities and towns, for help in subduing the powerful landowners who dominated the countryside. Townspeople replaced the nobility within the royal administration, and the monarchy circumscribed the power of the nobility by extending its authority over wealthy chivalric orders.

Spain had long been remarkable among European lands as a place where three religions—Islam, Judaism, and Christianity—coexisted with a certain degree of toleration. Ferdinand and Isabella ended this by imposing a state-controlled Christianity on all their subjects. They ran the church and used it to promote national unity. Of particular utility was the Inquisition, the ecclesiastical court that tried cases of heresy. In 1479 the Inquisition, run by Isabella's confessor Tomás de Torquemada (d. 1498), was assigned the task of monitoring the activities of the converted Spanish Jews (*conversos*) and Muslims (*Moriscos*). In

1492 the Jews who refused to convert were exiled and their properties were confiscated. In 1502 the same fate befell the Moors of Granada. The state's rigorous enforcement of orthodoxy kept Spain a loyal Catholic country and made it a base of operation for the Counter-Reformation, the Catholic response to the Protestant Reformation of the sixteenth century.

The marriages arranged for Ferdinand and Isabella's children were part of a grand plan to contain France, and they set the stage for Europe's politics in the sixteenth century. In 1496 their eldest daughter and heir, Joanna (later known as "the Mad") wed Archduke Philip, the son of Emperor Maximilian I. Charles, the child of this union, inherited a united Spain from his grandparents. This, augmented by his Habsburg patrimony and election as emperor in 1519, created a European kingdom almost as large as Charlemagne's. Ferdinand and Isabella's second daughter, Catherine of Aragon, wed Arthur, heir to England's King Henry VII. After Arthur's premature death, Catherine was betrothed to his brother, the future King Henry VIII. Henry's desire to end this marriage forced him to break with the papacy and declare England a Protestant nation.

Spain's power was also enhanced by the overseas explorations that Ferdinand and Isabella sponsored. The discoveries made in their names by the Genoese adventurer Christopher Columbus (1451–1506) founded Spain's empire in Mexico and Peru. Gold and silver from this "new world" enabled Spain to dominate Europe during the sixteenth century.

England

The last half of the fifteenth century was an especially difficult period for the English. While they were adjusting to their loss of the Hundred Years' War, a fight broke out between branches of their royal family, the House of York and the House of Lancaster. For thirty years (1455–1485) a dynastic struggle, now known as the Wars of the Roses (York's heraldic emblem was a white rose and Lancaster's a red rose) kept England in a state of turmoil.

Henry VI (r. 1422–1461), a weak king from the Lancastrian house, was challenged by his cousin, the duke of York, who had supporters in England's prosperous southern towns. In 1461 the duke of York's son seized power as Edward IV (r. 1461–1483). Although his reign was interrupted in 1470–1471, by a short-lived restoration of Henry VI, Edward retained the upper hand and greatly increased the power and wealth of the monarchy.

Edward's brother, Richard III (r. 1483–1485), usurped the throne from Edward's young son. He was, in turn, overthrown by Henry Tudor, a distant royal relation who had inherited the leadership of the Lancastrian faction. Henry established England's Tudor dynasty. Shakespeare's powerful play *Richard III* reflects the influence of Tudor propaganda in its portrayal of Richard as an unprincipled villain.

Henry Tudor, Henry VII (r. 1485–1509), married Edward IV's daughter (Elizabeth of York) to unite the rival branches of the royal family and create an uncontestable claim to the throne for their offspring. Henry also devised something called the Court of Star Chamber to bring the English nobility under tighter royal control. Created with the sanction of Parliament in 1487, the court was granted jurisdiction over cases involving the nobility. Since it was staffed by the king's chief councillors, the nobles could not use the tactics of intimidation and bribery that had enabled them to make a mockery of courts staffed by more vulnerable men. Henry construed legal precedents to the advantage of the crown, and he confiscated so much property from the nobility that he did not have to convene Parliament to raise the money he needed to govern. Henry shaped a monarchy that, during the reign of his granddaughter (Elizabeth I), became one of the most effective in early modern Europe.

The Holy Roman Empire

Germany and Italy were exceptions to the general trend toward political centralization seen in the histories of other European nations during the last half of the fifteenth century. Germany's rulers maintained the ancient practice of partitioning lands among all their sons. As a result, by the end of the Middle Ages Germany was divided into some 300 autonomous entities, and its fragmented authorities were powerless to halt the development of revolutionary movements like the Reformation.

German princes and cities worked together to maintain law and order, if not unity, within the Holy Roman Empire. In 1356 the emperor and the major German territorial rulers issued the *Golden Bull* and created a system that encouraged cooperation among regions of the empire. It allotted choice of an emperor to a seven-member electoral college: the archbishops of Mainz, Trier, and Cologne; the duke of Saxony; the margrave of Brandenburg; the count Palatine; and the king of Bohemia.

The emperor reigned more than ruled, for the extent of his powers, especially over the seven electors, was renegotiated with every imperial election. In the fifteenth century an effort was made to create some unity of purpose among the principalities. A regular national meeting—the imperial diet or *Reichstag* (composed of the seven electors, the nonelectoral princes, and the sixty-five imperial free cities)—began to be held.

In 1495 the diet won concessions from Maximilian I (r. 1493–1519) that were intended to promote order in the nation. Private warfare was banned. A court (the *Reichskammergericht*) was established to enforce internal peace, and an imperial Council of Regency (the *Reichsregiment*) was appointed to coordinate the development of policy. Although these reforms were important, they fell far short of the creation of a centralized state. During the sixteenth and seventeenth centuries, the territorial princes were virtually sovereign rulers in their domains.

⤳ The Northern Renaissance

The Humanist scholars of the Renaissance were responsible for the development of a climate in Europe favorable to religious and educational reform. Humanism spread to northern Europe from Italy through such intermediaries as students who studied in Italy and merchants who traded there. Reform was also promoted by the Brothers of the Common Life, an influential lay religious movement that began in the Netherlands and permitted men and women to live a shared religious life without making formal vows of poverty, chastity, and obedience.

The northern Humanists developed a distinctive culture. They tended to come from more diverse social backgrounds and to be more interested in religious reform than their Italian counterparts. They were also more willing to write for lay audiences. This latter was a crucial factor, for the invention of printing with movable type was about to create a world in which intellectual elites could argue their cases before the public and spark mass movements.

The Printing Press

Since the days of Charlemagne, kings and princes had encouraged literacy. Without people who could read, think critically, and write reliable reports, no kingdom, large or small, could be properly governed. During the late Middle Ages new schools spread literacy far beyond the ranks of the clergy, and the number of universities in Europe tripled from twenty to sixty.

An early printing press. Between 1435 and 1455, Johann Gutenberg worked out the complete technology of casting individual letters into rectangular metal type, composing the type into pages held together by pressure, and printing those pages on an adaptation of the wooden standing press using ink made of lampblack mixed with oil varnish. This new technology made it possible for the first time in the West to manufacture numerous identical copies of written works. [Huntington Library]

Medieval scribes had written books on expensive sheets of leather called vellum. Since it required 170 calfskins or 300 sheepskins to make a single vellum Bible, few people could afford the complete text. Whole pages were sometimes carved on wooden blocks for printing, but the production of such blocks was difficult and did not much reduce cost.

In the mid-fifteenth century Johann Gutenberg (d. 1468) of Mainz was stimulated by the growing market for books to invent printing with movable type. The development of a process of cheap paper manufacture also helped to bring down the costs of production and make books on subjects ranging from theology to farming and child-rearing available in all price ranges. The new technology generated a great demand, and the number of presses exploded. By 1500, about fifty years after Gutenberg opened his shop, printers were operating in over 200 European cities.

Literacy deeply affected people everywhere, nurturing self-esteem and a critical frame of mind. By standardizing texts and prompting discussions, the print revolution made anyone who could read an authority. As a result, ordinary men and women became less credulous and docile than their ancestors. But print also gave their rulers a powerful tool for manipulating their beliefs.

Erasmus

The career of Desiderius Erasmus (1466?–1536), the most famous of the northern Humanists, illustrates the impact of the printing press. Erasmus was both an educational and a religious reformer—a man who proves that some loyal Catholics advocated religious reform long before the Reformation erupted.

Erasmus published short Latin dialogues that were intended to teach students how to live as well as how to speak. In their later editions, these pieces (his *Colloquies*) included anticlerical dialogues and satires of religious superstitions that were designed to prompt reforms. Erasmus also published a collection of proverbs, the *Adages*. It grew from a first edition containing 800 examples to a final edition composed of over 5,000. It popularized common expressions that are still in use (e.g., "to leave no stone unturned," and "where there is smoke, there is fire").

Erasmus wanted to unite the classical ideals of humanity and civic virtue with the Christian virtues of love and piety. He believed that disciplined study of the classics and the Bible offered the best hope for reforming individuals and society. He taught the *philosophia Christi,* the philosophy of Christ: a simple, ethical piety modeled on Christ's life. Erasmus opposed anyone, Catholic or Protestant, who let doctrine and disputation overshadow humble piety and Christian practice.

Erasmus used his knowledge of classical languages to produce an improved version of the Bible based on the best manuscript sources available at the time. He believed that true reform was possible only if people were guided by a pure, unadulterated source. His Greek edition of the New Testament in 1516 made possible a more accurate Latin translation in 1519.

The church authorities were unhappy with Erasmus's "improvements" on their traditional Bible, the Latin Vulgate, and his popular anticlerical satires. At one point in the mid-sixteenth century all of Erasmus's works were placed on the Catholic church's *Index of Forbidden Books*. Luther, the Protestant leader, also condemned some of Erasmus's views. But friends and foes in both camps used the scholarly tools that Erasmus had created to promote reform.

Humanism and Reform

Germany. Rudolf Agricola (1443–1485) introduced Italian learning to Germany. Conrad Celtis (d. 1508), the first German poet laureate, and Ulrich von Hutten (1488–1523), a knight, promoted a nationalistic version of Humanism that was hostile to non-German cultures—especially that of papal Rome. Hutten, who attacked indulgences and published an edition of Valla's exposé of the *Donation of Constantine*, died in 1523 fighting in a hopeless revolt of the German knights against their princes.

A *cause célèbre* helped to unite reform-minded German Humanists. About 1506 a converted Jew named Pfefferkorn, assisted by the Dominican friars of Cologne, launched a campaign to suppress Jewish literature. Johann Reuchlin (1455–1522) was, at the time, Europe's foremost Christian authority on Hebrew and Jewish learning. He was the first Christian scholar to compile a reliable Hebrew grammar, and he was personally attracted to Jewish mysticism. When Pfefferkorn attacked Reuchlin, many German Humanists (motivated by a love of academic freedom rather than Judaism) rushed to Reuchlin's defense. The controversy produced one of the great books of the period, the *Letters of Obscure Men* (1515), a merciless satire of monks and Scholastics. It also predisposed the Humanists to rally around Martin Luther, for in 1517 some of the same people attacked Luther for publishing arguments challenging the validity of indulgences.

England. English scholars and merchants and touring Italian prelates brought Italy's learning to England. Erasmus lectured at Cambridge, and his close friend, Thomas More (1478–1535), became the most famous of the English Humanists. More's *Utopia* (1516), a critique of contemporary values, rivals the plays of Shakespeare as the most-read English work from the sixteenth century. *Utopia* described an imaginary society that overcame social and political injustice by holding all property and goods in common and requiring all persons to earn their bread by their own labor.

Humanism in England, as in Germany, paved the way for the Reformation, but some Humanists, like More and Erasmus, remained steadfastly loyal to the Roman Catholic Church. When More, one of Henry VIII's chief councillors, refused to accept the king's divorce of Catherine of Aragon and England's break with the papacy, Henry ordered his execution (July 1535).

France. When France invaded Italy, Italian learning invaded France. Guillaume Budé (1468–1540), an accomplished Greek scholar, and Jacques Lefèvre d'Étaples

(1454–1536), a biblical authority, were the leaders of French Humanism. Lefèvre's scholarly works exemplified the new critical scholarship that was to stimulate Martin Luther's thinking and bring on the Reformation. Marguerite d'Angoulême (1492–1549), sister of King Francis I, queen of Navarre, and a noted spiritual writer, was patron to a generation of young reform-minded Humanists that numbered among its members the Protestant reformer John Calvin.

Spain. In Spain Humanism was enlisted to defend the Catholic faith, not promote reform. Francisco Jiménez de Cisneros (1437–1517), confessor to Queen Isabella and (after 1508) the Grand Inquisitor and chief defender of orthodoxy, was the country's leading Humanist. In 1509 he founded the University of Alcalá near Madrid. He printed a Greek edition of the New Testament, and he translated many religious tracts that were used to reform clerical life and improve the clergy's direction of the piety of the laity. His greatest achievement was the *Complutensian Polyglot Bible*, a six-volume edition of the Hebrew, Greek, and Latin texts of the Bible in parallel columns.

∼ Voyages of Discovery and the New Empire in the West

The intellectual restlessness that marked the Renaissance and the Reformation was accompanied by a literal restlessness. In the fifteenth century, the Atlantic ceased to be regarded as a wall closing Europe in and began to be explored as a highway to global adventure (see Map 10-2). Henry the Navigator (r. 1394–1460), prince of Portugal, took the lead by sponsoring exploration of the African coast. By the last decades of the fifteenth century, the Portuguese were importing gold from Guinea by sea and competing with the land routes controlled by Arab traders.

The rush for Africa's gold became a search for India's spices. Spices, especially pepper and cloves, were in great demand in Europe. They were used to preserve food as well as to enhance its taste. In 1487 Bartholomew Dias (d. 1500) rounded the Cape of Good Hope at the tip of Africa. In 1498, Vasco da Gama (d. 1524) reached India, and the cargo he brought back to Portugal was worth sixty times the cost of his voyage. The Portuguese quickly built an empire in the East that gave them control of the European spice trade.

While Portugal explored the Indian Ocean, Spain attacked the Atlantic. Christopher Columbus (1451–1506) dreamed of finding a short route to the spice islands of the East Indies, but he blundered on to something much greater. On October 12, 1492, after a thirty-three-day voyage from the Canary Islands, he landed in San Salvador (Watlings Island) in the eastern Bahamas. He thought he was near Japan. Not until his third voyage to the Caribbean did Columbus realize that the island of Cuba was not Japan and that the South American continent beyond it was not China. Amerigo Vespucci (1451–1512) and Ferdinand Magellan (1480–1521) proved that the lands Columbus found were not, as he died believing, the edge of the Orient. They were a new continent separated

POLITICAL TRANSFORMATIONS

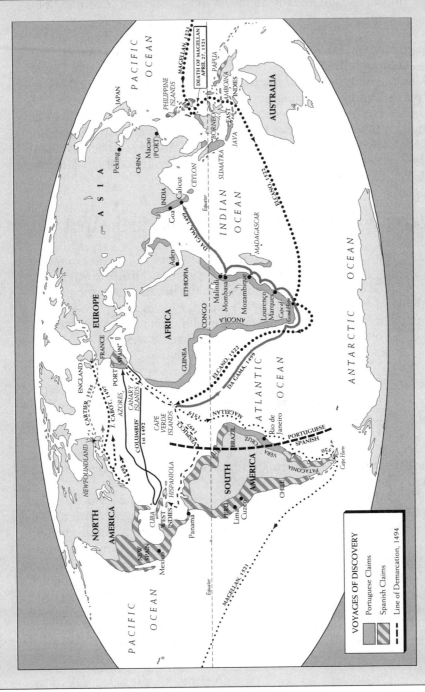

VOYAGES OF DISCOVERY

Portuguese Claims

Spanish Claims

Line of Demarcation, 1494

MAP 10-2

Voyages of Discovery and the Colonial Claims of Spain and Portugal

In 1487 Bartholow Diaz led an expedition around the Cape of Good Hope to map the geography of the African coast and assess the potential for trade with the people who lived there. Later voyages had less benign intents—particularly those to the West Indies, Central America, and Mexico. There, Europeans disrupted native populations and aggressively imposed Western governments and cultures. By the late sixteenth and seventeenth centuries, European diseases had so greatly reduced native populations that planters and developers began to import Europeans as indentured servants to replace native workers on colonial plantations. When Europeans proved inadequate, African slaves were imported by the tens of thousands.

The transition from reconnaissance to exploitation of the world beyond Europe began with Vasco da Gama's voyage in 1497. Focused strictly on commerce, da Gama made the first passage across the southern Atlantic, arriving in Calcutta in 1498. While rounding the Cape of Good Hope in early December 1497, he encountered the natives of South Africa for the first time. The journal that describes this encounter and the rest of the voyage was not written by da Gama, but by an unidentified sailor. It reveals the good intentions of the Portuguese and the friendliness of most of the natives, while also making clear the suspicion of both sides and European condescension and exploitation.

On Saturday [December 2] about two hundred negroes came, both young and old. They brought with them about a dozen oxen and cows and four or five sheep. As soon as we saw them we went ashore. They forthwith began to play on four or five flutes [known as "goras"], some producing high notes and others low ones, thus making a pretty harmony for negroes who are not expected to be musicians; and they danced in the style of negroes. The captain-major [da Gama] then ordered the trumpets to be sounded, and we, in the boats, danced, and the captain-major did so likewise when he rejoined us. This festivity ended, we landed . . . and bought a black ox for three bracelets. This ox we dined off on Sunday. We found him very fat, and his meat as toothsome as the beef of Portugal.

A Journal of the First Voyage of Vasco da Gama, 1497–1499, translated and edited by E. G. Ravenstein (London, Hakluyt Society, 1898), p. 11.

This map of Brazil, c1547, was drawn "upside-down," as if viewed from North America. Note Spanish cruelties to Indians, as well as scenes from daily life. [The Granger Collection, N.Y.]

from the East by an ocean even greater than the Atlantic. Magellan ventured onto this Pacific Ocean and died in the Philippines.

The Spanish Empire in the New World

Columbus's voyage in 1492 began more than three centuries of Spanish exploitation of a vast American empire. That empire transformed cultures on both sides of the Atlantic. As Europeans and their technologies entered the Americas, American goods and bullion flooded Europe's markets. In neither place was life ever again the same. In parts of both South and North America, Spain established a Roman Catholic faith, a system of economic dependence, and a hierarchical social structure that has endured to the present day.

Since Columbus was convinced that he had landed in the East Indies, he called the peoples he encountered "Indians." The name persisted even after it was clear that America was not the Indies. The ancestors of the Native Americans had migrated across the Bering Strait from Asia many thousands of years before the European voyages of discovery. As early as the first millennium B.C.E., those who lived in Mesoamerica (i.e., central Mexico to the Yucatan and Guatemala) and the Andean region (Peru and Bolivia) were pioneering advanced civilizations.

The earliest of the Mesoamerican civilizations was the Olmec, which dates from about 1200 B.C.E. By the first millennium C.E., its city of Teotihuacán was one of the largest urban centers in the world. The first millennium C.E. also saw the flowering of the civilization of the Mayas in the Yucatan region. The Mayans acquired considerable knowledge of mathematics and astronomy and built great cities centered on huge pyramids.

The first great interregional civilization in Andean South America, the Chavín, emerged during the first millennium B.C.E. Between 100 C.E. to 600 C.E., regional cultures, the Nazca on the southern coast of Peru and the Moche on the northern coast, appeared. The Huari-Tiahuanco culture again imposed interregional conformity from 600 to 1000, and the Chimu Empire flourished on Peru's northern coast from 800 to 1400. These early Andean societies built great ceremonial centers throughout the Andes; constructed elaborate irrigation systems, canals, and highways; and created exquisite pottery, textiles, and metalwork.

The Aztecs. When the Spanish explorers arrived, Mesoamerica was dominated by the Aztecs and Andean America by the Incas. The forebears of the Aztecs entered the Valley of Mexico early in the twelfth century. In 1428 a chief named Itzcoatl inaugurated an era of Aztec conquest that reached its climax just after 1500. The Aztec state, which centered on Tenochtitlán (modern-day Mexico City), was a collection of enslaved and terrorized tribes. Aztec religion involved the sacrifice of thousands of people a year to the gods of the sun and the soil. By extorting this grim tribute, the Aztecs nourished resentment among their subjects and caused them to dream of liberation.

In 1519 Hernán Cortés landed on Mexico's coast with a mere 600 men.

Montezuma, the Aztec ruler, initially believed Cortés to be a god, for an Aztec legend claimed that a priest (Quetzalcoatl) who had been driven into exile four centuries earlier would return about the time that Cortés appeared. Montezuma tried to appease Cortés with gold, for the Aztecs, who had recently been ravaged by epidemics of European origin (principally smallpox), were in no condition to fight. Gold only stimulated the Spaniards' appetites. Cortés's forces marched on Tenochtitlán and captured Montezuma, who died under unexplained circumstances. The Aztecs rose up to defend themselves. But by 1521 they were defeated, and Cortés named the former Aztec Empire "New Spain."

The Incas. The Incas of the highlands of Peru, like the Aztecs, had conquered many tribes. By the early sixteenth century they ruled harshly over several million subjects—using impressed labor to build roads and cities, to farm, and to fight.

In 1531 Francisco Pizarro, who was inspired by Cortés's example, invaded the Inca Empire. His army of 200 men was equipped with guns, swords, and horses—the military potential of which escaped the Incas. Pizarro lured the Inca chief Atahualpa to a conference where he captured him and killed several thousand Indians. Atahualpa raised a huge ransom in gold, but in 1533 Pizarro executed him. Division within the ranks of the Spaniards prevented them from establishing control of the sprawling Inca territories until the late 1560s.

The conquests of Mexico and Peru are among the most brutal episodes in modern Western history. In addition to loss of life, they prevented the Indian civilizations from having significant impact on Western civilization. The Spaniards and the Indians made some accommodations to each other, but in the end European values, religion, economic goals, and language dominated. South America became Latin America.

The Economy of Exploitation

The native peoples of America and their lands were immediately drawn into the Atlantic economy and the world of competitive European commercialism. For the Indians of Latin America—and later the blacks of Africa—that meant various forms of forced labor. The colonial economy of Latin America had three components: mining, agriculture, and shipping.

The early *conquistadores* ("conquerors") were primarily interested in gold, but by the middle of the sixteenth century, silver mining had become more profitable. The chief mining centers were Potosí in Peru and various smaller sites in northern Mexico. The Spanish crown received one-fifth (the *quinto*) of all mining revenues and monopolized the production and sale of the mercury that was required in the silver-mining process. Mining by native forced labor for the benefit of Spaniards epitomized the extractive economy that was fundamental to colonial life.

The West Indies (Cuba, Hispaniola, Puerto Rico, and other islands) evolved a plantation system that used the labor of black slaves from Africa to produce sugar for the European market. But the agricultural institution that characterized most of the Spanish colonies was the *hacienda,* a large landed estate owned by persons born in Spain *(peninsulares)* or persons of Spanish descent born in America *(creoles).* The *hacienda* economy was subordinate to the mining economy, for its major products—food and leather—were consumed by American mining communities. Laborers on the *hacienda* were usually bound to the land and prevented from moving from the service of one landowner to another.

The Spaniards initially developed a number of ways to use the Indian population to supply the labor needed for mining and agriculture in the New World. An *encomienda* was a grant of the right to the labor of a specific number of Indians for a particular period of time. Spain's monarchs opposed this arrangement, for they feared that the holders of *encomienda* might become a powerful independent nobility in the New World. The *repartimiento* required adult male Indians to devote a certain number of days of labor annually to Spanish economic enterprises. Although this sounded more humane, *repartimiento* service was often extremely harsh. The term limitation for laborers led some Spanish managers to work them to death on the assumption that new men were always scheduled to replace those currently employed.

Eventually a shortage of workers and the crown's opposition to extreme kinds of forced labor promoted the use of free labor. But the freedom of Indian workers was more apparent than real. They had to purchase the goods they needed from the landowners or mine owners for whom they worked. This created debts that bound them to their employers, a form of exploitation known as *debt peonage.*

The enslavement of Africans was introduced to the New World on the sugar plantations of the West Indies. It was an extension of a system of forced labor that the Spanish and the Portuguese had previously used in Europe.

The Impact on Europe

Deaths in combat, by forced labor, and from European diseases had devastating demographic consequences for the Indian population. Europeans lived in a far more complex human and animal environment than did Native Americans. Their interaction, over a long period, with different ethnic groups and animal species helped them develop strong immune systems that enabled them to survive the ravages of measles, smallpox, and typhoid. Native Americans evolved in a simpler, more sterile environment, and they were defenseless against Europe's diseases. Within a generation of the conquest, the Indian population of New Spain (Mexico) was reduced by 92 percent, from 25 million to 2 million.

The loss of life and destruction of cultures in the New World was a mixed blessing for the Old World. The bullion that flowed into Europe through Spain vastly increased the amount of money in circulation and created an inflation rate of 2 percent a year. Prices doubled in Spain by 1550 and quadrupled by 1600.

In Luther's Wittenberg, the cost of basic food and clothing increased almost 100 percent between 1519 and 1540. Wages and rents, on the other hand, lagged well behind the rise in prices.

The new money enabled governments and private entrepreneurs to sponsor basic research and industrial expansion and to promote the growth of capitalism. The economic thinking of the age favored the creation of monopolies, the charging of high interest for loans, and the free and efficient accumulation of wealth. The late fifteenth and the sixteenth centuries saw the maturation of this type of capitalism and its attendant social problems. Those who owned the means of production were ever more clearly separated from the workers who operated them. The new wealth raised the expectations of the poor and encouraged reactionary behavior by the rich. The social distinctions that became ever more visible in the new economic system prepared the way for the upheaval of the Reformation by making many people critical of traditional institutions and eager for new ideas—especially those that promised freedom and a chance at a better life.

During the late Middle Ages, previously divided lands came together as nations, and the foundations of modern France, Spain, England, Germany, and Italy were laid. Byzantine and Islamic scholars made ancient Greek science and scholarship available to the West, and Europeans reclaimed a classical cultural heritage from which they had been separated for almost eight centuries. This prompted renaissances of intellectual and artistic activity in both southern and northern Europe.

The new political unity spurred national ambition, and by the late fifteenth century Europeans were venturing far afield—to the shores of Africa, to the southern and eastern coasts of Asia, and to the New World of the Americas. For the first time, they confronted truly non-European civilizations. The savage exploitation of the peoples and lands of the New World revealed the dark side of Europe's culture, and the influx of New World gold and silver exacerbated Europe's economic and social problems. Some Europeans were driven by what they saw to question their traditional values.

⤳ Review Questions

1. How would you define the term *Renaissance* as it is used to explain what happened in fifteenth- and sixteenth-century Italy?

2. How would you define *Renaissance Humanism*? In what ways was the Renaissance a break with the Middle Ages? What lines of continuity did it maintain with medieval civilization?

3. Who were the leading, or most characteristic, literary and artistic figures of the Italian Renaissance? What was "the spirit of the Renaissance" that they all shared?

4. Why did the French invade Italy in 1494? How did this event trigger Italy's political decline? In what ways do the actions of Pope Julius II and the ideas of Niccolò Machiavelli signify the start of a new era in Italian civlization?

5. Does the history of Renaissance Italy support or refute the common assump-

tion that creative work proceeds best in periods of calm and peace?

6. How did the northern Renaissance differ from the Italian Renaissance? In what ways was Erasmus the embodiment of the northern Renaissance?

7. What prompted the voyages of discovery? How did the Spanish establish their empire in the Americas? What did native peoples experience during and after the conquest?

⌒ Suggested Readings

H. BARON, *The Crisis of the Early Italian Renaissance*, vols. 1 and 2 (1966). A major work, setting forth the civic dimension of Italian Humanism.

B. BERENSON, *Italian Painters of the Renaissance* (1957). Eloquent and authoritative.

C. BOXER, *Four Centuries of Portuguese Expansion, 1415–1825* (1961). Comprehensive survey by the leading authority.

G. A. BRUCKER, *Renaissance Florence* (1969). Comprehensive survey of all facets of Florentine life.

J. BURCKHARDT, *The Civilization of the Renaissance in Italy* (1867). An old classic that still has as many defenders as detractors.

A. W. CROSBY, *The Columbian Exchange: Biological and Cultural Consequences of 1492* (1973). A study of the epidemiological disaster that Columbus visited upon Native Americans.

E. L. EISENSTEIN, *The Printing Press as an Agent of Change: Communications and Cultural Transformations in Early Modern Europe*, 2 vols. (1979). Bold, stimulating account of the centrality of printing to all progress in the period.

W. K. FERGUSON, *Europe in Transition, 1300–1520* (1962). A major survey that deals with the transition from medieval society to Renaissance society.

C. GIBSON, *Spain in America* (1956). A splendidly clear and balanced narrative.

M. GILMORE, *The World of Humanism, 1453–1517* (1952). A comprehensive survey, especially strong in intellectual and cultural history.

J. HANKINS, *Plato in the Renaissance* (1992). An authoritative study of how Plato was read and interpreted by Renaissance scholars.

D. HERLIHY, *The Family in Renaissance Italy* (1974). Excellent on family structure and general features.

F. KATZ, *The Ancient American Civilizations* (1972). An excellent introduction.

C. KLAPISCH-ZUBER, *Women, Family, and Ritual in Renaissance Italy* (1985). Provocative, wide-ranging essays documenting Renaissance Italy as very much a man's world.

P. O. KRISTELLER, *Renaissance Thought: The Classic, Scholastic, and Humanist Strains* (1961). A master shows the many sides of Renaissance thought.

I. MACLEAN, *The Renaissance Notion of Women* (1980). An account of the views of Renaissance intellectuals and their sources in antiquity.

L. MARTINES, *Power and Imagination: City States in Renaissance Italy* (1980). Stimulating account of cultural and political history.

H. A. MISKIMIN, *The Economy of Early Renaissance Europe, 1300–1460* (1975). Shows interaction of social, political, economic, and cultural change.

E. PANOFSKY, *Meaning in the Visual Arts* (1955). Eloquent treatment of Renaissance art.

J. H. PARRY, *The Age of Reconnaissance* (1964). A comprehensive account of exploration in the years 1450 to 1650.

M. M. PHILLIPS, *Erasmus and the Northern Renaissance* (1956). A learned, rewarding account of the man and the movement.

11

The Age of Reformation

Society and Religion

> *Popular Religious Movements and Criticism of the Church*

Martin Luther and German Reformation to 1525

> *Justification by Faith Alone*
> *Election of Charles V*
> *Luther's Excommunication and the Diet of Worms*
> *Imperial Distractions: France and the Turks*
> *How the Reformation Spread*
> *The Peasants' Revolt*

The Reformation Elsewhere

> *Zwingli and the Swiss Reformation*
> *Anabaptists and Radical Protestants*
> *John Calvin and the Genevan Reformation*

Political Consolidation of the Lutheran Reformation

> *The Expansion of the Reformation*
> *Reaction and Resolution*

The English Reformation to 1553

> *The King's Affair*
> *The "Reformation Parliament"*
> *The King's Wives*
> *The Protestant Reformation under Edward VI*

Catholic Reform and Counter-Reformation

> *Ignatius of Loyola and the Jesuits*
> *The Council of Trent (1545–1563)*
> *The Church in Spanish America*

The Social Significance of the Reformation in Western Europe

> *The Revolution in Religious Practices and Institutions*
> *The Reformation and Education*
> *The Reformation and the Changing Role of Women*

Family Life in Early Modern Europe

> *Marriage*
> *Family Size*
> *Infant and Child Care*

KEY TOPICS

- ⌁ The social and religious background to the Reformation
- ⌁ Martin Luther's challenge to the church and the course of the Reformation in Germany
- ⌁ The Reformation in Switzerland, France, and England
- ⌁ Transitions in family life between medieval and modern times

In the second decade of the sixteenth century a powerful religious movement began in northern Germany. Protestant reformers, attacking what they believed to be burdensome superstitions that robbed people of money and peace of mind, led a revolt against the medieval church.

The Protestant Reformation opposed aspects of the Renaissance, especially the optimistic view of human nature that Hu- *manist scholars derived from classical literature. But the Reformation embraced some Renaissance ideas—particularly educational reform and training in ancient languages that equipped scholars to go to the original sources of important texts. Protestant challenges to Catholic practices originated in the study of the Hebrew and Greek Scriptures.*

✧ Society and Religion

A struggle between two political foes set the stage for the Reformation: the monarchies that were centralizing governments of nation-states, and the towns and regions that were fighting to preserve their traditional autonomy. Since the fourteenth century, the king's law and custom had been superseding local law and custom almost everywhere. Many townspeople and village folk viewed religious revolt as a part of a wider fight to limit encroachment on their liberties.

The Reformation began in the free cities of Germany and Switzerland. There were about sixty-five of them, most of which developed Protestant movements even if they did not ultimately come under Protestant control. These cities were troubled by more than a desire to defend themselves against intervention by princes. They suffered deep internal social and political divisions, and some of their factions favored the Reformation more than others. Guilds whose members were prospering and rising in social status were often in the forefront of the Reformation, but less distinguished groups were also attracted

The Reformation broke out against a background of deep social and political divisions that bred resentment against authority. This early-sixteenth-century woodcut by Georg Pencz presents a warning against tyranny. It shows a world turned upside down, with the hunted becoming the hunters. The message: tyranny eventually begets rebellion. [Hacker Art Books]

Significant Dates from the Period of the Protestant Reformation

1517	*Luther posts ninety-five theses against indulgences*
1519	*Charles V becomes Holy Roman Emperor*
1521	*Diet of Worms condemns Luther*
1524–1525	*Peasants' Revolt in Germany*
1527	*The* Schleitheim Confession *of the Anabaptists*
1529	*Marburg Colloquy between Luther and Zwingli*
1529	*England's Reformation Parliament convenes*
1531	*Formation of Protestant Schmalkaldic League*
1533	*Henry VIII weds Anne Boleyn*
1534–1535	*Anabaptists take over Münster*
1534	*England's Act of Supremacy*
1536	*Calvin arrives in Geneva*
1540	*Jesuits, founded by Ignatius of Loyola, recognized as order by pope*
1546	*Luther dies*
1547	*Armies of Charles V crush Schmalkaldic League*
1547–1553	*Edward VI, king of England*
1555	*Peace of Augsburg*
1553–1558	*Mary Tudor, queen of England*
1545–1563	*Council of Trent*
1558–1603	*Elizabeth I, queen of England; the Anglican settlement*

to the Protestant revolt. People who felt pushed around by either local or distant authorities tended, at least initially, to find an ally in the Protestant movement. The peasants on the land responded as much as the townsfolk, for their freedoms, too, were eroded by princely governments.

For many converts to Protestantism, religion and politics seemed to be sides of the same coin. When Protestant preachers scorned the authority of ecclesiastical landlords and ridiculed papal laws as arbitrary human inventions, they raised issues of political as well as religious liberty. An attack on the legitimacy of the one kind of authority translated easily into a critique of the other.

Popular Religious Movements and Criticism of the Church

The Protestant Reformation was, in part, a response to the crises that afflicted the late medieval church: the papacy's "exile" in Avignon, the Great Schism, the conciliar movement, and the flagrant worldliness of the Renaissance popes. These things led many clergy and laity to become increasingly critical of the traditional teaching and spiritual practice of the church. The late Middle Ages were marked by calls for reform and by widespread experimentation with new religious practices.

The laypeople of the late medieval period were less subservient to the clergy than their ancestors. The residents of cities had grown increasingly knowledgeable about the world and politics. As soldiers, pilgrims, explorers, and traders, they traveled widely. The establishment of postal systems and printing presses increased the information at their disposal. Improved access to books and libraries raised the rate of literacy among them and heightened their curiosity. Education equipped them to take the initiative in shaping the cultural lives of their communities.

The lay religious movements that preceded the Reformation all advocated religious simplicity in imitation of Jesus. They were inspired by an ideal of apostolic poverty which they saw in the Gospels' descriptions of the lives of Jesus and his disciples. They wanted a more egalitarian church that gave a voice to its members, not just its head. They wanted a more spiritual church, one that emulated the New Testament model.

The Modern Devotion. One of the most constructive lay religious movements of the period was led by the Brothers of the Common Life, advocates for the "Modern Devotion." The brothers urged ordinary people to adapt the spiritual disciplines of monasticism for their own uses. They took no formal vows and held no church offices. They supported themselves by working at secular jobs.

After Gerard Groote (1340–1384) began the movement in the Netherlands, the brother and (less numerous) sister houses spread rapidly throughout northern Europe. The Modern Devotion brought clerics and laity together to share a common life that stressed individual piety and practical religion. Thomas à Kempis (d. 1471) summarized the philosophy of the movement in what became the most popular devotional tract of the period, the *Imitation of Christ*. This guide to the inner life was intended primarily for monks and nuns, but it spoke also to the many laity who sought spiritual growth through the practice of ascetic disciplines.

The Brothers of the Common Life flourished during an age in which the laity wanted instruction from good preachers and were even taking the initiative to create endowments to provide this service. The brothers served the public's desire for better education by opening schools, working as copyists, sponsoring publications, and running hospices for poor students. Some famous scholars, such as Erasmus and Reuchlin, began their training with the brothers.

The Modern Devotion has been credited with inspiring Humanist, Protestant, and Catholic reform movements in the sixteenth century, but it was actually a very conservative movement. By integrating traditional clerical doctrines and values with an active common life, the brothers met the need of late medieval people for a more personal religion and a better-informed faith. The Modern Devotion helped laypersons develop fuller religious lives without turning their backs on the world.

Lay Control over Religious Life. The medieval papacy's successful campaign to win control over the appointment of candidates to church offices did not improve the administration of the church. The popes sold ecclesiastical posts to the highest bidders. The purchasers were entitled to the income from their offices, but they were not required personally to carry out the duties attached to the offices they bought. They hired inexpensive, often poorly trained and motivated substitutes to do their work, while they resided elsewhere. Rare was the late medieval German town that did not complain about clerical malfeasance or dereliction of duty.

City governments sometimes took the initiative in trying to improve religious life by endowing preacherships. These positions provided for well-trained, dedicated pastors who could provide regular preaching and pastoral care superior to the perfunctory services offered by other clergy. In many instances these preacherships became platforms for Protestant reformers.

Because medieval churches and monasteries were holy places, they had been exempted from secular taxes and laws. It was also considered inappropriate for holy persons (clergy) to do "dirty jobs" like military service, compulsory labor, standing watch at city gates, and other obligations of citizenship. Nor was it thought right that the laity, of whatever rank, should sit in judgment over God's priestly intermediaries. On the eve of the Reformation, however, secular governments were beginning to take steps to curtail clerical privileges that seemed undeserved.

Long before 1520, when Luther published a famous summary of economic grievances (*Address to the Christian Nobility of the German Nation*), communities were loudly protesting the financial abuses of the medieval church. Prominent among these was the sale of indulgences, papal letters that guaranteed sinners released time from purgatory. If rulers and magistrates were given a share of the profits, they usually did not object. But it was a different matter if local revenues were siphoned off for projects far from home. The state did not join the campaign against financial exactions like indulgences until rulers recognized how they themselves might profit from religion. The financial appeal of Protestantism lay in its rationale for the state's dissolution of monasteries and confiscation of ecclesiastical properties.

✧ Martin Luther and German Reformation to 1525

The kings of France and England were able to limit ecclesiastical taxation and papal jurisdiction over their churches. But Germany lacked the political unity needed to enforce "national" religious reforms. The restraints imposed on the church on a universal level in England and France were enacted locally and piecemeal in Germany as popular resentment of ecclesiastical abuses spread. By 1517 mass discontent was pervasive enough to win Martin Luther a widespread, sympathetic audience.

Luther (1483–1546) was the son of a successful Thüringian miner. He received his early education in a school run by the Brothers of the Common Life. Between 1501 and 1505, he attended the University of Erfurt, where the nominalist teachings of William of Ockham and Gabriel Biel (d. 1495) prevailed. After receiving his master of arts degree in 1505, Luther obeyed his parents and registered with the law faculty. But he never began the study of law. To the disappointment of his family, he entered the Order of the Hermits of Saint Augustine in Erfurt on July 17, 1505. This decision was an attempt to resolve a long-standing spiritual struggle. It came to a head during a lightning storm in which a terrified Luther promised Saint Anne, the patron of travelers in distress, that he would enter a monastery if he escaped death.

Luther was ordained in 1507 and led a conventional monastic life. In 1510 he went to Rome on business for his order and saw firsthand some of the things that were raising doubts about the church. In 1511 he moved to the Augustinian monastery in Wittenberg. A year later, he earned his doctorate in theology from Wittenberg's university and joined its faculty.

Justification by Faith Alone

Reformation theology was a response to the failure of traditional medieval religion to provide many laypeople and clergy with personal or intellectual satisfaction. Luther was especially plagued by his inability to achieve the perfect righteousness that medieval theology taught that God required for salvation. The church's teachings and sacrament of penance failed to console Luther and give him hope. The church seemed to demand of him a perfection he knew neither he nor any other human being could achieve.

The study of St. Paul's letters eventually brought Luther an insight into the process of salvation that quieted his fears. Luther concluded from his reading of the Scriptures that the righteousness that God demanded was not the product of religious works and ceremonies. It was a gift God gives to those who believe and trust in Jesus Christ, who alone is perfectly righteous. To believe in Christ meant to stand before God clothed in Christ's righteousness—to be justified solely by faith in him, not by confidence in one's record of good works.

The doctrine of justification by faith was incompatible with the church's practice of issuing indulgences, which remitted the obligation to perform a "work of satisfaction" for a sin. According to medieval theology, after the priest absolved a penitent of guilt, the penitent still had to pay the penalty for sin. The penitent could discharge the penalty here and now by prayers, fasting, almsgiving, retreats, and pilgrimages. But penitents whose works of satisfaction were inadequate could expect to suffer for them in purgatory.

Indulgences had originally been devised for Crusaders who fell in battle with the enemies of the church without an opportunity to do penance for their sins. Gradually, they were offered to laypeople who were anxious about the consequences of neglected penances or unrepented sins. In 1343 Pope Clement VI (1342–1352) declared the existence of a "treasury of merit," an infinite reservoir of excess good works which the saints had earned and which the pope could appropriate for others. Papal "letters of indulgence" were drafts on this treasury to cover the works of satisfaction owed by penitents. In 1476 Pope Sixtus IV (1471–1484) greatly expanded the market for these letters by proclaiming the church's power to grant indulgences not only to the living, but to souls in purgatory.

Originally, indulgences had been granted only for significant services to the church, but by Luther's day their price had been significantly discounted to encourage mass marketing. Pope Julius II (1503–1513) excited considerable interest by declaring a special Jubilee indulgence (to be sold in 1517) to raise funds for rebuilding Saint Peter's in Rome. In 1517 Archbishop Albrecht of Mainz was in debt to the Fugger bank of Augsburg for a loan he had taken out to pay the pope for permission to ignore church law and hold three profitable ecclesiastical offices—the archbishoprics of Mainz and Magdeburg and the bishopric of Halberstadt. In exchange for Albrecht's help in promoting sale of the Jubilee indulgence, Pope Leo X agreed to share the proceeds. A famous preacher, John Tetzel (d. 1519), was sent to drum up business in Luther's neighborhood.

According to tradition, Luther posted his ninety-five theses opposing the sale of indulgences on the door of Castle Church in Wittenberg on October 31, 1517. Luther especially protested Tetzel's insinuation that indulgences remitted sins and released the dead from punishment in purgatory. Luther believed Tetzel's claims went far beyond traditional practice and made salvation something that could be bought and sold.

Election of Charles V

The ninety-five theses made Luther famous overnight and prompted official proceedings against him. In April, 1518, he was summoned to appear before the general chapter of his order in Heidelberg, and the following October he was called to Augsburg to be examined by the papal legate and general of the Do-

A contemporary caricature depicts John Tetzel, the famous indulgence preacher. The last lines of the jingle read: "As soon as gold in the basin rings, right then the soul to Heaven springs." It was Tetzel's preaching that spurred Luther to publish his ninety-five theses. [Staatliche Lutherhalle, Wittenberg]

MAP 11-1 **The Empire of Charles V** *Dynastic marriages and simple chance concentrated into Charles's hands rule over the lands shown here, plus Spain's overseas possessions. Crowns and titles rained in on him; election in 1519 as emperor gave him new burdens and responsibilities.*

minican Order, Cardinal Cajetan. At that point the death of the Holy Roman Emperor Maximilian I, on January 12, 1519, diverted attention from Luther's case to the contest for a new emperor.

Charles I of Spain, a youth of nineteen, succeeded his grandfather and became Emperor Charles V (see Map 11-1). But the electors, who constantly sought to enhance their power, exacted a price for the office. They forced Charles to agree to consult with a diet of the empire on all major domestic and foreign issues. This ruled out unilateral imperial action in Germany—something for which Luther was soon to be thankful.

Luther's Excommunication and the Diet of Worms

While the imperial election was being held, Luther was in Leipzig (June 27, 1519) to debate an Ingolstadt professor, John Eck. This contest led Luther to question the infallibility of the pope and the inerrancy of church councils and, for the first time, to appeal to the Scripture as the sole authority governing faith.

In 1520 Luther described his position in three famous pamphlets. His *Address to the Christian Nobility of the German Nation* urged the German princes forcefully to reform the Roman Catholic Church and curtail its political and economic power. *The Babylonian Captivity of the Church* examined the sacraments, arguing that only two of the church's seven (Baptism and the Eucharist) were authentic. The pamphlet also claimed that the Scriptures, decrees of church councils, and decisions of secular princes were superior to the authority of a pope. The eloquent *Freedom of a Christian* explained Luther's key theological insight, salvation by faith alone.

On June 15, 1520, a papal bull, *Exsurge Domine*, condemned Luther for heresy and gave him sixty days to retract. The final bull of excommunication, *Decet Pontificem Romanum*, was issued on January 3, 1521. In April of that year, Luther appeared before a diet of the empire in Worms (over which the newly elected Charles V presided). Ordered to recant, Luther refused, for such an act, he claimed, would violate Scripture, reason, and conscience. On May 26, 1521, Luther was placed under the imperial ban. This meant that his heresy became a crime punishable by the state. Friends protected Luther by hiding him in Wartburg Castle. The year (April 1521 to March 1522) he spent in seclusion was put to good use. At Wartburg Luther produced one of the essential tools of Reformation: a German translation of Erasmus's Greek text of the New Testament.

Imperial Distractions: France and the Turks

Charles V was too preoccupied with military ventures to pay much attention to the Reformation that erupted in Wittenberg following Luther's trial. France wanted to move into Italy to drive a wedge through Charles's empire, and the Ottoman Turks were advancing on eastern Europe. Charles needed friendly relations with the German princes in order to recruit German troops for his armies.

In 1526 the Turks overran Hungary at the Battle of Mohacs, and in western Europe the French organized the League of Cognac in preparation for the second of four wars between the Habsburg and Valois dynasties (1521–1559). Thus preoccupied, the emperor, at the Diet of Speyer (1526), granted each German prince the right to deal as he saw fit with the situation Luther had created. This cleared the way for the Reformation to put down roots in places where the princes sympathized with it, and it inaugurated a tradition of princely control over religion that was to be enshrined in law by the Peace of Augsburg in 1555.

How the Reformation Spread

In the 1520s and 1530s, leadership of the Reformation passed from theologians and pamphleteers to magistrates and princes. City governments acted on the proposals of Protestant preachers and their growing flocks and mandated religious reforms. Reform ceased to be a matter of slogans and passed into law binding on all a town's residents. Like urban magistrates, some regional princes (e.g., the elector of Saxony and the prince of Hesse) implemented the reform in large states. They recognized political and economic advantages to themselves in the overthrow of the Roman Catholic Church and urged their neighbors to join them. Powerful alliances were negotiated, and Protestant leaders prepared for war with their Catholic emperor.

The Peasants' Revolt

In its first decade the Protestant movement suffered more from internal division than from imperial interference. By 1525, Luther had become as controversial a figure in Germany as the pope, and many of his early supporters had broken with him. Germany's peasants, who had welcomed Luther as an ally, had a particular reason for losing faith in him. Since the late fifteenth century, their leaders had been struggling to prevent the territorial princes from ignoring traditional restraints and imposing new regulations and taxes. Many peasants saw Luther's proclamation of Christian freedom and criticism of monastic landowners as a declaration of support for their cause.

Luther and his followers sympathized with the peasants, but Lutherans were not social revolutionaries. Luther's freedom of the Christian individual was an inner release from guilt and anxiety, not a restructuring of society by violent revolution. When the peasants rebelled against their masters in 1524–1525, Luther condemned them in the strongest possible terms and urged the princes to crush the revolt. Tens of thousands of peasants (possibly 100,000) died in the struggle. Had Luther supported the Peasants' Revolt, he would have contradicted his own teaching and would also probably have ended any chance for his reform to survive beyond the 1520s.

✧ The Reformation Elsewhere

Zwingli and the Swiss Reformation

Switzerland's political environment was as favorable to the success of a religious revolt as Germany's. Switzerland was a loose confederacy of thirteen autonomous cantons (states) and allied areas. Some (e.g., Zurich, Bern, Basel, and Schaffhausen) became Protestant, some (especially in the heartland around Lucerne) remained Catholic, and a few effected a compromise. Two developments prepared the ground for the Swiss Reformation: (1) a growth of national sentiment created by opposition to the practice of impressing Swiss soldiers into mercenary service outside the homeland, and (2) an interest in church reform that had been stimulated by the convocation of famous church councils in the Swiss cities of Constance (1414–1417) and Basel (1431–1449).

The Reformation in Zurich. Ulrich Zwingli (1484–1531), the leader of the Swiss Reformation, received a Humanist education and credited Erasmus for sparking his interest in reform. He was chaplain to Swiss mercenaries in Italy in 1515, and his experiences at a disastrous battle at Marignano prompted him to become an ardent critic of mercenary service. By 1518 he was also widely known for opposing the sale of indulgences and for denouncing religious superstitions.

In 1519 Zwingli applied for the post of people's priest in Zurich's main church. His fitness was questioned because of his acknowledged fornication with a barber's daughter. Many of his contemporaries, however, sympathized with the plight of celibate clergy, and Zwingli defended himself forcefully. Later he led the fight to abolish clerical celibacy and to establish the right of clergy to marry.

Zwingli's post as the people's priest in Zurich gave him a pulpit from which to campaign for reform. His reform program was simple: Whatever lacked literal support in Scripture was to be neither believed nor practiced. Application of that standard led him, as it did Luther, to question many traditional teachings and practices: fasting, transubstantiation, the worship of saints, pilgrimages, purgatory, clerical celibacy, and some of the sacraments. A public debate, held on January 29, 1523, ended with the city government endorsing Zwingli's ideas. Zurich took the lead in the Swiss Reformation and pioneered the kind of Protestantism that came to be called "puritanical."

The Marburg Colloquy. Landgrave Philip of Hesse (1504–1567) believed that Protestants had to cooperate if they hoped to fend off attacks from Catholics, and he tried to unite the Swiss and German reformations. He brought Luther and Zwingli together in his castle in Marburg in early October 1529. But theological disagreements—over the nature of Christ's presence in the Eucharist—prevented the two leaders from endorsing a political alliance. Luther concluded that Zwingli was a dangerous fanatic, and Zwingli believed that Luther was irrationally in thrall to medieval ideas.

The disagreement splintered the Protestant movement. Separate credal statements were issued, and separate defense leagues were formed. Semi-Zwinglian views were embodied in the *Confessio Tetrapolitana* prepared by the Strasbourg reformers Martin Bucer and Caspar Hedio. In 1530 this was presented to the Diet of Augsburg as an alternative to the *Augsburg Confession,* which the Lutherans proposed as a basis for unity.

Swiss Civil Wars. As Protestants and Catholics divided up the Swiss cantons, civil wars began. There were two major battles, both at Kappel (one in June 1529 and the second in October 1531). The first was a clear victory for the Protestants. The Catholic cantons were forced to repudiate their foreign alliances and recognize the rights of Protestants. The second battle cost Zwingli his life, but the treaty that ended the fighting confirmed the right of each canton to determine its own religion. Thereafter, things settled down. Heinrich Bullinger (1504–1575), Zwingli's protégé, assumed leadership of the Swiss Reformation and guided it toward the status of an established religion.

Anabaptists and Radical Protestants

The seeming failure of the Lutheran and Zwinglian reformations to elevate standards of ethical conduct and the slow pace of change discontented many people. Those who wanted a more rapid and thorough restoration of "primitive Christianity" (the church described in the New Testament) accused the reformers of going only halfway. These people formed radical Protestant movements, chief among which was that of the Anabaptists (the origin of the Mennonites and Amish). The Anabaptists ("rebaptizers") took their name from their rejection of infant baptism and their insistence on rebaptizing adults who had been baptized as infants.

Conrad Grebel (1498–1526) symbolically inaugurated Anabaptism by performing the first adult rebaptism in Zurich in January 1525. In October, 1523, Grebel's passion for biblical literalism had caused him to break with his mentor, Zwingli. He opposed Zwingli's support for the government's plea to proceed slowly in altering traditional religious practices. In 1527 Grebel's followers, the Swiss Brethren, published a statement of their principles, the *Schleitheim Confession*. They practiced adult baptism, opposed the swearing of oaths, committed themselves to pacifism, and refused to condone secular governments. Anabaptists literally withdrew from society to be free to live as they believed the first Christians had lived. State authorities interpreted their conduct as an attack on society's bonds.

The Anabaptist Reign in Münster. Lutherans and Zwinglians joined Catholics in persecuting the Anabaptists. In 1529 rebaptism became a capital offense throughout the Holy Roman Empire, and from 1525 to 1618 somewhere between 1,000 and 5,000 people were executed for undergoing rebaptism. Brutal punishments for nonconformists increased after state authorities witnessed the behavior of a group of Anabaptist extremists who took over the German city of Münster in 1534–1535.

Anabaptists converted the majority of the citizens of Münster and set up a town government that forced Lutherans and Catholics to convert or emigrate. Münster became an Old Testament theocracy, replete with charismatic leaders and the practice of polygamy. The latter was an attempt to provide for the women (widowed or deserted), who greatly outnumbered the men of the city.

The outside world was shocked, and Protestant and Catholic armies united to crush the radicals. After this bloody episode, Anabaptism reasserted its commitment to pacifism, and the movement spread largely among rural populations. Later Anabaptist leaders—like Menno Simons (1496–1561), the founder of the Mennonites—were moderates.

Other Nonconformists. The Anabaptists were not the only Protestant radicals. The Spiritualists were extreme individualists who believed that the only religious authority one ought to obey was the voice of God's spirit in one's heart. Thomas Müntzer (d. 1525), an early convert to Lutheranism and a leader of a peasants' revolt, belonged to this camp—as did Sebastian Franck (d. 1541), a freelance critic of all dogmatic religion, and Caspar Schwenckfeld (d. 1561), a prolific author for whom the tiny Schwenckfeldian denomination is named.

The Reformation's critique of religious superstition led some people to embrace extreme rationalism. The most prominent exponents of common-sense, rational, ethical religion were the Antitrinitarians. Their most famous spokesman, a Spaniard named Michael Servetus (1511–1553), was executed by the Protestant government of Geneva for rejecting the doctrine of the Trinity. Italian reformers, Lelio (d. 1562) and Faustus Sozzini (d. 1604), founded Socinianism, a Humanistic faith that opposed emerging Protestant orthodoxies and advocated religious toleration.

John Calvin and the Genevan Reformation

In the second half of the sixteenth century, Calvinism replaced Lutheranism as the dominant Protestant force in Europe. Although Calvinists believed strongly in divine predestination, they also believed that Christians ought to reorder society according to God's plan. They were zealous reformers who used the machinery of government to compel men and women to live according to codes of conduct that they believed were set forth in the Scriptures.

Calvinism's founder, John Calvin (1509–1564), was the son of a well-to-do secretary to the bishop of Noyon in Picardy. The church benefices the boy received at age twelve paid for the excellent education he received at Parisian colleges and the law school at Orléans. Young Calvin associated with a group of Catholic Humanists (led by Jacques Lefèvre d'Étaples and Marguerite d'Angoulême, the queen of Navarre) who advocated reform. Calvin eventually concluded that these people were ineffectual, but they helped awaken his interest in the Reformation.

It was probably in the spring of 1534 that Calvin converted to Protestantism, an experience he described as God's making his "long stubborn heart . . . teachable." In May 1534, he dramatically surrendered the benefices that had long supported him and joined the Reformation.

Geneva. In Luther's Saxony, religious reform paved the way for political revolution. In Calvin's Geneva, political revolution awakened an appetite for religious reform. The Genevans, assisted by the city-states of Fribourg and Bern, won their independence from the House of Savoy in 1527 and drove out their resident prince-bishop. The city councils assumed his legal and political powers.

Late in 1533 Bern sent the Protestant reformers Guillaume Farel (1489–1565) and Antoine Froment (1508–1581) to Geneva. In the summer of 1535, after much internal turmoil, the Genevans discontinued the traditional mass and other Catholic religious practices. On May 21, 1536, Geneva officially joined the Reformation.

Calvin arrived in Geneva in July 1536. He had been forced to flee France to avoid persecution for his religious beliefs, and he was intending to seek refuge in Strasbourg. The third Habsburg-Valois war forced him to detour to

Geneva, where Farel persuaded him to stay. Before a year had passed, Calvin had drawn up articles for the governance of Geneva's new church as well as a catechism to guide its people. Both were presented for approval to the city councils in early 1537. Because of the strong measures they proposed for governing the moral conduct of Genevans, the reformers were accused of creating a "new papacy." Both within Geneva and outside it, opponents attacked the attempt to impose a new orthodoxy. Bern, which had adopted a more moderate Protestant reform, pressured Geneva to restore ceremonies and holidays that Calvin and Farel opposed. In February 1538, the four *syndics* (the leading city magistrates) turned against the reformers and drove them out.

Calvin went to Strasbourg to become pastor to a group of French exiles. During his long stay in Strasbourg, he wrote a second edition of his masterful *Institutes of the Christian Religion.* Many scholars consider this to be the definitive theological explication of Protestant faith. Calvin married, took part in ecumenical discussions, and learned important lessons in practical politics from the Strasbourg reformer Martin Bucer.

In 1540 Geneva elected syndics who were eager to establish the city's independence from Bern. They believed that Calvin would be a valuable ally and invited him to return. Within months of his arrival in September 1540, the city implemented new ecclesiastical ordinances. Civil magistrates were pledged to work with the clergy to maintain discipline within the city.

The church Calvin designed was administered by four kinds of officials: (1) five presiding pastors; (2) various teachers or doctors who handled religious instruction; (3) twelve elders, laymen chosen by and from the Genevan councils to "oversee the life of everybody"; and (4) deacons, also laymen, who managed the church's charitable disbursements.

Calvin believed that a strong church government was needed to maintain the highest moral standards for the community, for no Christian city could tolerate conduct that was not pleasing to God. The *consistory*, a committee composed of the elders and the pastors of the church and presided over by one of the four syndics, was given this responsibility. It meted out punishments for a broad range of moral and religious transgressions—from missing church services (a fine of 3 sous) to fornication (six days on bread and water and a fine of 60 sous). The making of statements critical of Calvin and the consistory was listed among the sins meriting punishment.

Calvin branded his opponents wanton "Libertines" and showed them little mercy. His most prominent victim was the anti-Trinitarian Michael Servetus. Servetus fled to Geneva in 1553, seeking refuge from the Spanish Inquisition—only to be indicted by Calvin for heresy and burned at the stake.

After 1555 the city's syndics were all solidly behind Calvin, and he began to attract disciples from across Europe. Geneva welcomed the thousands of Protestants who were driven out of France, England, and Scotland, and at one point more than a third of the population of the city consisted of refugees (over 5,000 of them). They were utterly loyal to Calvin, for in their experience Geneva was Europe's only "free" city. Whenever they were allowed to return to their homes, they ardently championed Calvinistic reforms.

⤳ Political Consolidation of the Lutheran Reformation

The Expansion of the Reformation

Charles V, who spent most of his time in Spain and Italy, visited the empire in 1530 to convene a diet at Augsburg. The purpose of the meeting was to resolve the religious conflicts that had developed following Luther's break with the papacy in 1520. Charles adjourned the meeting with a blunt order to all Lutherans to revert to Catholicism.

The Reformation was too far advanced by that time to be halted by such a peremptory gesture. The emperor's mandate only served to persuade Lutherans that they needed to form a defensive alliance, the Schmalkaldic League. The league endorsed a common statement of faith, the *Augsburg Confession*—followed in 1538 by Luther's more strongly worded *Schmalkaldic Articles*. Regional consistories (judicial bodies composed of theologians and lawyers) were set up by Lutheran governments to replace the bishops who had formerly administered their churches.

Charles was prevented from doing much about this by the outbreak of new hostilities with France and with the Turks. Consequently, the league's leaders, Landgrave Philip of Hesse and Elector John Frederick of Saxony, were, for the time being, able to hold him at bay as Lutheranism spread.

Christian II (r. 1513–1523) introduced Lutheranism to Denmark, where it became the state religion. In Sweden in 1527, Gustavus Vasa (r. 1523–1560) persuaded a Swedish nobility that was eager to confiscate church property to embrace the reform. Poland, primarily because of the absence of a central political authority, became a model of religious pluralism and toleration. In the second half of the sixteenth century, it sheltered Lutherans, Anabaptists, Calvinists, and even Antitrinitarians.

Reaction and Resolution

In 1547 the armies of Charles V crushed the Schmalkaldic League, and the emperor issued the *Augsburg Interim*. It ordered Protestants to return to Catholic beliefs and practices. A few concessions were made to Protestant tastes. Clerical marriage was permitted in individual cases when the pope approved, and laypeople were allowed to receive both the bread and the wine at communion. Many Protestant leaders chose exile rather than comply with the terms of the *Interim*, but the Reformation was too entrenched by 1547 to be ended by imperial fiat.

Maurice of Saxony, whom Charles V hand-picked to replace Elector John Frederick as ruler of Saxony, recognized the inevitable and shifted his allegiance to the Protestants. Wearied by three decades of war, the emperor, too, finally surrendered his lifelong quest for the restoration of religious unity in Europe. In 1552 Charles reinstated John Frederick and Philip of Hesse and issued the Peace of Passau (August 1552), guaranteeing religious freedom for Lutherans. The Peace of Augsburg in September 1555 made the division of Christendom permanent. It legalized a principle well established in practice: *cuius regio, eius religio*—the ruler of a land determines the religion of that land. A subject who was discontented with the religion chosen by his ruler was permitted to migrate to a district that practiced his preferred faith.

⤳ The English Reformation to 1553

The king of England was the only major European monarch to break with the papacy, but England's Reformation owed more to nationalism than to sympathy with Lutheran or Calvinistic theology. England had a long history of maintaining the rights of the crown against the pope. Edward I (d. 1307) defeated Pope Boniface VIII's attempt to deny kings the right to tax their clergy. In the mid-fourteenth century, the English Parliament passed the first Statutes of Provisors and *Praemunire*. These curtailed the right of the pope to appoint candidates to church offices in England, limited the amount of money that could be sent out of England to Rome, and restricted the number of court cases that could be appealed to Rome from English jurisdiction.

In the late Middle Ages, Wycliffe and the Lollards fanned anticlerical sentiment among the English of all classes, and by the early 1520s advocates of reform were smuggling Lutheran writings into England. In 1524–1525 William Tyndale (ca. 1492–1536) translated the New Testament into English and had it published in Cologne and Worms. It began to circulate in England in 1526. Access to a Bible in the language of the people became the centerpiece of the English Reformation.

The King's Affair

Henry VIII (r. 1509–1547), the king who severed England's ties with the papacy, initially opposed the Reformation. When Luther's ideas began to circulate, Henry's chief ministers, Cardinal Thomas Wolsey (ca. 1475–1530) and, later, Sir Thomas More (1478–1535), urged him to rush to the pope's defense. Henry declared his Catholic convictions by publishing a treatise justifying the seven sacraments. It earned him a contemptuous response from Luther and the grant of a title, "Defender of the Faith," from Pope Leo X.

It was the king's unhappy marriage, not his doubts about theology, that allowed the seeds of reform to take root in English soil. Henry had married Catherine of Aragon (d. 1536), daughter of Ferdinand and Isabella of Spain and the aunt of Emperor Charles V. By 1527 the union had produced only one surviving child, a daughter, Mary. Since the precedent for women rulers was weak and the practice controversial, Henry feared that civil war would break out if he left his throne to a daughter.

Henry had wed Catherine in 1509 under unusual circumstances that had required a papal dispensation. Catherine had been the wife of Henry's elder brother, Arthur, the heir to their father's throne. When Arthur died, Catherine was betrothed to Henry, the new heir. This preserved England's alliance with

Spain. Catherine's numerous miscarriages and stillbirths convinced Henry that their union, despite papal permission, had been a sin and had violated God's laws against incest (see Leviticus 18:16, 20:21).

By 1527, Henry was thoroughly enamored of Anne Boleyn, one of the aging Catherine's young ladies in waiting. In order to wed Anne, who he believed would be a more fruitful mate, he needed a papal annulment of his marriage to Catherine. Legally, it would have been difficult for the pope to justify an annulment of a marriage that had been approved by a papal dispensation, and in practical terms it was impossible. The soldiers of the Holy Roman Empire had just mutinied and sacked Rome, and Pope Clement VII was a prisoner of Catherine's nephew, Charles V.

Cardinal Wolsey, Henry's Lord Chancellor and a papal legate who had aspirations to become pope, was given the job of securing the annulment. After two years of profitless diplomatic maneuvering, Henry concluded that Wolsey had failed and dismissed him in disgrace (1529). Thomas Cranmer (1489–1556) and Thomas Cromwell (1485–1540), both of whom harbored Lutheran sympathies, then became the king's chief advisers. They proposed a different course: Why not simply declare the king supreme in England's spiritual affairs as he was in England's temporal government? Once that was done, no foreign permission would be needed to legalize a new marriage for the king.

The "Reformation Parliament"

In 1529, Parliament convened for a seven-year session, and began to issue a flood of legislation to establish the king's authority over the clergy. In January 1531, Convocation (a legislative assembly representing the English clergy) recognized Henry as head of the church in England "as far as the law of Christ allows." In 1532 Parliament passed a decree (Submission of the Clergy) that gave the king jurisdiction over the clergy and canon law. Another act (Conditional Restraint of Annates) recognized the king's power to withhold from Rome the payment of dues traditionally owed the pope.

In January 1533, Thomas Cranmer secretly wed Henry to the pregnant Anne Boleyn. In February 1533, Parliament's Act for the Restraint of Appeals forbade appeals from the king's courts to those of the pope. In March 1533 Cranmer became archbishop of Canterbury, England's primate—or highest ranking clergyman—and declared that the king had never been validly married to Catherine. In 1534 Parliament ended all payments by the English clergy and laity to Rome and gave Henry sole jurisdiction over high ecclesiastical appointments. The Act of Succession in the same year declared Anne Boleyn's children legitimate heirs to the throne, and the Act of Supremacy proclaimed Henry "the only supreme head on earth of the Church of England." In 1536 the first Act for Dissolution of Monasteries closed the smaller houses, and three years later all English monasteries were shut and their endowments confiscated by the king.

Not all of Henry's subjects approved of the nationalization of their church, but Henry encouraged compliance by making examples of two of his most prominent critics. When Thomas More and John Fisher, bishop of Rochester, refused to accept the Act of Succession and the Act of Supremacy, Henry had them executed.

Henry was far bolder in politics than in piety. Except for his break with Rome and his approval of the use of English Bibles in English churches, Henry opposed changes in doctrine and practice. The Ten Articles of 1536, a program for England's nationalized church, made only mild concessions to Protestant tenets. In 1539 the king issued the Six Articles, which were intended to stem a rising tide of enthusiasm for Protestantism. These reaffirmed transubstantiation, denied the Eucharistic cup to the laity, preserved mandatory celibacy for the clergy, authorized private masses, and ordered the continuation of auricular confession. England had to await Henry's death before it could become a genuinely Protestant country.

The King's Wives

Henry was more successful as a politician than as a husband. In 1536 Anne Boleyn, who had disappointed Henry by bearing him another daughter (Elizabeth), was executed for alleged treason and adultery. Henry married four more times. His third wife, Jane Seymour, died in 1537, shortly after giving birth to the long-desired male heir, Edward VI. Henry then wed Anne of Cleves as part of a plan that Cromwell promoted to forge an alliance among Protestant princes. Neither the alliance nor Anne—whom Henry found to have a remarkable resemblance to a horse—proved worth the trouble. The marriage was annulled by Parliament, and Cromwell was executed. Catherine Howard, Henry's fifth wife, was beheaded for adultery in 1542. His last wife, Catherine Parr, was a patron of Humanists and reformers. Henry was her third husband, and she survived him to marry a fourth time.

The Protestant Reformation Under Edward VI

When Henry died, his son, Edward VI (r. 1547–1553), was only ten years old. The young king's regents gave him a Protestant education—enlivened by correspondence with John Calvin. Edward's pro-Protestant government repealed Henry's Six Articles and laws against heresy, and it sanctioned clerical marriage and lay communion with both cup and bread. In 1547 the chantries, endowments supporting priests who said masses for the dead, were dissolved. In 1549 the Act of Uniformity imposed Thomas Cranmer's *Book of Common Prayer* on all English churches, and a year later images and altars were ordered removed from churches.

The Second Act of Uniformity, passed in 1552, revised the *Book of Common Prayer* and published a forty-two-article confession of faith written by Thomas Cranmer. The confession endorsed the Protestant doctrines of justification by faith and supremacy of Holy Scripture. It recognized only two sacraments and denied transubstantiation—although it affirmed the real presence of Christ in the Eucharistic elements.

The turn toward Protestantism that took place during Edward's reign was reversed by his heir, Catherine of Aragon's fervently Catholic daughter, Mary. In 1553 Mary succeeded her teenaged half-brother and made it her mission, as queen, to restore England to the Catholic community. Despite a bloody persecution of Protestants, she was unable completely to undo the work her father and brother had begun. When she died childless in 1558, Anne Boleyn's daughter, Elizabeth (d. 1603), inherited her throne and engineered a religious compromise. The Elizabethan "settlement" left England with a stable, moderately Protestant national church.

⌁ Catholic Reform and Counter-Reformation

Before Luther spoke out, proposals had already been made for reforming the Roman Catholic Church. One of the boldest came on the eve of the last church council that met before the Reformation, the Fifth Lateran Council (1513–1517). But the pope, remembering how the councils of Constance and Basel had usurped the authority of his predecessors, squelched the initiative.

The Modern Devotion inspired many of the laity and clergy who pushed for reform. In 1517 it prompted the foundation of a new kind of religious organization in Rome, the Oratory of Divine Love. The Oratory encouraged cooperation among learned laity and clergy who were deeply committed to the cul-

The Ecstasy of St. Teresa of Avila, by Gianlorenzo Bernini (1598–1680). Mystics like Saint Teresa and Saint John of the Cross helped revive the traditional piety of medieval monasticism. [Scala/Art Resource, N.Y.]

tivation of inner piety, the promotion of Christian living, and the reform of the church.

The fervent Catholic faith of the sixteenth century generated many new religious orders. The Theatines were founded in 1524 to groom devout, reform-minded leaders for the higher levels of the church hierarchy. The Capuchins were established in 1528 to minister to ordinary people by returning to the ideals of Saint Francis. The Somaschi, in the mid-1520s, and the Barnabites, in 1530, dedicated themselves to caring for the residents of war-torn areas of Italy. The Ursulines, founded in 1535, undertook the religious education of girls from all social classes. The Oratorians, established in 1575, promoted religious literature and church music—the great hymnist and musician Giovanni Palestrina (1526–1594) was one of them. And, thanks to the inspiration of Spanish mystics Saint Teresa of Avila (1515–1582) and Saint John of the Cross (1542–1591), older monastic orders also underwent renewal.

Ignatius of Loyola and the Jesuits

The most influential of the new orders, the Society of Jesus, was organized in the 1530s by Ignatius of Loyola (1491–1556). Ignatius, a dashing courtier and *caballero*, began his spiritual pilgrimage in 1521 when he was seriously wounded in battle. He passed a lengthy and painful convalescence reading Christian classics and studying the techniques developed by the church's saints for overcoming mental anguish and pain. A dramatic conversion experience determined him to do whatever was necessary to become a "soldier of Christ."

The lessons Ignatius learned from his struggles with himself evolved into a program for personal individual renewal. Ignatius believed that a person could create a new self through study and discipline, and he wrote a devotional guide (*Spiritual Exercises*) to teach techniques for achieving spiritual self-mastery.

The Protestant reformers of Ignatius's day made a virtue of opposing the authority of the traditional church. Ignatius, however, urged Catholics to deny themselves and submit without question to the church. Perfect discipline and self-control were to be cultivated—as were enthusiasm for traditional spirituality, mystical experience, and willingness to subordinate all personal goals to those of the church. People imbued with these qualities were well equipped to counter the Reformation. Within a century the ten original "Jesuits" were joined by more than 15,000 ardent recruits. They recovered districts initially lost to Protestantism in Austria, Bavaria, and the Rhineland, and staffed missions as far afield as India, Japan, and the Americas.

The Council of Trent (1545–1563)

Pope Paul III (1534–1549), in response to pressure from Emperor Charles V, finally called a general council to address the crisis created by the Reformation. The commission, appointed by the pope to prepare for the council, was chaired by Caspar Contarini (1483–1542), a member of the Oratory of Divine Love. Contarini was such an advocate of reform that his critics branded him a "semi-

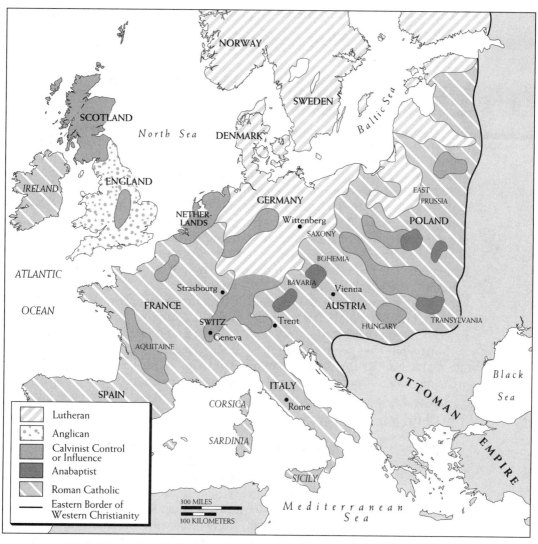

MAP 11-2 **The Religious Situation About 1560** *By 1560 Luther, Zwingli, and Loyola were dead, Calvin near the end of his life, the English break from Rome fully accomplished, and the last session of the Council of Trent about to assemble. Here is the religious geography of western Europe at this time.*

Lutheran." The report he presented to the pope in February 1537 was so blunt an indictment of the papal curia that Protestants circulated it to justify their break with the papacy.

The opening of the council, which met in Trent in northern Italy, was delayed until 1545, and its three sessions spread over eighteen years (1545–1563) (see Map 11-2). Long interruptions were caused by war, plague, and politics. Unlike the late medieval councils, Trent was strictly under papal control—and dominated by Italian clergy. Only high-ranking churchmen could vote. Theologians from the universities, the lower clergy, and laypersons did not have a voice in the council's decisions.

The council focused on the restoration of internal church discipline. It curtailed the selling of church offices and other religious goods. It ordered bishops who resided outside their dioceses to return home and to take steps to elevate the conduct of their charges. Bishops were enjoined to preach and to conduct frequent tours of inspection of the clergy. Trent also sought to increase respect for the parish priest by requiring him to be neatly dressed, better educated, strictly celibate, and active among his parishioners. To this end Trent called for the construction of a seminary in every diocese.

Trent made no doctrinal concessions to Protestantism. On the contrary, it ringingly affirmed most of the things to which Protestants objected: traditional Scholastic education; the role of good works in salvation; the authority of tradition; the seven sacraments; transubstantiation; the withholding of the Eucharistic cup from the laity; clerical celibacy; purgatory; indulgences; and the veneration of saints, relics, and sacred images.

Trent was not designed to heal the rifts that had developed within Christendom, but to strengthen the Roman Catholic Church in opposition to Protestantism. Some secular rulers were initially leery of Trent's assertion of papal authority, but they were reassured as the new legislation took hold and parish life revived under the guidance of a devout and better-trained clergy. The increasing religious polarization of Europe was, however, a source for anxiety.

The Church in Spanish America

The Roman Catholic priests who accompanied the expeditions that explored and conquered the Americas were imbued with the Christian Humanism that flourished in sixteenth-century Spain. They wanted to convert the Indians not only to Christianity but to European civilization as well.

The early Spanish conquerors and the mendicant friars who worked among the Indians were often at odds. Many priests believed that conquest was a necessary prerequisite for the conversion of the Indians, but they deplored exploitation of native peoples and tried to defend them. Bartolomé de Las Casas, a Dominican, contended that conquest was not necessary for conversion. The campaign he began in 1550 for royal legislation regulating conquest was successful, but his rhetoric encouraged the growth of the "Black Legend"—a condemnation of all Spanish colonists for inhumanity toward the Indians. Although the "Black Legend" contained elements of truth, it exaggerated the case against Spain. The Aztec demands for human sacrifice prove that Indian rulers could also be exceedingly cruel. Had the Aztecs discovered Spain and won the upper hand, they would have dealt with Europeans much as Spaniards dealt with Indians.

By the end of the sixteenth century, the church in Spanish America had made peace with colonialism. On numerous occasions, individual priests defended the rights of Indian tribes, but the church also profited from the growing prosperity of the Spanish colonists. As a great landowner with a stake in the colonial status quo, it did not challenge Spanish domination or any but the most extreme modes of economic exploitation. By the time the colonial era drew to a close in the late eighteenth century, the Roman Catholic Church had become one of the strongest and most conservative institutions in Latin America.

The Social Significance of the Reformation in Western Europe

Luther, Zwingli, and Calvin believed that Christians were called not to separate themselves from the world, but to take up their Christian duties as citizens of the state. Consequently, they have been called "magisterial reformers," meaning not only that they were leaders of major Protestant movements but also that they were willing to use the magistrate's sword to advance their causes.

To some modern observers this looks like a compromise of the highest religious principles, but the reformers did not see it that way. They assumed that their reforms had to conform to the realities of the societies of which they were members. The reformers were so sensitive to what they believed was politically and socially possible that some scholars claim that they actually encouraged acceptance of the status quo. But despite this political conservatism, the Reformation, in some places, contributed to radical changes in traditional religious practices and institutions.

The Revolution in Religious Practices and Institutions

Religion in Fifteenth-Century Life. On the eve of the Reformation, the clergy and the religious made up 6 to 8 percent of the total population of the central European cities that were about to become Protestant. In addition to their spiritual authority, they exercised considerable political power. They legislated, taxed, tried cases in special church courts, and enforced laws with threats of excommunication. The church calendar regulated daily life. About one-third of the year was given over to some kind of religious observance, fast, or celebration. Cloisters, which educated the children of prominent citizens and enjoyed the patronage of powerful aristocratic families, had great influence. There was booming business at religious shrines, where pilgrims gathered by the hundreds or thousands. Begging friars constantly worked the streets, and several times each year special preachers arrived to sell letters of indulgence.

The conduct of many of the religious was a source of concern. Despite the fact that clergy were sworn to celibacy and forbidden legal marriages, many had concubines and children. Society's response to these relationships was mixed, but the church tolerated them upon payment of penitential fines. Everywhere there were complaints about the clergy's exemption from taxation and immunity from prosecution in civil courts, and people grumbled about having to support church offices whose occupants lived and worked elsewhere.

Religion in Sixteenth-Century Life. The Reformation made few changes in the politics or class structures of the cities where it triumphed. The same aristocratic families governed as before, and the same people were rich and poor. The Reformation did, however, have a profound impact on the clergy. Their numbers fell by two-thirds; religious holidays shrank by one-third. Monasteries and nunneries nearly disappeared—transformed into hospices or educational institutions. Parish churches were reduced in number by at least one-third. Worship was conducted in the vernacular. In some places, particularly those influenced by the Zwinglian reform, the walls of sanctuaries were stripped bare and whitewashed.

The laity observed no obligatory fasts. Local shrines were closed down, and anyone found venerating saints, relics, and images was subject to punishment. Copies of Luther's translation of the New Testament or excerpts from it could be found in private homes. Instead of controlling access to the Scriptures, the new clergy encouraged laypersons to study them. Protestant clergy could marry, and many did. They paid taxes and were punished for their crimes in civil courts. The moral life of the community was supervised by committees composed of equal numbers of laity and clergy, and secular magistrates had the last word in resolving disputes. Not all Protestant clergy were enthusiastic about lay authority in religion. The laity complained about "new papists" among the Protestant preachers—men who sought the strict control over the lives of the laity that the Catholic clergy enjoyed.

The laity themselves were no less ambivalent about certain aspects of the Reformation, and they could be just as reactionary as some clergy. Over half of the original converts returned to the Catholic fold before the end of the sixteenth century.

The Reformation and Education

The Reformation's implementation of Humanistic educational theories in new Protestant schools and universities had significant cultural impact. Even when the Reformers' views on doctrine and human nature separated them from the Humanists, they shared the Humanists' belief in the unity of wisdom, eloquence, and action. The Humanist program of study, which emphasized language skills and a reliance on original sources, was essential for the practice of a Protestant faith that acknowledged no authority higher than that of Scripture.

When, in August 1518, Philip Melanchthon (1497–1560), a young professor of Greek, joined Luther at the University of Wittenberg, his first act was to champion Humanist curricular reforms. In his inaugural address, *On Improving the Studies of the Young,* Melanchthon defended classical studies against medieval Scholasticism, and he and Luther completely restructured the University of Wittenberg's program of study. Canon law and commentaries on

Lombard's *Sentences* were dropped. Old-fashioned Scholastic lectures on Aristotle were replaced by a straightforward historical approach. Students read primary sources directly, not as interpreted by Scholastic commentators. Candidates for theological degrees relied on exegesis of the Bible, not the citation of "authorities," to defend their theses. New chairs of Greek and Hebrew were created. Luther and Melanchthon also pressed for universal compulsory education so that both boys and girls could learn to read the Bible in vernacular translation.

In Geneva, John Calvin and his successor, Theodore Beza, founded an academy that developed into the University of Geneva. Their school, which concentrated on training Calvinist ministers, developed a program similar to the one designed by Luther and Melanchthon. Calvinist refugees trained in the academy carried Protestant educational reforms to France, Scotland, England, and the New World. Thanks to them, a working knowledge of Greek and Hebrew became commonplace in educated circles in the sixteenth and seventeenth centuries.

Some contemporaries complained that the original Humanist program narrowed its focus as Protestants took it over, but Humanist culture and learning profited from the Reformation. Protestant schools and universities consolidated and preserved for the modern world many of the basic pedagogical achievements of Humanism.

The Reformation and the Changing Role of Women

The Protestant reformers rejected ascetic disciplines, like celibacy, as vain attempts to earn salvation, and they urged clergy to marry to dispel the belief that the lives of clergy were spiritually more meritorious than those of laypersons. The development of a more positive attitude toward marriage translated into a more positive attitude toward women.

Medieval thinkers often degraded sexually active women as temptresses (like Eve) and exalted virginal women as saints (like Mary). Protestants praised woman in her own right, but especially in her biblical vocation as mother and housewife. The reformers acknowledged the contribution their wives made to their ministries, and Protestants stressed as no religious movement before them had the sacredness of home and family. The ideal of companionate marriage—that is, of husband and wife as co-workers in a special God-ordained community of the family—greatly improved women's legal status. Since Protestant marriage was not a sacrament, divorce was easier, and women had the right to leave husbands who flagrantly violated marriage contracts. Although from a modern perspective, Protestant women remained subject to men, new marriage laws gave them greater security and protection.

Because they wanted women to become pious housewives modeling their lives on biblical precepts, Protestants encouraged vernacular literacy for girls. Some women became authors and contributed to the literature of the Reformation. Many, in the course of their studies, pondered the significance of biblical passages that suggested they were equal to men in the presence of God.

The discussion of woman's role that Protestant theology encouraged inched society marginally closer to the emancipation of women.

✧ Family Life in Early Modern Europe

Marriage

The Reformation was one factor among many that worked changes in domestic life at the end of the Middle Ages. Men and women began to delay first marriages to later ages than they had in previous centuries. Grooms tended to be in their mid- to late twenties rather than in their late teens and early twenties, and brides in their early to mid-twenties rather than in their teens. The church-sanctioned minimum age for marriage remained fourteen for men and twelve for women. Betrothal could still occur at these young ages if parents approved.

Later marriages were a reflection of the difficulty couples encountered in amassing enough capital to establish independent households. Family size and population increased in the fifteenth and early sixteenth centuries. That meant that property tended to be divided among more heirs, and an average couple had to work longer to prepare materially for marriage. Many—possibly 20 percent of all women in the sixteenth century—never married. Single women often

A young couple in love (ca. 1480), by an anonymous artist. [Bildarchiv Preussischer Kulturbesitz]

grew increasingly impoverished as they aged without the support of a husband or children.

Marriages tended to be "arranged" in the sense that the male heads of two families met and discussed the terms of a marriage before they informed the prospective bride and bridegroom. It was rare, however, for the two people involved not to know each other in advance or to have no prior relationship. Children had a legal right to protest and resist an unwanted marriage. A forced marriage was, by definition, invalid, and no one believed an unwanted marriage would last. The best marriage was one desired by both parties and approved by their families.

Later marriages to older partners shortened the length of the average marriage and elevated the rate of remarriage. Maternal mortality increased with late marriage and, as the rapid growth of orphanages and foundling homes between 1600 and 1800 testifies, so did out-of-wedlock pregnancies.

Family Size

The early modern family was conjugal or nuclear. It consisted of a father and a mother and an average of two to four surviving children. A wife endured a pregnancy about every two years. About one-third of the children born died by age five, and one-half were gone by age twenty. Rare was the family at any social level that did not suffer the loss of children. Martin Luther fathered six children, two of whom died—one at eight months and another at thirteen years.

Birth control methods of limited effectiveness had been available since antiquity: acidic ointments, sponges, and *coitus interruptus.* The church's growing condemnation of contraception in the thirteenth and fourteenth centuries suggests that its use was increasing. St. Thomas Aquinas defended the church's position by asserting that a natural act, like sex, was moral only when it served the end for which it was created—in this case, the production of children and their subsequent rearing to the glory of God. Christian moral teachings may, however, have increased some couples' use of contraception by encouraging husbands to empathize with the burden frequent pregnancies placed on their wives.

Infant and Child Care

Theologians and physicians joined in condemning the widespread custom of putting newborn children out to wet nurses. Wet nurses were mothers who made money by suckling other women's children. Wet nursing often exposed an infant to great risks from disease or neglect, but nursing a child was a chore many upper-class women found distasteful. Husbands also disliked it, for the church forbade sexual intercourse while a woman was lactating on the theory that sexual intercourse spoiled a woman's milk. Nursing also has a contraceptive effect, and there is evidence that some women prolonged nursing to fend off new pregnancy. For wealthy burghers and noblemen who wanted an abundance of male heirs, time spent nursing was time wasted.

In addition to wet nursing, other practices common to early modern families cause them to appear cold and unloving. A child who spent the first year of his life with a wet nurse might, between the ages of nine and fourteen, find himself sent away from home again for an apprenticeship or employment. Also, the gap in ages between husband and wife was often great, and a widower or widow sometimes remarried very quickly.

The forms love and affection take, however, are as relative to time and culture as other values. Depending on the options that are available, a kindness in one historical period can seem a cruelty in another. Primitive living conditions, which made single life difficult, necessitated quick remarriages. A competitive economic environment with limited opportunities for vocational education encouraged early apprenticeships if children were to have jobs. There is no convincing evidence that people of the Reformation era were less capable of loving one another than modern people are.

The Lutheran Reformation, which made pluralism a fact of Western religious life, was the product of an age of widespread discontent. People at all levels of society had come to resent a church that failed to hold clergy accountable for their spiritual conduct while exempting them from many burdens imposed on the laity. Spiritual and secular grievances combined to fuel a revolution that restructured both the church and the state.

Luther's declaration that Scripture was the only authority governing faith opened a Pandora's box, for people proved to have very different ideas about what Scripture taught. Lutheran, Zwinglian, Anabaptist, Spiritualist, Calvinist, and Anglican versions of biblical religion ap-peared in rapid succession, and Protestants had difficulty containing their revolution.

A move to reform the Catholic church was underway long before the Reformation broke out in Germany, but, lacking papal support, it made little progress until the mid-sixteenth century. Catholic reform, when it came, was doctrinally reactionary but administratively and spiritually innovative. The church demanded strict obedience and conformity, but it also provided the laity with a better-educated and disciplined clergy. The result was a smaller but more vigorous church, prepared to fight for its place in an increasingly pluralistic culture.

⤳ Review Questions

1. What were the main problems of the church that contributed to the Protestant Reformation? Why was the church in the early sixteenth century unable to suppress dissent as successfully as it had earlier?

2. On what did Luther and Zwingli agree? On what did they disagree? What about Luther and Calvin? Did differences and splits among Protestants lessen the effectiveness of the Protestant movement or increase the range of its influence?

3. Why did the Reformation begin in Germany? How did the political context Germany provided for a reform movement differ from the situation in France or Italy?

4. What was the Catholic Reformation?

What were the major reforms instituted by the Council of Trent? Did the Protestant Reformation have a healthy effect on the Catholic Church?

5. Why did Henry VIII break with the Catholic Church? Did he establish a truly Protestant religion in England? What problems did his successors face as a result of his religious policies?

6. What impact did the Reformation have on women in the sixteenth and seventeenth centuries? What new factors and pressures affected relations between men and women, family size, and child care during this period?

↜ Suggested Readings

W. BOUWSMA, *John Calvin: A Sixteenth Century Portrait* (1988). Interpretation of Calvin against the background of Renaissance intellectual history.

J. DELUMEAU, *Catholicism Between Luther and Voltaire: A New View of the Counter Reformation* (1977). Programmatic essay on a social history of the Counter-Reformation.

A. G. DICKENS, *The English Reformation* (1974). The best one-volume account.

H. O. EVENNETT, *The Spirit of the Counter Reformation* (1968). Essay on the continuity of Catholic reform and its independence from the Protestant Reformation.

B. GOTTLIEB, *The Family in the Western World* (1992). Accessible overview, with up-to-date annotated bibliographies.

J. L. IRWIN (ed.), *Womanhood in Radical Protestantism, 1525–1675* (1979). Sources illustrating images of women in sectarian Protestant thought.

D. L. JENSEN, *Reformation Europe: Age of Reform and Revolution* (1981). Excellent, up-to-date survey.

J. F. MCNEILL, *The History and Character of Calvinism* (1954). The most comprehensive account, and very readable.

H. A. OBERMAN, *Luther: Man Between God and the Devil* (1989). Perhaps the best account of Luther's life, by a Dutch master.

J. O'MALLEY, *The First Jesuits* (1993). Extremely detailed account of the creation of the Society of Jesus and its original purposes.

S. OZMENT, *Protestants: The Birth of a Revolution* (1992). The Reformation in Germany.

S. OZMENT, *When Fathers Ruled: Family Life in Reformation Europe* (1983). A survey of sixteenth-century attitudes toward marriage and parenthood.

J. J. SCARISBRICK, *The Reformation and the English People* (1990). Eloquent argument that the Reformation changed little religiously; that it was a political, not a spiritual, triumph.

D. STARKEY, *The Reign of Henry VIII* (1985). Portrayal of the king as in control of neither his life nor his court.

J. STAYER, *Anabaptists and the Sword* (1972). The political philosophies of sectarians.

L. STONE, *The Family, Sex and Marriage in England, 1500–1800* (1977). Controversial but in many respects still reigning view of English family history.

R. H. TAWNEY, *Religion and the Rise of Capitalism* (1947). Advances beyond Weber's arguments relating Protestantism and capitalist economic behavior.

M. WEBER, *The Protestant Ethic and the Spirit of Capitalism*, trans. by Talcott Parsons (1958). First appeared in 1904–1905 and has continued to stimulate debate over the relationship between religion and society.

F. WENDEL, *Calvin: The Origins and Development of His Religious Thought*, trans. by Philip Mairet (1963). The best treatment of Calvin's theology.

G. H. WILLIAMS, *The Radical Reformation* (1962). Broad survey of the varieties of dissent within Protestantism.

12

The Age of Religious Wars

KEY TOPICS

- The war between Calvinists and Catholics in France
- The Spanish occupation of the Netherlands
- The struggle for supremacy between England and Spain
- The devastation of central Europe during the Thirty Years' War

Political rivalries and religious conflicts combined to make the late sixteenth and the early seventeenth centuries an "age of religious wars." The era was plagued both by civil conflicts within nations and by battles among nations. Catholic and Protestant factions struggled for advantage within France, the Netherlands, and *England. The Catholic monarchies of France and Spain attacked Protestant regimes in England and the Netherlands. Ultimately, every major nation in Europe was drawn into a conflict that devastated Germany, the Thirty Years' War (1618–1648).*

↭ Renewed Religious Struggle

During the first half of the sixteenth century, religious war was confined to central Europe—to parts of the empire where Lutherans fought for recognition. In the second half of the sixteenth century, the battles shifted to western Europe (France, the Netherlands, England, and Scotland) as Calvinists struggled for their cause.

The Peace of Augsburg (1555) ended the first phase of the war in central Europe by granting each ruler of a region of the empire the right to determine the religion of his subjects. The only kind of Protestantism that Augsburg recognized, however, was Lutheranism. Lutherans and Catholics joined forces to oppose Anabaptists and other sectarians, and Calvinists were not yet strong enough to demand legal standing.

By the time the Council of Trent adjourned in 1563 the Roman Catholic Church had been reinvigorated, and the Jesuits were spearheading a counteroffensive to recover regions lost to Protestantism in western Europe. John Calvin, who died in 1564, made Geneva both a refuge for Protestants fleeing persecution and a school to equip them to meet the Catholic challenge.

Genevan Calvinism and Tridentine Catholicism were equally dogmatic and aggressive, and mutually incompatible. Calvinism mandated a presbyterian organization that distributed authority among local governments. Boards of *presbyters* (elders), composed of both clergy and laity and representing individual congregations, set policy for the church at large. The Roman Catholic Church was, by contrast, a centralized, hierarchical system that stressed absolute obedience to the pope. The pope and bishops ruled supreme without the necessity of consulting with the laity. Calvinism attracted people who favored the decentralization and distribution of political power and who opposed authoritarian rule, whereas Catholicism was preferred by advocates of absolute monarchy—those who favored "one king, one church, one law."

The contrast between the two religions appears in the art of the period. The Baroque, a successor to Mannerism, was favored by Catholic countries. Baroque artists, like Peter Paul Rubens (1571–1640) and Gianlorenzo Bernini (1598–1680), produced grandiose works bursting with life and energy. Protestant patrons often preferred simpler, more rationally controlled, and less exuberantly emotional art—such as the churches designed by the English architect Christopher Wren (1632–1723) and the gentle portraits painted by the Dutch Mennonite, Rembrandt van Rijn (1606–1669).

As religious wars engulfed Europe, intellectuals perceived the wisdom of religious pluralism and toleration. Skepticism, relativism, and individualism in religion increasingly came to be seen as virtues. Valentin Weigel (1533–1588), a Lutheran who surveyed a half-century of religious strife in Germany, spoke for many when he advised people to look within themselves for religious truth and not to churches and creeds.

Politicians were slower than intellectuals to see the wisdom of toleration. The rulers who succeeded best at holding religious strife and civil war in check were the *politiques*—monarchs (like Elizabeth I of England) who urged toler-

In stark contrast to the Baroque style, this seventeenth-century Calvinist church in the Palatinate has no interior decoration to distract the worshiper from the Word of God. The intent was to create an atmosphere of quiet introspection and reflection on one's spiritual life and God's Word. [German National Museum, Nuremberg]

ance, moderation, and compromise in religious matters. Governments led by people who took religion with utmost seriousness (e.g., Mary I of England, Philip II of Spain, and England's Oliver Cromwell) failed to maintain stability.

❧ The French Wars of Religion (1562–1598)

Anti-Protestant Measures and the Struggle for Political Power

In the 1520s Lutheran ideas began to circulate in Paris and to excite the suspicions of the French government. French Protestants were dubbed *Huguenots*—after Besançon Hugues, the leader of the revolt that established an independent, Protestant Geneva.

In 1525, when Emperor Charles V captured King Francis I of France at the Battle of Pavia, the French authorities began actively to prosecute Protestants. They hoped that by cooperating with Charles's anti-Protestant campaign they might win favorable terms for the king's release. A second crackdown followed a decade later. It was a response to a major Protestant publicity campaign that (on October 18, 1534) plastered Paris and other cities with anti-Catholic placards. The government's reaction convinced some that the monarchy was committing itself to exterminating Protestantism, and John Calvin and other members of the French reform decided to leave France.

Hostilities between the French and the empire (the Habsburg-Valois wars) ended with the Treaty of Cateau-Cambrésis in 1559. The treaty marked a shift in the European balance of power from France to Spain, and it was a prelude to an outbreak of civil conflict within France. Both these developments began with an accident. In 1559 the French king, Henry II, was mortally wounded in a tournament, and his sickly fifteen-year-old son, Francis II, ascended the throne. The queen mother, Catherine de Médicis, governed France as the boy-king's regent. The weakness of her administration tempted three great families to struggle for leadership of France: the Bourbons, whose power lay in the south and west; the Montmorency-Chatillons, who controlled the center of France; and the Guises, whose lands were in the east.

The Guises were initially the strongest, and they dominated the young king. Francis, duke of Guise, had commanded Henry II's army, and his brothers, Charles and Louis, were cardinals of the church. They arranged for their niece, Mary Stuart, Queen of Scotland, to marry Francis II. The Guise family championed a militant, reactionary Catholicism, and Protestants rallied to their opponents—the Bourbon prince of Condé, Louis I (d. 1569), and the Montmorency-Chatillons admiral, Gaspard de Coligny (1519–1572).

Appeal of Calvinism

Ambitious aristocrats and discontented townspeople had different reasons for joining Calvinist churches in opposing the Guise-dominated French monarchy. Although there were more than 2,000 Huguenot congregations in France by 1561, Huguenots were a majority of the population in only two regions: Dauphiné and Languedoc. Huguenots made up only about one-fifteenth of France's population, but they controlled important districts and were heavily represented among the more powerful segments of French society. Over two-fifths of the country's aristocracy became Huguenots. Many probably saw Protestantism as a way to strengthen their authority over their domains. They hoped to establish within France a principle of territorial sovereignty akin to that endorsed for the Holy Roman Empire by the Peace of Augsburg.

The military organization of Condé and Coligny progressively merged with the Huguenot churches. Each side had much to gain from the other. Calvinism provided both a theological justification and a practical motive for political resistance to the Catholic monarchy. Armed strength was essential if Calvinism hoped to become a viable religion in France, but the confluence of secular and religious motives cast suspicion on the sincerity of some Calvinist leaders. Religious conviction was neither the only nor always the main reason for their conversion to Protestantism.

Catherine de Médicis and the Guises

Francis II died in 1560, but his mother, Catherine de Médicis, continued to rule France as regent for her second son, Charles IX (r. 1560–1574). Catherine's first concern was always to preserve the monarchy. Hoping to balance the power of the Guises, she sought allies among the Protestants. In 1562, after conversations with Coligny and Theodore Beza, Calvin's successor, she issued the *January Edict.* This granted Protestants freedom to hold synods and public worship services outside towns—but only private meetings within them. Royal efforts to promote toleration ended abruptly in March 1562, when the duke of Guise massacred a Protestant congregation at Vassy and began a war with the Huguenots.

Had Condé and the Huguenot armies rushed immediately to the queen's side after this attack, they might have secured an alliance with Catherine, who feared the powerful Guises. But the Protestant leaders hesitated, and the Guises won control of the young king and his mother.

The Peace of Saint-Germain-en-Laye. During the first French war of religion (April 1562 to March 1563), the duke of Guise was assassinated. A brief resumption of hostilities in 1567 was followed (from September 1568 to August 1570) by the bloodiest phase in the conflict. Condé was killed, and Huguenot leadership passed to Coligny, who was far the better military strategist. He negotiated the Peace of Saint-Germain-en-Laye (1570) which won Huguenots religious freedoms within their territories and the right to fortify their cities.

Queen Catherine tried to survive by balancing the fanatical Huguenot and Guise extremes. Like the Guises, she preferred a Catholic France and tolerated Protestants only as a counter to Guise domination of the monarchy. But after the Peace of Saint-Germain-en-Laye strengthened the Huguenots, Catherine switched sides. She began to plot with the Guises to prevent the Protestants from winning over her son.

Catherine had reason to fear Coligny. He was on the verge of persuading the young king to invade the Netherlands to help the Dutch Protestants against their Catholic Habsburg ruler. Such a move would have set France on a collision course with Spain, and Catherine knew that France stood little chance in such a contest.

The Saint Bartholomew's Day Massacre. On August 18, 1572, the French nobility gathered in Paris for the wedding of the king's sister (Marguerite of Valois) to Henry of Navarre, a Huguenot leader. Four days later an attempt was made on Coligny's life. Catherine had apparently been party to a plot by the Guises to eliminate Coligny, and when it failed, she panicked. She feared both the king's reaction to her complicity with the Guises and what the Huguenots and Coligny might do in seeking revenge. In desperation she convinced Charles that a Huguenot coup was afoot and that only the swift execution of the Protestant leaders could save the crown.

On August 24, Saint Bartholomew's Day, 1572, Coligny and 3,000 fellow Huguenots were ambushed in Paris and butchered. Within three days an estimated 20,000 Huguenots were executed in coordinated attacks throughout France. Protestants across Europe were horrified, while Pope Gregory XIII and Philip II of Spain greeted the news of the Protestant deaths with special religious celebrations.

Catholics came to regret the slaughter of the French Protestants, for Saint Bartholomew's Day changed the nature of the struggle between Protestants and Catholics everywhere. The disastrous outcome of France's internal squabbling over political power and religious freedom convinced Protestants in many lands that they were engaged in an international war for survival—a fight to the death with an adversary whose cruelty justified any means of resistance.

Protestant Resistance Theory. At the start of the Reformation, Protestants tried to honor the biblical mandate (Romans 13:1) that directed subjects to obey the rulers God placed over them. Luther only grudgingly approved resistance to Charles V after the emperor ordered Protestants to return to Catholicism in 1530. Calvin, secure in his control of Geneva, had always condemned willful disobedience and rebellion against lawfully constituted governments. But he also taught that lower magistrates, as part of lawfully constituted governments, had the duty to oppose higher authorities if these became tyrannical.

An early Calvinist rationale for revolution was developed by John Knox, a Scot driven into exile by the Catholic regent for Scotland, Mary of Guise. Knox's *First Blast of the Trumpet Against the Terrible Regiment of Women* (1558) declared that the removal of a heathen (i.e., Catholic) tyrant was not only permissible, but a Christian duty. The Saint Bartholomew's Day massacre persuaded other Calvinists to adopt a similar point of view. François Hotman's *Franco-Gallia* (1573) argued that France's representative assembly, the Estates General, was an authority superior to the crown. Theodore Beza's *On the Right of Magistrates over Their Subjects* (1574) justified the overthrow of tyrants by lower authorities. And Philippe du Plessis Mornay's *Defense of Liberty Against Tyrants* (1579) urged princes, nobles, and magistrates to cooperate in rooting out tyranny in any land where it appeared.

The Rise to Power of Henry of Navarre

Henry III (r. 1574–1589), the last of Henry II's sons to wear the French crown, was caught between the vengeful Huguenots and a radical Catholic League formed in 1576 by Henry of Guise. Like his mother Catherine, Henry sought a middle course—appealing to the neutral Catholics and Huguenots who put the political survival of France above its religious unity.

In May 1576, Henry, in the Peace of Beaulieu, promised the Huguenots almost complete religious and civil freedom. The move was premature, for the Catholic League was able to force Henry to reverse himself. In October, 1577, the Edict of Poitiers again restricted Huguenots to limited areas.

By the mid-1580s the Catholic League, with Spanish help, was supreme in Paris. In 1588 Henry III launched a surprise attack to rout the league (the "Day of the Barricades"). The coup failed, and the king had to flee. News of the English victory over the Spanish Armada then emboldened him to order the assassinations of both the duke and the cardinal of Guise. These murders enraged the Catholic League, led by another Guise brother, Charles, duke of Mayenne. By April 1589, the king was left with no choice but to seek an alliance with the Protestant leader, Henry of Navarre, the Bourbon heir to his throne.

As the two Henrys prepared to attack the Guise stronghold in Paris, a Jacobin friar assassinated Henry III and cleared the way for Henry of Navarre to become King Henry IV (r. 1589–1610) of France. Pope Sixtus V and King Philip II of Spain were aghast at the prospect of France becoming a Protestant nation. Philip dispatched troops to support the Catholic League and to claim the throne of France for his daughter, Isabella, Henry II's granddaughter.

The threat of Spanish intervention in their affairs rallied the people of France to Henry IV's side and strengthened his hold on the crown. Henry was a popular man who had the wit and charm to neutralize any enemy in a face-to-face meeting. He was also a *politique*, a leader who considered religion less important than peace. Henry concluded that since most of his subjects were Catholics, he could best rule as a Catholic who was committed to protecting Protestants. Consequently, on July 25, 1593, he embraced Catholicism—reputedly claiming that "Paris is worth a mass." The Huguenots were horrified, and Pope Clement VIII remained skeptical. But the majority of the French people, both clergy and laity, were relieved. They had had enough of war.

The Edict of Nantes

On April 13, 1598, Henry issued the Edict of Nantes to end the civil wars of religion, and the following month (May 2, 1598) the Treaty of Vervins made peace between France and Spain.

The Edict of Nantes confirmed a promise of toleration that Henry IV had made the Huguenots at the start of his reign. By granting some religious rights to a dissenting Protestant minority within what was to remain an officially Catholic country, Nantes came close to creating a state within a state. It designated certain towns and territories as places where Huguenots, who by this time numbered well over a million, could openly conduct worship, hold public offices, enter universities, and maintain forts. Nantes was a truce more than a peace. It turned a hot war into a cold one—a war that eventually claimed Henry IV as a victim. In May 1610, he was assassinated by a Catholic fanatic.

◦—∽ Imperial Spain and the Reign of Philip II (1556–1598)

Pillars of Spanish Power

Philip II of Spain dominated international politics for much of the latter half of the sixteenth century. Bitter experience had led his father, Charles V, to conclude that the Habsburg family lands were too large to be governed by one man.

A view of the Escorial, Philip II's massive palace-monastery-mausoleum northwest of Madrid. Built between 1563 and 1584, it was a monument to the piety and power of the king. Philip vowed to build the complex after the Spanish defeated the French at Saint-Quentin on St. Lawrence's Day in 1577. The floor plan of the Escorial resembles a grill, the symbol of St. Lawrence (who, according to legend, was martyred by being roasted alive on a grill). [Robert Frerck/Odyssey Productions]

He, therefore, divided them between his son and his brother. Philip inherited the intensely Catholic and militarily supreme western half. The eastern portion (Austria, Bohemia, and Hungary) went to Philip's uncle, Emperor Ferdinand I. The imperial title, thereafter, remained with the Austrian Habsburgs.

Philip was a reclusive man who preferred to rule as the remote executive manager of a great national bureaucracy. His character is reflected in the unique residence he built outside Madrid, the Escorial. A combination palace, church, tomb, and monastery, it was a home for a monkish king. Philip was a learned and pious Catholic, a regal ascetic with a powerful sense of duty to his office. He may even have arranged the death of his son Don Carlos (1568), when he concluded that the prince was too mad and treacherous to be entrusted with the power of the crown.

New World Riches. Philip's home base was Spain's populous and prosperous district of Castile. The wealth of the New World that flowed through the port of Seville gave Philip great sums with which to fight wars and underwrite international intrigues. Despite this flood of bullion, Philip's expenses exceeded his income. Near the end of his life he destroyed one of Europe's great banks, the house founded by the Fuggers of Augsburg, by defaulting on his loans.

The American wealth that entered Europe through Spain had a dramatic impact on society. Increased prosperity led to increased population. By the early seventeenth century, the towns of France, England, and the Netherlands had tripled and quadrupled in size, and Europe's population had reached about 100 million. Growth in wealth and numbers of consumers triggered inflation—a steady 2 percent a year rise in prices. More people with more currency to spend meant more competition for food and jobs, and that caused prices to double and triple while wages stagnated.

This was especially the case in Spain, where the new wealth was concentrated in the hands of a few. Nowhere did the underprivileged suffer more than in Spain. The Castilian peasants, the backbone of Philip II's great empire, were the most heavily taxed people in Europe.

Supremacy in the Mediterranean. At the start of Philip's reign, his attention focused almost exclusively on a struggle with the Turks in the Mediterranean. During the 1560s, the Turks had advanced deep into Austria, and their fleets had spread out across the Mediterranean.

Between 1568 and 1570, armies under Philip's half-brother, Don John of Austria, the illegitimate son of Charles V, suppressed and dispersed the Moors in Granada. In May 1571, Spain, Venice, and the pope formed the Holy League—again under Don John's command—to counter Turkish maneuvers in the Mediterranean. On October 7, 1571, Don John's fleet engaged the Ottoman navy off Lepanto in the largest naval battle of the sixteenth century and a clear victory for the Christians. The Mediterranean belonged to Spain.

In 1580 Philip confirmed his dominance of the south by annexing Portugal. This augmented Spanish seapower and brought the magnificent Portuguese overseas empire in Africa, India, and the Americas into the Spanish orbit.

The Revolt in the Netherlands

Philip was far less successful in northern Europe than he was in the Mediterranean. A rebellion in the Netherlands set in motion a chain of events that ended Spain's dreams of world empire.

The Netherlands, the richest district in Europe, was governed for Philip by his half-sister, Margaret of Parma. She was assisted by a council headed by Cardinal Granvelle (1517–1586). Granvelle hoped to check the advance of Protestantism in the Netherlands by promoting church reform. He also planned to reduce the autonomy of the seventeen Netherlands provinces and to create a centralized royal government directed from Madrid. The merchant towns of the Netherlands were, however, accustomed to their independence, and many, like magnificent Antwerp, had become Calvinist strongholds. Two members of the royal council opposed their Spanish overlords: the Count of Egmont (1522–1568) and William of Nassau, the Prince of Orange (1533–1584).

William of Orange placed the political autonomy and well-being of the Netherlands above religious creeds. In 1561 he married Anne of Saxony, but he remained a Catholic until his conversion to Lutheranism in 1567. After the Saint Bartholomew's Day massacre in 1572, Orange became a Calvinist.

In 1561 Cardinal Granvelle began an ecclesiastical reorganization of the Netherlands that was intended to tighten the Catholic hierarchy's control over the country and to accelerate its assimilation as a Spanish dependency. Orange and Egmont, with the support of the Dutch nobility, engineered Granvelle's removal from office in 1564. But the aristocrats who took his place proved inept at running the government, and popular unrest mounted.

In 1564 Philip unwisely insisted that the decrees of the Council of Trent be enforced throughout the Netherlands. Opposition materialized under the leadership of William of Orange's younger brother, Louis of Nassau, who had been raised a Lutheran. The Calvinist-inclined lesser nobility and townspeople joined him in a national covenant, the *Compromise,* a solemn pledge to oppose Trent and the Inquisition. In 1566, when Margaret's government spurned the protesters as "beggars," Calvinists rioted, and Louis called for help from French Huguenots and German Lutherans. A full-scale rebellion against the Spanish regency seemed about to erupt.

The Duke of Alba. A revolt failed to materialize, for the Netherlands' higher nobility were repelled by the behavior of Calvinist extremists and unwilling to join their rebellion. Philip dispatched the duke of Alba to restore order.

In 1567 an army of 10,000 was transferred from Milan, and responsibility for the Netherlands was delegated to a special tribunal, which inaugurated a reign of terror. It executed the counts of Egmont and Horn and several thousand suspected heretics, and it imposed high taxes to force the Netherlanders to pay the costs for the suppression of their revolt. Persecution and taxation drove tens of thousands of refugees from the Netherlands during Alba's cruel six-year rule, and the duke came to be more hated than Granvelle or the radical Calvinists.

Resistance and Unification. William of Orange, who was an exile in Germany during these turbulent years, now emerged as the leader of an independence movement in the Netherlands. The northern, Calvinist-inclined provinces of Holland, Zeeland, and Utrecht became his base. Here, as elsewhere, a fight for political independence was combined with a struggle for religious liberty.

The uprising in the Netherlands was a true popular revolt that enlisted all kinds of people. William even endorsed the raids of the "Sea Beggars," an international group of anti-Spanish exiles and criminals who were brazen pirates. In 1572 the Beggars captured Brill and other seaports in Zeeland and Holland. They incited the native population to join the rebellion, and resistance spread steadily southward. In 1574 the people of Leiden heroically withstood a long Spanish siege, and the Dutch opened the dikes and flooded their country to repulse the hated Spanish. The faltering Alba had by that time ceded power to Don Luis de Requesens, who replaced him as commander of Spanish forces in the Netherlands in November 1573.

The greatest atrocity of the war followed Requesens's death in 1576. Leaderless and unpaid Spanish mercenaries ran amok in Antwerp on November 4, 1576. Seven thousand people lay dead in the streets as a result of what came to be called "the Spanish Fury." This brief event did more to unify the Netherlanders than all previous appeals to religion and patriotism. The ten largely Catholic southern provinces (approximating modern Belgium) joined the seven largely Protestant northern provinces (roughly the modern Netherlands) in opposing Spain.

The Pacification of Ghent declared the unification of the Netherlands on November 8, 1576. The Netherlanders resolved religious differences by agreeing to a territorial settlement like the one the Peace of Augsburg had defined for the Holy Roman Empire in 1555. In January 1577, the last four provinces joined the all-embracing Union of Brussels, and for the next two years the Spanish faced a unified and determined Netherlands.

In November 1576, Don John, the victor over the Turks at Lepanto, took command of Spain's land forces and promptly suffered his first defeat. In February 1577, he signed the Perpetual Edict, a humiliating treaty that promised the removal of all Spanish troops from the Netherlands within twenty days.

The Spanish were, however, nothing if not persistent. The nobility's fear of Calvinist extremism caused a break-up of the Union of Brussels, and Don John and Alessandro Farnese of Parma, the regent Margaret's son, re-established Spanish control in the southern provinces. In January 1579, the southern provinces formed the Union of Arras and made peace with Spain. The northern provinces responded by organizing the Union of Utrecht.

Netherlands' Independence. Seizing the opportunity to break the back of Netherlands' resistance, Philip II declared William of Orange an outlaw and placed a bounty of 25,000 crowns on his head. This stiffened the resistance of the northern provinces, and in a famous speech to the Estates General of Holland in December 1580, (the *Apology*), Orange denounced Philip as a heathen tyrant whom the Netherlands need no longer obey.

On July 22, 1581, most of the northern provinces belonging to the Union of Utrecht formally repudiated Philip's authority and pledged themselves to the French duke of Alençon, Catherine de Médicis's youngest son. Alençon was seen as a compromise between the extremes of Spanish Catholicism and Calvinism, and he was expected to aspire to nothing more than titular authority over the provinces. When he rashly attempted to impose his will on them in 1583, he was deposed and sent back to France.

William of Orange was assassinated in July 1584, and his son, Maurice (1567–1625), became leader of the Dutch resistance. Fortunately for him and his cause, Philip II overextended himself by meddling in the affairs of France and England. Spain's power waned after England defeated Philip's great Armada (see page 281) in 1588. By 1593 the northern provinces had driven out all Spanish soldiers, and in 1596 France and England recognized the independence of these provinces. Peace with Spain was concluded in 1609, and full international recognition came in the Peace of Westphalia in 1648.

⤳ England and Spain (1553–1603)

Mary I

In an effort to protect England's Reformation, Edward VI (d. 1553) sought to disinherit his Catholic half-sister, Mary Tudor (r. 1553–1558). He named as heir to his throne, not his sister, but his cousin—Lady Jane Grey, a grandniece of Henry VIII's. The people of England felt, however, that Mary was the rightful heir, and they rose up to support her. Jane Grey lost her crown and her head.

As queen, Mary exceeded the worst fears of the Protestants. Her Parliaments repealed Edward's Protestant statutes and reverted to the strict Catholic religious practice of her father, Henry VIII. She executed as heretics the great Protestant leaders who had served her brother: John Hooper, Hugh Latimer, and Thomas Cranmer. The names of 282 Protestants whom she burned at the stake are recorded. Many others avoided martyrdom by fleeing to the continent. The "Marian exiles" settled in Germany and Switzerland, where they established communities of worship, wrote tracts justifying armed resistance, and waited for the time when a Protestant counteroffensive could be launched in their homelands. Many absorbed religious beliefs that were much more radical than those they had brought from England.

In 1554 Mary chose a highly unpopular husband, Prince Philip (later King Philip II) of Spain. She favored him because he was the leader of the militant Catholicism that Mary hoped to establish in England, but many of Mary's subjects feared that the marriage would lead to Spain's dominance of England. The politically troublesome marriage was childless, and Mary died knowing that her half-sister, Elizabeth, the daughter of her father's first Protestant marriage, would follow her to the throne.

Elizabeth I

Elizabeth I (r. 1558–1603), the daughter of Henry VIII and Anne Boleyn, was perhaps the most astute politician of the sixteenth century. Assisted by a shrewd adviser, Sir William Cecil (1520–1598), she built a true kingdom on the ruins of Mary's reign. Between 1559 and 1563, she and Cecil guided a religious settlement through Parliament. It merged a centralized episcopal system, which the queen controlled, with broadly defined Protestant doctrine and traditional Catholic ritual. The resulting Anglican church avoided inflexible religious extremes and spared England the religious conflicts that were bloodying continental nations.

Catholic and Protestant Extremists. Religious compromises were unacceptable to zealots of both persuasions, and subversive groups worked to undermine Elizabeth. When she ascended the throne, most of her subjects were Catholics. The extremists among them, encouraged by the Jesuits, plotted to replace her with Mary Stuart, Queen of Scots. Unlike Elizabeth, whose father had declared her illegitimate, Mary Stuart had an unblemished claim to the throne inherited from her grandmother Margaret, sister of Henry VIII. Elizabeth responded swiftly to Catholic assassination plots, but rarely let emotion override her political instincts. Despite proven cases of Catholic treason and even attempted regicide, she executed fewer Catholics during her forty-five years on the throne than Mary Tudor had executed Protestants during her brief five-year reign.

Elizabeth dealt cautiously with the extreme Protestants—the "Puritans" who wanted to "purify" the national church of every vestige of "popery." The Puritans had two major grievances: (1) the retention of Catholic ceremony and vestments within the Church of England, which made it appear to the casual observer that no Reformation had occurred, and (2) the continuation of the episcopal system of governance, which enabled the queen to take the pope's place in dominating the church.

The more extreme Puritans, the Congregationalists, wanted every congregation to be autonomous, a law unto itself, with neither higher episcopal nor presbyterian control. But most sixteenth-century Puritans were not separatists. They campaigned in Parliament for an alternative national church of semiautonomous congregations governed by representative presbyteries (hence, their name "Presbyterians"). Their model was the system Calvin had established in Geneva. Elizabeth conceded nothing that lessened the hierarchical unity of the Church of England and her control over it. The Conventicle Act of 1593 gave separatists the option of either conforming to the practices of the Church of England or facing exile or death.

Deterioration of Relations with Spain. Despite the sincerest desires on the part of both Philip II and Elizabeth to avoid a direct confrontation, events led inexorably to war between England and Spain. In 1567, when the Spanish duke of Alba marched his army into the Netherlands, many in England feared that Spain intended to use the Netherlands as a base for an invasion of England. In 1570 Pope Pius V (1566–1572) branded Elizabeth a heretic and proposed a military expedition to recover England for Catholicism. His mischievous act only complicated a difficult situation.

Following Don John's demonstration of Spain's awesome seapower at the battle of Lepanto in 1571, England signed a mutual defense pact with France. Throughout the 1570s, Elizabeth's famous seamen, John Hawkins (1532–1595) and Sir Francis Drake (1545?–1596), preyed on Spanish shipping in the Americas. Drake's circumnavigation of the globe between 1577 and 1580 was one in a series of dramatic demonstrations of England's growing ascendancy on the high seas.

The Saint Bartholomew's Day massacre forced a change in Elizabeth's foreign policy. Protestants in France and the Netherlands appealed to her as their only protector. In 1585 she signed the Treaty of Nonsuch which sent English soldiers to the Netherlands. Funds she had previously funneled covertly to Henry of Navarre's army in France now flowed openly. These developments strained relations between England and Spain, but the event that brought on war was Elizabeth's decision to execute Mary, Queen of Scots (1542–1587).

Mary, Queen of Scots. Mary Stuart, the daughter of King James V of Scotland and Mary of Guise, had resided in France from the time she was six years old—training for her role as the future wife of King Francis II. The death of her young husband in 1561 sent Mary back to Scotland to rule a land she barely knew. A year earlier, a fervent Protestant Reformation had won legal recognition in the Treaty of Edinburgh. Mary, who had been raised a Catholic in France, had no sympathy with Scotland's new religion or with its dour morality. She wanted to replicate in Scotland the gaiety and sophistication of French court life.

John Knox, the leader of the Scottish Reformation, railed openly about the queen's private mass and Catholic practices (which Scottish law made capital offenses for everyone else). Although Queen Elizabeth personally despised Knox, she recognized that his defense of Protestantism served her foreign policy. It limited Mary's ability to persuade the Scots to cooperate with France against England.

In 1568 a scandal cost Mary her throne. Mary had married Lord Darnley, a youth with connections to the royal houses of both England and Scotland. Although she had a son by him (the James who was eventually to inherit both Scotland and England), Darnley proved an impossible husband. Mary reputedly took the earl of Bothwell as her lover, and he, allegedly, murdered Darnley. Acquitted of this crime, Bothwell abducted Mary and married her. This amounted to usurpation of the throne, and outraged Protestant nobles forced Mary to abdicate in favor of her infant son and to flee Scotland.

Mary unwisely entered England seeking refuge from her cousin Elizabeth. Elizabeth distrusted Mary, for in the opinion of Catholics, Mary had the superior claim to the English throne. Elizabeth, therefore, held Mary under house arrest—for nineteen years. In 1583 Elizabeth's vigilant secretary, Sir Francis Walsingham, uncovered a plot against Elizabeth involving the Spanish ambassador Bernardino de Mendoza. In 1586 Walsingham exposed still another Spanish scheme to unseat Elizabeth, and this time he had proof of Mary's involvement. Elizabeth was loath to execute Mary. She feared that such an act would diminish the aura of divine right that was one of the props of monarchy, and she knew that it would raise a storm of protest among Catholics. In the end, however, she concluded that she had no choice, and Mary was beheaded on February 18, 1587. Mary's death dashed Catholic hopes for a bloodless reconversion of England and persuaded Philip II that the time had come for a military assault on the Protestant nation.

The Armada. Spain's preparations for war were interrupted in the spring of 1587 by successful raids Sir Francis Drake led on the port city of Cadiz and the coast of Portugal. These strikes forced Philip to postpone his invasion of England until the spring of 1588.

On May 30, 1588, the ill-fated Armada of 130 ships, bearing 25,000 sailors and soldiers under the command of the duke of Medina-Sidonia, set to sea. The barges that were to transport Spanish soldiers from their galleons onto England's shores were prevented from leaving Calais and Dunkirk to rendezvous with the fleet. While the Spanish vessels waited, an "English wind" sprang up and helped the swifter English and Dutch ships scatter the Spanish forces.

Spain never fully recovered from this defeat. By the time Philip died on September 13, 1598, his armies had suffered reversals on all fronts. His successors, Philip III (r. 1598–1621), Philip IV (r. 1621–1665), and Charles II (r. 1665–1700), were all inadequate men. They allowed the French to emerge as the leading continental power and the Dutch and English to whittle away at Spain's empire.

When Elizabeth died on March 23, 1603, she left behind a strong nation poised on the brink of acquiring a global empire. Since Elizabeth had never married—choosing instead to use the hope of winning her hand as a tool for English diplomacy—her death ended the Tudor dynasty. Ironically, her heir, James I of England, was Mary's son (James VI of Scotland).

✧ The Thirty Years' War (1618–1648)

The Thirty Years' War in the Holy Roman Empire was the last and most destructive of the wars of religion, and it was unusually devastating. Religious passions escalated entrenched hatreds on all sides, and virtually every major European land was drawn into the conflict. When the hostilities ended in 1648, the agreements among the victorious nations shaped the map of northern Europe as we know it today.

Preconditions for War

Fragmented Germany. In the second half of the sixteenth century, Germany was a collection of about 360 autonomous political entities: secular principalities (duchies, landgraviates, and marches), ecclesiastical principalities (archbishoprics, bishoprics, and abbeys), free cities, and regions dominated by knights with castles. The Peace of Augsburg (1555) had given each a degree of sovereignty within its borders. Since each levied its own tolls and tariffs and coined its own money, travel and trade were difficult. Many little states had pretensions that exceeded their powers.

During the Thirty Years' War, Germany, Europe's crossroads, became Europe's stomping ground. The great conflict had many causes. Most related in some way to a fear of German unification. The Council of Trent raised Protestant suspicions about an imperial-papal conspiracy to use the Holy Roman Empire to restore Catholic dominance throughout Europe. The imperial diet, which was controlled by the German magnates, was leery of any attempt to consolidate the empire at the expense of the liberties of the territorial princes. It countered every move by the emperor to impose his will in the empire, and individual German rulers called on allies outside of Germany for help in defending their rights. Allies were eager to help, fearing what might happen to the balance of power if Germany was brought under the control of a Catholic emperor.

Religious Division. Religious differences accentuated political divisions among states both internationally and within Germany (see Map 12-1). By 1600, there may have been slightly more Protestants than Catholics in the Holy Roman Empire. The territorial principle proclaimed by the Peace of Augsburg in 1555 was designed to freeze Lutherans and Catholics in place by forcing each territory to declare its faith. But as time passed, there were troublesome shifts of opinion.

Lutherans were more successful in securing rights to worship in Catholic lands than Catholics were in securing such rights from Lutherans. Catholic rulers, weakened by the Reformation, had no choice but to make concessions to Protestant communities within their territories, and these Protestant enclaves became constant sources of tension. Protestants were also reluctant to enforce the "Ecclesiastical Reservation" provision of the Peace of Augsburg, which called for the restoration to Catholic control of ecclesiastical principalities when their rulers converted to Protestantism.

Protestant and Catholic antipathies were not the only sources of religious strife. Warring factions emerged among Protestants in the second half of the sixteenth century. Liberal and conservative branches of Lutheranism opposed each other, and Calvinists failed to come to terms with either of these. Calvinism had not been recognized as a legal religion by the Peace of Augsburg, but it won a foothold in the empire when Frederick III (r. 1559–1576), Elector Palatine (ruler within the Palatinate), made it the official religion of his domain. His royal city of Heidelberg became the German "Geneva," an intellectual center for Calvinism and a staging area for Calvinist penetration of the empire.

The Lutherans came to fear the Calvinists almost as much as they did the Catholics, for the bold missionary forays of the Palatine Calvinists threatened to undo what the Peace of Augsburg had done to stabilize the empire. Some Lutherans were also shocked by outspoken Calvinist criticism of their doctrines (e.g., Lutheran faith in Christ's real presence in the Eucharist).

Like the Calvinists, the Jesuits also actively undermined the Peace of Augsburg. Catholic Bavaria, supported by Spain, became for the Counter-Reformation what the Palatinate was for Calvinism. Jesuit missionaries, operating from Bavaria, returned major cities (e.g., Strasbourg and Osnabrück) to the Catholic fold. In 1609 Maximilian, duke of Bavaria, organized a Catholic League to counter a Protestant alliance formed in the same year by the Calvinist Elector Palatine, Frederick IV (r. 1583–1610). The army the league assembled under the command of Count Johann von Tilly tipped Germany into war (see Map 12-2).

Four Periods of War

The Bohemian Period (1618–1625). The war broke out in Bohemia after the ascent to the Bohemian throne in 1618 of Ferdinand, Habsburg archduke of Styria and heir to the empire. Ferdinand, who had been educated by Jesuits, was determined to restore Catholicism to the Habsburg lands. No sooner had he become king of Bohemia than he revoked the religious freedoms of Bohemia's Protestants. The Protestant nobility responded in May 1618 by literally throw-

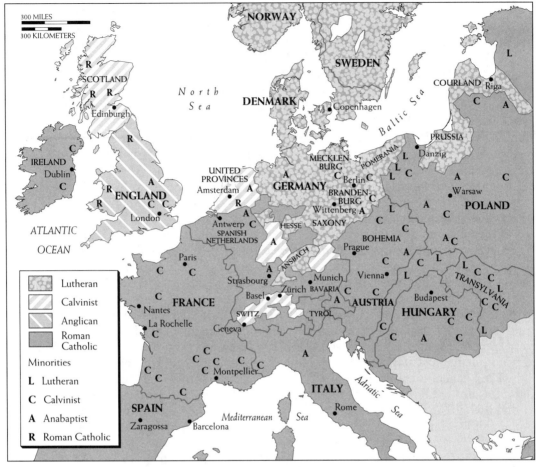

MAP 12-1 Religious Divisions About 1600 *By 1600 few could seriously expect Christians to return to a uniform religious allegiance. In Spain and southern Italy, Catholicism remained relatively unchallenged, but note the existence elsewhere of large religious minorities, both Catholic and Protestant.*

ing his regents out a window—an event described as the "defenestration of Prague." A year later, when Ferdinand (II) became Holy Roman Emperor, the Bohemians refused to recognize his jurisdiction and declared their allegiance to the Calvinist Elector Palatine, Frederick V (r. 1616–1623).

The Bohemian revolt escalated into an international war. Spain, Maximilian of Bavaria, and the Lutheran Elector John George I of Saxony (r. 1611–1656)—who saw a chance to weaken the Elector Palatine—sided with Ferdinand. Tilly, the empire's general, routed Frederick V's troops at the Battle of White Mountain in 1620. By 1622 Ferdinand had subdued Bohemia and conquered the Palatinate. As the remnants of Frederick's army retreated north, the Duke Maximilian followed—claiming land as he went.

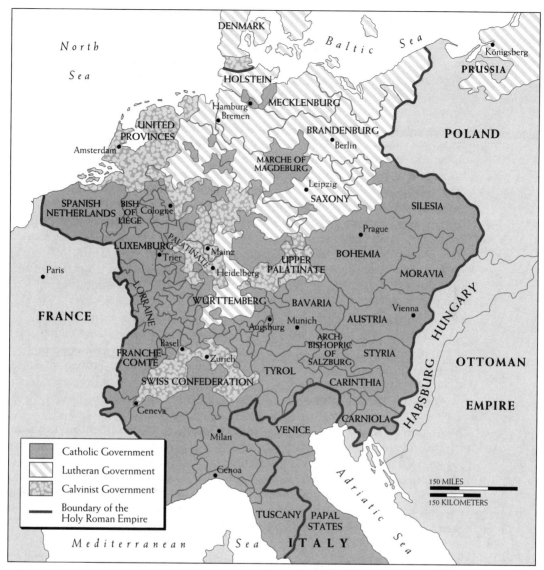

MAP 12-2 The Holy Roman Empire About 1618 *On the eve of the Thirty Years' War, the empire was politically and religiously fragmented, as this somewhat simplified map reveals. Lutherans dominated the north and Catholics the south, while Calvinists controlled the United Provinces and the Palatinate and were important in Switzerland and Brandenburg.*

The Danish Period (1625–1629). Maximilian's forays into northwestern Germany raised fears of a Catholic consolidation of the empire. Christian IV (r. 1588–1648), king of Lutheran Denmark and duke of German Holstein, was encouraged by the English, French, and Dutch to undertake the defense of

Protestantism. He invaded Germany in 1626, but was quickly forced to retreat.

Ferdinand II, who feared that he would not be able to control the ambitious Maximilian, turned the conduct of the war over to a mercenary, Albrecht of Wallenstein (1583–1634). A brilliant and ruthless military strategist, Wallenstein became a law unto himself, but he so effectively broke the back of Protestant resistance that Ferdinand was able to issue an Edict of Restitution in 1629. It ordered the return of all church lands acquired by the Lutherans since 1552. Compliance would have meant Protestant concession of sixteen bishoprics and twenty-eight cities and towns to Catholic governors. The edict struck panic in the hearts of the Habsburgs' opponents and reignited resistance.

The Swedish Period (1630–1635). Gustavus Adolphus of Sweden (r. 1611–1632), a deeply pious Lutheran monarch and a military genius, took up the gauntlet for Protestantism. He was handsomely bankrolled by two very interested bystanders: Cardinal Richelieu, the minister of the Catholic king of France, who wanted to prevent a powerful Habsburg empire from materializing on his border; and the Dutch, the Habsburgs' Protestant opponents of long standing. The Swedish king won a stunning victory at Breitenfeld in 1630 that reversed the course of the war. The battle was decisive, but far from final.

Gustavus Adolphus died fighting Wallenstein's forces at the Battle of Lützen in November 1632, and in 1634 Ferdinand arranged for Wallenstein, who had outlived his usefulness, to be assassinated. The German Protestant states reached a compromise agreement with Ferdinand (the Peace of Prague of 1635). But when the Swedes refused to join them, the war continued.

The Swedish-French Period (1635–1648). The French openly entered the war in 1635 and prolonged it for thirteen more years. French, Swedish, and Spanish soldiers looted the length and breadth of Germany. The Germans, who were too disunited to repulse the foreign armies, simply watched and suffered. By the time peace talks began in the Westphalian cities of Münster and Osnabrück in 1644, an estimated one-third of the German population had died. It was the worst catastrophe in Europe since the Black Death of the fourteenth century.

The Treaty of Westphalia

The Treaty of Westphalia ended hostilities in 1648 by ensuring the continued fragmentation of Germany (see Map 12-3). The territorial principle that rulers could determine the religions of their subjects was reasserted. Calvinism was added to the list of legal religious options, and the German princes were acknowledged supreme over their principalities. Bavaria was elevated to the rank of an elector state, and Brandenburg-Prussia emerged as the most powerful north German principality. The independence of the Swiss Confederacy and of the United Provinces of Holland, long a fact, was proclaimed in law. And France acquired considerable territory.

War between France and Spain continued outside the empire until 1659,

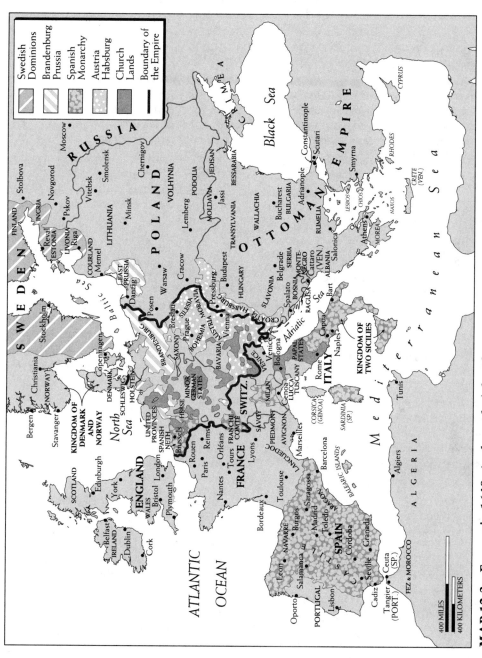

MAP 12-3 Europe in 1648 At the end of the Thirty Years' War, Spain still had extensive possessions. Austria and Brandenburg-Prussia were prominent, the independence of the United Provinces and Switzerland was recognized, and Sweden held important river mouths in north Germany.

when the French forced the Spanish to accept the humiliating Treaty of the Pyrenees. Germany's fragmentation and Spain's humbling left victorious France the dominant power in Europe. The competitive nationalisms of the modern world are rooted in these religious conflicts of the seventeenth century.

Politics, as well as religion, contributed to the great conflicts of the Age of Religious Wars: France's civil strife, Spain's struggle with the Netherlands, England's resistance to Spain, and the devastation of Germany by a consortium of European powers. But neither religion nor politics alone explains the course of the wars. The religious differences that occasioned a war were sometimes ignored in pursuit of political objectives shared by Catholics and Protestants, and wars ended with agreements to disagree—with the recognition of minority religious rights and a guarantee of the traditional boundaries of political sovereignty. The result was that at mid-century Europe had a real, but unsustainable, peace.

✧ Review Questions

1. What part did politics play in determining which religions were adopted by France's leaders? What led to the Saint Bartholomew's Day Massacre? What did it achieve?

2. How did Spain acquire the dominant position in Europe in the sixteenth century? What were its strengths and weaknesses as a nation?

3. How does the term *politique* apply as a description of Henry of Navarre (Henry IV of France), Elizabeth I, and William of Orange?

4. What changes occurred in the religious policies of England's government in the process of establishing the Anglican Church? What were Mary I's political objectives? What was Elizabeth I's "settlement"?

5. Why was the Thirty Years' War fought? How did politics affect the outcome of the war? What were the objectives of the Treaty of Westphalia?

✧ Suggested Readings

F. BRAUDEL, *The Mediterranean and the Mediterranean World in the Age of Philip the Second*, vols. 1 and 2 (1976). Widely acclaimed work of a French master historian.

R. DUNN, *The Age of Religious Wars, 1559–1689* (1979). Excellent brief survey of every major conflict.

P. GEYL, *The Revolt of the Netherlands, 1555–1609* (1958). The authoritative survey.

J. GUY, *Tudor England* (1990). A standard history and good synthesis of recent scholarship.

J. LYNCH, *Spain under the Hapsburg I: 1516–1598* (1964). Political narrative.

K. THOMAS, *Religion and the Decline of Magic* (1971). Provocative, much-acclaimed work focused on popular culture.

C. V. WEDGWOOD, *The Thirty Years' War* (1939). Extremely detailed account that downplays the war's achievements.

J. WORMALD, *Mary, Queen of Scots: A Study in Failure* (1991). Mary portrayed as a queen who did not understand her country and was out of touch with the times.

The first efforts by people to draw images to describe their vision of the world were Paleolithic cave paintings. This depiction of bulls and horses is found in the Dordogne valley of southern France.

This fresco painting is of Queen Ahmose-Nefertari of the Twentieth Dynasty, the last dynasty of the New Kingdom period.

Greek vase paintings are both works of art and invaluable sources of information for historians. This picture of a fight between a lapith and a centaur (a scene from mythology) is found on a red figure vase from the fifth century B.C. Only the figures' black background has been painted. The red areas are the natural color of the vase's fired clay.
[Firenze Museo Archaeologico. (Art Resource)]

This cameo shows profiles of the Emperor Claudius and his wife, Agrippina the younger, superimposed over profiles of Germanicus, the nephew of the Emperor Tiberius, and his wife, Agrippina the elder.
[Kunsthistorisches Museum, Vienna]

This mosaic depicts the Empress Theodora and her attendants at a church service. Its rich, but abstract, style marks a break with the naturalism of classical art. The change probably reflects the other-worldly values of early medieval Christianity.
[Scala/Art Resource, NY]

This page from the Lindisfarne Gospel (ca. 700 A.D.) illustrates the artistic vision of northern Europeans, who were little influenced by Greece and Rome. It uses plant and animal shapes from nature to create wildly energetic abstract patterns.
[Lindisfarne Gospels: Decorated initial to the Gospel according to St. Matthew manuscripts. Courtesy of the British Library, London. (Superstock)]

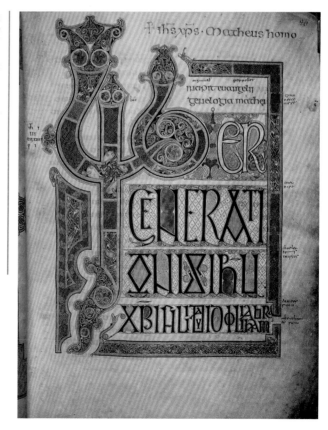

This portrayal of the funeral of St. Francis of Assisi was created by Giotto (1266–1336), a Florentine painter whose work heralded the Italian Renaissance. Giotto and most later painters thought of pictures not as pages to be read, but as windows offering views of a coherently organized world. [Scala/Art Resource, NY]

These scenes, representing events in the story of Adam and Eve, are from the frescoes that Michelangelo Buonarroti painted for the ceiling of the Vatican's Sistine Chapel (1503–1513). They illustrate how the Renaissance adapted ideals from classical pagan art for use by a Christian culture. [The Vatican, Rome. (Superstock)]

13

Paths to Constitutionalism and Absolutism: England and France in the Seventeenth Century

Two Models of European Political Development

Constitutional Crisis and Settlement in Stuart England

James I
Charles I
Oliver Cromwell and the Puritan Republic
Charles II and the Restoration of the Monarchy
James II and Renewed Fears of a Catholic England
The "Glorious Revolution"

Rise of Absolute Monarchy in France

Henry IV and Sully
Louis XIII and Richelieu
Young Louis XIV and Mazarin

The Years of Louis's Personal Rule

King by Divine Right
Versailles
Suppression of the Jansenists
Louis's Early Wars
Revocation of the Edict of Nantes
Louis's Later Wars
Louis XIV's Legacy

KEY TOPICS

- ↣ The factors behind the divergent political paths taken by England and France in the seventeenth century
- ↣ The conflict between Parliament and the king over taxation and religion in early Stuart England, the English Civil War, and the abolition of the monarchy
- ↣ The Restoration of the English monarchy and the development of Parliament's supremacy over the throne after the "Glorious Revolution"
- ↣ The establishment of an absolutist monarchy in France under Louis XIV
- ↣ The wars of Louis XIV

During the seventeenth century, England and France evolved contrasting political systems. England became a parliamentary monarchy with a policy of religious toleration. France developed an absolutist, highly centralized monarchy that *enforced religious conformity. Both systems defy simple description. English monarchs did not share all power with Parliament, and the kings of France were not free of all institutional or customary restraints on their authority.*

Significant Dates from the Seventeenth Century

1603	*James I, king of England*
1611	*Authorized, or King James, Version of the Bible*
1625	*Charles I, king of England*
1642	*Outbreak of the English Civil War*
1643	*Louis XIV, king of France*
1648	*Treaty of Westphalia*
1649	*Charles I executed*
1649–1652	*The Fronde*
1649–1660	*England, Puritan Commonwealth*
1660	*Charles II restores the English monarchy*
1667–1668	*War of Devolution*
1685	*James II, king of England*
1685	*Louis XIV revokes Edict of Nantes*
1688	*England's "Glorious Revolution"*
1689	*William and Mary rule England*
1689–1697	*Nine Years' War*
1701	*Act of Settlement, the Hanoverian Succession*
1702–1714	*War of the Spanish Succession*
1702	*Queen Anne, the last of the Stuarts*
1715	*Deaths of Louis XIV and Anne, queen of England*

⌒ Two Models of European Political Development

In the second half of the sixteenth century, changes in military technology sharply increased the cost of warfare and forced governments to look for new sources of revenue. Monarchs who, like France's kings, developed sources of income that were not controlled by nobles or by assemblies representing their wealthy subjects achieved absolute power. In places like England, where rulers had insufficient funds and limited powers of taxation, royal authority was compromised. Kings had to negotiate policy with groups on which they depended for financial support.

The contrast between the French and English political systems was visible by the end of the seventeenth century, but not in 1603 when England's Elizabeth I died. The much revered queen had broad support, and Parliament met during her reign only to approve taxes. The Stuart kings who succeeded Elizabeth to the throne had a different experience. They pursued fiscal and religious policies that alienated their nation's propertied classes and united them against the crown.

Elizabeth's contemporary, Henry IV (r. 1589–1610) of France, struggled with a divided nation emerging from the turmoil of religious war. His successor, Louis XIII (r. 1610–1643), began to reassert the crown's authority, and in the second half of the seventeenth century, Louis XIV brought the French nobles under control. The aristocratic *Parlement* of Paris won the right to register royal decrees to give them the authority of law, and the king allowed regional *parlements* considerable latitude to deal with local issues. But when the nobles discovered that a strong king was a source of patronage and a guardian of their privileged place in society, they lost interest in organizing anything like England's Parliament. An Estates General had developed in France in the late Middle Ages, but once the monarchy won control over taxation, there was little reason for it to meet. No sessions were held from 1614 until the eve of the French Revolution in 1789.

ᔓ Constitutional Crisis and Settlement in Stuart England

James I

When the childless Elizabeth died in 1603, no one contested the right of James VI of Scotland (the son of Mary Stuart, Queen of Scots) to claim her throne as James I of England. But a formidable task lay ahead of him. As a Scot, James was an outsider who had no native constituency to help him deal with England's religious factions and substantial national debt. James's advocacy of the divine right of kings, a subject on which he had written a book *(A Trew Law of Free Monarchies)* in 1598, also set him on a collision course with English tradition.

England's Parliament, its chief check on royal power, met only when summoned by the monarch to authorize tax levies. James hoped to develop alternative resources that would enable him to fund his government without calling Parliament. Relying on the authority of ill-defined privileges that he alleged were royal prerogatives, James created new customs duties called *impositions.* Members of Parliament resented these, but they preferred to wrangle and negotiate behind the scenes rather than risk serious confrontation.

Religious problems added to political tensions during James's reign. Puritans within the Church of England had hoped that James's upbringing as a Scottish Presbyterian would dispose him to support the reformation of the English church. They wanted to eliminate elaborate priestly rituals and end government of the church by bishops—establishing in their places simple services of worship and congregations run by presbyters elected by the people. James, however, had no intention of using his national church to promote representative government—which he condemned as a trespass on the divine right of kings.

In January 1604, James responded to a list of Puritan grievances (the so-called Millenary Petition) by pledging to maintain and even enhance the Anglican episcopacy. As he explained: "A Scottish presbytery agreeth as well with monarchy as God and the devil. No bishops, no king." James did, however, accept the Protestant demand for the use of vernacular Scriptures, and in 1611 the royal commission he appointed issued an eloquent new translation of the Bible. For generations the Authorized, or King James, Version remained the standard English text.

James had no sympathy with the moral agenda implicit in English Puritanism. The recreations and sports of which the Puritans disapproved were, to the king, innocent activities that were good for people. James also believed that Puritan rigidity about such things discouraged Roman Catholics from converting to the Church of England. Consequently, in 1618 James tried to force a change by ordering the clergy to read his *Book of Sports* (legalizing games on Sunday) from their pulpits. When they refused, he backed down.

James's lifestyle seemed designed to give offense to the Puritans, for the royal court was a center of scandal and corruption. James governed by favorites, the most influential of whom, the duke of Buckingham, was rumored to be the king's homosexual lover. Buckingham controlled royal patronage and openly sold peerages and titles to the highest bidders. There had always been court favorites, but never before had a single person controlled access to the monarch.

Disappointed and disgusted by James, some Puritans began voluntarily to leave England for the New World. In 1620 Puritan separatists founded Plymouth Colony in Cape Cod Bay. Later in the same decade a larger, better-financed group of Puritans founded the Massachusetts Bay Colony.

In addition to his domestic policy, James's conduct of foreign affairs also roused opposition. James made peace and avoided war, for he feared that wars would generate debts that would force him to beg assistance from Parliament. The treaty he signed with Spain in 1604, although long overdue, was interpreted by some of his subjects as confirmation of his pro-Catholic sentiment. Their suspicions increased when James tried unsuccessfully to relax the penal laws against Catholics. The situation further deteriorated when, in 1618, James wisely hesitated to rush English troops to the aid of German Protestants involved in the Thirty Years' War and when he suggested that his son Charles marry the Infanta, the daughter of the king of Spain.

As James aged and his health failed, the reins of government passed to Charles and to Buckingham, and parliamentary opposition and Protestant sentiment combined to undo his pro-Spanish foreign policy. The marriage alliance was rejected, and in 1624, shortly before James's death, Parliament pushed England into a war with Spain.

Charles I

Although Parliament supported war with Spain, distrust of Buckingham diminished its willingness to finance the venture. This forced Charles I (r. 1625–1649), with the help of the unpopular Buckingham, to pursue the same fiscal strategy as his father. Without consulting Parliament, he imposed new tariffs and duties, collected discontinued taxes, and subjected people of property (under threat of imprisonment) to the "forced loayn"—a tax that, theoretically, was to be repaid. Soldiers in transit to war zones were also quartered in English homes.

When Parliament met in 1628, its members were furious. They refused to acquiesce to the king's request for funds unless he agreed to abide by terms they set forth in a Petition of Right: (1) no more forced loans or taxation without the consent of Parliament, (2) no imprisonment of citizens without due cause, and

(3) an end to billeting troops in private homes. Though Charles promised what was demanded, Parliament did not trust him to keep his word.

Years of Personal Rule. In August 1628, Buckingham, Charles's chief minister, was assassinated. Although his death led some to rejoice, it was not enough to reconcile king and Parliament. In January 1629, Parliament issued more decrees critical of the king. The levying of taxes without parliamentary consent and Charles's high-church policies were declared acts of treason. Charles responded by dissolving Parliament. It did not reconvene until a war with Scotland created a fiscal crisis in 1640.

Without funds from Parliament, Charles could not continue his foreign wars. But when he made peace with France in 1629 and Spain in 1630, some of his subjects accused him of wanting to strengthen his ties with Roman Catholic nations. Many Protestant leaders feared that Catholics were establishing ascendancy over the king. Charles had wed a French princess whose marriage contract gave her the right to hear mass daily at the English court. Charles also favored a group within the Church of England (the Arminians) that opposed some Puritan doctrines and advocated elaborate services of worship.

To allow Charles to rule without having to negotiate with Parliament for money, the king's chief minister, Thomas Wentworth, earl of Stafford (after 1640), instituted the policy of *thorough*. By promoting strict efficiency and administrative centralization, the monarchy hoped to establish absolute royal control over England. Toward this end, Charles's men exploited every legal fundraising device. They enforced previously neglected laws and extended existing taxes into new areas. Charles won challenges to his policies in the courts, but at the cost of alienating the propertied men who would sit in any future Parliament he might be forced to call.

During his years of personal rule, Charles lived expensively. He surrounded himself with an elaborate court and patronized some of the greatest artists of the day. Like his father, he sold titles of nobility to raise money—and to diminish the prestige of the aristocracy. Nobles and great landowners saw their fortunes and their local influence and social standing diminishing, and they began to fear that Charles would avoid ever having to call another Parliament.

Charles might have ruled indefinitely without Parliament had he not departed from the tolerant example set by his father and tried to impose religious conformity within England and Scotland. William Laud (1573–1645), Charles's religious advisor and archbishop of Canterbury (after 1633), encouraged the king's preference for high-church Anglicanism (or Anglo-Catholicism), a state-supported church with a powerful episcopacy and a preference for elaborate liturgies in place of the preaching-centered worship favored by Puritans. In 1637 Charles and Laud, over objections by English Puritans and the Scots, attempted to impose the English episcopal system and prayerbook on Scotland. The Scots rebelled, and Charles, having insufficient resources for a war, had to call Parliament.

The members of Parliament were in the peculiar position of wanting to oppose their king's policies while crushing the rebellion against him. Led by John Pym (1584–1643), they refused to discuss funding for the war until Charles agreed to redress their list of grievances. The king responded by dissolving what came, for obvious reasons, to be known as the Short Parliament (April–May 1640). When the Presbyterian Scots invaded England and defeated an English army at the Battle of Newburn in the summer of 1640, Charles had no choice but to reconvene Parliament—on its own terms—for a long, fateful session.

The Long Parliament. The landowners and the merchant classes whom Parliament represented resented the king's financial exactions and paternalistic rule. Those who were Puritans also disliked his religious policies. The Long Parliament (1640–1660), therefore, enjoyed support from many important factions.

The House of Commons began by impeaching the king's chief advisors, the earl of Stafford and Archbishop Laud. (Stafford was executed for treason in 1641 and Laud in 1645.) Parliament then abolished the instruments the king used to implement the political and religious policy of *thorough*, the Court of Star Chamber and the Court of High Commission. The levying of new taxes without consent of Parliament was declared illegal, and Parliament proclaimed itself to be a permanent branch of England's government. It said that it could not be dissolved without its own consent and that no more than three years could elapse between its meetings.

Members of Parliament were united on the subject of curtailing the powers of the monarchy, but divided on the issue of religious reform. Moderate Puritans (Presbyterians) and extreme Puritans (Independents) wanted to abolish the episcopal system and the *Book of Common Prayer*. The Presbyterian majority also hoped to impose a Calvinist system in which the church would be governed by presbyteries, committees composed of representatives from local congregations. The Independents wanted a radical decentralization of the church that would allow each congregation to govern itself. A considerable number of conservatives in both houses of Parliament did not want any changes at all.

These divisions intensified in October 1641, when a rebellion erupted in Ireland and Parliament was asked to raise funds for a royal army to suppress it. Pym and his followers argued that Charles could not be trusted with an army and that Parliament should take command of England's armed forces. Conservatives in Parliament were appalled at the thought of such a radical departure from tradition.

Eruption of Civil War. Charles saw the division within Parliament as his chance to regain the upper hand. On December 1, 1641, Parliament presented him with the "Grand Remonstrance", a summary of over 200 grievances against the crown. In January 1642, he responded by sending soldiers into Parliament to arrest Pym and other leaders. When they managed to escape, Charles withdrew from London and began to raise an army against Parliament. The House of Commons hastened to pass the Militia Ordinance, giving Parliament authority to raise its own army, and for the next four years (1642–1646) civil war engulfed England.

The royal army (the Cavaliers) was based in the northwestern half of England. It defended strong monarchy and an Anglican, episcopal church. Its parliamentary opponents, the "Roundheads" (for their short haircuts), had their stronghold in the southeastern half of the country. They wanted parliamentary government and a decentralized, Presbyterian church.

Oliver Cromwell and the Puritan Republic

Two things contributed to Parliament's victory. The first was an alliance struck between Parliament and Scotland in 1643. It was made possible by Parliament's acceptance of the Scots' Presbyterian system of church government. The second was the reorganization of the parliamentary army under Oliver Cromwell (1599–1658), a middle-aged country squire who favored the Independents. Cromwell and his "godly men" wanted neither the king's episcopal system nor

Oliver Cromwell's New Model Army defeated the royalists in the English Civil War. After the execution of Charles I in 1649, Cromwell dominated the short-lived English republic, conquered Ireland and Scotland, and ruled as Lord Protector from 1653 until his death in 1658. [Historical Pictures/Stock Montage, Inc.]

the Presbyterian organization endorsed by Parliament's Solemn League and Covenant with Scotland. The only established state church they would accept was one that granted freedom of worship to Protestant dissenters.

In 1644 Parliament won the largest engagement of the war, the Battle of Marston Moor, and in June 1645, Cromwell's newly reorganized and fanatical forces, the New Model Army, defeated the king at Naseby. Charles tried to exploit the divisions within Parliament by winning the Presbyterians and the Scots over to his side, but Cromwell foiled him. In December 1648, Colonel Thomas Pride used Cromwell's soldiers to prevent the Presbyterians, who had a majority in Parliament, from taking their seats. After "Pride's Purge," only a "rump" of fewer than fifty members remained. This Rump Parliament was dominated by Independents who did not shy away from bold action. On January 30, 1649, after trial by a special court, the Rump Parliament executed the king and abolished the monarchy, the House of Lords, and the Anglican Church. Civil war had become revolution.

From 1649 to 1660 England was officially a Puritan republic. In reality, Cromwell ruled. Cromwell's military achievements were impressive. His army conquered Ireland and Scotland and unified what we know today as Great Britain. The general was less gifted as a politician, for he was easily frustrated by the necessity of working with the dawdling members of Parliament. When in 1653 the House of Commons entertained a motion to disband his expensive army of 50,000, he marched in and disbanded Parliament.

Calling himself "Lord Protector," Cromwell set up a military dictatorship. It had minimal popular support. Cromwell's army and foreign adventures cost three times as much as Charles's government had, and still the Protector could not prevent near chaos from erupting in many parts of England. Commerce suffered, and people chafed under Cromwell's rigorous enforcement of Puritan codes of conduct. The Lord Protector was as intolerant of Anglicans as the king had been of Puritans.

Cromwell failed to build a political system that provided a workable alternative to the monarchy and Parliament. He tried various arrangements, none of which succeeded. By the time he died in 1658, a majority of the English were ready to end the Puritan republican experiments and return to traditional institutions of government. In 1660 the exiled Charles II (r. 1660–1685), son of Charles I, was invited home to restore the Stuart monarchy.

Charles II and the Restoration of the Monarchy

Charles II, a man of considerable charm and political skill, ascended the throne amid great rejoicing, and England returned to the institutions it had abandoned in 1642: a hereditary monarchy with no obligation to summon Parliament, and a state religion (an Anglican Church with bishops and an official prayerbook). Since Charles had secret Catholic sympathies, he favored a policy of religious toleration—the best that Catholics could hope for in England. Few in Parliament, however, believed that patriotism and religion could be separated. Between 1661 and 1665, Parliament enacted the Clarendon Code. It excluded Roman Catholics, Presbyterians, and Independents from religious and political offices. Penalties were imposed for attending non-Anglican worship services. Adherence to the *Book of Common Prayer* and the *Thirty-Nine Articles* (the Anglican Church's statement of faith) was demanded, and oaths of allegiance to the Church of England were required of persons who wished to serve in local government. Charles also tried to tighten his grip on the rich English colonies in North America and the Caribbean, many of which had been developed by separatists who wanted independence from English rule.

Charles's foreign policy was dominated by a series of naval wars with Holland that were caused by England's Navigation Acts. These acts required that goods brought to England be carried either in English ships or in ships registered to the country in which their cargo originated. Since Dutch vessels carried goods from many nations, this was a direct attack on Holland's shipping industry. In 1670 Charles allied with the French, who were also at war with Holland, and received French aid to underwrite the cost of his campaign. In exchange for the promise of a substantial subsidy from Louis XIV of France, Charles also secretly pledged to announce, at some propitious moment, his conversion to Catholicism. The time to fulfill that pledge never came.

To unite the English people behind the war with Holland and to show good faith with Louis XIV, Charles issued a Declaration of Indulgence (1672) that suspended all laws against Roman Catholics and Protestant nonconformists. But again, Parliament blocked the king's efforts to promote religious tolerance by refusing to grant money for the war until Charles rescinded the Declaration. Parliament then passed the Test Act, which excluded Roman Catholics from public office by requiring all royal officials to swear an oath repudiating the doctrine of transubstantiation.

The Test Act was aimed in large measure at the king's brother, James, duke of York, heir to the throne and a recent, devout convert to Catholicism. In 1678 a notorious liar, Titus Oates, accused Charles's Catholic wife of plotting with Jesuits and Irishmen to kill her husband and bring his Catholic brother to the throne. Parliament, caught up in the hysteria of Oates's "Popish Plot," executed several people, and a faction in Parliament, the Whigs, nearly won passage for a bill excluding James from the succession.

Chronically short of money and having little hope of adequate grants from Parliament, Charles II increased customs duties and extracted more financial aid from Louis XIV. This allowed him to avoid convening a Parliament after 1681. By the time of his death in 1685 (after a deathbed conversion to Catholicism), he had cowed his opponents and positioned James to call a Parliament filled with royal friends.

James II and Renewed Fears of a Catholic England

James II (r. 1685–1688) did not know how to use his opportunities. He alienated Parliament by insisting on the repeal of the Test Act. When Parliament balked, he dissolved it and flaunted the Test Act by openly appointing known Catholics to high offices. In 1687 he issued a Declaration of Indulgence that suspended religious tests and permitted free worship. Candidates for Parliament who opposed the Declaration were evicted by the king's soldiers and replaced by Catholics. In June 1688, James imprisoned seven Anglican bishops who had refused to publicize his suspension of laws against Catholics.

James's policy of enlightened toleration was actually a drive to bring all English institutions under royal control. His goal was absolutism, and even conservative, loyalist "Tories" (as the monarchy's allies were called) could not abide this. The English had reason to fear that once James had the power, he would imitate Louis XIV. In the year James came to the throne Louis had revoked the Edict of Nantes and used soldiers to suppress Protestant worship in France.

A birth galvanized James's enemies into action against him. They had hoped that he would die without a male heir and that the throne would pass to Mary, his eldest daughter. She was a Protestant—the wife of William III of Orange. William was *stadtholder* of the Netherlands, great-grandson of William the Silent, and the leader of the European states that were threatened by Louis XIV's schemes to expand France's power. On June 20, 1688, James's second wife alarmed England's Protestants by giving birth to a son, a Catholic heir to their throne. Within days of the boy's birth, Whig and Tory members of Parliament had agreed to invite William and Mary to invade England to preserve "traditional liberties."

The "Glorious Revolution"

When the English people failed to oppose the landing that William of Orange's army made in November 1688, James accepted defeat and fled to France. Parliament completed the bloodless "Glorious Revolution" by declaring the throne vacant and proclaiming William and Mary its heirs. They, in turn, issued a Bill of Rights that limited the powers of the monarchy and guaranteed the civil liberties of England's privileged classes. Henceforth, the English monarch would be subject to law and would govern with the consent of a Parliament that met regularly. The Bill of Rights also prohibited Roman Catholics from occupying the English throne. The Toleration Act of 1689 legalized all forms of Protestantism—save those that denied the Trinity—and outlawed Roman Catholicism.

In 1701 the Act of Settlement closed the "century of strife" (as the seventeenth century came to be known in England) by providing for the English crown to go to the Protestant House of Hanover in Germany if none of the children of Queen Anne (r. 1702–1714), the second daughter of James II and the last of the Stuart monarchs, survived her. Since she did outlive her children, the Elector of Hanover became King George I of England—the third foreigner to occupy the English throne in just over a century.

Although the "Glorious Revolution" of 1688 was not a popular revolution like those that erupted in America and France a hundred years later, it established a framework for a government by and for the governed, a permanent check on monarchical power by the classes represented in Parliament. English philosopher John Locke's *Second Treatise of Government* (1690), which was written prior to the revolution, came to be read as a justification for it. Locke claimed that the relationship between a king and his people was a bilateral contract. If the king broke that contract, the people (by whom Locke meant those with property) had the right to depose him. Locke's political theory and England's parliamentary monarchy were destined to have wide appeal.

❧ Rise of Absolute Monarchy in France

In seventeenth-century France, unlike England, absolute monarchy established itself, limited the freedom of the nobility, and enforced religious conformity. The dictum of Louis XIV (r. 1643–1715) was "one king, one law, one faith."

Louis's predecessors had provoked a rebellion among the nobles by trying to impose direct rule on the nation at all levels. Louis chose to work through established social and political institutions rather than to destroy them. His genius lay in his ability to make the monarchy the most powerful political institution in France while assuring the nobles and other wealthy groups that it posed no threat to their private power bases and their standing. Once nobles understood that the king would protect their local authority, they supported his central authority. The king and the nobles agreed that they needed each other—but that Louis XIV was the senior partner in the relationship.

Henry IV and Sully

Louis XIV learned much from his predecessors. Henry IV (r. 1589–1610), who came to the throne at the end of the French wars of religion, sought to rein in the French nobility—particularly the provincial governors, the regional *parlements*, and the powerful *Parlement* of Paris. These groups were divisive elements within the state. Their chief interest was the protection of their privileges.

Since the war-weary French were eager for the restoration of order, Henry and his finance minister, the duke of Sully (1560–1641), were able to expand government control over the economy. They established royal monopolies on gunpowder, mines, and salt. They began construction of a canal system that linked France's rivers to create a waterway from the Atlantic to the Mediterranean. They introduced the *corvée,* a labor tax that drafted workers to build and maintain roads. Sully even dreamed of joining the whole of Europe in a kind of common market.

Louis XIII and Richelieu

Henry IV was assassinated in 1610, and the following year Sully retired. Louis XIII (r. 1610–1643), Henry's son, was only nine years old at the time, so the task of governing fell to the queen mother, Marie de Médicis (d. 1642). Sensing a lack of support from the French nobility, Marie sought to make a friend of France's arch-rival, Spain. In 1611 she negotiated the Treaty of Fontainebleau. It provided for a ten-year mutual defense pact and marriage alliances between the royal houses of the two nations. Louis XIII was to wed the Spanish Infanta, and his sister, Elizabeth, was engaged to the heir to the Spanish throne. The queen's best move was the appointment of Cardinal Richelieu (1585–1642) as the king's chief adviser. The loyal, shrewd Richelieu was the architect of the success the French monarchy enjoyed in the first half of the seventeenth century.

Richelieu was a devout Catholic, but he believed that France's interests were best served by curbing the growth of the power of the Catholic Habsburgs. Although he endorsed the queen's treaty with Catholic Spain and encouraged conformity to Catholic practices in France, Richelieu was determined to contain Spain—even if that meant aiding Protestants. In the Thirty Years' War, Richelieu helped to fund the Protestant army of Gustavus Adolphus. This enabled him to save Catholic Bavaria from attack and to win freedom of religion for Catholics in places his Protestant allies conquered. Thanks to Richelieu, France emerged from the war with substantial gains in land and political influence.

At home, Richelieu implemented a rigorous centralization of royal government. Supported by a king who let him make most decisions of state, Richelieu stepped up the campaign Henry IV had begun against separatist provincial governors and *parlements.* He appointed civil servants (the *intendants*) to guard against abuses in the sale of royal privileges, such as the right to collect taxes or sell licenses. He made it clear to everyone that there was only one law in France. If noblemen disobeyed the king's edicts, they were imprisoned or executed. Such treatment of the nobility won Richelieu much enmity—even from his patron, the queen mother.

In 1629 Richelieu began a campaign against the Huguenots. Royal armies occupied important Huguenot cities and imposed the Peace of Alais. It truncated the Edict of Nantes by denying Protestants the right to maintain garrisoned cities, separate political organizations, and independent law courts. Richelieu was prevented from doing more to limit religious freedoms by France's alliances with Protestant powers in the Thirty Years' War. But in 1685 Louis XIV completed his work by revoking the Edict of Nantes.

Richelieu was a modern politician in the sense that he understood the use of propaganda and the importance of mobilizing popular support for government policies. He employed the arts and the printing press to defend his actions and to persuade the French people to accept things done for *raisons d'état* ("reasons of state"). Louis XIV's masterful use of propaganda to develop royal power was a tribute to Richelieu's example.

Young Louis XIV and Mazarin

Louis XIII survived Richelieu by only five months. Since his heir, Louis XIV (r. 1643–1715), was five years old, the son's reign began, as the father's had, with a regency government. The queen mother, Anne of Austria (d. 1666), placed the reins of government in the hands of Cardinal Mazarin (1602–1661), Richelieu's protégé.

Since many members of the aristocracy and the wealthy commercial classes had deeply resented Richelieu's efforts to build a strong, centralized monarchy, Mazarin was confronted by a violent political backlash. From 1649 to 1652, there were widespread rebellions. They are known collectively as the *Fronde* (after the name of a slingshot used by street boys). The uprisings were exploited by nobles and townspeople who wanted to reverse the drift toward absolute monarchy and to preserve local autonomy.

The *Parlement* of Paris initiated the revolt in 1649, and "the many" (the nobles) briefly triumphed over "the one" (the monarchy). Mazarin released some aristocratic prisoners in February 1651, and he and Louis XIV went briefly into exile. (Mazarin left France, and Louis fled Paris.) When the nobles failed to restore order and near anarchy ensued, support for the young king materialized and Louis and Mazarin returned (October 1652). The Fronde convinced most French people that a strong king was preferable to the chaos created by many competing regional powers. On the other hand, Louis XIV and his later advisers concluded that heavy-handed policies (like those of Richelieu and Mazarin) might endanger the monarchy.

✧ The Years of Louis's Personal Rule

On the death of Mazarin in 1661, Louis XIV assumed personal control of the government. Unlike his royal predecessors, he appointed no single chief minister. This had the advantage of making revolt more difficult to rationalize. It made it impossible for rebellious nobles to claim that they were opposing their king's wicked ministers, but not the crown itself. Mazarin had prepared Louis well for the duties of government, and the young king's experiences during the Fronde had stiffened his resolve to be a strong ruler. Louis wrote in his memoirs that the Fronde caused him to loathe "kings of straw."

Louis devised two successful strategies for enhancing the power of the monarchy. First, he became a master of propaganda and political image-making. Louis never missed an opportunity to remind the French people of the grandeur of his crown. Second, Louis made sure that the French nobles and other major social groups benefited from the growth of his authority. Although he maintained control over foreign affairs, he usually conferred informally with regional *parlements* before making rulings that would affect them. Likewise, he rarely enacted economic regulations without consulting local opinion, and local *parlements* were given considerable latitude in regional matters.

King by Divine Right

Reverence for the king, the personification of government, had been nurtured in France since Capetian times, and it was widely accepted that the king's wish was the law of the land. Louis XIV transformed this traditional reverence for the crown into a belief in the king's divine right to absolute authority.

Bishop Jacques-Bénigne Bossuet (1627–1704), the king's tutor, provided the theoretical rationale for Louis's concept of the royal office. Bossuet was an ardent champion of the so-called "Gallican liberties," traditional exemptions the French clergy claimed from interference in their affairs by the papacy. The theory of the "divine right of kings" that Bossuet outlined also gave kings spiritual legitimacy as caretakers of national churches. Bossuet drew his evidence from the Old Testament whose rulers were divinely appointed by and answerable only to God. Just as medieval popes had insisted that only God could judge a pope, so Bossuet argued that none save God could judge a king. Kings were duty-bound to honor God's will, but as God's regents on earth they could not be made accountable to mere princes and parliaments. This argument justified Louis XIV's alleged declaration, *"L'état, c'est moi"* ("I am the state").

Versailles

One of the most successful instruments of Louis XIV's propaganda was the splendid palace he built to house his court at Versailles on the outskirts of Paris (1682). Versailles was a temple to royalty—a proclamation of the glory of its "Sun King." It was also home to Louis and thousands of his subjects: France's more important nobles and numerous royal officials and servants. The maintenance of Versailles and its expansion and elaboration, which continued throughout Louis's lifetime, consumed over half the royal income. The political dividends Versailles paid proved well worth the investment.

By organizing life at court around his personal routine, Louis demonstrated that he alone was the sole source of power and privilege in France. Nobles scrambled for the honor of being present at intimate moments in the king's day—his rising, dressing, or retiring—in hopes of having a chance to whisper special requests in his ear. Like menial servants, the most distinguished of aristocrats fought for the privilege of holding the king's candle or assisting him with the left sleeve of his nightshirt. These duties were choreographed by an extraordinarily elaborate court etiquette.

Court life was carefully planned to domesticate and trivialize the nobility. Barred by law from high government positions, the nobles were kept busy and dependent with ritual and play so that they had little time to plot revolt. Luxurious dress codes and high-stakes gambling drove them into debt and dependency on the king. Members of the court spent the afternoons hunting, riding, or strolling about the lush gardens of Versailles. Evenings were given over to plays, concerts, gambling, and the like—followed by supper at 10:00 P.M.

The real business of government was handled by Louis and members of councils charged with responsibility for foreign affairs, domestic relations, and the economy. The chief ministers of these councils were talented self-made men or members of families with long histories of loyal service to the crown. Louis trusted them with power, for, unlike the nobility, they had no indepen-

"Perspective View of Versailles," as painted in 1668 by Pierre Patel the Elder (1605–1676). The central building is the hunting lodge built for Louis XIII earlier in the century. The wings that appear here were some of Louis XIV's first expansions. [Chateau, Versailles, France. Giraudon/Art Resource, N.Y.]

dent bases in the provinces and depended solely on the king for their places in government and society.

Suppression of the Jansenists

Like Richelieu before him, Louis believed that political stability required religious conformity. The first deviant religious group to attract his attention were the Roman Catholic Jansenists.

Catherine de Médicis had prevented the Jesuits from working in France because of their close connections to Spain, but following Henry IV's conversion to Catholicism, the ban was lifted (1603). Jesuits who swore an oath of allegiance to the king and acquired special licenses were permitted to set up a limited number of colleges and conduct various public activities. The Jesuits were not, however, easily harnessed. They became the royal confessors. They dominated the education of the upper classes, and they pushed for implementation of the decrees of the Council of Trent throughout France.

Jansenism, which appeared in the 1630s, was a Catholic movement named for a Flemish theologian and bishop who was critical of the Jesuits, Cornelius Jansen (d. 1638). Jansenists followed the teachings of Saint Augustine, who emphasized the role divine grace played in human salvation. They objected to the Jesuits' emphasis on free will, for they believed with Saint Augustine that original sin so corrupted humankind that individuals could do nothing good nor secure their own salvation without divine grace. Jansenist emphasis on salvation by grace led the Jesuits to accuse the Jansenists of being crypto-Protestants.

The fight between the Jansenists and the Jesuits had political as well as theological dimensions. Jansen had ties with a prominent Parisian family, the Arnaulds, who, like many others in France, believed that the Jesuits had arranged the assassination of Henry IV in 1610. The Arnaulds dominated Jansenist communities at Port-Royal and Paris during the 1640s. In 1643 a book by Antoine Arnauld *(On Frequent Communion)* attracted attention by charging that the Jesuits use of the confessional allowed people too easily to escape responsibility for their sins.

On May 31, 1653, Pope Innocent X declared that five Jansenist theological propositions concerning grace and salvation were heresies. In 1656 the pope banned a book by Cornelius Jansen (*Augustinus,* 1640), and the Sorbonne censured Antoine Arnauld. In the same year Antoine's friend, Blaise Pascal (d. 1662), published a defense of Jansenism, the first of his *Provincial Letters.* Pascal was a deeply religious man who objected to Jesuit moral theology not only because it was lax, but also because its rationalism failed to do justice to the profound mysteries of religious experience.

In 1660 Louis banned Jansenism and closed down the Port-Royal community. This drove Jansenism underground, where it apparently continued to thrive; in 1710 Louis found it necessary to order a more thorough purge of Jansenist sentiment. His suppression of Jansenism—a kind of Catholicism broad enough to appeal to Huguenots—eliminated the best hope for peacefully unifying France's religions.

Louis's Early Wars

Governing for Warfare. The economy of France was overwhelmingly agrarian, as was true of other nations in Louis's day. But Jean-Baptiste Colbert (1619–1683), Louis's brilliant financial adviser, managed it so skillfully that France was able to support a huge standing army.

Colbert centralized France's economy as Louis centralized France's government. The kind of economic policy Colbert instituted has been called *mercantilism.* Its aim was to maximize exports and conserve the bullion their sale brought to the exporting nation. Colbert relied on state supervision of industries and tariffs to regulate the flow of imports and exports. He established new national industries and imposed a strict regimen for workers in state-run factories. He simplified the administrative bureaucracy; reduced the number of tax-exempt nobles; and increased the *taille,* the direct tax on the peasantry that provided much of the king's income.

Thanks to Colbert, France became one of the world's commercial powers, and Louis was able to afford ambitious military ventures. An army of about 250,000 men was created for him by a father-son team of war ministers: Michel Le Tellier (minister to 1666) and Tellier's son, the marquis of Louvois (minister from 1667 to his death in 1691).

Before Louvois, the French army had been an amalgam of local companies of recruits and mercenaries who supplemented their irregular pay by pillaging the countryside. Louvois made soldiering a respectable profession: discipline was improved; a system of promotion by merit was introduced; enlistment, for terms of four years, was restricted to single men; pay was good; and military conduct at all levels was monitored by civil servants. New technology was also provided for Louvois's new army by a brilliant military engineer, Sebastien Vauban (1633–1707). He perfected the arts of fortifying and besieging towns, invented trench warfare, and developed the concept of the defensive frontier—an idea that remained basic to military tactics through World War I.

The War of Devolution. Louis's first great foreign adventure was the War of Devolution (1667–1668). Like the later War of the Spanish Succession, it was fought to press a claim Louis's wife, Marie Thérèse (1638–1683), had to Spain's Belgian provinces. In 1659 Marie had surrendered her place in the line of succession to the Spanish throne in exchange for a huge dowry to be paid to Louis. The dowry was never paid, and Philip IV of Spain, who died in September 1665, left a will disinheriting Marie in favor of a sickly four-year-old son by a second marriage, Charles II (r. 1665–1700). Louis decided to contest the will, and the legal grounds he chose gave the war its name. Louis argued that in certain regions of Brabant and Flanders, which were part of Philip's estate, property "devolved" to the children of a first marriage rather than to those of a second. Therefore, Marie had a better claim to these districts than Charles.

In 1667 Louis sent his armies into Flanders and the Franche-Comté, and England, Sweden, and the United Provinces of Holland reacted by forming the Triple Alliance. In 1668 Louis signed the Treaty of Aix-la-Chapelle and agreed to a peace that gave him control of some towns bordering the Spanish Netherlands (see Map 13-1).

Invasion of the Netherlands. In 1670 France persuaded England to join an alliance against the Dutch. The Triple Alliance crumbled, and in 1672 Louis struck directly at Holland, the power that had organized the Triple Alliance. Without neutralizing Holland, Louis knew he could make no progress in the Spanish Netherlands—nor could he fulfill his dream of winning European hegemony.

Louis's attack on the United Provinces of Holland was countered by the young Prince of Orange, the future William III of England. Orange was the great-grandson of William the Silent, the native leader who had repulsed Philip II and established the independence of Holland. Orange persuaded the Holy Roman Emperor, Spain, Lorraine, and Brandenburg to join him in stopping the

MAP 13-1 The Wars of Louis XIV *This map shows the territorial changes resulting from Louis XIV's first three major wars. The War of the Spanish Succession was yet to come.*

"Christian Turk," the voracious French king who was becoming a menace to the whole of western Europe. In 1676 a victory over the Dutch fleet gave France control of the Mediterranean. The United Netherlands retained all its territory, but the war ended in 1679 with no clear winner.

Revocation of the Edict of Nantes

Following the Peace of Nijmwegen which ended the war in the Netherlands and halted (for the moment) France's aggression in Europe, Louis imposed religious conformity on his subjects. The Edict of Nantes of 1598 had established a legal Protestant minority in France, but the Huguenots' relations with the Catholic majority (nine-tenths of the French population) were never good. The French Catholic Church denounced Calvinists as heretics and traitors and declared their persecution a pious, patriotic duty.

Louis hounded the Huguenots from public life by banning them from government office and excluding them from the professions. He raised their taxes, quartered his troops in their towns, and in October 1685, he outlawed their faith by revoking the Edict of Nantes. Protestant churches and schools closed. Protestant clergy went into exile. Nonconverting laity were enslaved on the galleys, and Protestant children were turned over to Catholic priests for baptism.

Louis's flaunting of religious intolerance was a major blunder, for it persuaded Protestant countries that he had to be stopped at all costs. More than a quarter-million French people fled their homeland to stiffen opposition to France in England, Germany, Holland, and the New World. Many of the Huguenots who remained in France formed guerilla bands to fight the king. But Louis, to his death, was persuaded that the revocation of Nantes was his most pious act, one that put God in his debt.

In 1685, Louis XIV revoked the Edict of Nantes, *thus ending religious toleration in France. [Robert Harding Picture Library, London]*

Louis's Later Wars

The League of Augsburg and the Nine Years' War. In 1681 Louis's forces conquered the free city of Strasbourg, prompting new defensive coalitions to form against him. One of these, the League of Augsburg, expanded to include England, Spain, Sweden, the United Provinces, and the electorates of Bavaria, Saxony, and the Palatinate—with the support of Emperor Leopold. From 1689 to 1697, the league and France fought the Nine Years' War, while in North America England and France fought King William's War, a struggle for the colonies.

In 1697, mutual exhaustion forced an interim settlement, the Peace of Ryswick. The treaty was a triumph for William of Orange, now William III of England, and the Emperor Leopold. It secured Holland's borders and thwarted Louis's expansion into Germany.

War of the Spanish Succession. Louis tried a fourth time to win dominance over Europe. Charles II of Spain (surnamed "the Sufferer" because of his genetic deformities and lingering illnesses) died on November 1, 1700. Louis and the Austrian Emperor Leopold each claimed the Spanish inheritance for a grandson. Louis's grandson, Philip of Anjou, had the better claim, for his grandmother, Marie Thérèse, was the older sister of the Spanish princess, Margaret Thérèse, who had married Leopold. But Marie Thérèse had renounced her right to the Spanish throne when she married Louis.

Louis feared that the Habsburgs would dominate Europe if they ruled both Spain and the Holy Roman Empire. Most of the nations of Europe, however, feared France more than the Habsburgs. As a result, even before Charles II died, international negotiations were underway to partition his inheritance in a way that would preserve the balance of power.

Charles II upset these negotiations by bequeathing his estate to Philip of Anjou. Louis, finding himself the unexpected winner, ignored partition agreements, sent his grandson to Madrid to become Philip V of Spain, and invaded Flanders. In September 1701, England, Holland, and the Holy Roman Empire formed the Grand Alliance. They hoped to secure Flanders as a neutral barrier between Holland and France and to gain a share of the Spanish inheritance for the Habsburgs. The result was the War of the Spanish Succession (1702–1714), another total war enveloping all of western Europe.

The French army was poorly financed, poorly equipped, and poorly led. England, on the other hand, had advanced weaponry, superior tactics, and a splendid general—John Churchill, the duke of Marlborough. Marlborough routed French armies in two decisive engagements: Blenheim in August 1704, and Ramillies in 1706. In 1708–1709 famine and excessive taxation spawned revolts that tore France apart, and Louis wondered aloud how God could forsake one who had done so much for Him.

Louis could not bring himself to accept the stiff terms the alliance demanded for peace, and hostilities continued. A clash at Malplaquet (September 1709) created carnage unsurpassed until modern times. France and England fi-

MAP 13-2 Europe in 1714 *The War of the Spanish Succession ended in the year before the death of the aged Louis XIV. By then France and Spain, although not united, were both ruled by members of the Bourbon family, and Spain had lost its non-Iberian possessions.*

nally declared an armistice at Utrecht (July 1712) and came to an agreement with Holland and the emperor (the Treaty of Rastadt, March 1714). Philip V remained king of Spain, but England won Gibraltar and a chance to become a Mediterranean power (see Map 13-2). The eighteenth century was to belong to England as the sixteenth had to Spain and the seventeenth to France.

Louis XIV's Legacy

Louis XIV left France a mixed legacy. Although the monarchy was still strong when he died, it was more feared than admired. Its finances were insecure, and its debts great. Its tightly centralized control of political and economic life had suppressed the development of representative institutions, and its use of Versailles to trivialize the lives of aristocrats had diminished their capacity to provide the nation with effective leadership.

On the positive side, Louis erected magnificent buildings, provided patronage for important artists, and brought a new majesty to France. He skillfully handled the fractious French aristocracy and bourgeoisie. He appointed talented ministers, councillors, and *intendants*. And he created a French empire by expanding trade with Asia and by colonizing North America.

The Sun King's rule was not so absolute as to oppress the daily lives of his subjects. Louis's France was not a modern police state. His interests were those that traditionally had been assumed to be the responsibilities of kings: the making of war and peace, the regulation of religion, and the oversight of economic activity. Even at the height of his power, local elites enjoyed considerable independence so long as they did not interfere with his plans on the national level. The French people showed little interest in representative government before a severe financial crisis revealed the impotency of their monarchy at the end of the eighteenth century.

In the seventeenth century, England and France developed divergent forms of government: parliamentary monarchy in England and absolute monarchy in France. The politically active nobility and wealthy commercial classes of England struggled throughout the century to limit the authority of their rulers. They were not advocates of democracy or religious freedom in a modern sense, but they did establish representative government in England and extend legal recognition to a variety of religious beliefs.

In France, the monarchy remained supreme. Although the king had to mollify local elites, France developed no national institution like the English Parliament. Louis XIV was able, on his own, to build the largest army in Europe and to crush religious dissent. The model of effective centralized monarchy he created had great appeal to later generations of European rulers.

⌁ Review Questions

1. What similarities and differences do you see between the systems of government and religious policies in place in England and France at the end of the seventeenth century? What accounts for the path each nation took?

2. Why did the English king and Parliament come into conflict in the 1640s? Does one of these parties bear more responsibility than the other for the war that broke out? What role did religion play in the struggle?

3. What was the Glorious Revolution? Why did it take place? What were James II's mistakes? What were the issues involved in the events of 1688? What kind of settlement emerged from the revolution? How did England in 1700 differ from England in 1600?

4. By what stages did absolutism develop in France? How did the policies of Henry IV and Louis XIII contribute to the creation of absolute monarchy?

5. How did Louis XIV consolidate his monarchy? What limits were there on his authority? What was Louis's religious policy?

6. How successful was Louis XIV's foreign policy? What were its aims? Were they realistic? To what extent were they attained?

✎ Suggested Readings

W. BEIK, *Absolutism and Society in Seventeenth-Century France* (1985). An important study that questions the extent of royal power.

R. BONNEY, *Political Change in France Under Richelieu and Mazarin, 1624–1661* (1978). A careful examination of the manner in which these two cardinals laid the foundation for Louis XIV's absolutism.

P. BURKE, *The Fabrication of Louis XIV* (1992). Examines the manner in which the public image of Louis XIV was forged in art.

P. COLLINSON, *The Religion of Protestants: The Church in English Society, 1559–1625* (1982). The best recent introduction to Puritanism.

R. S. DUNN, *The Age of Religious Wars, 1559–1715* (1979). Lucid survey setting the conflicting political systems of France and England in larger perspective.

R. HUTTON, *Charles the Second, King of England, Scotland, and Ireland* (1989). Replaces all previous biographies.

C. RUSSELL, *The Causes of the English Civil War* (1990). A major revisionist account, which should be read with Stone below.

L. STONE, *The Causes of the English Revolution, 1529–1642* (1972). Brief survey stressing social history and ruminating over historians and historical method.

V. TAPIÉ, *France in the Age of Louis XIII and Richelieu* (1984). A narrative account.

G. TREASURE, *Mazarin: The Crisis of Absolutism in France* (1996). An examination not only of Mazarin, but also of the larger national and international background.

D. UNDERDOWN, *Fire from Heaven: Life in an English Town in the Seventeenth Century* (1992). A lively account of the manner in which a single English town experienced the religious and political events of the century.

J. B. WOLF, *Louis XIV* (1968). Very detailed political biography.

14

New Directions in Thought and Culture in the Sixteenth and Seventeenth Centuries

The Scientific Revolution

Nicolaus Copernicus: Rejection of the Earth-Centered Universe
Tycho Brahe and Johannes Kepler: New Scientific Observations
Galileo Galilei: A Universe of Mathematical Laws
Isaac Newton: The Laws of Gravitation
Newton's Reconciliation of Science and Faith

Continuing Superstitions: Witch Hunts and Panics

Village Origins
Influence of the Clergy
Role of Women
Witch Panics

Literary Imagination in Transition

Miguel de Cervantes Saavedra: Rejection of Idealism

William Shakespeare: Dramatist of the Age
John Milton: Puritan Poet
John Bunyan: Visions of Christian Piety

Philosophy in the Wake of Changing Science

Francis Bacon: Empirical Method
René Descartes: The Method of Rational Deduction
Blaise Pascal: Reason and Faith
Baruch Spinoza: The World as Divine Substance
Thomas Hobbes: Apologist for Absolutism
John Locke: Defender of Moderate Liberty

KEY TOPICS

- The astronomical theories of Copernicus, Brahe, Kepler, Galileo, and Newton, and the emergence of the scientific worldview
- Witchcraft and witch hunts
- The literary imagination in a changing world
- The philosophical foundations of modern thought

During the sixteenth and seventeenth centuries, science created a new view of the universe that challenged many previously held beliefs. The earth moved from the center of things to become only one of several planets orbiting a sun that was only one of countless stars. This new cosmology forced people to rethink humanity's place in the larger scheme of things. Traditional religion and the new science came into apparent conflict, and the grounds for faith and morality had to be reconsidered.

The achievements of science were so impressive that the scientific method was assumed to be applicable to researching issues of every kind. In the West, not only students of natural phenomena, but philosophers, theologians, and politicians came to believe that all truths ought to be verifiable by scientific techniques.

The Scientific Revolution

For a thousand years, medieval European high culture had rested on a nearly universal consensus: a single Christian faith supported by a single worldview. But during the sixteenth century, the Reformation and the religious wars shattered confidence in the correctness of that consensus. The result was skepticism and an inclination to reconsider all traditional teachings about nature and humanity.

The intellectual breakthroughs of the sixteenth and seventeenth centuries have been described as a *Scientific Revolution*. The metaphor is misleading if it is assumed to imply a rapid, widespread transformation of culture. The development of scientific attitudes was a slow process that never involved more than a few hundred people.

Nicolaus Copernicus: Rejection of the Earth-Centered Universe

Less than revolutionary methods were sometimes employed to achieve the Scientific Revolution. Such was the case with Nicolaus Copernicus (1473–1543), an Italian-educated Polish astronomer with an international reputation. Copernicus was assumed to be a fairly conventional thinker until, in the year of his death (1543), he published *On the Revolutions of the Heavenly Spheres*. The book provided Copernicus's successors with an intellectual springboard for a criticism of the previously accepted view of the position of the earth in the universe.

The maps of the universe commonly accepted in Copernicus's day were variants of one found in the ancient Greek astronomer Ptolemy's *Almagest* (c. 150 C.E.). They assumed that the earth was the center point of a ball-shaped universe composed of concentric, rotating crystalline spheres to which the heavenly bodies were attached. At the outer regions of these spheres lay the realm of God and the angels.

The laws of physics that the Greek philosopher Aristotle had described lay behind Ptolemy's model. The earth was at the center because it was the heaviest of objects. It did not move, for motionlessness was the natural state of

Major Works of the Seventeenth Century

1543	*On the Revolutions of the Heavenly Spheres* (Copernicus)
1605	*The Advancement of Learning* (Bacon)
	King Lear (Shakespeare)
	Don Quixote, Part I (Cervantes)
1609	*On the Motion of Mars* (Kepler)
1620	*Novum Organum* (Bacon)
1632	*Dialogues on the Two Chief Systems of the World* (Galileo)
1637	*Discourse on Method* (Descartes)
1651	*Leviathan* (Hobbes)
1656–1657	*Provincial Letters* (Pascal)
1667	*Paradise Lost* (Milton)
1677	*Ethics* (Spinoza)
1678	*The Pilgrim's Progress* (Bunyan)
1687	*Principia Mathematica* (Newton)
1690	*Treatises of Government* (Locke)
	An Essay Concerning Human Understanding (Locke)

physical things. The heavenly bodies moved because they were attached to spheres that transferred motion down from the highest level where a "prime mover" imparted movement to the system. Christians, of course, identified Aristotle's "prime mover" with God.

Medieval astronomers were aware of problems with Ptolemy's system. Ptolemy claimed that planets were attached to spheres, but planets appeared to move in noncircular patterns around the earth. Sometimes they actually seemed to go backward. Ptolemy and his disciples credited these strange motions to epicycles—orbits around orbits. Like spinning jewels on rings, planets were said to revolve in cycles around the paths of their primary orbits around the earth. This was plausible, but it produced a very cluttered model for the universe.

Copernicus's *On the Revolutions of the Heavenly Spheres* was meant not to destroy Ptolemy's theory, but to propose a refinement that would provide a more elegant solution to some of the mathematical problems it raised. Copernicus suggested that if the earth were assumed to move about the sun in a circle, the epicycles could be, if not eliminated, at least reduced in number. If the earth moved, it could be assumed that its motion distorted the perspective astronomers had on the heavens, making it appear that the planets moved elliptically.

Except for modifying the position of the earth, Copernicus maintained most of the other assumptions of Ptolemaic astronomy: circular orbits, epicycles, etc. He utilized no new data, and his system was no better than the earlier ones at predicting the location of the planets. The importance of his work was its illustration of a new approach to solving scientific problems. By focusing attention on the relationship between mathematics and the observed behavior of planets, Copernicus illustrated the methods of the new science—the utilization of mathematics to organize empirical data and clarify observation. Mathematics provided the models for the new scientific thinkers, but it was empirical evidence that persuaded the learned public of the validity of their ideas.

Tycho Brahe and Johannes Kepler: New Scientific Observations

Tycho Brahe (1546–1601), a Danish astronomer, spent most of his life trying to refute Copernicus and advocating a revised version of Ptolemy's earth-centered model for the universe. (Brahe suggested that the moon and the sun revolved around the earth and that the other planets revolved around the sun.) To make his case, Brahe collected the most accurate astronomical data that had ever been acquired by observation with the naked eye.

When Brahe died, his astronomical tables passed to Johannes Kepler (1571–1630), a German astronomer and a convinced Copernican. After much work, Kepler discovered that if the Copernican concept of circular orbits was abandoned, Brahe's data could be reconciled with the theory that the sun was at the center of things. Brahe's measurements suggested that the orbits of the planets were elliptical. Kepler published his views in 1609 (*On the Motion of Mars*), but their acceptance was hampered by the fact that no one could explain why planets would revolve in ellipses. The solution to that puzzle appeared eighty years later when Isaac Newton proposed the theory of gravity. Newton's insights were the result of new data and a new way of thinking about nature provided by another astronomer, Galileo.

Galileo Galilei: A Universe of Mathematical Laws

Ptolemy could have acquired most of the astronomical data available to Kepler, for it had all been gathered with the naked eye. But in the year that Kepler published his theories, an Italian scientist, Galileo Galilei (1564–1642), first turned a telescope on the heavens. He saw stars where none had been known to exist, mountains on the moon, spots moving across the sun, and moons orbiting Jupiter. This made the heavens seem far more complex than anyone had formerly suspected—far too complex to be explained by a mere revision of the Ptolemaic model.

Galileo's *Dialogues on the Two Chief Systems of the World* (1632) published his discoveries and put forth his arguments supporting the Copernican view. The Roman Catholic Church responded by indicting him for heresy, and Galileo recanted to avoid punishment. After making his formal submission to the church, he allegedly muttered under his breath; "It [the earth] still moves."

Galileo's most important achievement was to establish belief in a universe governed by laws that could be described by mathematics. The mathematical regularity that Copernicus saw in the heavens, Galileo believed, was characteristic of all physical nature. The smallest atom behaved with the same

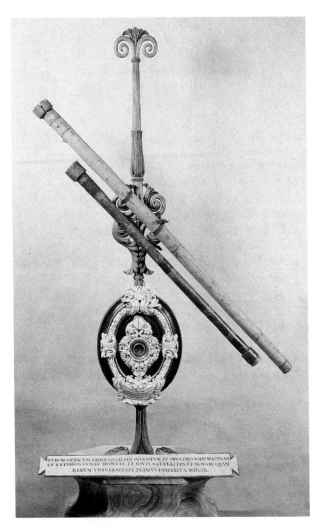

The telescope with which Galileo worked after 1609. He observed earth's moon and the cyclical phases of the planet Venus and discovered the most prominent moons of Jupiter. These observations had revolutionary intellectual and theological implications in the seventeenth century. [Instituto e Museo de Storia della Scienza, Scala/Art Resource N.Y.]

mathematical precision as the largest heavenly sphere. This insight led scientists to look for explanations of things by focusing exclusively on phenomena that could be quantified. Qualities (e.g., color, beauty, flavor, etc.) were assumed to be secondary functions of basic realities whose fundamental property was quantity (i.e., something measurable by numbers). This led scholars to try to develop mathematical models to explain things like social relationships and political systems.

The new science promoted a new concept of reality. If the real was what could be measured by mathematics, nature was not a living thing with will, understanding, and intention. It was a cold, rational, mechanistic system.

Isaac Newton: The Laws of Gravitation

Isaac Newton (1642–1727), an English mathematician, established a basis for physics that endured for over two centuries. His thinking was prodded by the search for a solution to a question that plagued the scientists who accepted the Copernican model for the universe: What force kept the heavenly bodies moving in an orderly fashion? Aristotelian physics had solved this problem for Ptolemy by suggesting that the universe was a system of concentric spheres arranged according to their weights—from the heaviest, the stationary earth at the center, outward to the ethereal realms of the highest heavens.

In 1687 Newton published *The Mathematical Principles of Natural Philosophy* (or *Principia Mathematica*, its Latin title). Newton shared Galileo's faith that reality could be described mathematically, and he was influenced by Galileo's theory of inertia. Earlier scientists had assumed that rest (motionlessness) was an object's natural state and that movement had to be explained. Galileo proposed instead that what the physicist ought to ask is not why there is motion instead of rest, but why there is a change in an existing state—be it rest or movement.

Newton theorized that the revolutions of the heavenly bodies were controlled by gravity, an attraction emanating from each physical thing for all other things. Since the strength of this attraction is proportional to the mass and proximity of each object, the order that exists among the planets can be explained as the balance they have achieved among their mutual forces. Newton demonstrated the effects of gravity mathematically, but he made no attempt to explain what gravity was in itself.

Newton believed that mathematics held the key to understanding nature, but, like the other advocates of the new science, he also believed that the ultimate test of a theory was its ability to explain empirical data and observation. The final test of any hypothesis was whether it described what could be observed. Science began and ended with empirical observation of what was actually in nature, not with a rational argument about what ought to be there. Consequently, religious dogma could not dictate conclusions to science.

Newton's Reconciliation of Science and Faith

After Newton, spirits and divinities were no longer needed to explain the operation of the universe. Newton demonstrated that natural phenomena were not chaotic expressions of arbitrary decisions made by supernatural beings. They were predictable functions of regular laws that could be described by mathematical formulae.

Newton and most scientists of his day were very devout. They knew that by altering the picture of the created world they were changing the image of its Creator. They concluded that the Creator of a universe ruled by reason must be rational and that the study of the world the Creator made must lead to a better understanding of the Creator. Science and religious faith were, therefore, not only compatible but mutually supporting. The search for an explanation for natural phenomena led scientists to reconstruct a chain of causes and effects that led ultimately to a first, or divine, cause.

At the very time when Europeans were tiring of the wars of religion and of irresolvable disputes over dogma, the new science offered them a peaceful means for arriving at a common view of God. Faith in science's rational deity also promoted faith in the rationality of human beings and in their capacity to progress—once science liberated them from dogma and superstition. The Scientific Revolution thus made virtues out of the pursuit of change and the criticism of inherited views—activities that earlier generations had opposed as leading to dangerous, destabilizing heresies. It remained to be seen whether the God of reason could take the place of the personal deity traditionally worshiped in the West.

✨ Continuing Superstition: Witch Hunts and Panics

Loss of faith in traditional certainties drove some thinkers to seek a new grounding for truth in reason and science. But there was a darker alternative. Many people responded to the intellectual challenges of the age with fear and suspicion. In their desperate search for security, they crossed the line that divides religion from magic and the occult. This was as true for the learned as for the less educated.

The centuries that fostered the growth of Western science also nurtured superstition. Witch hunts and panics erupted almost everywhere. Between 1400 and 1700, an estimated 70,000 to 100,000 people were sentenced to death for practicing harmful magic (*malificium*) and diabolical witchcraft. Belief in demons was virtually universal, and witches were said to fly to *sabbats* (sexual orgies with the Devil where they practiced every indecency imaginable). These beliefs had roots in both popular and elite cultures—especially the culture of the clergy.

Village Origins

Village societies dealt with the threats and terrors of life by identifying certain people as "cunning folk." These were persons who were believed to have special powers. Their communities turned to them for help with problems caused by disease and infertility and for aid in averting or mitigating natural disasters. The witch cultures of village societies probably thrived as a form of peasant rebellion. They may have perpetuated ancient, pre-Christian religious practices, and they were part of a belief system that empowered peasants who felt oppressed by the wealthy, urbanized classes. The church's campaign to defend Christian society against witchcraft served to expand the church's authority. Since the "cunning folk" were revered local spiritual leaders who were outside the control of the church, they were the priests' competitors. They had to be destroyed if the clergy hoped to establish dominance over village society.

Influence of the Clergy

Widespread faith in magic was the essential precondition for the great witch hunts of the sixteenth and seventeenth centuries, and such beliefs were not limited to ordinary people. They were shared by intellectuals and the Christian clergy. Exorcism of demons had been one of the traditional functions of the clergy, and the clergy found that fear of demons and the Devil was useful in persuading people to accept the discipline of the church.

Many Christians would have been hard pressed to distinguish between magic and the sacramental rituals performed by their clergy. In the late thirteenth century, the church declared that its priests were the only possessors of legitimate magical power. Inasmuch as such power was not human, theologians reasoned that it had to come either from God or from the Devil. If it came from God, it belonged exclusively to the church. Persons who practiced magic, but who were not clergy, had to derive their power from pacts with the Devil.

Role of Women

Since a reputation for magical powers enhanced one's standing in a village society, claims to such powers were made by the people most in need of security and influence: the old and the impoverished—especially single or widowed women. A good 80 percent of the victims of witch hunts were women, most of whom were single and between forty-five and sixty years of age.

It is possible that persecution of witches provided a male-dominated society with a means for ridding itself of unconventional women who were not under some man's control. Or it may simply be that older single women were perceived, along with other poor people, as burdens on society. Some female professions (e.g., midwifery) linked women with the unexplained deaths of beloved wives and infants, and this, too, exposed them to suspicion and accusations of malfeasance.

Witch Panics

The great witch panics occurred in the second half of the sixteenth and early seventeenth centuries. They were, in part, a response to the suffering caused by the religious divisions and wars of the era. Increasing levels of violence exacerbated fear and hatred and inspired a search for scapegoats on which to vent these emotions. Witch hunts also helped church and state enforce conformity and eliminate competition for the loyalty of their subjects.

The Reformation may bear some responsibility for fueling the witch panics. By challenging the legitimacy of traditional Catholic practices that had previously been assumed to provide protection against demons and the Devil, the Reformation encouraged people to take things into their own hands. The Reformation, however, may also have helped to end the witch craze. By ridiculing the sacramental magic of the old church and preaching faith in a God who was absolutely sovereign, Protestantism subordinated the Devil to God's divine plan and reduced fear of demonic powers. Ultimately, for Protestants, God was the only significant spiritual force in the universe, and his freely offered grace, not magic, was the only defense against the power of evil. This faith, the growing influence of science, and stronger governments (able to deal with mobs) helped end the pursuit of witches.

❧ Literary Imagination in Transition

The world of the seventeenth century was no longer medieval, but it was also not yet modern. The intellectual life of the period may have been so remarkably rich and vital because it issued from the interplay of both points of view. The great literary figures of the era were capable of defending traditional values while exploring popular new ideas that encouraged people to take responsibility for themselves.

Miguel de Cervantes Saavedra: Rejection of Idealism

There was religious reform in Spain, but no Protestant Reformation. The Spanish state empowered the Inquisition to enforce uniformity of opinion in Spain, and the religion of which the state approved was the mystical, ascetic piety of the early Middle Ages. It was this that colored Spain's literature.

For centuries Spain had been a nation of crusaders, and the union of Catholic piety with secular power, which is characteristic of a crusade, shaped a culture based on the ideals of medieval chivalry—particularly, honor and loyalty. The novels and plays of the period are almost all devoted to stories in which these virtues are tested.

Miguel de Cervantes Saavedra (1547–1616), who is generally acknowledged to be the greatest writer Spain has produced, devoted himself to exploring the strengths and weaknesses of religious idealism. Cervantes was self-educated, reading widely and immersing himself in the "school of life." As a youth, he worked in Rome for a Spanish cardinal. He entered the army and was decorated for gallantry in the Battle of Lepanto (1571). He was also captured by pirates and enslaved in Algiers for five years. He later found work as a tax collector and was imprisoned for padding his accounts. It was in prison in 1603 that he began to write his most famous work, *Don Quixote*.

Cervantes set out to satirize the chivalric romances popular in Spain in his day, but he developed a deep affection for Don Quixote, the deluded knight whose story he tells. *Don Quixote* is satire only on the surface. The work raises serious questions about the things that give meaning to human lives.

Cervantes's Don Quixote is a none-too-stable, middle-aged man who is driven mad by reading too many chivalric romances. He aspires to become the knight of his own imagination and sets out to prove his worthiness by performing brave deeds. He dedicates himself as a courtly lover to the service of

Dulcinea, a quite unworthy peasant girl whom he imagines to be a refined and noble lady. Sancho Panza, a clever, worldly-wise peasant, accompanies him as his squire and watches with bemused skepticism as the Don repeatedly makes a fool of himself. The story ends tragically when a well-meaning friend tries to restore Don Quixote's reason by defeating him in battle and forcing him to renounce his quest for knighthood. Stripped of the delusion that gave meaning to his life, the Don returns to his village to die a shamed and broken-hearted old man.

Don Quixote examines side by side the modern realism of Sancho Panza and the old-fashioned religious idealism of the Don. It comes to the conclusion that both are respectable and both are necessary for human fulfillment.

William Shakespeare: Dramatist of the Age

Little is known about William Shakespeare (1564–1616), the greatest playwright in the English language. He married young (at age eighteen), and by 1585 he and his wife, Anne Hathaway, had three children. He may have worked for a time as a schoolteacher. The wide, but erratic, knowledge of history and classical literature that informs his plays suggests that he was not schooled as a professional scholar.

Once he could afford it, Shakespeare chose to live the life of a country gentleman. He entered eagerly into the commercialism and the bawdy pleasures of the Elizabethan Age, and his work shows no trace of Puritan anxiety about worldliness. He was radical in neither politics nor religion, and his few allusions to Puritans are more critical than complimentary. By modern standards he was a political conservative, accepting the social rankings and the power structure of his day and demonstrating unquestioned patriotism.

Shakespeare experienced every aspect of life in the theater—as playwright, actor, and owner-producer. He wrote and performed for a famous company of actors, the King's Men, and, between 1590 and 1610, many of his plays were staged at Elizabeth's court. Although the French drama of the period was dominated by classical models, the Elizabethan audience that Shakespeare wanted to please welcomed a mixture of styles: classical comedies and tragedies, medieval morality plays, and contemporary Italian short stories.

Shakespeare wrote all kinds of plays that synthesized the best from the past and from the work of his contemporaries. The most original of Shakespeare's tragedies may be *Romeo and Juliet* (1597), but four of his greatest were the products of one short period in his career: *Hamlet* (1603), *Othello* (1604), *King Lear* (1605), and *Macbeth* (1606). Shakespeare also wrote comedies and plays based on real historical events. The later were strongly colored by the propaganda that served the Tudor monarchy, but almost all of Shakespeare's plays have demonstrated a remarkable ability to transcend the limits of the world for which they were written. Their keen analyses of human motivation, stirring evocations of human emotion, and stunning poetry keep them alive and capable of filling theaters.

John Milton: Puritan Poet

John Milton (1608–1674) was a devout Puritan with a deep appreciation for classical literature and the Italian Renaissance. Youthful travels in Italy shaped his thinking, but England's political and religious crises drove him to take up his pen. Like his Catholic contemporaries in Spain, the Protestant Milton believed that standing a test of character was the most important thing in a person's life. This theme runs through much of his work, and his strong sense of commitment to principle inspired him with the desire to create a body of work that would influence the course of public events in England.

In 1639 Milton spoke out against Charles I and Archbishop Laud in defense of the Presbyterian form of church government and various Puritan reforms. In 1642 a brief failed marriage (which was later reconciled) led him to publish several tracts defending the right to divorce. When Parliament subjected these pamphlets to censorship, Milton wrote an eloquent defense of freedom of the press, *Areopagitica* (1644). Milton believed—at least until the upheavals of civil war moderated his views—that government should exert as little control as possible over the private lives of individuals. He sided with the Independents in Parliament who wanted to dissolve the national church and grant autonomy to individual congregations, and he defended the decision to execute Charles I (*On the Tenure of Kings and Magistrates*).

Milton's eyesight began to fail in the 1650s, and he was blind by the time he composed the poems for which he is best remembered. *Paradise Lost* (1667) recounts the story of Satan's revolt in heaven and Adam's fall on earth. It is a study of the destructive effects of pride and the redemptive power of humility. The Satan of *Paradise Lost* is a proud but sorry figure who prefers reigning over hell to serving in heaven. He epitomizes the tragedy that occurs when sin distorts the virtues that are intended to be the source of human greatness.

Milton hoped that *Paradise Lost* would become England's *Iliad* or *Aeneid*. Just as those poems articulated the values that underlay Greek and Roman civilization, Milton sought to capture the theological ideals that were fundamental to the culture of Puritan England. Unlike the extreme Calvinists, Milton did not believe that all earthly events, among which he included Adam's first sin, were part of a divinely predestined plan. Like the Dutch theologian Jacob Arminius (d. 1609), who accused the Calvinists of determinism, Milton defended human free will. He maintained that human beings had to take responsibility for their fates and that their efforts to improve their characters could, with God's grace, bring them salvation.

The failure of the Puritan revolution led Milton to contemplate the nobility of those who do the best they can in the face of certain defeat. This was the theme of his last works: *Samson Agonistes* (1671), the biblical tale of Samson, and *Paradise Regained* (1671), the story of Christ's temptation in the wilderness.

John Bunyan: Visions of Christian Piety

A more extreme Puritan point of view than that espoused by Milton is found in the works of John Bunyan (1628–1688). Bunyan does not approach Milton in poetic artistry, but he movingly describes the religious beliefs held by England's ordinary people. Bunyan, who had only the most basic education and who earned his living as a tinker, became the great spokesman for a fading cause: radical Puritanism in Restoration England.

Bunyan served in Oliver Cromwell's revolutionary army. After the restoration of the monarchy in 1660, his fiery preaching landed him in prison. During his incarceration, which lasted for twelve years, he wrote a famous autobiography, *Grace Abounding*. The Puritan conviction that individuals could do nothing to earn God's forgiveness made them anxious and introspective. They kept diaries and wrote autobiographies, hoping that the record of their daily lives would reveal some sign of God's saving grace at work in them. Although their struggle against the flesh and the world did not earn them salvation, so long as it was successful they had some confidence that they were already saved.

The anxious quest for salvation is the subject of Bunyan's *The Pilgrim's Progress*, a work unique in its contribution to Western religious symbolism and imagery. It is a huge allegory, a story of the journey of Christian and his friends Hopeful and Faithful to the Celestial City. It warns that one must give up all earthly distractions to search for "Life, life, eternal life."

⌖ Philosophy in the Wake of Changing Science

The intellectual revolution that launched modern science and created a theology based on reason also transformed Western philosophy. The new methods of science—empirical observation and mathematical description—appealed to philosophers who were disillusioned by the logic chopping of medieval Scholasticism. They hoped that better answers to questions about matters of faith, morality, and political authority might be found if these subjects were analyzed scientifically.

Francis Bacon: Empirical Method

Francis Bacon (1561–1626), the English lawyer, statesman, and author who is often honored as the father of the scientific method of research, was not himself a scientist. His contribution to science was to help create an intellectual climate conducive to its growth.

In books such as *The Advancement of Learning* (1605), the *Novum Organum* (1620), and the *New Atlantis* (1627), Bacon attacked medieval Scholasticism's reverence for authority: its belief that most truth had already been discovered and only needed to be explicated. He urged his contemporaries to strike out on their own to search for a new understanding of nature. Bacon was a leader among the early European writers who defended the desirability of innovation and change.

Bacon believed that knowledge was not just an end in itself. It should produce useful results. It should improve the human condition. He claimed that

Scholasticism had nothing more to contribute toward this end, for its practitioners did nothing but rearrange old ideas. If any real progress were to be made, philosophers had to go back and reexamine the foundations of their thought. If they relied on empirical observation more than logical speculation, Bacon promised that they would discover new information that would open new possibilities for humankind.

Bacon's rejection of past methods of inquiry sprang from his awareness that the world was becoming a much more complicated place than it had been for his medieval forebears. Like Columbus, and partially because of him, Bacon claimed that he had to chart a new route to intellectual discovery. The new territories that were being explored on the globe were opening new vistas for the mind. Most people in Bacon's day assumed that the best era in human history lay in antiquity, but Bacon disagreed. He looked to a future of material improvement achieved through the empirical examination of nature.

René Descartes: The Method of Rational Deduction

René Descartes (1596–1650), the gifted French mathematician who invented analytic geometry, popularized a scientific method that relied more on deduction than empirical observation and induction. Thinkers all over Europe eagerly applied his techniques to all kinds of subject matters.

Descartes's *Discourse on Method* (1637) tried to put all human thought on a secure mathematical footing. In order to arrive at truth, Descartes said that it was necessary to doubt all ideas except those that were clear and distinct. An idea was worthy of trust not because some authority vouched for it, but because all rational beings could intuit its validity for themselves. Descartes began his search for truth by seeing if he had any ideas he could not doubt—ideas that were self-substantiating. He discovered that he could not question his own act of thinking without assuming his existence. To doubt doubting, one had to accept the existence of the doubter. With this clear and distinct idea as his premise, Descartes was able to construct arguments deducing the existence of God and a real world external to the human mind.

Descartes divided existing things into two basic categories: things in thought and things in space. Thinking was characteristic of the mind, and extension (things occupying space) of the body. Since space was measurable by mathematical means, mathematical laws governed the world of extension. These laws can be discovered by reason, for mathematical truths form coherent systems in which each part can be deduced from some other part. Spirits, divinities, or immaterial things have no place in the world of extension. That realm belongs to the scientist who explains it by using mathematical reason to discover the mechanical properties of matter.

Natural scientists eventually abandoned Descartes's deductive method for induction, the process of formulating a hypothesis by generalizing from discrete bits of empirical data. Deduction, however, remained popular with people who pondered subjects for which little empirical data was available—political theory, psychology, ethics, and theology.

The microscope of Robert Hooke (1535–1703). The microscope became the telescope's companion as a major optical instrument in the seventeenth century. Several scientists, including Galileo, had a hand in its development, but the Englishman Hooke and the Dutchman Anton von Leeuwenhoek (1632–1723) did the most to perfect it. [Historical Collections, National Museum of Health and Medicine, Armed Forces Institute of Pathology]

Blaise Pascal: Reason and Faith

Blaise Pascal (1623–1662), a French mathematician and physical scientist, warned against what seemed to him to be a false optimism promoted by the new rationalism and science. He was a deeply religious man who surrendered his wealth to pursue a life of austerity. The seriousness with which he took human sinfulness made him distrustful of those who claimed that science could perfect human nature.

Pascal opposed both dogmatism and skepticism. His hope was to find a middle ground between the Jesuits' dogmatic *casuistry* (i.e., clever argumentation that minimizes the paradoxes of faith) and the rationalist's skepticism. The latter led either to atheism or to *deism* (a philosophy that substituted a rational

Pascal invented this adding machine, the ancestor of mechanical calculators, around 1644. It has eight wheels with ten cogs each, corresponding to the numbers 0–9. The wheels move forward for addition, backward for subtraction. [Bildarchiv Preussischer Kulturbesitz]

principle—a "prime mover"—for the Bible's personal God). Pascal never completed this project, but he did produce a provocative collection of reflections on faith, his posthumously published *Pensées.*

Pascal's sister was a member of the Jansenist community of Port-Royal, and Pascal wrote his *Provincial Letters* to defend the Jansenists against their Jesuit enemies. Jansenism was a kind of Catholicism based on Saint Augustine's claim that original sin robbed humanity of the ability to do good and made it completely dependent on God's grace for salvation. Pascal insisted that human reason and science could not comprehend the two essential truths of the Christian faith: (1) that the loving God, to whom people aspire, exists, and (2) that human beings, because they are corrupt by nature, are utterly unworthy of this God's perfection. Pascal argued that rational analysis of the human condition did reveal humanity's utter corruption and did demonstrate that reason itself could not solve the mystery of human destiny. Reason could go no further, but those who properly heeded its lessons were driven to make the "leap of faith" and profess their total reliance on divine grace.

Pascal proposed an ingenious "wager" to demonstrate the unreasonableness of skepticism. He noted that it is a better bet to believe that God exists than to doubt. If God does exist, the believer wins everything. If it turns out that God does not exist, the believer has not lost much by believing. Furthermore, Pascal argued, religious faith is valuable in and of itself apart from the issue of God's existence. It provides motivation for discipline and helps one maintain an important perspective on life. Pascal urged people to pursue self-understanding through "learned ignorance" (i.e., through contemplation of the significance of human limitations).

Baruch Spinoza: The World as Divine Substance

Where Pascal claimed that reason could do little to establish faith, the most controversial thinker of the seventeenth century, Baruch Spinoza (1632–1677), tried to reduce faith to reason. His arguments led both Jews and Protestants to brand him an atheist. When Spinoza's *Ethics* was published after his death in 1677, religious leaders universally condemned it for espousing *pantheism* (the equation of God with nature).

The *Ethics* was organized, in the spirit of the new science, as a geometrical system of definitions, axioms, and propositions. The most controversial part of the book deals with the nature of substance and of God. According to Spinoza, a true substance must be self-caused, free, and infinite. This definition corresponds to the traditional description of God and implies that substance and God are the same, that everything that exists is contained in God. Spinoza's doctrine is not literally pantheistic, for God could be assumed to be greater than the created world that He, as primal substance, embraces. But if Spinoza is correct, everything that is true of the natural world is also true of God. Everything that transpires in the world is an expression of God. Mind and matter must also fundamentally be the same, for both are extensions of the divine substance.

Since Spinoza seemed to imply that the substance of the world was eternal and that human actions were unfree expressions of its attributes, Jews and Christians rejected him. They believed the world to be created by God in time, and they insisted that human beings had to have been given enough freedom to enable them to be held responsible for their actions. Spinoza's most enthusiastic followers were nineteenth-century thinkers who rejected revelation and theism and sought a purely rational religion.

Thomas Hobbes: Apologist for Absolutism

Thomas Hobbes (1588–1679), the most original political philosopher of the seventeenth century, turned to reason and empirical observation to find an explanation for social institutions. Hobbes was an urbane and much-traveled man who enthusiastically supported the new scientific movement. He visited Paris and made Descartes's acquaintance. He spent time in Italy with Galileo, and he was interested in the work of William Harvey (1578–1657), the man who discovered that blood circulated through the human body. Hobbes was also a superb classicist. His translation of Thucydides' *History of the Peloponnesian War*, the first in English, is still read.

The English Civil War made Hobbes a political philosopher and inspired him to write *Leviathan* (1651)—a thoroughly materialistic and mechanical explanation for human conduct. Hobbes theorized that all psychological processes derive from bare sensation and that, therefore, all motivations are ego-istical. Their intent is always to increase pleasure and minimize pain. The human power of reasoning is nothing more than a process of adding and subtracting the implications of the general names people agree to give to things.

Despite his mechanistic view of human nature, Hobbes believed that people could progress by using scientific reasoning. Progress was contingent, however, on the correct and prior use of the greatest of human creations, the commonwealth. The commonwealth created the conditions that were essential for rational, civilized life.

The key to Hobbes's political philosophy is found in a brilliant myth he devised to explain humanity's original state. Hobbes claimed that nature inclines people to a "perpetual and restless desire" for power. Because all people want, and in the state of nature possess, a right to everything, their equality breeds enmity, competition, diffidence, and perpetual quarreling—"a way of every man against every man." Whereas earlier and later philosophers saw the original human condition as a paradise from which people had fallen, Hobbes described it as a corrupt environment from which people could be delivered only by the establishment of a politically organized society. Unlike Aristotle and Christian thinkers like Thomas Aquinas, Hobbes did not believe human beings were naturally sociable. He claimed that they were self-centered beasts who were utterly without discipline unless it was imposed on them by force.

People escape their terrible natural state by entering a social contract; that is, by agreeing to live in a commonwealth ruled by law. A desire for "commodious living" and a fear of death drives them to accept the constraints of communal life. The social contract obliges every person, for the sake of peace and self-defense, to agree to set aside his or her right to all things and be content with as much liberty against others as he or she would allow others against him or herself. Because words and promises are insufficient to guarantee this agreement, the social contract also authorizes the coercive use of force to compel compliance.

Believing the dangers of anarchy to be greater than those of tyranny, Hobbes thought that rulers should have unlimited power. There is little room in Hobbes's political philosophy for protest in the name of individual conscience, nor for resistance to legitimate authority by private individuals. Contemporary Catholics and Puritans alike criticized these features of the *Leviathan*, but Hobbes insisted that loss of rights for some individuals was clearly preferable to the suffering everyone experienced in a civil war. It mattered little to Hobbes whether his ruler was Charles I, Oliver Cromwell, or Charles II (each of whom Hobbes supported), so long as he kept his subjects from reverting to the chaos that was their natural condition.

John Locke: Defender of Moderate Liberty

John Locke (1632–1704) studied the works of Francis Bacon, René Descartes, and Isaac Newton, and he tried to synthesize the rationalism of Descartes and the experimental science advocated by Bacon and Newton. Although he was not as original as Hobbes, he had a greater impact on events. His ideas assisted opponents of absolutist monarchies in organizing both the American and the French revolutions.

Locke's sympathies were with the leaders of popular revolutions. His father fought with the parliamentary army during the English Civil War. In 1682 Locke himself joined a rebellion against Charles II led by Anthony Ashley Cooper, the earl of Shaftesbury. Its failure forced him to seek asylum in Holland.

Locke's *Essay Concerning Human Understanding* (1690) offered a scientific explanation for the human thought process. Locke claimed that the mind of a newborn was a blank tablet on which no ideas had yet been inscribed. No knowledge was innate; all was acquired from sensory experience. What people knew, therefore, was not the external world in itself, but the impressions interaction with the world made on the mind.

If there were no innate ideas, there could be no innate moral norms. Morals were the products of a person's rational decision to subordinate self-love to a concern for others. Such a decision was rational, for it enhanced the pleasures of human social life. Locke believed that the moral precepts taught by Christianity were identical to the ideals that uncorrupted reason would embrace without the aide of revelation. Reason and religion were but two guides along the same path.

During the reign of Charles II, Locke wrote *Two Treatises of Government*, an attack on theories of absolute monarchy. Sir Robert Filmer, the author of *Patriarcha*, or the *Natural Power of Kings* (1680), had compared the rights of kings over their subjects to those of fathers over their children. Locke disputed this by insisting that both fathers and rulers are bound by the law of nature that creates everyone equal and independent. People enter into social contracts that empower legislatures and monarchs to "umpire" their disputes. They do this, however, to preserve their natural rights, not to surrender them. The job of a ruler is to serve the law of nature.

Locke's differences with Hobbes stemmed from the latter's negative views of human nature. Locke believed that the natural human state was not Hobbes's jungle of selfish egomaniacs, but a community of perfect freedom and equality in which everyone enjoyed rights to life, liberty, and property. The warfare that Hobbes feared broke out, Locke believed, only when rulers failed to preserve people's natural freedom and tried to enslave them.

The Scientific Revolution and the thought of writers whose work was contemporaneous with it mark a major turning point in history. During the seventeenth century, many of the fundamental premises of the medieval worldview were abandoned. The earth was displaced from the center of the universe, and the universe seemed much larger and more complex than had previously been imagined. New knowledge of the physical universe called into question dogmas that rested on the authority of the church and Scripture. Theology and metaphysics yielded to mathematics as the preferred discipline for exploring nature. Political thought became much less concerned with religious issues and much less in awe of traditional authorities. Arguments were developed to promote greater freedom of religious and political expression. People began to comprehend the influ-ence of environment on human character and action. Life on earth became the chief preoccupation of Western intellectuals, and they demonstrated greater self-confidence in their capacity to realize its potentials.

∾ Review Questions

1. What contributions to the Scientific Revolution were made by Copernicus, Brahe, Kepler, Galileo, and Newton? What did Bacon contribute to the foundation of scientific thought? Who do you think made the most important contribution? Why?

2. Was the Scientific Revolution truly a revolution? Which has a greater impact on history: a political or an intellectual revolution?

3. How did Newton reconcile his scientific discoveries with his faith in God? How did his efforts compare with those of Galileo and Pascal? Are reason and faith compatible?

4. How do the political philosophies of Hobbes and Locke compare? How did each view human nature? Would you rather live under a government designed by Hobbes or by Locke? Why?

5. How do you explain the fact that witchcraft and witch hunts flourished during an age of scientific enlightenment? Were there unique aspects of life in the late sixteenth and early seventeenth centuries that encouraged witch panics? Might the Reformation have contributed to them?

6. What concerns about the adequacy of past values were raised by Cervantes, Shakespeare, and Milton? What new worldview did they shape for their generation?

∾ Suggested Readings

R. Ashcraft, *Revolutionary Politics and Locke's Two Treatises of Government* (1986). The most important study of Locke to appear in recent years.

H. Butterfield, *The Origins of Modern Science, 1300–1800* (1949). An authoritative survey.

H. F. Cohen, *The Scientific Revolution: A Historiographical Inquiry* (1994). Supplants all previous discussions of the history and concept of the Scientific Revolution.

M. Duran, *Cervantes* (1974). Detailed biography.

M. A. Finocchiaro, *The Galileo Affair: A Documentary History* (1989). A collection of all the relevant documents and introductory commentary.

A. R. Hall, *The Scientific Revolution, 1500–1800: The Formation of the Modern Scientific Attitude* (1966). Traces undermining of traditional science and rise of new sciences.

I. Harris, *The Mind of John Locke: A Study of Political Theory in Its Intellectual Setting* (1994). The most comprehensive recent treatment.

C. Hill, *Milton and the English Revolution* (1977). A major biography.

M. Hunter, *Science and Society in Restoration England* (1981). Examines the social relations of scientists and scientific societies.

M. Jacob, *The Newtonians and the English Revolution* (1976). A controversial book that attempts to relate science and politics.

R. Kieckhefer, *European Witch Trials: Their*

Foundations in Popular and Learned Culture, 1300–1500 (1976). Excellent background for understanding the great witch panic.

T. S. Kᴜʜɴ, *The Copernican Revolution* (1957). A scholarly treatment.

B. Lᴇᴠᴀᴄᴋ, *The Witch Hunt in Early Modern Europe* (1986). Lucid up-to-date survey of research.

D. Lɪɴᴅʙᴇʀɢ ᴀɴᴅ R. L. Nᴜᴍʙᴇʀs (eds.), *God and Nature: Historical Essays on the Encounter Between Christianity and Science* (1986). The best collection of essays on the subject.

K. Tʜᴏᴍᴀs, *Religion and the Decline of Magic* (1971). Provocative, much-acclaimed work focused on popular culture.

R. S. Wᴇsᴛғᴀʟʟ, *Never at Rest: A Biography of Isaac Newton* (1981). An important major study.

B. H. G. Wᴏʀᴍᴀʟᴅ, *Francis Bacon: History, Politics, and Science, 1561–1626* (1993). The most extensive recent study.

15

Successful and Unsuccessful Paths to Power (1686–1740)

KEY TOPICS

- ➣ The decline of Spain and the Netherlands, as maritime powers, relative to France and England
- ➣ Opposition to the French monarchy from the nation's aristocrats
- ➣ The political stability of Britain in the early eighteenth century
- ➣ The efforts of the Habsburgs to secure their holdings
- ➣ The emergence of Prussia as a major power under the Hohenzollerns
- ➣ The efforts of Peter the Great to transform Russia into a powerful, centralized nation along Western lines

The late seventeenth and early eighteenth centuries witnessed significant shifts of power within Europe. Great Britain, France, Austria, Russia, and Prussia emerged as the dominant states, while Spain, the United Netherlands, Poland, Sweden, and the Holy Roman and Ottoman empires declined.

The most successful countries were those that developed strong central governments. During the seventeenth cen-

tury, the turmoil created by the English civil wars and the Fronde in France had impressed people with the value of a monarch as a guarantor of domestic tranquility. On the continent, this created support for the kind of absolutist government pioneered by France's Louis XIV. The path a nation took was often a function of the character, personality, and energy of its ruler.

Events and Reigns

1533–1584	*Ivan the Terrible*
1584–1613	*Time of Troubles*
1613	*Michael Romanov becomes tsar*
1640–1688	*Frederick William, the Great Elector*
1682–1725	*Peter the Great*
1683	*Turkish siege of Vienna*
1688–1713	*Frederick I of Prussia*
1697	*Peter the Great's European tour*
1700–1721	*The Great Northern War*
1703	*Saint Petersburg founded*
1711–1740	*Charles VI, the Pragmatic Sanction*
1713	*War of the Spanish Succession ends*
1713–1740	*Frederick William I of Prussia*
1714	*George I founds the Hanoverian dynasty*
1715	*Louis XV becomes King of France*
1720–1742	*Robert Walpole dominates British politics*
1726–1743	*Cardinal Fleury*
1727	*George II*
1740	*Maria Theresa succeeds to the Habsburg throne*
1740	*Frederick II invades Silesia*

⤳ Spain and the Netherlands

Spain

At the end of the seventeenth century, Spain yielded its position as the dominant power in western Europe to Britain and France. Spain's political decline was linked to the failure of an economy that had never been healthy. Spain developed few industries. Wool remained virtually its only export, and the nation paid for imported goods with the gold and silver mined in its New World empire. This income was often imperiled by raids on Spain's treasure fleet carried out by pirates and hostile navies.

Spain also had serious internal political problems. The monarchy, which had never been strong, was dependent on the cooperation of the local nobility and the church. After the defeat of the Spanish Armada in 1588, whatever prestige the crown had earned began to fade. Things reached a nadir between 1665 and 1700, when the royal government was headed by the physically malformed, dull-witted, and sexually impotent Charles II. Following his death, foreign powers fought the War of Spanish Succession to impose a candidate of their choice on Spain.

The Treaty of Utrecht (1713) finally recognized Philip V (r. 1700–1746), the grandson of Louis XIV, as Spain's king. His new Bourbon dynasty should have concentrated on consolidating its position in Spain. Instead, Philip's wife,

Elizabeth Farnese, persuaded him to use his resources to advance her family's ambitions in Italy. Not until Charles III (r. 1759–1788) ascended the throne did Spain have a king who was concerned with domestic administration and the management of the empire. He was able to improve Spain's government, but it was too late for him to become a player in Europe's game of power politics.

The Netherlands

Like Spain, the United Provinces of the Netherlands ceased to be a great power during the eighteenth century. Wars with Louis XIV and England enabled the British to win naval supremacy. After the death of William III of England in 1702, the provinces blocked the succession of another strong *stadtholder* who could maintain their political unity. Their fishing industry declined, and the Dutch lost their technological superiority in shipbuilding. Countries that had relied on Dutch ships to transport their goods began to trade directly with each other, and Dutch domestic industries stagnated. Only in the area of international finance did the United Provinces retain much influence.

❖ France and Great Britain

France

France, although less strong in 1715 than in 1680, was still a great power. It had a large population, an advanced economy, and a highly developed administrative structure. France's resources were drained by the last of Louis XIV's wars, but the conflicts had similarly debilitated the other major European states. All that France needed in order to recover economically was intelligent leadership and a less ambitious foreign policy.

France did begin to recover, but not because of an improvement in the quality of its leadership. The prestige of the monarchy was already faltering when Louis XIV passed the crown to his five-year-old great-grandson Louis XV (r. 1715–1774). The young king's regent—his uncle, the duke of Orléans—made a deteriorating situation worse.

Orléans was a gambler who turned over the financial management of the government to a Scottish speculator, John Law (1671–1729). Law believed that an increase in the money supply would stimulate postwar economic recovery, so he established a bank to issue paper money. Law transferred responsibility for the national debt to the "Mississippi Company," a corporation that had a monopoly on trading privileges with France's Louisiana colony in North America. The company issued shares of its stock in exchange for government bonds and relied on profits from stock speculation to redeem those bonds. Initially the price of the stock rose handsomely, but smart investors took their profits and redeemed the paper currency from Law's bank in gold. The bank lacked sufficient bullion to back up the money it printed, and in February 1720, the government had to halt gold trading in France. Law fled the country, and the "Mississippi Bubble" (as the affair was called) burst. The fiasco brought disgrace on the government and cast a shadow over economic activity in France for the rest of the century.

***Renewed Authority of the* Parlements.** The duke of Orléans further weakened the monarchy by trying to recreate a role for the French nobility in the decision-making processes of the government. Louis XIV had filled governmental offices with commoners and kept aristocrats distracted and competing for symbolic honors at Versailles. The regent was pressured by the aristocrats to restore a balance of power, and he set up a system of councils on which nobles were to serve with bureaucrats. The experiment failed, for the nobles, who had been thoroughly domesticated, lacked both the talent and the desire to govern.

The great French families were not, however, prepared to yield ground in their ancient fight to limit the power of the monarchy over their landed domains. Their most effective weapons in this struggle were the *parlements,* the aristocratically dominated courts.

The French *parlements* were different from the English Parliament. They did not have the power to legislate, but as courts that enforced the law, their formal approval was required to make a royal law valid. Louis XIV had curtailed the authority of stubborn, uncooperative *parlements,* but the duke of Orléans restored their right to register laws. For the rest of the century, until the revolution that overthrew the monarchy in 1790, the aristocrats used the *parlements* to resist royal authority.

Cardinal Fleury and Louis XV. After 1726 things briefly improved for the monarchy. A seventy-three-year-old churchman, Cardinal Fleury (1653–1743), became the king's chief minister. Like his seventeenth-century predecessors, the cardinals Richelieu and Mazarin, Fleury was a political realist who understood that the nobles were both politically ambitious and irresponsible. He believed that steps had to be taken to enable France to recover economically. To this end, he avoided expensive military ventures, repudiated part of the national debt, built new roads and bridges, and encouraged the growth of new industries. He was never able, however, to impose sufficient taxes on the nobles or the church to put the state on a stable financial footing.

Following Fleury's death in 1743, his work was speedily undone. Despite the cardinal's best efforts to train Louis XV for the responsibilities of office, the king possessed all the vices and none of the virtues of his great-grandfather. He wanted absolute power but would not work the long hours required to use it. He became a pawn of the intrigues of his court, and his personal life was scandalous. Louis XV was too mediocre a man to be evil, but in a monarch mediocrity could do as much damage as wickedness.

Despite its lack of able leadership, France remained a major power. At mid-century its army was still the largest and strongest on the continent. Its commerce and production were expanding. Its colonies were producing wealth and spurring the growth of domestic industries. France had great potential, but it lacked a head capable of exploiting its opportunities.

Great Britain

The British monarchy was not as degraded as the French, but it was not entirely stable. In 1701 Parliament's Act of Settlement had positioned the German house of Hanover to inherit the throne. But a challenge was mounted to the ascension of the first member of the dynasty, George I (r. 1714–1727). In December 1715, James II's son, James Edward, the "Stuart pretender" (1688–1766), landed in Scotland and began to rally an army. His men were soon dispersed, but the experience alerted the new dynasty to the necessity of consolidating its position.

Whigs and Tories. During the seventeenth century, England had been one of the most politically restive countries in Europe, and as Queen Anne's reign (1702–1714) came to a close, there were sharp clashes between political factions called Whigs and Tories. Neither group was organized like a modern political party. Each was a network of like-minded local politicians whose points of view were articulated by a few national spokesmen. The Tories favored a strong monarchy, low taxes for landowners, and the Anglican Church. The Whigs believed that the monarchy should acknowledge the sovereignty of Parliament. They defended urban commercial interests and rural landowners, and they ad-

Cardinal Fleury (1653–1743) was the tutor and chief minister of Louis XV from 1726 to 1743. Fleury gave France a period of peace and prosperity, but was unable to solve the state's long-term financial problems. This portrait is by Hyacinthe Rigaud (1659–1743). [Ets. J. E. Bulloz]

vocated religious toleration for Protestant nonconformists. Both groups were conservative in that they defended the status quo.

The Tories wanted peace with France, but the Elector of Hanover, who was to succeed Queen Anne as George I, believed that it was in Hanover's interest to keep France at war. The Whigs sought his support, and in the final months of Anne's reign, some Tories opened channels of communication with the Stuart pretender. Given this, it was little wonder that the Whigs won the confidence of the new king. For the forty years following his succession, the chief difference between Whigs and Tories was that the former were given public offices and patronage and the latter were not.

The Leadership of Robert Walpole. English politics remained in a state of flux until Robert Walpole (1676–1745) persuaded the king to redesign the nation's government. Walpole, a Norfolk squire, had been active in the House of Commons and had served as a cabinet minister. A British financial scandal similar to France's Mississippi Bubble scheme brought him to the king's attention.

Management of Britain's national debt had been assigned to the South Sea Company. The company exchanged government bonds for its stock, and, as in the French case, the price of its stock soared until speculators began to sell their holdings. Parliament intervened in 1720 to prevent a crash and, under Walpole's leadership, adopted measures to honor the national debt. Walpole's contemporaries credited him with saving the financial integrity of the nation.

Walpole has often been described as the first prime minister of Great Britain. He originated England's system of administration by a cabinet of ministers, each of whom has responsibility for a separate branch of government. But unlike a modern prime minister, he was not chosen by the House of Commons. His power depended on his ability to manipulate the House while retaining the favor of his kings, George I and George II (r. 1727–1760).

Walpole's slogan, "Let sleeping dogs lie," summarized his policy of maintaining peace abroad while promoting the status quo at home. Corruption was the glue that held his government together, for politicians quickly learned that to oppose him was to risk the almost certain loss of government patronage for self, family, and friends.

The Structure of Parliament. The eighteenth-century British House of Commons was neither a democratic nor a representative body. Members of Parliament were chosen by property owners and expected to protect their economic and social interests. Each county elected two members. But if the more powerful landed families in a county agreed on the candidates, there was no contest. Other members were chosen by units called boroughs. A few boroughs were large enough to hold truly democratic elections, but most boroughs had a very small number of electors. A rich family could buy up most of the property to which the votes of a borough were attached and, in effect, "own" a seat in Parliament.

Members of Parliament did not pretend to represent the people at large, but they provided England with unified government. Owners of property were suspicious of the bureaucrats who worked for the crown and preferred them-

This series of four Hogarth etchings satirizes the notoriously corrupt English electoral system. Hogarth shows the voters going to the polls after having been bribed and intoxicated with free gin. (Voting was then in public. The secret ballot was not introduced in England until 1872.) The fourth etching, "Chairing the Member," shows the triumphal procession of the victorious candidate, which is clearly turning into a brawl. [Metropolitan Museum of Art, Harris Brisbane Dick Fund, 1932. Acc. #32.35.(124)]

selves to bear the burdens of local administration (e.g., as judges, militia commanders, tax collectors). In this sense Britain's nobles and substantial landowners governed the nation. Since Parliament represented their interests, they acknowledged its sovereignty as a central political authority. Parliament thus provided Britain with the kind of unity that was possible elsewhere in Europe only under an absolutist monarchy.

Parliament also provided the British government with a sound financial base. Continental kings could impose taxes unilaterally, but the British monarch could do so only with the consent of Parliament. Since the property owners represented in Parliament levied taxes on themselves, in England, unlike France, there were virtually no exemptions from taxation. Consequently, vast sums could be raised to fight the wars that Parliament endorsed. By 1693, when the Bank of England was set up to regulate credit, financial policies were in place that enabled Britain to become a great power.

The British people enjoyed more political freedom than the citizens of continental states. Patronage did not stifle divergent points of view among members of the government. Newspapers and public debate flourished. Free speech and freedom of association were possible, and there was no standing army to intimidate the populace.

Rights that the English regarded as traditional raised a real barrier to the government's arbitrary use of power. If public outcry was loud enough, Parliament would rescind unpopular measures or allow itself to be persuaded to begin or end wars. Despite manifest corruption, Britain became a European power of the first order with a form of government and an economy that inspired progressive thinkers across Europe.

⌁ Central and Eastern Europe

The maritime nations of western Europe had well-defined borders and strong central governments. Their battles were more often fought on the high seas and in their overseas empires than on European territory.

East of the Elbe River, political organization was "soft." Economies were largely agrarian. Serfdom persisted. Cities were few. And since no states had overseas empires, wars were fought out at home rather than abroad. The wars of the seventeenth century accustomed people to frequently shifting political loyalties, and the rulers of the region's numerous small states and principalities resisted the development of any centralized monarchy.

In the last half of the seventeenth century, political and social institutions emerged that were to characterize eastern and central Europe for the next 200 years. Following the Peace of Westphalia, the Austrian Habsburgs resigned themselves to the weakness of Germany's Holy Roman Empire and turned their attention to developing a base of power farther east. At the same time in northern Germany, Prussia evolved as a challenger to Habsburg domination. By the start of the eighteenth century, Russia, too, was becoming a major military power. As Sweden, Poland, and the Ottoman Empire faded, Austria, Prussia, and Russia began to flourish.

Sweden: The Ambitions of Charles XII

Sweden had seized the opportunity of the Thirty Years' War to make a bid for empire. During the seventeenth century, it won control of the Baltic—permitting Russia and Germany access to the sea only on its terms. Sweden's economy was not strong enough, however, to sustain its political success.

In 1697 a headstrong (possibly insane) king, Charles XII (r. 1697–1718), ascended Sweden's throne. Three years later Russia launched the Great Northern War (1700–1721) to win a foothold on the Baltic. Charles XII fought vigorously and often brilliantly, but he mismanaged the campaign. After an initial victory and a distracting foray into Poland, he invaded Russia. His army bogged down in the brutal winter weather and suffered decisive defeat at Poltava in 1709. The war ended in 1721, when Sweden ran out of resources. Russia occupied a large section of the eastern Baltic coast and broke Sweden's monopoly of the sea. After Charles XII's death, the Swedish nobles limited the power of the monarchy, and Sweden abandoned foreign adventures.

The Ottoman Empire

The Ottoman Empire was the chief barrier to expansion of Europe's major southeastern states: the Austrian Habsburg domain and Russia. Late in the seventeenth century the Ottomans still controlled most of the Balkan peninsula and the entire coastline of the Black Sea.

Although officially Islamic, the Ottoman Empire contained an ethnically and religiously diverse population. Its government worked through religiously defined political entities called *millets*. Laws and regulations applied to people according to the *millets* to which they belonged rather than to the districts in which they lived. The non-Islamic residents of the empire (the *zimmis*) could practice their faiths, but they were second-class citizens who could not rise in the service of the empire. This arrangement limited interaction among and integration of people of different faiths.

From its beginnings in the fifteenth century, the Ottoman Empire had been an aggressive power pressing westward from Istanbul (Constantinople) into Europe. By 1683 it was besieging the city of Vienna and forcing Christians in the Balkan peninsula and on the islands of the eastern Mediterranean to convert to Islam. Many of these people had previously been compelled by the Venetians to accept Roman Catholicism, and they welcomed the Turks as liberators.

By the end of the seventeenth century, the Ottomans were overextending themselves. Since military campaigns left Ottoman sultans little time to attend to civilian affairs, political factions in the capital acquired considerable independence. They resisted attempts to strengthen the central government, and rivalries among them weakened the effectiveness of the empire's administration. Control of distant provinces came to depend on the goodwill of native rulers, and commercial agents representing foreign nations dominated the empire's trade and its economy.

By the early eighteenth century, the weakness of the Ottoman Empire was creating a political vacuum on the southeastern perimeter of Europe. For the next two centuries European states probed and appropriated parts of the empire. In 1699 the Turks surrendered Hungary, Transylvania, Croatia, and Slavonia to the Habsburgs. Russia also moved into Ottoman territory, and early in the nineteenth century many of the peoples who lived in the Balkans and around the Black Sea launched campaigns to establish independent states. The result was political and ethnic turmoil that has yet to end.

Poland: Absence of Strong Central Authority

In no other part of Europe was the failure to maintain a competitive political position so complete as in Poland. The fault lay with the Polish nobility, who defeated all attempts to establish an effective central government—even one of their own making.

The Polish monarchy was elective, and divisions among the noble families prevented them from choosing one of their own to be king. Most of Poland's monarchs, therefore, were outsiders—puppets of foreign powers. The Polish nobles belonged to a central legislative body called the *Sejm* (Diet). It was an aristocratic assembly that excluded representatives from corporate bodies, such as towns. The Diet was virtually powerless. Its rule of *liberum veto* permitted any one of its members unilaterally to disband its meetings—a practice known as "exploding" the Diet. The need to achieve unanimity on every issue made it extremely difficult for the Diet to do much. Government as it was developing elsewhere in Europe simply was not tolerated in Poland. Consequently, during the last half of the eighteenth century, Poland disappeared from the map of Europe.

The Habsburg Empire and the Pragmatic Sanction

The Thirty Years' War was a turning point for the Austrian Habsburgs. It ended their dream of winning control over Germany and returning it to the Catholic fold. The decline of the Spanish branch of the family freed the Austrian Habsburgs to strike out in a new direction of their own.

The Treaty of Westphalia had legalized Protestantism and recognized the autonomy of more than 300 political entities within the Holy Roman Empire. The Habsburg family retained its hold on the imperial title, but the effectiveness of the title depended on the emperor's ability to elicit cooperation from the members of the imperial Diet. Although the post-Westphalian Holy Roman Empire resembled Poland in its lack of central authority, the Diet (which met at Regensburg from 1663 until its final dissolution in 1806) achieved some coordination of economic and political interests. The Habsburgs' domains and the emerging Prussian state also helped stabilize Germany.

Consolidation of Austrian Power. The Habsburgs began by consolidating their power within their hereditary possessions (see Map 15-1). These included the Crown of Saint Wenceslas (encompassing the kingdom of Bohemia in what was until recently Czechoslovakia and the duchies of Moravia and Silesia) and the

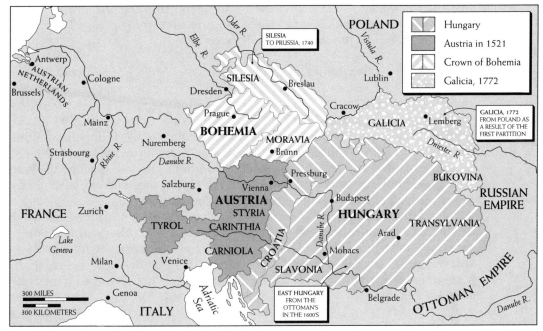

MAP 15-1   The Austrian Habsburg Empire, 1521–1772 *The empire had three main units: Austria, Bohemia, Hungary. Expansion was mainly eastward: east Hungary from the Ottomans (in the seventeenth century) and Galicia from Poland (1772). Meantime, Silesia was lost, but Habsburgs retained influence in Germany as Holy Roman Emperors.*

Crown of Saint Stephen (Hungary, Croatia, and Transylvania). In the early eighteenth century the family acquired the former Spanish (thereafter Austrian) Netherlands, Lombardy (northern Italy), and, for a brief time, the Kingdom of Naples (southern Italy). For most of the eighteenth and nineteenth centuries, the Habsburgs' power derived from lands outside Germany.

The Habsburgs' possessions were extremely difficult to rule. The various properties that composed the empire were held by different titles, and in most areas the Habsburgs could govern only with the cooperation of the local nobles. Geographical barriers and differences of language and custom prevented the Habsburgs' subjects from developing a common identity. Even the Habsburg zeal for Roman Catholicism was no bond for unity, for many of the Magyar nobles of Hungary were zealous Calvinists. The Habsburgs tried to chart common policies for their far-flung domains, but they repeatedly found it necessary to make concessions to nobles in one part of Europe to maintain their position in another.

Despite these difficulties, Leopold I (r. 1657–1705) was able to fight off the Turks and France's Louis XIV. In 1699 the Ottomans recognized his sovereignty over Hungary, and Leopold's increasing strength in the East enhanced his political leverage in Germany. He began to bring his Magyar subjects under control and to extend his reach into the Balkan peninsula and western Romania. These new possessions made it possible for him to turn the port of Trieste into a base for Habsburg power in the Mediterranean.

The Habsburg Dynastic Problem. Leopold was succeeded by Joseph I (r. 1705–1711) and Charles VI (r. 1711–1740). Charles, who had no male heir, feared that after his death the European powers would intervene in the Austrian Habsburg lands just as they had in the Spanish Habsburgs' domains in 1700. To prevent this and to provide his realm with a semblance of legal unity, he devoted most of his reign to winning the approval of his family, the various diets representing his subjects, and Europe's chief nations for a document called the Pragmatic Sanction. It recognized a single line of inheritance for the Habsburg dynasty through Charles VI's daughter Maria Theresa (r. 1740–1780).

Charles established a clear line of succession and a basis for legal bonds among the Habsburg holdings, but he could not prevent other nations from attacking his daughter. Less than two months after his death, the fragility of his foreign agreements was clear. In December, 1740, Frederick II of Prussia invaded the Habsburg province of Silesia, and Maria Theresa had to fight to defend her inheritance.

Prussia and the Hohenzollerns

Like the Habsburgs, the Hohenzollerns of Prussia held a scattered collection of lands by a variety of different feudal titles. But the Hohenzollerns were more successful than the Habsburgs in forging their diverse properties into a centrally administered state. They constructed a powerful bureaucratic machine to mobilize every social class and most economic pursuits in support of the institution on which the state was founded: the army. As a result, "Prussian" has become synonymous with administrative rigor and military discipline.

A State of Disconnected Territories. The Hohenzollern family rose to prominence in 1417 as rulers of the German territory of Brandenburg (see Map 15-2). To this they added the duchy of Cleves and the counties of Mark and Ravensburg in 1609, the duchy of East Prussia in 1618, and the duchy of Pomerania in 1637. At Westphalia in 1648 the Hohenzollerns lost part of Pomerania to Sweden but were compensated by the grant of three bishoprics and the promise of the archbishopric of Magdeburg (1680). By the late seventeenth century the scattered Hohenzollern holdings constituted a block of territory within the Holy Roman Empire second in size only to that of the Habsburgs.

Despite its size, the Hohenzollern conglomerate was weak. Except for Pomerania, none of the new acquisitions was contiguous with the home base in Brandenburg. All were exposed to foreign aggression. All were poor in natural resources. Many had been devastated during the Thirty Years' War. Each was dominated by a native aristocracy that limited the power of the Hohenzollern ruler. They shared no single concern that might encourage their unification.

MAP 15-2 Expansion of Branden-burg-Prussia *Seventeenth-century Brandenburg-Prussia expanded mainly by acquiring dynastic titles in geographically separated lands. Eigh-teenth-century expansion occurred through aggression to the east: Silesia seized in 1740 and various parts of Poland in 1772, 1793, and 1795.*

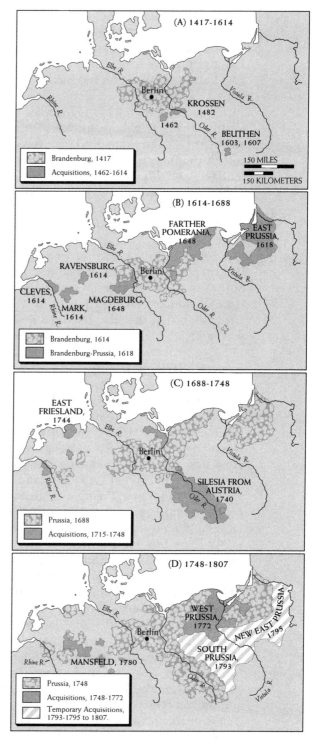

Frederick William, the Great Elector. Frederick William (r. 1640–1688), "the Great Elector," transformed this unlikely mix of possessions into a powerful modern state. His instruments were a tightly centralized bureaucracy and a rigorously disciplined army. The threat of invasion by Sweden or Poland helped persuade his subjects to cooperate in the creation of these institutions.

The army with which Frederick William began his reign was too small to intimidate his neighbors. In 1655, when the Brandenburg estates refused his request for taxes to finance a larger force, he used the soldiers at his disposal to collect the money he needed to employ more. He also skillfully co-opted potential opponents. In exchange for supporting the Hohenzollerns, the Prussian nobles—the Junkers—were granted complete control over the serfs on their estates. Frederick William also used the Junkers to collect his taxes, which fell most heavily on the peasants and the urban classes. The privilege of joining the army officer corps became an honor reserved to men of noble family.

Since the army was the one institution that drew members from all the Hohenzollern territories and all its soldiers and civilian personnel took an oath of loyalty to the elector, the army defined the state. Total mobilization of the state's resources enabled Frederick William to build a military machine far larger than that usually sustained by a small country. Prussia thus became a power with which other (and larger) nations had to reckon.

Frederick William I, King of Prussia. The house of Hohenzollern had created a nation, but it did not yet possess a crown. The acquisition of a royal title was the achievement of the Great Elector's son, Frederick I (r. 1688–1713). Frederick was the least "Prussian" member of his family. He built palaces, founded Halle University (1694), supported the arts, and lived luxuriously. In 1700, when the War of the Spanish Succession broke out, he made a deal with the Holy Roman Emperor. In exchange for the use of the Prussian army, the emperor permitted Frederick to assume the title "King in Prussia."

Frederick's heir, Frederick William I (r. 1713–1740), was both the most eccentric and the most effective of the Hohenzollern monarchs. After giving his father a funeral that would have pleased the luxury-loving Frederick I, Frederick William I imposed policies of strict austerity. He increased the size of the army and consolidated an obedient, compliant bureaucracy. He ruled alone without the assistance of ministers. His officials submitted reports in writing to him in his office (his *Kabinett*). Then he alone examined the papers, made decisions, and issued orders.

Frederick William's civilian bureaucrats worked under military discipline. All departments were centrally managed by the General Directory (*General-Ober Finanz-Kriegs-und-Domänen-Direktorium*). The nobility were subjected to taxation, and most remaining feudal dues were transformed into money payments. Service to the state and the monarch became an automatic impersonal reflex—a mechanical and unquestioning recognition of a duty to a public office, not a loyalty engendered by any feeling for the unique qualities of the individual who held that office.

The Prussian Army. Frederick William was a near fanatic where his army was concerned. He required each district in his kingdom to provide him with a certain number of men. They were trained with rigorous discipline. A show regiment composed of the tallest men in Europe was recruited. There were different laws for soldiers and for civilians, and royal patronage made the officer corps society's highest class. Frederick William merged the army, the Junker nobility, and the monarchy into a single political entity. In 1725 he began the practice of always appearing in military uniform in order to publicize his concept of the state.

Frederick William's military force grew from about 39,000 in 1713 to over 80,000 in 1740. Prussia was only the thirteenth most populous nation in Europe, but it fielded Europe's third or fourth largest army. Military priorities and values dominated Prussian government, society, and daily life as in no place else in Europe. Other nations possessed armies, but Prussia was possessed by its army.

Having built the best army in Europe, Frederick William avoided using it. He enjoyed drilling his soldiers but not sending them into battle. He was capable of terrorizing his family and associates—occasionally knocking out teeth with his walking stick. But he did not pursue aggressive foreign policies. He regarded the army as a symbol of Prussian power and unity, not an instrument to be used for foreign adventures.

Frederick II, "the Great" (r. 1740–1786) inherited his father's superb military machine, but not his father's self-restraint. He celebrated his ascension to the throne by invading Silesia and challenging Austria for control of Germany. The struggle dominated central European affairs for over a century.

↔ The Entry of Russia into the European Political Arena

The rise of Prussia and the consolidation of the Austrian Habsburg domains doubtless seemed to many at the time only one more shift in the ancient game of German politics. But the entrance of Russia into European affairs was something wholly new. Russia had long been considered a part of Europe only by courtesy. Hemmed in by Sweden on the Baltic and by the Ottoman Empire on the Black Sea, it had no warm-water ports. Archangel, a port on the White Sea, was its chief outlet to the West, but it was closed by ice during part of the year. Russia was a land of vast, but unfocused, potential.

Birth of the Romanov Dynasty

The reign of Ivan IV, "the Terrible" (1533–1584), the first Muscovite prince to use the title "Tsar of Russia," was followed by a period of anarchy and civil war. In 1613 an assembly of nobles tried to end the confusion of this "Time of Troubles" by recognizing the seventeen-year-old Michael Romanov (r. 1613–1654) as their tsar. He founded the dynasty that ruled Russia until 1917.

Michael Romanov and his two successors, Alexis I (r. 1654–1676) and

Theodore III (r. 1676–1682), stabilized Russia's government, but their nation remained weak and poor. Russia's administrative bureaucracy was dominated by the old nobility (the *boyars*), and it was only barely capable of maintaining order. The chief sources of instability were peasant revolts, raids by *cossacks* (horsemen who lived on the steppe frontier), and the possibility of mutiny by the *streltsy*, Moscow's garrison.

Peter the Great

In 1682 two boys ascended Russia's shaky throne: Peter I, "the Great" (r. 1682–1725), and Ivan V. The succession was bloodily disputed, and the *streltsy* had decided the outcome. Sophia, the boys' sister, served as regent until Peter's followers overthrew her in 1689. Peter then ruled personally, although in theory he shared the crown with the sickly Ivan until Ivan's death in 1696.

Like Louis XIV of France, whose youthful development had also been shaped by the experience of social upheaval, Peter resolved to establish a strong central monarchy. For ideas about how this could be done, he turned to the West. Products and workers from the West had filtered into Russia, and Europe's culture, particularly its military science, intrigued Peter.

Peter the Great (r. 1682–1725) seeking to make Russia a major military power, reorganized the country's political and economic structures. His reign saw Russia enter fully into European power politics. [The Bettmann Archive]

In 1697 Peter made a famous tour of Europe. For convenience, he traveled officially incognito rather than as a head of state. (This minimized ceremonial functions.) The European leaders whom he visited found their almost seven-foot-tall guest both crude and rude. But Peter was thoroughly at home in their shipyards and munitions factories. These offered him what he had come to find.

Peter returned to Moscow determined to Westernize Russia. He set himself four objectives which he pursued ruthlessly: taming the *boyars* and the *streltsy*, extending royal authority over the church, reorganizing governmental administration, and developing the economy. Policy in each of these areas was intended to strengthen the military power of the nation and the authority of the monarchy.

***Taming the* Boyars *and* Streltsy.** In 1698, immediately on his return from abroad, Peter launched an attack on the *boyars*. He personally shaved their long beards and sheared off the dangling sleeves of their shirts and coats—Russian peculiarities that western Europeans mocked. More important, he pressed the *boyars* into government service. In 1722 he published a Table of Ranks to peg a person's social status to his position in the bureaucracy or the army, not the nobility. This induced *boyars* to submit to the service of the state, but the Russian nobles were never as thoroughly domesticated as Prussia's aristocrats.

The *streltsy* fared less well than the *boyars*. They rebelled while Peter was on his European tour. When he returned, he brutally suppressed their revolt and executed about 1,200 of them. Their corpses were publicly displayed to demonstrate the consequences of disloyalty to the tsar.

Winning Secular Control of the Church. Peter was similarly ruthless in his dealings with the Russian Orthodox Church, which was firmly opposed to westernization. In 1667 Patriarch Nikon had attempted to reform the church by introducing some changes into its texts and ceremonies. Since the Russian church had always claimed to be the protector of the most ancient and authentic Christian rituals, these reforms stirred up considerable unrest. A group known as the Old Believers resisted the patriarch's mandates, and late in the century thousands of them committed suicide rather than submit to the new liturgies. The tragedy dissuaded the church hierarchy from making any further substantial moves toward modernization.

Peter wanted to make sure that the clergy did not blunder into another Old Believer schism or organize to oppose westernization. Consequently, he abolished the office of patriarch in 1721 and ceded its power over the church to a synod headed by a layman, the Procurator General. This was the most radical of Peter's breaks with tradition.

Reorganizing Domestic Administration. Peter modeled his domestic administration on Sweden's government. Rather than set up departments under a single minister to handle things like tax collection, foreign affairs, wars, and the economy, he established "colleges" with numerous members. In 1711 Peter created a central senate of nine members which was to run the government when the tsar was in the field with the army. The chief purpose of Peter's reforms, like those of Prussia's kings, was to construct a bureaucracy that would support an efficient army.

Developing the Economy and Waging War. The economic projects Peter sponsored were those that served the military. To get the men needed to staff them, young Russians were sent abroad for training and western European craftsmen were invited to immigrate. Although few of Peter's enterprises met with much success, the iron industry he began in the Ural Mountains had by mid-century made Russia the largest iron producer in Europe.

Peter believed that Russia's economic development and its future political power depended on the acquisition of warm-water ports that would allow Russia to communicate with the West. To acquire these, the tsar went to war with the Ottoman Empire and with Sweden. In 1696 his armies drove the Turks from Azov on the Black Sea, but Russia held this prize only until 1711.

Achievements on the Swedish front were more lasting. In 1700 Russia invaded Swedish territory on the Baltic. When Charles XII, the erratic king of Sweden, failed to follow up a victory over Peter at Narva, Peter was able to regroup. In 1709 Charles renewed the war, and Peter defeated him at the Battle of Poltava. In 1721 the Peace of Nystad ended the "Great Northern War" and confirmed Russia's conquest of Estonia, Livonia, and part of Finland. Their ports gave Russia access to the markets and capitals of western Europe.

Peter moved the capital of Russia to a new city he built on the Gulf of Finland, Saint Petersburg. Like other monarchs of his day, he followed the example of Louis XIV and constructed a kind of Versailles. The Russian aristocrats were compelled to move to Saint Petersburg, where the tsar could keep an eye on them. The city filled with lavish buildings modeled on those that housed the courts of western Europe. It was intended to stake Russia's claim to a place among Western nations.

Despite Peter's determination to strengthen the Russian monarchy, he could not bring himself to secure its future. After he quarreled with his only son (Alexis), the heir to the throne died mysteriously in his father's prison. Although Peter claimed the right to name a successor, he had not done so by the time he died in 1725. Consequently, for the next thirty years soldiers and nobles struggled to thrust their candidates onto the throne. Peter had made Russia a modern state, but not a stable one.

By the second quarter of the eighteenth century, the major European powers were not yet nation-states in which citizens were united by a shared sense of community, culture, language, and history. They were still monarchies in which the cohesion of the state was a function of the personality of the ruler and personal relationships among great noble families. Monarchs had generally grown stronger, but nobles were still able to resist or obstruct the policies of their rulers.

In foreign affairs there were two long-term conflicts. In central Europe, Austria and Prussia contested leadership of Germany. In western Europe, France and Great Britain fought on two fronts. During the reign of Louis XIV, the French bid for dominance in Europe was at the heart of the struggle. But throughout the eighteenth century, their duel was for control of overseas commerce. These wars *were accompanied by economic and social developments that, in the long run, were more significant contributors to the transformations that were taking place in Europe.*

✧ Review Questions

1. Why did Britain and France remain leading powers while Spain and the United Netherlands declined?

2. How did the structure of British government change under the political leadership of Walpole? What were the chief sources of Walpole's political strength?

3. How was the Hohenzollern family able to forge a conglomerate of diverse land holdings into the state of Prussia? Who were the major personalities involved in this process? What were their individual contributions? Why was the military so important in Prussia?

4. How do the Hohenzollerns and the Habsburgs compare with respect to their approach to dealing with the problems that confronted their domains?

Which family was more successful? Why? Why were the rulers of Sweden, the Ottoman Empire, and Poland less successful?

5. How did Russia become a great power? Why? How would you describe the character of Peter the Great? What were Russia's domestic problems before he came to power? What were his methods of reform? To what extent did he succeed? How were his reforms related to his military ambitions?

6. Can you support the claim that "Peter the Great was a rational ruler who was interested in the welfare of his people"? Can you make a case for Peter as a bloody tyrant who was concerned only with promoting his own glory?

✧ Suggested Readings

J. BLACK, *Eighteenth Century Europe, 1700–1789* (1990). An excellent survey.

J. BREWER, *The Sinews of Power: War, Money and the English State, 1688–1783* (1989). An extremely important study of the financial basis of English power.

F. L. CARSTEN, *The Origins of Prussia* (1954). Discusses the groundwork laid by the Great Elector in the seventeenth century.

J. C. D. CLARK, *English Society, 1688–1832: Social Structure and Political Practice During the Ancien Régime* (1985). An important, controversial work that emphasizes the role of religion in English political life.

A. COBBAN, *A History of Modern France,* 2nd ed., vol. 1 (1961). A lively and opinionated volume.

N. DAVIS, *God's Playground,* vol. 1 (1991). Excellent on pre-partition Poland.

P. M. G. DICKSON, *Finance and Government Under Maria Theresa* (1987). A definitive work.

W. DOYLE, *The Old European Order, 1660–1800* (1992). The most thoughtful treatment of the subject.

P. DUKES, *The Making of Russian Absolutism: 1613–1801* (1982). An overview based on recent scholarship.

R. J. W. EVANS, *The Making of the Habsburg Monarchy, 1550–1700: An Interpretation* (1979). Places much emphasis on intellectual factors and the role of religion.

F. FORD, *Robe and Sword: The Regrouping of*

the French Aristocracy After Louis XIV (1953). An important book for political, social, and intellectual history.

H. HOLBORN, A History of Modern Germany, 1648–1840 (1966). The most comprehensive survey in English.

R. A. KANN AND Z. V. DAVID, The Peoples of the Eastern Habsburg Lands 1526–1918 (1984). A helpful overview of the subject.

R. K. MASSIE, Peter the Great: His Life and His World (1980). A good popular biography.

D. MCKAY AND H. M. SCOTT, The Rise of the Great Powers, 1648–1815 (1983). Now the standard survey.

J. H. PLUMB, The Growth of Political Stability in England, 1675–1725 (1969). An important interpretive work.

N. V. RIASANOVSKY, A History of Russia, 5th ed. (1992). The best one-volume introduction.

P. F. SUGAR, Southeastern Europe Under Ottoman Rule, 1354–1804 (1977). An extremely clear presentation.

E. N. WILLIAMS, The Ancien Régime in Europe (1972). Very high quality state-by-state survey.

Index